Pirate Hunting

Also by Benerson Little

The Sea Rover's Practice:
Pirate Tactics and Techniques, 1630–1730

The Buccaneer's Realm:
Pirate Life on the Spanish Main, 1674–1688

Pirate Hunting

*The Fight Against Pirates,
Privateers, and Sea Raiders from
Antiquity to the Present*

BENERSON LITTLE

Potomac Books, Inc.
Washington, D.C.

Maps by Benerson Little and Mary Crouch.

Library of Congress Cataloging-in-Publication Data
Little, Benerson.
  Pirate hunting : the fight against pirates, privateers, and sea raiders from antiquity to the present / Benerson Little. – 1st ed.
      p. cm.
  Includes bibliographical references and index.
  ISBN 978-1-59797-291-8 (hardcover : alk. paper)
  1. Pirates–History. 2. Piracy–History. I. Title.
  G535.L578 2010
  364.16'4–dc22

                                        2010022457

Potomac Books, Inc.
22841 Quicksilver Drive
Dulles, Virginia 20166

First Edition

10 9 8 7 6 5 4 3 2 1

For
Courtney and Bree
Ben and Margaret
and Mary

Contents

Preface

Rebels, romantics, and writers have long been enamored with sea rovers, and understandably so. After all, the image is compelling—who hasn't at some point dreamed of setting sail on a rakish sloop or small frigate to plunder the Main? It is easy to imagine this, even in our modern daydreams, turning greedy owners, incompetent managers, and inadequate service providers into the objects of our fantasy rebellion. We plunder their corporate reserves and sink their corporate headquarters into a sea of bloody red ink then sail into the sunset, beyond which is a beach on which to retire with an infinite supply of rum, entertainment, and adventure.

The reality, of course, was and is far different. Whatever the motivations of sea rovers, the "salt water thief's" plundering, lawful or unlawful, has left destruction, enslavement, and death in its wake, and those who could least afford to bear the burden have often been harmed more than the merchant owners and traders whose goods were stolen or destroyed. It is from the point of view of those who sought to stop or prevent sea rovers of all sorts that this book is written, and in a way, it is an homage to all past and present who have fought to defend life, liberty, and, yes, even property from the rover.

In writing this book, I have tried not to forget Alfred Korzybski's dictum: *the map is not the territory*. Although Korzybski was never mentioned, this concept was drilled into me decades ago as a Navy SEAL. We understood that acting on facts, on reality, and not on wishful thinking or tenuous hypothesis, would help keep us alive in a very hazardous profession. The captain of a ship vitally relies on his or her charts yet he or she is constantly verifying them, and ultimately they are not the most vital navigation tool. The depth finder is. The theory of depth beneath the keel is subordinate to the fact of depth beneath the keel, at least if the captain hopes to keep his or her vessel from running aground. And so it was with us, for the ignorance or distortion of facts often had fatal consequences.

In this book, I have tried to avoid the trap of forcing or cherry-picking facts to fit a hypothesis or theory, and I have especially tried to avoid theory as ideology or faith, a common trap that too many scholars step into, and which invariably leads to the belief that all opposing ideas are more or less blasphemy and thus must be rooted out with the very tools of misdirection scholars are supposed to decry: obfuscation, distraction, distortion, blind eyes, and deliberate misinterpretation. My goal has been, as far as a hypothesis is even necessary, to let one build itself from the facts and not the other way around.

The rest is very much a descriptive and democratic history and analysis applied in the end to the present circumstances of piracy. I understand that descriptive history is not in vogue with some scholars, notwithstanding its practical value. In the case of pirate hunting, description is vital, for the history of pirate hunting is a grand "post op" which we today can look to in order to deal with current piracy and that which is likely to crop up again. This condition is especially important to me, as I intend this book not only for the general reader interested in the subjects of piracy and pirate hunting, but also for those who are working at this moment to solve the problems of modern piracy—violence, robbery, and hostage-taking at sea in the real world.

In writing this book, whose scope is far broader than I estimated when I first considered it, I owe thanks to several people without whose help the book could not be what it is, notwithstanding that all of them would probably deny this.

At Potomac Books, my thanks and appreciation go to Kathryn Owens, Claire Noble, Don McKeon, Bud Knecht, and Melaina Phipps for their outstanding efforts in making this book possible. To Philip P. Boucher, Distinguished Professor of History (Emeritus) at the University of Alabama at Huntsville, my thanks for our several wide-ranging conversations over coffee, for they provided me with a better understanding of the process of researching and writing history, and of the academic side of this process as well. To Mike Greene and Roland Vincent—old friends and fellow épée fencers—my thanks as well for the helpful information they provided. To Shelley Barber, librarian and curator extraordinaire at Boston College, my many thanks not only for her enthusiasm for the written piratical word (not to mention the written word in general), but also for the many related articles she pointed out to me. My thanks also to Rachel Lindstrom for forwarding several useful articles to me.

My thanks and high regard to Capt. Derek B. Creamer and former SEAL Team Two member Lt. Brad "Pappy" Hamilton of the Lee County, Florida, Sheriff's Department Waterborne Strike Team for their suggestions and assistance, particularly for their review of certain tactical descriptions, for permitting me to use a couple of photographs, for their enthusiasm for the subjects of piracy and pirate hunting, and for their efforts toward maritime security at the local and national level. Capt. John Dorozynski, a former master of liquefied natural gas (LNG) vessels plying the eastern seas, provided me with a very useful personal perspective, and likewise has my thanks.

My many thanks and high regard also to Capt. Michael R. Howard, USN (Ret.)—a member of NSWU-1 at Naval Station Subic Bay when I first deployed there, a teammate at SDV Team One as well as the officer in charge to whom I reported at SDV Team One Detachment Hawaii two decades ago, and the director of the National Navy UDT-SEAL Museum in Fort Pierce, Florida, not to mention an old dive buddy and old friend—for his assistance on the subject of modern anti-piracy operations, and particularly for his passion for the subject of pirates and pirate hunting, past and present. (Captain Howard has even acquired the lifeboat from the *Maersk Alabama* piracy incident for the museum.) My thanks also to Suzi Howard, likewise an old friend and the museum's education coordinator, for her enthusiasm, assistance, and hospitality when I visited in 2009. I'd also like to thank the museum staff and volunteers for their courtesy and assistance, and for their service in helping maintain the honorable history of U.S. Navy SEALs and their forbearers.

To Mary Crouch, my many thanks for her assistance in reviewing the text and my Spanish (and even Catalan and Italian) translations, as well as for assisting me in drawing the maps for this book and reviewing draft chapters. In particular, she has my thanks for her general support, and for putting up with me in my inevitable state of distraction.

My parents, Margaret and Ben, and my daughters, Courtney and Bree, as ever have my utmost thanks and respect for their patience, love, and support (and my daughters as well for not taking too much advantage of my willingness to say yes to anything when I'm writing).

List of Illustrations

List of Maps

1

Of Black Flags and Bloody Banners

The Pursuit of Pirates and Privateers

The sea, our birth mother and life's blood, has often been described as a deadly beauty: warm and enticing one moment, cold and murderous the next. Used, worshiped, even abused but never mastered, the sea reminds us of our mortality daily by returning some of us to the eternal depths from which our distant ancestors rose. But not all of the sea's dangers are of "wind and weather . . . sands and rocks."[1] The sea can be doubly dangerous, as mariner Charles May noted:

> On the 17th of August 1688, the ship *Terra Nova,* Capt. Daniell commander, arriv'd at Port Royal in Jamaica. [Four months later the] ship being well fitted, and the provisions and passengers aboard, we sail'd from Port Royal on the 24th of December, being Christmas-eve. We were richly loaden with sugar, logwood, Jamaica pepper, hides, indigo, sarsaparilla, &c. . . . But above all, in the great cabin, was a large chest . . . full of pigs of silver, bags of pieces of eight, and some gold. This treasure brought us into some danger, for the night after our departure, a sloop came up with us, and bearing along our side, after haling us, pretended to be sent on purpose with some letters . . . [but] Our commander suspecting some knavery, commanded them to keep off . . . our guns and small-arms being all ready to fire upon them if they offer'd to come near us.[2]

The danger, of course, was that the sloop was filled with pirates, and indeed it was. How the scene played out from here might have made for an exciting book or after-dinner tale, but for those caught up in the uncertainty of the unknown, the excitement was only worth its price if all turned out well. Happily, this time the pirates stood away and sought a prize elsewhere, deterred by the merchant crew's apparent willingness and ability to make a resolute fight.

We are all familiar with pirates and other sea rovers, or at least we think we are, whether from Rafael Sabatini's swashbuckling novels *Captain Blood*, *The Black Swan*, and *The Sea Hawk*; from Robert Louis Stevenson's adventurous coming-of-age tale *Treasure Island*; or, and more likely today, from cinema's classic swashbucklers and Disney's pirate fantasies.[3] Most recently, the headline grabbing depredations of the Somali pirates have made them the archetype of the modern sea rover. But it is the popular historical image that still predominates, and much of it derives from the very real Anglo-American pirates of the early eighteenth century and the novelists and Hollywood writers and directors who turned pirates from thieving cutthroats into near-harmless caricatures based as much on fiction and fantasy as on reality. Charles Johnson, a contemporary of these rovers, fairly accurately described the deeds of dozens of them, albeit with a bit of poetic license. One will serve as typical:[4]

> [Howell] Davis first came up with the enemy, and standing alongside of them, showed his piratical colours. They, much surprised, called to Davis telling him they wondered at his impudence in venturing to come so near them, and ordered him to strike. But he answered, that he intended to keep them in play till his consort [which was not a pirate, but a captured merchantman] came up, who was able to deal with them, and that if they did not strike to him they should have but bad quarter. Whereupon he gave them a broadside, which they returned.
>
> In the meantime the prize drew near, who obliged all the prisoners to come upon deck in white shirts, to make a show of force, as they had been directed by Davis. They also hoisted a dirty tarpaulin, by way of black flag, they having no other, and fired a gun. The Frenchmen were so intimidated by this appearance of force that they struck.[5]

The incident has all the classic marks of our image of the pirate: the black flag, the intimidation, the deceptive tactics, the broadsides, the swagger and bluster. If we add details from the journals of actual pirate prisoners—a pirate gunner wearing a gold-laced hat, pirate captains fighting over coats with gold and silver lace, pirates of all sorts cursing and swearing, "You Dog you! if you will not Sign our Articles, and go along with me, I'll shoot you thro' the Head," and, "You lie, by God, we are pirates, by God," and other colorful phrases—it might seem like something right out of Hollywood.[6] And, paraphrasing J. M. Barrie in *Peter Pan*, it seems all very familiar too, like a familiar friend or recurring dream (even though we have never experienced it firsthand), right down to the smell of the salty air, tarred rigging, and burnt gunpowder; the bright sun glinting off cutlass blades and pistol barrels; and the pirate captain waving his sword to signal the prey to "Strike amain!" lest the Jolly Roger be replaced by the bloody red banner whose message is "No quarter!"[7]

Nearly three centuries later, we see something similar but more ominous, given that it is contemporary: pirates off the coast of Somalia, some of them former fishermen who now make their livelihood by chasing and capturing any vessel within range. Their vessels are small boats supported by "mother ships" which are sometimes large fishing vessels and sometimes mere boats ferrying fuel in drums. They are poor men, these rovers. Many claim to be part of a Somali coastguard protecting Somali waters from foreign incursion, but they are in fact pirates, part of well-organized, large-scale piracy that may have originally developed from attacks on foreign "pirate" fishing vessels illegally plundering Somali waters. Somalia is a poor country with a failed government and no viable economy.[8]

In April 2009, four of these pirates attacked and boarded the cargo ship *Maersk Alabama*. The crew fought back: they disabled the ship and lured one pirate away from the others, then attacked and captured him, stabbing him in the hand in the process. In the standoff that followed, the crew held a pirate prisoner, but the pirates held the disabled ship and threatened the crew. The vessel's captain, Richard Phillips, courageously offered himself up as a hostage in exchange for the release of his ship and crew, and the pirates agreed. Because they no longer had their boat, they took to sea in the ship's lifeboat, intending to hold Phillips for ransom. The crew soon offered to exchange their prisoner for their captain, and the pirates again agreed. The crew released the prisoner pirate, but the pirates went back on their word and did not release Captain Phillips. The stage was set: four pirates and their hostage were underway in a lifeboat at sea, a U.S. destroyer was on the way, and the world was watching.[9]

This attack was not an isolated instance, but one of many in the waters off East Africa. Piracy is not a historical aberration or the mere stuff of fiction and film, but a historical constant and a threat even today.

THE SEA-ROVING FAMILY

To understand pirate hunting, we must first understand the various sea-going professions of profit by plunder. The modern international definition of piracy is "any illegal acts of violence or detention, or any act of depredation, committed for private ends by the crew or the passengers of a private ship or a private aircraft, and directed . . . on the high seas, against another ship or aircraft, or against persons or property on board such ship or aircraft."[10] For most of us, an eighteenth century definition remains valid: "A Pirate is a Sea-Thief, or *Hostis humani generis* [Enemy of all mankind], who to enrich himself, either by surprise or open force, sets upon Merchants and others trading by Sea, ever spoiling their Lading, if by any possibility he can get the master, sometimes bereaving them of their Lives and sinking their Ships; the Actors wherin, Tully calls Enemies to all, *with whom neither Faith nor Oath is to be kept.*"[11] Under most laws of the past as well as under U.S. law today, a pirate is also one who plunders the shore from the sea. Until recently, the penalty for piracy was the same: the guilty pirate was usually beheaded, crucified, strangled in the chair, broken on the wheel, or hanged, as law and custom dictated.

Unfortunately, such apparently simple definitions—clear enough for the merchant captain or passenger robbed, beaten, and terrorized at sea, or the coastal inhabitant raided and pillaged ashore—are not so simple as they seem, at least not to lawyers. For many centuries, the pirate has been considered "an enemy of all mankind," and as such may be captured and tried by any nation: "It is because a pirate is dangerous to everybody that he bears a *caput lupinum* [literally, the head of a wolf; in Old English law, the sign of an outlaw], may be seized by anybody, and punished anywhere."[12] However, the ancient pirate, although his victims probably held him in revulsion as great as any pirate in history, was not always held as such in law. In fact, in spite of the centuries-old obsession of many criminal lawyers and jurists with the concept of the pirate as enemy of all mankind, some have been well aware that it was "neither a Definition, nor so much as a Description of a pirat [sic], but a rhetorical invective to show the odiousness of that crime."[13]

One seventeenth-century judge asked sarcastically, "Whether there ever was any such thing as a Pirate, if none could be a Pirate but he that was actually in War with all Mankind?"[14] Even Roman orator Cicero, usually credited with the phrase's origin (although Polybius had used it a century earlier in regard to the Illyrian pirates), was aware of this flaw: "You acted as pirates are accustomed to act, who, though they are the common enemies of all men, still select some friends, to whom they not only spare, but even enrich with their booty."[15] Nonetheless, the idea has stuck and is one of the reasons some legal scholars today believe the law of piracy should be significantly revised, or even scrapped, and pirates prosecuted under other laws.[16]

The terms *piracy* and *pirate* have often seemed insufficient alone to describe those who steal on the seas, if we consider how many various epithets and other terms are commonly added to them. A sixteenth-century letter notes the authority to seize "pirattes and rovers on the seas" and "pyrattes, rovers, or men of warre," for example, while another of the same period orders two ships to "repress the pirates and freebooters infesting the Narrow Seas."[17] An early eighteenth-century warrant authorizes two captains "for seizing pyrates, freebooters and sea-rovers etc."[18] A letter written in 1664 asks for protection from "sea pirates, and forreigne men of warr," while the preface to a deposition made by a pirate victim in 1691 describes the capture of a ship "which was acted and done in a most Treacherous and Pyratticall manner by certain Rovers or pirates."[19]

We see this proliferation of piratical terms for at least two reasons. First, given that there are several other terms for pirate and piracy, prosecutors and lawmakers in the past may have considered it best to use them all, lest other lawyers advise pirates on how to abuse the potential loophole. Such redundancy, including synonyms and terms for similar yet distinct concepts, is a distinct attribute of British and derivative American law. This sort of legal jargon, which often annoys those who have to hire a lawyer to interpret it, apparently derives from the Middle Ages, when English, French, and Latin law terms intermingled.[20] Nonetheless, such repetition is found in the laws of non-English speaking lands as well, and probably for a similar reason. In 1691, for example, Louis XIV ordered that English privateers captured on French rivers be treated as *"Pirates & Forbans,"* the latter word being a synonym for pirate.[21] Words also change meanings over time, and to ensure that the correct meaning was understood, synonyms were probably added.

Second, and more importantly, pirates were not always the only thieves on the sea: some rovers were "lawful thieves," of whom more will be said shortly. Using additional terms probably ensured that a captain commissioned to seize pirates had the authority to seize anyone suspected of piracy, no matter the color of the rover's purported authority. After all, one man's pirate might be his neighbor's licensed entrepreneur.

But we can also make a third argument, that the addition of other terms makes for more colorful rhetoric when describing or verbally abusing those who steal on the sea. These anti-pirate tautologies, as they might be called, are often quite colorful and have a good ring: "*[H]ijos de puta, borrachos, infames ladrones . . .piratas!*" ("Sons of whores, drunkards, infamous thieves . . . pirates!") shouted enraged Spanish seamen and passengers aboard an early seventeenth-century galleon after watching English or Dutch sea rovers capture a companion ship.[22] Likewise was thirteenth century sea-robbing monk and mercenary Eustace Le Moine referred to by a variety of terms, including *villainous pirate, archpirate, Spanish tyrant, most wicked man, apostate,* and *traitor,* the first two terms actually being the least offensive at the time.[23] Adding other epithets, besides being an enjoyable exercise in venting and wordplay (often composed of elegantly rendered expletives), ensured that the pirate was understood to be more than a mere sea robber: he was scum of the sea.

The confusion surrounding the question of piracy does not end with the law. The terms *pirate* and *piracy* are commonly misused in news media, books, television documentaries, cinema, advertising, political rhetoric, and general conversation, often deliberately. After all, *pirate* sounds better; it's sexier than the correct terms. It has been misapplied to a variety of sea-going troublemakers, not to mention to some legitimate privateers and men-of-war. Homeric adventurers, Viking raiders, Spanish New World *guardas costas* and privateers, Malay sea raiders, Jacobite privateers, American colonial rebel privateers, Barbary corsairs, Confederate commerce raiders, German commerce raiders under both the Kaiser and the Nazi regimes, post-World War II Communist and Nationalist Chinese gunboats, North Korean naval gunboats, seagoing anti-nuclear activists, anti-whaling activists, various politically motivated ship hijackers, and terrorists at sea have all been referred to, incorrectly most of the time, as pirates. Many of these various parties have been labeled pirates for political purposes, often as a pretense for legal or military action. The pirate label naturally makes for good headlines as well: "U.S. Captain Is Hostage of Pirates; Navy Ship Arrives," was one of many newspaper headlines and television news crawls after Somali pirates attacked the *Maersk Alabama.*[24]

The problem is further compounded by the modern, typically distorted, yet understandably and undeniably romantic view in which the pirate has become a tongue-in-cheek symbol of social rebellion. Indeed, most of us at one time or another want (and some of us even try) to break free of the confines of corporate cubicles, assembly lines, the boss's thumb, or suburban blandness, and set sail for plunder as did the make-believe employees of The Crimson Permanent Assurance in *Monty Python's The Meaning of Life.*[25] In the sketch, suffering employees mutiny against their managers, hoist the Jolly Roger, and set sail in their small office building to plunder the fat merchant banks of the Corporate Main, all to a swashbuckling score as rousing as any. Conversely, some modern corporate CEOs are viewed as pirates as well, although, other than a perceived ruthless greed, they lack the attributes we have come to associate with pirates of the Golden Age: they do not risk their lives, as pirate captains were expected to, when necessary; they cannot be deposed by a vote of their employees, as these pirate captains could by their crews; and their income is not limited to a few times more than their average employees, as these pirate captains' shares were, relative to those of the common member of the crew.

Even some modern military units and law enforcement organizations refer to themselves as pirates or buccaneers, if only in jest. Warships and combat aircraft are sometimes named for sea rovers. Two U.S. Navy surface combatants have been named USS *Pirate*, for example, and several fighter and fighter-bomber aircraft have been variously named Buccaneer, Corsair, and Pirate.[26] Some combat aircraft squadrons use the Jolly Roger as part of their insignia, British submarines commonly fly it after successful combat operations, and some naval commando and maritime law enforcement units display the black pirate flag on patches or insignia.[27] Sports teams ranging from youth to professional are similarly engaged with the theme, many of them being variously named Pirates, Privateers, Buccaneers, Rovers, Raiders, Marauders, Corsairs, and Vikings. With this tongue-in-cheek label comes a certain honest swashbuckling pride as well. Nonetheless, in this wishful plundering, we forget that pirates were and are often quite literally cutthroats— the sort of people we expect our naval forces to hunt down and capture or kill.

Last, and to complicate the issue even more, the terms *pirate* and *piracy* fail to encompass all the various sorts who have roved the seas for profit by plunder. We might therefore best organize the subject by referring to all of them as *sea rovers*—as those who roam the seas for plunder, legitimately or otherwise, or whose purpose is otherwise to attack or destroy merchant vessels or to plunder ashore from the sea. Although the term *sea rover* has often been narrowly applied only to pirates, from the point of view of the victim, it is a more than adequate description of any sort of sea-going plunderer.

Of the various sorts of sea rover, we have already defined the *pirate*, who is by definition a criminal. His first cousin is the *privateer*, whose name derives from *private man-of-war*. The privateer is an armed vessel lawfully commissioned by its government to attack the merchant shipping of an enemy in times of war and to profit from the goods, vessels, and other valuables captured in such attacks. From a strategic point of view, the privateer's purpose is political, or public; his job is to harass enemy commerce. But from the point of view of those who outfit and man the privateer, its purpose is private, given that crew and investors seek personal gain via plunder. The privateer has often been held in esteem little better than the pirate: "Privateering is nothing more than piracy organized and legal," noted a nineteenth-century legal analyst, reflecting the view of many.[28] The privateer also has a little brother, called a *letter-of-mart-man* (or *letter-of-marque-man*), who is a merchantman (a merchant ship) of sufficient force that in time of war, his government grants him a letter of marque authorizing him to attack and capture enemy shipping encountered in the course of his trade route.

The privateer also has a big brother, often called a *cruiser*: a man-of-war tasked to cruise for enemy merchantmen and who can likewise profit from their capture. The term is also often applied to privateers and pirate hunters. The bastard progeny of the cruising man-of-war is the nineteenth- and twentieth-century *commerce raider*, whose primary purpose is the destruction of enemy shipping as a means of weakening the enemy. The true sea roving elders are the *sea raiders*, the peoples for whom sea roving is a way of life or a significant part of it—the Vikings and Mycenaeans, for example, and the Sea Dyaks and some of the Polynesians, among many others. Last is the *pirate hunter*, half-brother to both the cruising man-of-war and the privateer, and the last of our sea rover family tree, so to speak. The issue or family tree is clouded by the fact that the distinctions are often transient. For example, some pirates became privateers in time of war, just as a some privateers became pirates in time of peace—and both privateers and pirates at times became pirate hunters.[29]

The destruction of these sea rovers is the subject of this book. Only the pirate hunter is excepted, and even then not always, for often the pirate hunter has been simultaneously a plunderer or raider as well. But of all of these rovers, only the pirate and pirate hunter are active today. The rest have been laid to rest or have outgrown their bloody-minded way of life, except for the commerce raider who slumbers deeply and waits, hopefully forever, for a war of sufficient scale to warrant again the wholesale destruction of merchant shipping.

WHY ROVERS ROVE

If we ask why rovers rove, the answer is most often "for money" or "for adventure." Occasionally, some suggest rebellion. Scholars usually and quite understandably provide some variety of the first answer and tend to view sea roving largely via economic models. Some view piracy strictly through Marxist eyes, as the rebellion of the oppressed against the capitalists or tyrants who exploit them, and by implication ennobling the pirate and his violent behavior, forgetting that much of the pirate's violence is directed against the weak, typically the common working seafarer and, in past centuries, the often-poor coastal resident.[30] In the most reasonable models, piracy is the product of poverty, the need to ensure or increase critical resources, or mere economic opportunism. In fact, all three theories play a variously greater or lesser role, depending on circumstances.[31] Related theories of revenge and rebellion deriving from economic or political conditions—one reaps what one sows, so to speak—are discussed in chapter 9.

However, no matter the theory of crime or piracy, it is a given that under the right conditions, a minority of people, whatever the ethics and mores of their society, will take by force when the opportunity presents itself, deterrents and consequences be damned. Even more will do so when social and physical deterrents and consequences are diminished, need is great, or society itself promotes material gain by force of arms. After all, there is a good reason piracy persists even today where there is both reasonable opportunity *and* reasonable means of escape with the booty, and why in the past, privateering seldom wanted recruits. Thucydides put it well: "[A]s communication by sea became more common, [they] were tempted to turn pirates, under the conduct of their most powerful men; the motives being to serve their own cupidity and to support the needy."[32] Need and greed are likewise principal motives today.

One key economic element of sea roving often overlooked, and generally disregarded or deemphasized in many pirate novels and films, is slavery. Throughout history, sea roving has invariably been involved to some degree in this terrible practice, and in many eras, slaves were the principal source of plunder and profit. Sea rovers not only captured slaves and sold them, but often also captured and sold free men, women, and children into slavery. Throughout much of history, there has been a market for slaves, and sea rovers were by their sea-going nature well-placed to profit from it. The involvement of pirates and privateers in the slave trade has crossed all cultural boundaries, including race and religion, and not even our modern age of piracy is immune to human trafficking in the form of ransom for hostages.

Although simple economics—the need or desire to profit by plunder—is the sea rover's ultimate motive, there are other factors at play. In particular, opportunism, tradition, individual rebellion (often combined with a need to belong), the lure of adventure, and the allure of the sea all play a role. The unwillingness to give up privateering when peace is declared has been a significant factor in piracy in the past in some cultures. Charles Johnson pointed out that "privateers in time of war are a nursery for Pirates in time of peace."[33] Machiavelli was more direct: "War makes thieves, and Peace hangs them."[34] Lawlessness, unemployment, employment under inadequate or brutal conditions, and poverty have significant roles in piracy as well, past and present.[35] In the case of the privateer and the commerce raider, there is the strategic requirement of reducing enemy shipping in order to hinder the supply of war material and to harm the enemy economy, although the privateer and his investor have historically been far more concerned with profit than with military strategy. In the case of many sea-raiding peoples, there is the need or impulse to raid, and often with it the need to explore and expand. Although it might be tempting to avoid speculating on pirate motivation, the most effective use of strategy and tactics requires an understanding of why an adversary does what he or she does. To understand, after all, is to predict and often thus to prevent.

THE NECESSITIES

Another way to look at sea roving is to look at the conditions necessary for this ancient trade to exist as more than an occasional aberration.

First, there must be the sine qua non—commerce by sea. Piracy and privateering by definition cannot exist without something to plunder. In the case of coastal raiding, there must be coastal towns or villages worthy of plundering.

Second, there must be those willing and able to undertake sea roving. Many of piracy's recruits have been seamen, often displaced from their common trades as merchant seamen, fishermen, or privateer sailors. Recruits have also been drawn from the poor, disenfranchised, and itinerant adventurers of all classes. Even "men of wealth and noble birth" have been known to undertake piracy.[36] Privateers often recruited from merchant seamen who hoped for better working conditions and wages or profit, were lured by "golden dreams," or both. Throughout history, the common perception of sea roving as "easy money" with little real risk attached has probably served to inspire recruits. At least some of those who undertake sea roving must be mariners, for managing a vessel at sea, even a small one, is no task for the lubber. Sea-raiding peoples by definition lived as sea rovers.

Third, the sea rover must have adequate arms with which to attack, seaworthy vessels in which to attack, an adequate source of food, ammunition (if required), naval stores, and a secure base for outfitting, refitting, and rest and recreation.

Fourth, the sea rover must be able to escape with his plunder. Although the second and third conditions have much to do with this—rovers need capable armed crews, swift vessels, and secure bases in order to avoid capture—escape also requires the complicity of a state or nation, either directly by support (protection, arms, vessels, other supplies, intelligence, markets for plunder) or indirectly by negligence or incapacity, typically by failing to protect merchant shipping or suppress piracy or the sale of plunder.[37]

Fifth, there must be someone to take the rover's plunder (both goods and money) off his hands. In some cases, this may be his own family or village.

Last, sea roving must be sufficiently profitable to be worth the risk—both the financial risk to the investor and the risk to life and liberty of the rover himself. This is a relative standard; one sea thief might risk jail or physical harm for the theft of a few paltry ship's stores, while another might find such risk acceptable only in the case of plunder that will feed or enrich him for months or years.

None of the foregoing is intended to suggest that piracy can only occur under these conditions. Fools, some of whom are at times strangely lucky, may attempt piracy even when conditions are entirely unfavorable and still occasionally be successful. After all, there is tactical value in the unexpected; surprise, allied with determination, can often make up for other tactical and environmental deficiencies, even if only briefly.

OF PIRATES AND PIRATE HUNTERS

The need for pirate hunting is obvious. Throughout history, sea rovers have hindered trade, harmed commerce, and caused economic loss and even crisis. They have killed or murdered innocent seafarers and passengers, imprisoned or enslaved some, held others for ransom, sometimes tortured and raped them, and in general have terrorized the sea traveler and coastal resident. To claim, as some pirates or their apologists have, that they have not harmed or do not intend to harm those they attack and capture, is mere sophistry, for the pirate's threat of deadly force is exactly that: do as you are told or you will be harmed, even murdered.[38] Although the sea rover would prefer to steal without a fight—"What bandit was ever so wicked, what pirate was ever so barbarous, as to prefer stripping off his spoils from his victim stained with his blood, when he might possess his plunder unstained, without blood?"—he will use violence as necessary, and often has.[39] Privateers, although legitimate and even heroic at times, have interfered with trade and caused similar and often greater economic harm. Merchant crews captured by privateers have often been imprisoned or enslaved for years. Sea-raiding peoples have plundered ships and towns, exacted tribute, and enslaved captives. Even the commerce-raiding warship has terrorized the seas by sinking merchantmen, including passenger liners, without warning. The cost of the failure to suppress sea roving can be enormous, even today. In 2008, for example, Somali pirates attacked at least 111 vessels, captured 42, held 242 mariners hostage, and, according to some estimates, exacted as much as $150 million in ransoms, a small part of the estimated $16 billion in annual losses due to piracy. The toll on the victims of piracy can bear no financial accounting.[40]

No matter one's political or philosophical perspective, it must be agreed that trade has facilitated the advance of mankind, and, perhaps in the manner of two steps forward and one step back, has usually improved its condition as well, in spite of the unrestrained greed that often characterizes it, and which indeed characterizes much of human history in general. Trade must therefore be protected.

And so must the victims of piracy, those who have directly experienced the pirate's violence or threat of violence. Throughout history, captains of industry of all political and economic systems have typically ventured only their own capital, or that of their nations, in trade by sea. With rare exceptions, they did not and do not "venture their own skins." "He's in no daunger of the losse of life by cut throate Sea-theeves" wrote John Taylor, the "Water Poet," of the merchant owner.[41] Instead, it has been the common seafarer who has borne much of the physical, psychological, and even economic burden of attacks by rovers at sea. Similarly have the sea-going passenger, often a migrant, and coastal resident suffered, in particular the poor and others who could not afford to ransom themselves from slavery or other imprisonment, or who could not bear the loss of goods and other property gained from years of hard work.

Thus the pirate hunter. Merchants have pressed for them, the public has pleaded for them, and governments have authorized them whenever sea rovers have wrought havoc on shipping or coastal towns, and thus on economies. Often the plight of rovers' victims has inspired action as well. Naval and privateer captains and crews—repulsed by piratical acts, incited by the opportunity of advancement granted by a successful naval action, lured by reward, enticed by adventure, or simply doing their duty—have rightly leapt at the opportunity to capture or kill sea rovers.

Although this book is a history of the methods and men intended to thwart the various rovers of the sea, it is also necessarily a history of sea roving itself. The history of piracy is obviously useful in the study of pirate hunting, for "honest men may lawfully learn something from thieves for their own better defence."[42] The study of pirate hunting even holds lessons beyond sea roving and its suppression, making this book also a primer on the principles of strategy and tactics, as well as a partial history of naval warfare, including the various weapons systems and tactics made available by technological innovation. Further, the history of pirate hunting is a history of the development of speed at sea under oar, sail, steam, and other systems of propulsion. This book also touches upon the history of the expansion of some of the sea peoples, of exploration by sea, and of commerce by sea as well, for without such trade there would be little, if any, piracy, and no privateering or commerce raiding. Last, it is a small but vital part of the history of mankind itself.

THE PIRATE HUNTERS STRIKE BACK

Returning to the acts of piracy that introduced this chapter, we continue with Captain Johnson's account, largely corroborated by the journal of one of Davis's prisoners, Capt. William Snelgrave, a slaver. Not long before, Davis, a clever man, had been the prisoner of pirate Edward England but wisely refused to join England's crew. He did, however, fraternize and become familiar with England's crew, which resulted in three months in jail at Barbados on charges of piracy. Soon after his release, Davis passed from befriending pirates to piracy itself. After capturing the French merchantman described earlier, Captain Davis and crew eventually found themselves at Prince's Island in the Gulf of Guinea off the coast of West Africa, pretending to be the crew of a pirate-hunting English man-of-war. At Prince's Island, Davis made a present of a dozen slaves to the local Portuguese governor and, according to Johnson, invited the governor and his chief officers to visit his ship, intending to clap them all in irons and hold them for ransom. Snelgrave, however, noted no such plot but did write that the Portuguese governor, realizing he had been trading with pirates and fearing the consequences should word of this get out, had his own plot in mind.[43]

The next morning, Davis went ashore with "his first surgeon, the trumpeter, and some others" to escort the governor and company aboard, according to Johnson, or simply to visit the governor, according to Snelgrave.[44] Unfortunately, the pirates were met with neither governor nor friendly smiles and open arms, but with volleys of shot, for, according to Johnson, a slave who knew of the supposed plot had escaped and warned the governor. "[T]hey every man dropped except one, this one fled back and escaped into the boat and got on board the ship. Davis was shot through the bowels, yet he rose again, and made a weak effort to get away, but his strength soon forsook him and he dropped down dead."[45]

Johnson's account of Davis's death is confirmed by Snelgrave, who referred to Davis as "my generous friend," having been treated well (unlike some) by the pirate commander, who himself claimed to have known Snelgrave in the past: "Captain Davis, though he had four shots in diverse parts of his body, yet continued running towards the boat, but being closely pursued, a fifth shot made him fall, and the Portuguese being amazed at his great strength and courage, cut his throat that they might be sure of him."[46] With the death of Davis, Bartholomew Roberts was elected commander and vowed revenge against the Portuguese, but after a desultory attack on the town, they departed, fearing ambush if they marched upon it. Roberts went on to become an infamously successful pirate, in terms of merchant vessels captured, until his death at the hands of the Royal Navy. [47]

The Somali pirates who held Captain Phillips certainly hoped to fare better and put their faith in the belief that if the pirates were holding a hostage, the U.S. Navy would not take action. They expected a ransom—after all, hostage taking had been working well—which would be shared among themselves, their supporters, and their warlord. The pirates, if successful, would likely spend the money as other Somali pirates have: on cars, houses, and wives.[48]

But the U.S. government had not been idle. A U.S. Navy P-3 Orion surveillance aircraft arrived on scene, followed by the destroyer USS *Bainbridge* and a number of Navy SEAL commandos. The lifeboat attempted to head to the Somali coast, but naval vessels and a navy helicopter prevented it.

Negotiations stalled. The on-scene commander directed the *Maersk Alabama* to continue on its course, fearing another pirate attack; Navy SEALs were ordered aboard to ensure its protection.

Meanwhile, a second Navy SEAL unit, this one specializing in counterterrorism, parachuted into the sea with the necessary light boats, arms, and equipment, and boarded the USS *Bainbridge*. In the lifeboat, Captain Phillips attempted to escape by leaping into the water and swimming away, but shots from the pirates forced him back to the lifeboat. Abduwali Abdukhadir Muse, the pirate who had been stabbed in the hand, chose to go aboard the *Bainbridge* for treatment and to negotiate a ransom. Soon the lifeboat's fuel ran out. The *Bainbridge* offered to take the lifeboat under tow, ostensibly to Somalia, and the pirates accepted. At night, the *Bainbridge* drew the lifeboat closer. Tensions had risen even further among the pirates aboard the small craft. Time passed. In the darkness, eventually all three of the pirates were revealed to observers on the stern of the USS *Bainbridge*. The observers were armed.[49]

With multiple simultaneous shots, three Navy SEAL snipers killed the three pirates.[50]

Presented with an opportunity it helped to create, the rescue force successfully seized it. The shots—made at night aboard a moving ship, aimed at targets aboard a moving boat, and with a hostage's life at stake—were a credit to the training, expertise, and cool nerves of the snipers. The pirate Muse, still aboard the *Bainbridge*, was arrested and brought to the United States for trial. He was later charged in two previous acts of piracy.[51]

Sea roving has its swashbuckling glories, great and small, but so has pirate hunting. And it is pirate hunting—the fight against pirates, privateers, and sea raiders—that this book is about: its history, strategies, tactics, vessels, arms, victories, defeats, consequences, and, above all, the hunters who sought battle against those who would plunder by force of arms on or from the sea.

2

Heroes of the Fantastic

Pirate Hunting in the Age of the Iliad

"Hiis heart was mailed in oak and triple brass who was the first to commit a frail bark to the rough seas," wrote the Roman poet Horace in a farewell ode dedicated to fellow poet Virgil, who was about to sail from Italy to Greece.[1] We will never know who this first stout-hearted sailor was, nor the vessel, nor when this first mariner first put out from shore to sea, nor how many others first did of their own accord, not knowing that anyone else ever had before them.

To take to the sea for the first time, ignorant of what lay beyond the horizon and beneath the surface; ignorant of the actual expanse; ignorant of wind, current, and swell on the open waters; ignorant of navigation beyond the sight of land; ignorant of how to manage a rude vessel in a storm; and in all of this having to overcome the fear of the great unknown—surely this first mariner must have had a stouter heart than even the first who flew into the sky or beyond it into space. Even to those who know the sea, it can be daunting: "For I tell thee there is nought else worse than the sea to confound a man, how hardy soever he may be," observed a Phaeacian, a member of one of a great but mythical sea-going people from the island of Corcyra.[2]

The sea is alluring, exciting, entrancing, and, taken for granted or not, often deadly. Were the sea a person, we might describe it as warm-hearted in a calm, cold-hearted in a storm, fickle in temperament, and perversely irresistible. It has as many stunning vistas as all of the many varied environments of the inland world put together. It is filled with strange creatures who lie hidden below most of the time, and when they appear may seem as monsters and even leviathans to those who have known only the land. Its surface changes daily, from a softly undulating, almost oily calm one moment, to a raging tempest of great swells whose white foam and breaking waters spill violently from crest to trough the next. It is variously every shade of blue, gray, and green, and contrasting above is the vast expanse of the heavens, an endless horizon all around, with all the various colors of night and day, of sunrise and sunset, between. The sea provides us with food, oxygen, and energy from its depths. It serves as a vast road over which to travel, explore, and transport goods ranging from critical necessities to outrageous luxuries. It is a source of rest and recreation, of beauty and poetry, of contemplation and reflection.

And it has drowned uncounted thousands upon thousands of sailors and ships. In spite of modern technology, the sea still draws many each year into its eternal embrace, and science and exploration notwithstanding, the unknowns of the sea and its depths still far outnumber the knowns. Indeed, it is this confounding and often deadly unpredictability of the sea that has helped make the pirate more despised than the bandit. This point is typically overlooked by legal commentators who contend that pirates merit severe punishment because they are at war with all mankind, or perhaps more realistically, because they harm everyone when they rob sea-going commerce, for it benefits everyone: "It is no wonder if piracy be reckoned a much greater and more pernicious crime than robbery upon the land, because the consideration of the general navigation, and commerce of nations, is far beyond any man's particular property."[3] Instead, they should also look even more narrowly at what makes the pirate different from other thieves: the sea. The sea is often deadly of itself alone, and the pirate adds to this danger by subjecting the innocent mariner not only to the cruelty of the sea, but to the cruelty of his fellow man as well. He places the mariner in double jeopardy.

In the *Odyssey*, Homer noted this theme well, writing of "the wars of men and the grievous waves of the sea," and of Odysseus escaping "both war and sea."[4] Cicero asked, "Who ever put to sea without being aware that he was committing himself to the hazard of death or slavery, either from storms or from the sea being crowded with pirates?"[5] Heliodorus wrote, "Alas, do you not see how to our banishment fortune hath added the robberies of pirates, [and] ingag'd us in all the dangers of the sea?"[6] These and other writers—not to mention seafarers themselves—understood that to subject anyone without good reason to this combination of force of nature and evil of man is to commit an enormity. The man who would attack and rob the innocent and leave them adrift at sea with their food, water, and other stores plundered and their masts cut down—or worse, murder them—is surely an enemy of all mankind. "Some the Sea swallowes, but that which most grieves,

Some turne Sea-monsters, Pirates, roaving theeves," wrote John Taylor in the first half of the seventeenth century, refusing to forgive the pirate for his ultimate sin, that of preying on his fellow mariners.[7]

It is possible, of course, that the first person to take to the sea did so in the name of such violence—to raid a neighbor, perhaps—but this is much less likely than the purpose of fishing, travel, exploration, or trade. Chemical analysis of obsidian found on Crete has proved that sea trade has existed since at least 6000 BC, and the recent discovery on Crete of tools believed to date back at least 130,000 years confirms the antiquity of sea travel among hominids, if not necessarily among our own direct ancestors. Almost certainly as soon as people took to the sea, for whatever reason, the pirate followed.[8] The fisherman had his catch, the traveler his personal possessions, and the trader his goods—all waiting to enrich the "salt water" thief. Violence was also, by this early date, certainly long-practiced among peoples, dating back uncounted millennia before them to primate ancestors, and before them eventually to ancestors in the sea. It is not only the sea that is in our blood, but also violence in the name of self-preservation and competition, tempered only by instinct, culture, diversion, and, sometimes, intelligence. It would thus have required no great intellect to discover the profit to be had by raiding on and from the sea. Thus was the sea rover born, and almost immediately, his nemesis, the pirate hunter.

HOMER'S ADVENTURERS

"Tell me, Muse, of that man, so ready at need, who wandered far and wide, after he had sacked the sacred citadel of Troy," wrote Homer in the seventh or eighth century BC of the legendary and largely mythical voyage home several centuries earlier of Odysseus, known later to the Romans as Ulysses.[9] Odysseus's story is told largely in the *Odyssey*, an epic seafaring tale of raiding, adverse fortune, homecoming, and revenge—that is, a tale of sea roving and sea rovers, and some of the earliest evidence of them as well. Chronologically, the *Odyssey* follows the *Iliad*, Homer's epic of the siege of Troy, an attack ostensibly in retaliation for the abduction of the Greek beauty Helen by the Trojan Paris. It completes parts of the *Iliad* as well, including the sack of the great city whose downfall in the tale came at the hands of clever sea warriors, Odysseus among them, who slipped by night from the Trojan Horse, opened the gates, and led the Mycenaean host in pillage, rapine, and slave raiding.

The names of the leading participants are legend: Agamemnon, Achilles, Nestor, Menelaus, Hector, Priam, Ajax, and many others. Further details are known through fragments of other epic poems, which, when added to the *Iliad* and *Odyssey*, complete an epic cycle. They include *Cypria*, which tells of the events that led up to the siege, and *Telegony*, which tells of Odysseus after the *Odyssey* ends.[10] Some seven centuries later, the Roman poet Virgil wrote the epic *Aenead*, telling of the wanderings by sea of Aeneas and other refugee Trojans, and of the wars leading to the mythical founding of Rome. These are timeless tales based in historical fact, set in a universe ruled chaotically by numerous gods and in which mankind competes with sirens, cyclopes, sea monsters, and other creatures, not to mention with his brother, neighbor, and others of his own race.

The late Mycenaeans of whom Homer writes—or as he also variously calls them, the Achaeans, Danaans, and Argives—were an amphibious people with strong ties to land and sea. As mariners, they were particularly adept as rovers and traders, although their leaders appear to have scorned the merchant trade, as have many warriors throughout history.[11] However, they were not known as the greatest of all seamen. Homer reserves this honor for the mythical Phaeacians, who were "skilled beyond all others in driving a swift ship upon the deep."[12] Still, Mycenaean prowess at sea roving was the equal of any and is borne out by Homer's detailed description of the siege of Troy, although his heroes did not in fact conduct warfare on the scale he describes. Homer's is an epic, after all, put into written word from an oral tradition several centuries old when he inscribed it, and as such we not only excuse but praise his magnificent literary license.

On the other hand, historians all the way back to Thucydides point out that Mycenaean warfare did actually consist largely of plundering raids from the sea, the siege of Troy being an exception in scale.[13] Herodotus even writes that the Greek-Persian wars had their ultimate origin in a "series of outrages" that go all the way to the Phoenician theft of Io, daughter of Inachus, in Greece. This was followed by a Cretan raid on the Phoenician coast in which the king's daughter Europé was seized (and from whom the name of the European continent ultimately derives), followed by a Greek raid into the Black Sea during which the princess Medea was carried off, followed by a Trojan raid in which Helen was abducted, followed finally by the siege and sack of Troy.[14]

In all such raids, cattle, horses, sheep, and goats were common booty, as were men, women, and children carried away as slaves. Women were a popular plunder, both as concubines and slaves: "[E]ven to Ismarus," tells Odysseus of his wanderings, "whereupon I sacked their city and slew the people. And from out the city we took their wives and much substance, and divided them amongst us, that none through me might go lacking his proper share."[15] Menelaus roved the sea after the sack of Troy, ranging from Cyprus to Phoenicia, Egypt, Ethiopia, Libya, and beyond, "gathering much livelihood."[16] Helen of Troy may well have been plundered in such raiding: "Wait, with the first Northwind that lying pirate will desert us, setting sail on the high seas, our virgin as his loot! Isn't that how the Phyrgian shepherd [Paris] breached Sparta and carried Leda's Helen off to the towns of Troy?"[17] However, Herodotus notes that, "Men of sense care nothing for such women, since it is plain that without their own consent they would never be forced away.[18]

The Mycenaean rovers apparently felt no sense of wrongdoing in attacking the towns or vessels of another people, and to them a pirate, such as we think of when we use the word today, was probably one who stole at sea from his own people or who stole indiscriminately from all—a renegade, in other words, who claimed allegiance to none, or at least to none of the greater clans or peoples. Odysseus confirmed that roving against foreigners was common and acceptable: "I had nine times been a leader of men and of swift-faring ships against a strange people, and wealth fell ever to many hands. Of the booty I would choose out for me all that I craved, and much thereafter I won by lot. So my house got increase speedily, and thus I waxed dread and honourable among the Cretans."[19] Still, pirates and other rovers were not well-regarded by their victims: "[M]uch less would pirates coming to his land be let go scatheless for long, men whose care it was to lift their hands and seize the goods of others, and to weave secret webs of guile, and harry the steadings of herdsmen with ill-sounding forays."[20]

Sea roving or "sea robbing" in this Greek Bronze Age was largely indistinguishable from legitimate warfare. Raiding had a two-fold purpose: pillaging the enemy for immediate profit and weakening him over the long term. The tactics of pirate hunting were usually indistinguishable from those of legitimate warfare as well, for raiding the enemy's towns and villages and robbing his ships was the common solution to the enemy's roving, after defending against his attacks. After all, what the foreigner or enemy steals, one may steal back—or at least its equivalent, not to mention whatever else one can carry away. This age of roving was a vicious cycle of violent theft and violent retaliation, often one and the same. We must not forget what most of these rovers were at their core: slave raiders who often murdered the innocent, destroyed families, and left great carnage in their wakes.

OF CURVED SHIPS AND STRAIGHT SWORDS

In this early age, sea-going vessels were of two sorts: the merchant ship (broad abeam and relatively slow) and the fighting ship or galley (light, narrow, open, shallow drafted, and swift). While the merchant ship was often "a roomy slow-moving craft propelled by sail alone," the fighting ship was propelled by sail and oar.[21] Merchant ships of the period were typically deep-bellied, with vertical stem and stern timbers, and often very large (up to 450 tons), yet were managed by a single square sail.

However, the Mycenaean fighting ships, of which their crews were immensely proud, were black (probably tarred), with painted bows, un-decked except at bow and stern, with thwarts for rowing, thole pins to work the oars against, a stone for an anchor, a single mast and loose-footed sail, simple rigging of plant fiber or twisted ox-hide, low gunwales, a sharp prow, and a bow and stern that rose fairly vertically then curved amidships like "cattle horns," giving the ships a distinctive appearance. Odysseus, for example, refers to them as "my curved ships."[22]

Both types of vessel were constructed "outside in" by first forming a shell of external planking connected at their edges by pinned mortise and tenon joints, then adding the internal frames. Good shipwrights were highly regarded: Argus has gone down in history, and "Noeman, famous son of Phromius" was so well-regarded that Athena herself "craved" one of his ships for Odysseus's son, Telemachus. The ships themselves were light enough to be easily run ashore, but relatively fragile in stormy seas. As Homer describes them, they were of either twenty or fifty oars, although other sizes were common as well. A twenty-oared ship was, by maritime historian Lionel Casson's educated estimate, approximately forty feet long and nine or ten feet abeam amidships. A fifty-oared ship would have been roughly ninety feet long. Stores—"wine in jars and barley-flour, the marrow of men, in well-sewn skins," for example—were stowed beneath the thwarts, but arms may have been stowed on the thwarts to keep them from bilge water.[23]

Whenever possible, the Mycenaean rover came ashore at night, running his ship onto the beach. At sea, he used his sail when there was a fair wind and his oars in calms and battle, first un-stepping the mast and laying it amidships in order to reduce drag. Unlike some of the galley crews who came millennia later, the Mycenaean oarsman was a free warrior, not a slave, proud of his strength and his ability to row his vessel at top speed. Rowing and racing at sea and exercises ashore—running, boxing, wrestling, training in arms—made these warriors fit, strong in both muscle and wind. Odysseus's words probably summarized the attitude of many real Mycenaean rovers, and of many rovers in general who came for many centuries after them: "Such an one was I in war, but the labour of the field I never loved, nor homekeeping thrift, that breeds brave children, but galleys with their oars were dear to me, and wars and polished shafts and darts."[24]

Fighting ships and sailors require weapons, and the Greek weapons of this age, as Homer described them and scholars confirm, were primarily the spear, shield, sword, ax, sling, club, and bow. Armor was not as Homer described—of leather shield, bronze helmet, bronze corselet (torso armor), and bronze greaves—but of leather shield, leather helmet, and quite probably no corselet in most cases, given the size of the shield, although there are a few examples of Mycenaean body armor extant. Greaves as such were probably "gaiters of leather or cloth" worn over the shins in order to protect them from the shield rubbing against them, as some scholars believe. Swords were of bronze, some of them three feet long or longer and tapering from a broad hilt to a point, a form intended primarily for thrusting. Spear heads were also of bronze, with a socket for the shaft, which was probably made of ash. Shields—the primary means of defense—were large, three or four feet in diameter, and of ox-hide stretched over a wooden frame. Some were in figure eight form. Axes were both single- and double-headed.[25]

These weapons were far deadlier than we tend to realize, given our firsthand unfamiliarity with their effects. Of the numerous descriptions of wounds in the *Iliad* (many of them quite graphic), most are from spear thrusts, and this was probably the case in the Mycenaean Age. Given that the shield and spear were the primary arms of warfare for thousands of years, it is not surprising that Homer describes so many spear wounds, most of them from thrusts, as is the case with sword wounds as well. Although the Mycenaean swords could be used to cut, bronze does not take or keep an edge well, and as previously noted, the shape of the sword is designed for thrusting. The sword thrust is also clearly shown in various Mycenaean designs.[26]

If the Mycenaeans had worn the bronze armor of Homer's epic, most quickly-mortal sword and spear wounds would likely have been given by thrusts to unprotected areas. Graphic descriptions of wounds, while perhaps disturbing to some, are necessary to remind us that warfare on any scale is bloody and brutal. Common locations of wounds included the face (often a mortal wound, given the breadth of the blade and the depth of the wound), the throat (carotid artery, esophagus, cervical spine), armpit (axillary artery), lower abdomen (bladder, bowels, iliac arteries), and groin or upper thigh (femoral artery). Almost certainly what would in the Renaissance be called *le coup de Jarnac*—severing the femoral artery in the lower thigh with a cut or thrust, or the popliteal artery behind the knee, named for the baron de Jarnac after he killed the seigneur de la Châtaignerie in this way—was known as well. Given the apparent general lack of chest armor among most Mycenaean warriors, sword thrusts to the torso were probably common. The abdomen and the base of the neck extending to the clavicle were particularly vulnerable. Cuts would have had their place, weakening the adversary through loss of blood, blinding him via scalp or other head wounds, or cutting through softer tissues such as the neck. Even a sword that cuts poorly can still inflict significant damage if heavy enough and wielded well, with blows to the head that stun or kill, with those that break bones (for example, the skull, the clavicle, and the bones of the forearm, wrist, and hand), and with those that cleave limb from body.

It is a prideful and patronizing modern myth that all forms of Western swordplay prior to the Renaissance were inferior. Rather, their technique was much simpler, given the weights of their various swords and that defense was usually provided primarily by a shield. However, to learn any of their forms demanded just as much diligent practice, and in their timing, tactics, strategy, courage, and cunning, all of these forms were almost certainly as sophisticated as Western swordplay of the past four centuries. Evolutionary changes in swordplay have primarily occurred with the introduction of new types of swords that arose in response to changes in warfare or social customs, to improvements in metallurgy, or to take advantage of a weakness in existing arms, armor, or tactics, and seldom because a better way was found to wield an existing sword.

THE TACTICS OF RAIDERS FROM THE WINE DARK SEA

Most roving attacks were made ashore, for here lay the great booty, slaves especially, not to mention that towns and cities need not be discovered or chased at sea. If a target village were poorly defended, a rover might sail or row directly to the town if built on the shore, or as close as they could if built inland. If rovers expected significant resistance, they beached or anchored their vessels some distance from their target, made a reconnaissance, then moved by land to attack by surprise at dawn.[27] Surprise was necessary whether or not the target village or city was fortified or otherwise capable of resistance. Without it, the most valuable plunder—inhabitants as slaves-to-be—

would flee inland with their material wealth, including livestock. Surprise was best effected by attacking at dawn or by ruse. In myth, Theseus, slayer of the Minotaur, captured Crete after his ships were mistaken for some of those of King Minos, perhaps as the result of a ruse.[28]

Reconnaissance was likewise vital and was described by Odysseus: "And in the River Aegyptus [the Nile] I stayed my curved ships. Then verily I bade my loved companions to abide there by the ships, and to guard the ship, and I sent forth scouts to range the points of outlook."[29] Prior intelligence was also advisable; Theseus was guided by Cretan fugitives.[30] If the attackers were successful, they looted the town, made appropriate sacrifices if it were safe to do so, loaded their ships, and put out to sea again.

Homer does not describe attacks at sea. Perhaps they were relatively uncommon, or perhaps the bards who passed the epic tales down to him had not found them suitable to epic description. Worse, Homer barely even hints at warfare at sea, other than brief mention of Ajax's "boarding pike," for example, and of lying in wait for a ship.[31] The latter was probably the usual tactic for hunting a merchant ship or pirate. "But come, give me a swift ship and twenty men, that I may lie in watch and wait even for him on his way home, in the strait between Ithaca and rugged Samos, that he may have a woeful end of his cruising in quest of his father," spoke Antinous in the *Odyssey* of his plan to murder Telemachus.[32] A swift fighting galley could put to sea quickly from ashore, and its oars and large crew gave it an advantage over a slow merchantman, assuming wind and sea cooperated by providing light airs and a calm surface. A merchant ship of the day made four to six knots with the wind large and two or so close-hauled. The speed of oared fighting galleys is more difficult to estimate. Later Greek triremes could cruise at four knots and make brief high-speed bursts of up to nine knots under ideal conditions.[33] In comparison, heavy seventeenth-century war galleys cruised at two to three knots, depending on conditions, and sprinted for up to an hour at five.[34]

If they laid their ambush well, rovers could easily run up on a slow merchantman. Most of these vessels of commerce, given the large number of rovers required to man a fighting galley, probably surrendered immediately to be pillaged and enslaved—and to ensure their survival. Ships of this age were not fitted with rams, and in any case, ramming and sinking a merchant ship would have defeated the purpose of capturing it. If it were well defended, boarding was the solution, preceded by flights of arrows to thin the ranks and force defenders to take cover. The rover's best tactic was probably to board in parallel fashion from astern, his bow alongside the victim's waist, his oars shipped. The rover may have boarded at the merchantman's stern, his bow overlapping it, if either vessel had oars out. In either case, this would have permitted him to board multiple men at once. If the attacker put his bow perpendicular to his prey, he would have been forced to board singly, over his narrow prow. Grappling hooks of some sort were mandatory. These circumstances—gangs of armed men in small, swift vessels chasing and attacking large, slow merchant vessels—characterize sea roving throughout the millennia, right up to the present.

DEFEATING THE HOMERIC ROVER ASHORE

The principal defense against these rovers and raiders was ashore. Early on, unfortified seaside towns and villages found themselves vulnerable to swift raids from the sea, and so most moved inland or to nearby areas of difficult access in order to give inhabitants time to spot an attack and prepare for it. Watchmen in the hills scanned the seas for sails, and lit fires to give warning. Towns at the edge of the water relied on lookouts and especially on their fortifications as their primary initial defense.[35]

There were two likely, viable means of defending against attacks ashore, especially if the attackers outnumbered the defenders and the town or village were not well-protected by fortification. First, by attacking fiercely as the raiding vessels came ashore, defenders could halt the raid at its inception. This was the tactic used in myth by the Coans, who mistook Heracles for a pirate and tried "to prevent his approach by pelting his ship with stones," probably from slings.[36] Jason, of Argonaut fame, was attacked at both Arcon and Lemnos as he came ashore. At the former place he was taken for a pirate, at the latter as a raiding Thracian enemy. Further, at Lemnos, he was attacked not by male warriors, but by women in their dead husbands' armor. The women had killed all but one of their husbands for complaining that their wives stank, or as Apollonius Rhodius has it, because they were enamored of the captive Thracian "maids" they had taken in slave raids.[37] Either reason was probably sufficient.

Second, if the raiders' ships were beached, defenders could attack and burn them while the main part of the attackers were away, for rovers usually left only a small guard with the ships, although in the case of major expedition, they built a "Trench and Rampier [rampart or wall]" with sharp stakes for protection, as described in the *Iliad*.[38]

Well-fortified towns were probably able to withstand all but the largest and longest of sieges, and sallies could be made against the besiegers. Such attacks were probably fairly rare, for they required large numbers of men, which in turn required alliances and unified leadership, difficult in an age of petty kingdoms.

If all else failed, a counterattack as the invaders engaged in rapine and plunder was the last resort, and often a good one. Looting is a distraction to discipline and security, and thus a weakness to be exploited. The raider, drunk and busy filling his bag with booty, taking slaves, and quite probably assaulting women, is not fit to fight effectively. "Howbeit, thereafter I commanded that we should flee with a swift foot," recounted Odysseus of his raid on Ismarus, "but my men in their folly hearkened not. There was much wine still a drinking. . . . Meanwhile the Cicones went and raised a cry to other Cicones their neighbours, dwelling inland, who were more in number than they and braver withal. . . . They set their battle in array by the swift ships, and the hosts cast at each other with their bronze-shot spears . . . then at last the Cicones drave in the Achaeans and overcame them, and six of my goodly-greaved company perished from each ship."[39] He described a similar defeat in Egypt, where his crew "gave place to wantonness, being the fools of their own force." The Egyptian counterattack slaughtered many and enslaved others.[40] Odysseus's men would not be the last to die from the folly of a withdrawal delayed by plunder and rapine, or from the distraction they bred.

Last, a likely tactic may have been to pursue the successful raiders. Because rovers in this age beached their ships at night whenever possible, and because the routes among the Greek islands were well-known, pursuers may have occasionally followed at a distance, then attacked the raiders as they slept on sandy beaches.

DEFEATING THE HOMERIC ROVER AT SEA

Attacks on rovers at sea were far more difficult, given that finding a pirate at sea was often purely a matter of chance. Chasing another well-crewed fighting galley was difficult as well, and surprise via lying in wait was almost certainly necessary. A long chase in the wake of a swift ship would leave oarsmen, in Virgil's words describing a race, "gasping for breath, their chests wracked, mouths parched, sweat rivering down their backs"—not to mention in less than ideal condition to fight.[41]

The fight at sea, whether between rovers or between rover and merchantman, probably began with bow and arrow, assuming the attackers were so armed, and perhaps the sling as well, until the attacker was close enough to board or ran out of projectiles. Initially, the assault with bow or sling would have been more harassing than damaging unless extra men were available as archers, for most would have been at the oars. A few archers, or even none, would probably have sufficed for rovers attacking a small merchantman, but to attack a fighting galley, or even a well-armed merchantman (which was expensive and probably justified only in the case of a rich cargo), would certainly have required more. In many cases, merchant prey probably surrendered out of resignation or terror when they realized they would be overtaken.

Oared fighting galleys engaged against each other would have each maneuvered to best advantage, probably trying to wear the adversary down at longer ranges with the bow and arrow, then boarding when he was sufficiently weakened. Use of the bow would have continued during boarding. Josiah Burchett, secretary of the Admiralty of the Royal Navy in the early eighteenth century, considered the Mycenaean ships unsuitable to naval warfare, particularly as they could only be fought from the bow and stern, given the oars in between.[42]

Boarding a rover was probably done most often as it probably was when boarding a merchant vessel: with bow overlapping stern. The adversary's oars may have prevented boarding alongside, given how light fighting galleys were. The "hollow ships" of the Mycenaeans lacked a deck, thus boarding was probably an even more haphazard affair than in later centuries. Long spears or boarding pikes such as Ajax wielded in the Trojan attack on the Greek ships would have been ideal for both attack and defense as the hunter came close to board the rover, or the rover to board the merchantman. Although Ajax fought from the decks of ships drawn ashore, wielding his weapon against attackers on the beach, the pike, "jointed with rings, two and twenty cubits in length," would have served just as well at sea.[43] Homer's description of its length is surely a gross exaggeration, however; ten to twelve feet is probably the greatest manageable length for a pike at sea. Some seventeenth- and eighteenth-century boarding pikes were this long, and among pikemen ashore, sixteen feet was common.[44] Longer pikes were difficult to manage, and one suspects that Mycenaean pikes were no longer than twelve feet. Boarding pikes might also have been used to help fend off an attacking vessel, as might oars. Light booms and even boathooks were used for this purpose in the seventeenth and eighteenth centuries.[45]

According to Homer, as Ajax fought with his pike, he bore his shield with his left arm, probably hanging free from it, or from his shoulder or neck, depending on its size.[46] The shield at sea would have been an excellent defensive weapon during the chase, behind which static defenders could find protection from arrows at longer distance and from arrows and spears alongside. Attackers would likewise use it for protection as they approached. Perhaps some shields lined the bulwarks, if this could have been done without interfering with the oars, as was done in later centuries. An illustration circa 1190 BC of a fight between Egyptians under Ramses III and those who were called the "Sea People" shows many shields in use, the bow wielded to great effect, as well as the sword and the spear (see figure 3). In the illustration, the bow and spear account for many of the casualties, some of whom lay across the gunwales, and battle may have been largely decided by them as the vessels came near.[47] If, however, attackers did actually board, battle in the narrow quarters would have been even closer and more vicious, and the wounds at least as horrible, as in the fight among the ships: "Now round his ship the Achaians and Trojans warred on each other hand to hand, nor far apart did they endure the flights of arrows, nor of darts, but standing hard each by other, with one heart, with sharp axes and hatchets they fought, and with great swords, and double-pointed spears."[48]

In the long run, though, the best defense against any sea rover may have been the alliance. Although such associations did not prevent all attacks, they did tend to prevent those among members, and may have deterred some foreign attacks as well. Most importantly, alliance helped with retaliation, invariably in the form of a raid. When Helen (daughter of Leda and Zeus, wife to Menelaus of Sparta) was abducted by Paris, it was an alliance of Greek clans that led to the retaliation against Troy and its allies, and eventually to the destruction of the great city by these now-pirate hunters. Trojan raiding ended with the loss of its citadel and the cities of many of the Trojan allies (many of which were sacked by Achilles), as well as the death or enslavement of many of its people. In reality, the reason for the attack on Troy is unknown. The citadel had been attacked in fact and in myth before. Heracles had already successfully sacked and burned it and put Priam on its throne.[49] The great siege recounted in the *Iliad* may have been in retaliation for repeated Trojan raids, the result of conflict over trade routes (access to the Bosporus, for example), or both: a raid for great booty that would also put a raiding and trading rival out of business. Wars have been fought over far less.

Finally, there is evidence that at least one treaty—"a decree consented to by all Greece"—was specifically enacted to control piracy in the time of King Minos by limiting ships in Greek waters to crews no larger than five. Anyone else would obviously be a pirate. Minos, however, almost immediately violated the accord by pursuing the escapee Daedalus, said by some to have invented the sail.[50]

Ultimately, the best means of dealing with pirates or "sea robbers" in this age was to track them to their lairs and destroy them ashore. Unfortunately, as many of these rovers belonged to large clans allied with other large clans, long-term suppression of sea rovers often required large-scale warfare.

HEROES AND HUNTERS

"Strangers, who are ye? Whence sail ye over the wet ways? On some trading enterprise, or at adventure do ye rove, even as sea-robbers, over the brine, for they wander at hazard of their own lives bringing bale to alien men?"[51] The line is from the *Odyssey*, but something like it was doubtless spoken to all those who appeared armed for war from the sea.

One of the great sea-roving tales is that of Jason and his crew of Argonauts, and similar words were probably spoken to him when he arrived at Colchis on the Black Sea in search of the Golden Fleece. The myth is better known than any other sea-roving tale of the age, excepting only of the sack of Troy. Even Heracles's great sea-roving voyages—he sacked Troy, Astypalaea and the surrounding Cos, Elis (after first being defeated there), and Pylus, for example—are unknown to most.[52] The Argonaut myth historically has been so well-known that three late-seventeenth century Caribbean sea rovers— the pirates Joseph Banister and John Beare, as well as the privateer Bernard Lemoyne—even named their ships the *Golden Fleece* (in Lemoyne's case, *La Toison d'Or*), and others probably did as well.[53]

Mythologically, Jason sought the Golden Fleece on behalf of his uncle, Pelias, son of Poseidan, who had seized the Iolcan throne from his half-brother Aeson, Jason's father. If Jason were successful in the quest, his uncle would give up the throne, rightfully Jason's by heredity. In fact, the voyage was little more than a voyage of exploration and raiding, probably lured by either amber or by gold "panned" using fleece laid in the Phasis River. Jason prepared his voyage well. His ship was crafted in Pagasae by the finest ship-wright of the time, Argus the Thespian, with the aid of Athena. In its bow was an "oracular beam" put there by Athena. The *Argo* was also a symbol of the importance of swift, well-crafted vessels to a sea roving people.[54]

Jason sent word far and wide of his intended voyage and recruited more than fifty heroes, enough to row a warship of fifty oars, enough to defend against attacks, and especially enough to make swift raids on small coastal villages. Accounts of the crew list vary somewhat, but we know it was composed largely of warriors, including among others Heracles (taking a break from his labors), Hylas his squire, Ancaeus with bear skin and double-bladed battle ax, Polyphemus the old warrior, and, in some accounts, Atalanta the virgin huntress, whom we should rightly name as the first known female pirate, or at least the first known female sea rover. Orpheus the poet came aboard. There must be mariners on such a voyage, and three of the crew were sons of Neptune himself. One of them, Euphemus, was so fleet afoot that he could run across the surface of the sea, and the others, Erginus and Ancaeus, "both boasted their skill in seacraft and war." There was Argus the Thespian, who built the ship and who at sea probably went as a combination boatswain and carpenter. Lynceus was the lookout, and Nauplus, who surpassed all others in naval skill, navigated. Tiphys could foretell wind and wave of the sea, and Idmon had the skill of prophecy. Castor and Polydeuces (Pollux in the Roman pantheon), brothers to Helen of Troy, went along, as did Cepheus, king of Ethiopia and husband of Cassiopeia. Benches were chosen by lot, except for Heracles and Ancaeus, who had the middle bench. It was a well-balanced company of sea-going soldiers and fighting sailors, of strong-willed, independent souls willing to work together for a common goal, each seeing himself both as a prince (which indeed many were) and as an equal to his comrades, much as many companies of sea rovers have been throughout history. The adventurers named themselves the Argonauts, and are said to have taken the name from their ship, the *Argo*, named in turn for its shipwright, Argus, although there are other stories regarding the origin of the name.[55] Some called these rovers the Minyans.[56]

We have to wonder why the crew was not larger—why were there not more ships on a raiding foray into a foreign sea and shore? Perhaps there were, if the tale is based in fact, but in mythological terms, they were unnecessary. The Argonauts were heroes, after all, heroes of heroes in an age of heroes. Even so, Heracles attacked Troy with at least six small ships and perhaps as many as eighteen fifty-oared fighting galleys.[57]

The voyage itself is best recounted elsewhere in many forms, from epic poetry to novel to film. Suffice it to say that Jason was successful after many trials, including those of fire-breathing bulls, a terrible dragon, princess-stealing (which led eventually to tragedy), and battle against female warriors descended from the Amazons, besides his mere piratical raiding.[58] However, one point stands out beyond simple sea roving and literary adventure. Combination voyages of exploration and plundering, like Jason's, often tempted invasion and conquest. In particular, raids on neighboring or distant lands provided intelligence of wealth in the form of precious metals and gemstones, goods, livestock, agricultural produce, timber, useful minerals, fishing grounds, and availability of fresh water, not to mention the land itself, including its fertility, accessibility, and defensibility. Hand-in-hand went intelligence of the prepared defenses of coastal peoples and their wealth. This functional knowledge often led eventually to invasion, conquest, colonization, and even the permanent expansion of a people and its lands or the wholesale migration of a people itself. Jason's voyage epitomized such sea-roving voyages for the next three thousand years, including those of the Vikings and Polynesians, not to mention the wide-ranging Elizabethans and their European counterparts.

But there is more to the story of Jason and the Argonauts than sea roving on distant shores. King Minos, keeper of the labyrinth-confined Minotaur slain by Theseus, had used his navy to clear the local waters of pirates, and some archaeologists believe this is borne out by the fact that many Minoan towns along the shore were apparently unfortified.[59] Indeed, Crete may well be the cradle of both piracy and pirate hunting. We know the names of none of these early pirate-hunting captains for certain, except for one: Jason.[60] According to the ancient writer Clidemus, Jason was excepted from the limitation of five men to a vessel, and was "made captain of the great ship *Argo*, to sail about and scour the sea of pirates."[61] We might rightly therefore refer to Jason, or at least to the man or men on whom he is based, as the first named pirate hunter. Like many who came after him, he was first a pirate, then the pirate's nemesis. Minos deserves credit as well for commanding the first known pirate hunters. His chief captain, Taurus, killed by Theseus, may have been a pirate hunter as well. Theseus is also considered by some to have been a pirate hunter, not to mention a sea rover, having fought and killed a number of various piratical rogues on his journey to Athens.[62]

But the gods never placed Jason in the heavens, where he might have ruled as the patron of all those who followed in his wake. Argonauts Castor and Polydeuces, the Discouri, are there, though, as the brightest stars of the constellation Gemini. In the Age of Sail, they were known as the "Gods of the Sea, because they support Pirates," as a shipwrecked French explorer put it in 1708.[63] Today they occasionally descend from the heavens as a form of St. Elmo's Fire or as the Corposants (Holy Bodies) and display their ghostly light on the yards and mastheads of vessels at sea. Cepheus is there too, in the heavens, and Heracles and Orpheus. Some say that Theseus was once there, and that his lyre still is. Even the *Argo* sails eternally in the firmament sea, and thus does the soul of her shipwright as well. But not their captain. Perhaps the gods determined that pirate hunting was not a fitting occupation for a sea-roving hero. Sir Isaac Newton, who in addition to his other accomplishments had a hand in the advancement of navigation at sea, believed that because the Argonaut Musaeus had created the first celestial sphere, all of the Greek constellations were in some way related to the voyage of the *Argo*.[64] But if so, why then not Jason? Maybe the answer is there, overlooked at first: ships must be captained, even those in the firmament. Jason—pirate, explorer, and pirate hunter—is there after all, commanding in the heavens from the small aft deck of his famous fifty-oared ship.[65] Perhaps most of his crew of heroes are with him as well, pulling on their oars to propel the *Argo* on its celestial circumnavigation.

The age of Mycenaean sea roving—a "Golden Age" of roving, if you will—collapsed with its civilization into a dark age circa 1100 BC when the iron-armed Dorians or, as the Greeks called them, the *Heracleidae* (the descendants of Heracles) invaded, only to spring forth several centuries later into the Hellenic or Classical Age of Greece.[66] It had taken wholesale invasion and cultural change to suppress Mycenaean "sea robbing" and raiding. However, sea roving in the ancient Mediterranean did not begin with the Homeric Mycenaeans, nor did it end with them. For centuries before and after, the Mediterranean, with its rugged, tortuous coastlines and numerous islands, was a sea rover's haven and heaven in which many "hoisted their sails to fate" and pulled on "oars which served as wings to ships."[67]

3

In the Age of Ancient Empires

Pirate Hunting in the Mediterranean, 1450–700 BC

If for some fantastic reason anyone ever had to design a region ideally suited to piracy, he or she could do no better than what nature and mankind created by accident in the Mediterranean. The region's long tortuous coastline, many scattered islands, diverse topography, and natural chokepoints provide the perfect natural geography. Several thousand years ago, human circumstances conspired with this geography not only to make the Mediterranean seem the center of the world to the peoples who lived on its shores and nearby, but also to provide sea roving's essential element, trade by sea.[1]

We forget how large this great middle sea in the center of Europe, Africa, and Asia must have seemed and how few men or women would have known of, much less visited, its entire expanse even during a lifetime. Of those who might have, most would have been mariners. A passage from the *Odyssey* provides a glimpse into the perceived expanse of distant shores and peoples known to so few:

> Tell me of thy land, thy township, and thy city, that our ships may conceive of their course to bring thee thither. For the Phaeacians have no pilots nor any rudders after the manner of other ships, but their barques themselves understand the thoughts and intents of men; they know the cities and fat fields of every people, and most swiftly they traverse the gulf of the salt sea, shrouded in mist and cloud, and never do they go in fear of wreck or ruin.[2]

As already noted, the Phaeacians were a mythical people, and to the average person, perhaps only those with advanced ships and apparently magical technology and navigational skills could travel such a vast, unknown realm by sea.

In reality, in the ancient Mediterranean were great empires and great sea peoples who pushed the boundaries of trade, exploration, and conquest. These were not mythical peoples with magic ships, but men and women of flesh and blood who braved the known and unknown dangers of sea and shore near and far. The earliest of these known peoples of empire were the Egyptians, whose ships traded as far as Somalia. In the region of modern Lebanon were the Phoenicians, widely known as outstanding mariners and far-ranging traders. The nearby Mesopotamians traded by sea as far away as India. In Crete were the Minoans, a great trading people. Following them in Greece were the sea raiding Mycenaeans, and later came the Athenians, not a maritime people, but one that permitted foreigners to carry out their maritime trade.[3] The economies of these ancient empires filled the sea with ships, themselves filled with common goods and uncommon riches: cedar and other timber, olive and other oils, livestock, wine, copper, papyrus, linen and other fabrics, incense, ivory, carnelian, lapis, various other precious stones, gold, and many other cargoes besides.[4]

But just as we forget how large this ancient world must have seemed (and actually was), just as we forget that it was not of one age, but of many, so we also forget how many "Golden Ages" of piracy must have risen and fallen during this ancient period of great empires and vast sea-going trade. The maritime nature of the entire period—of every ebb and flood of every empire and age of these two thousand years—was of sea trading peoples, and of sea raiding peoples, pirates, and vessels of reprisal. The latter corresponded roughly with those granted "letters of marque and reprisal" in the sixteenth and seventeenth centuries.[5] Throughout much of history, the reprisal has been a common, often respected, and often quite lucrative means of justice, and in the ancient Mediterranean, it was routine.

The words *pirate* and *piracy* are ultimately derived from the Greek word for attempt, attack, or assault, and many scholars argue that even outright piracy was not regarded with the same contempt in this ancient age as it is today, or at least that the term *pirate* itself did not hold the connotation of outcast and outlaw, or of malfeasance by criminals at sea.[6] These same authorities, who include Thucydides, note that the pirates and sea raiders of this ancient age were referred to as men who plundered, who took booty, but not as pirates per se, and they were often regarded with honor.[7] However, one suspects that this may be mere quibbling or hair-splitting, for the victim then by all accounts regarded the sea robber as the victim does now: as one deserving abject contempt and swift severe justice. Even Thucydides himself suggests that as nations engaged in greater and greater trade, and thus grew wealthy, the sea rover became an enemy in the eyes of the wealthy "tyrants" of the Mediterranean and was no longer the practitioner of an acceptable, if unwelcome, trade.[8]

EARLY PIRATES AND ROVERS

The earliest records of pirates and their piracies are not of the Mycenaeans or, by inference from their pirate hunting, of the Minoans. They are instead of the fourteenth century BC Lukka of Lycia. We know little of them, and what we do know comes from a series of cuneiform tablets, called the Amarna letters, that recorded the correspondence between Egypt and several kingdoms during the reign of Amenhotep III. One letter from the king of Alasiya (Cyprus) vigorously denies that the Alasiyans are allied with the Lukkan pirates, whom he claims routinely plunder the Alasiyan city of Zikhra. Based at Lycia, the Lukkans were well-placed to plunder the Levant, as the Eastern Mediterranean is known. Unfortunately, the clay tablet reveals nothing about how these raiders were dealt with, except to note that if Alasiyans were involved, they would be punished.[9] Other letters describe attacks on the merchant shipping of Byblos and Simyra by rovers from Beirut, Tyre, and Sydon, and a raid by the "Milim people" into northern Syria.[10]

There are also sparse records of a large confederation of raiders known today as the Sea Peoples, whose members were bands of roving sea raiders from the coasts of Asia Minor and from some of the northern coasts of the Mediterranean from 1200 to 1100 BC: the Peleset, Tjeker, Shekelesh, Denyen, and Weshesh.[11] Scholars conclude that the Peleset were the people later known as the Philistines, but the identity of the others is still debated, as are their origins in general. Some may have been Greeks, possibly the Achaeans. The Sea Peoples raided from the sea, causing havoc across much of the eastern Mediterranean, and by all accounts were seeking new lands in which to settle.[12] Some scholars suggest they may been responsible for the collapse of a number of local civilizations, including the Mycenaean.

A probably fictional account written circa 1100 BC during the reign of Ramses III describes the power held by some of these sea raiding peoples. It describes how Egyptian priest Wenamen was dispatched to Byblos in Syria for a large quantity of Lebanese cedar. En route he was robbed in Dor, a Tjeker port, and the local king refused to recompense him, given that the thief

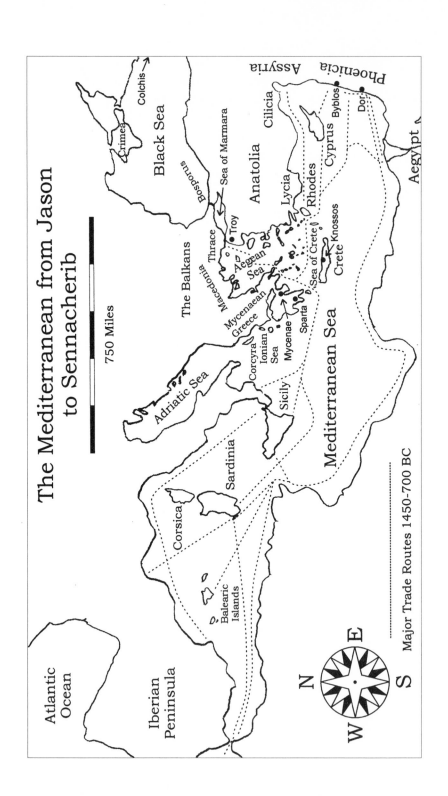

The Mediterranean from Jason to Sennacherib

750 Miles

Atlantic
Ocean

Iberian
Peninsula

Corsica

Balearic
Islands

Sardinia

Sicily

Adriatic Sea

Corcyra
Ionian
Sea

Mycenaean
Greece

Mycenae
Sparta

The Balkans

Macedonia

Thrace
Troy

Aegean
Sea

Sea of Crete
Crete Knossos

Mediterranean Sea

Black Sea

Crimea

Colchis

Bosporus

Sea of Marmara

Anatolia

Lycia
Rhodes

Cilicia

Cyprus

Assyria

Phoenicia

Byblos

Dor

Aegypt

N
W   E
S

Major Trade Routes 1450-700 BC

was apparently one of Wenamen's own crew members. From Dor, Wenamen sailed to Byblos, where he seized valuables from a Tjeker ship, intending to hold them until his loss at Dor was made good. At Byblos, insult was added to injury when he was informed that he would have to pay for the timber, which had in the past been provided as tribute. Egypt's power was waning, and other Mediterranean peoples, including the various sea raiders, were flexing their muscles in spite of their defeat at the hands of the Egyptians a century before. When it came time to set sail for Egypt, Wenamen's passage was blocked by eleven Tjeker sea raider ships. Zakar-Baal, the local ruler, advised the raiders that they could not plunder Wenamen within the city harbor, for he was an Egyptian emissary and suggested they do it on the open sea instead. Fortunately for Wenamen, the weather was in his favor and he escaped.[13]

Other rovers threatened the Mediterranean as well: the Carians, Ionians, and Phoenicians, for example, and the Taphians, Pelasgians, Agyllians, and Lemnians, among others. Even honest traders sometimes raided for slaves. But detailed records are few.[14] Suffice it to say that the age was doubtless one in which sea roving played a significant role in the success of many Mediterranean peoples.

COUNTERING THE ANCIENT ROVER

Until roughly 800 BC, pirate hunting beyond the Aegean was probably identical to that of the Mycenaeans and Minoans. At the most fundamental level, towns were built away from the shore in order to give defenders time to identify the pirates and prepare for an attack. As wealth grew, newer towns were built on the shore itself and protected by fortifications.[15] To physically clear even local areas of pirates required more than just a navy to patrol straits, headlands, other danger zones, and islands known to make good pirate haunts. It required naval stations and garrisons as well. According to Thucydides, the Minoan navy did not simply "clear the seas" by cruising for pirates and attacking them on sight. Rather, Minos used his navy, and probably his army as well, to force pirates from their strongholds in the Aegean, which he then colonized, appointing his sons as governors. His navy in turn was able to patrol the routes between Crete and her colonies. Many of the islands' rovers and original inhabitants were probably absorbed into the Minoan empire.[16] A similar but narrower form of this strategy can be seen in the case of the pirates who attacked the shipping of Byblos and Simyra: their ruler pleaded for the Egyptian pharaoh to place forces, probably naval, into the offending ports so that rovers could not use them.[17]

As for Minos's motives, Thucydides believed that he purged the sea of pirates not merely to protect his own trade, but also to expand his empire.[18] Naval operations against sea rovers have often been conducted as part of colonial expansion, and the fall of such empires has often led in turn to significant increases in piracy. The collapse of Minos's Cretan empire set loose the Mycenaean sea rovers described in the last chapter, for example.[19] Throughout history, naval control and economic order have worked to suppress piracy, while economic disorder or political anarchy coupled with a lack of control of the sea has usually resulted in an increase in piracy. One can often discern a paradoxical cycle as well: piracy is suppressed in order to protect trade and grow the economy, which in turn gives rise to piracy again as wealth and trade increase.

As for the actual means of fighting a sea rover at sea or ashore, we remain hindered by the lack of written and physical record. Few records of early naval warfare of any sort exist. The earliest record of a naval battle may be that between the Hittites and Cypriots circa 1207 BC, but there are no details.[20] Similarly, Thucydides dated the first naval battle to roughly 690 BC between the Corinthians and the Corcyraeans, but he provided no details.[21]

The first detailed record of both naval warfare and pirate hunting is that of Egyptian pharoah Ramses III and his armed forces defeating a great coalition of the Sea Peoples on sea and on land roughly a century later after having beaten off three previous raids.[22] In Ramses's own words:

> Behold ye, the great might of my father, Amon-Re. The countries which came from their isles in the midst of the sea, they advanced to Egypt, their hearts relying upon their arms. The net was made ready for them, to ensnare them. Entering stealthily into the harbor-mouth, they fell into it. Caught in their place, they were dispatched, and their bodies stripped. . . . My arrow struck, and none escaped my arms nor my hand. I flourished like a hawk among the fowl; my talons descended upon their heads.[23]

Another inscription continues just as poetically: "Capsized and perishing in their places, their hearts are taken, their souls fly away, and their weapons are cast out upon the sea. His arrows pierce whomsoever he will among them, and he who is hit falls into the water."[24] Accompanying the inscriptions at Medinet Habu in Egypt is a great bas-relief graphically illustrating the bloody chaos of close combat at sea. (See figure 3.) Ramses's "net"—an ambush or trap—remains a staple of naval warfare, whether the adversary be a single pirate vessel or a fleet of warships. Unfortunately, little other evidence exists of naval actions, pirate hunting or otherwise, and what does exist has little information on tactics.

There are other known successes against sea rovers. The Phoenicians, for example, one of the great trading empires in the Mediterranean and well-known for "sharp" trading, expanded even into the western part of the sea. Such expansion would have required strong, active defenses against the various sea rovers of the age, not forgetting, of course, that the Phoenicians were occasionally rovers themselves. The naval forces of Assyrian king Sargon II captured pirates in the early eighth century BC. His son, Sennacherib, put down a revolt in Cilicia in 698 BC in which Greek rovers had a hand, and destroyed one of their fleets near the mouth of the Saros. In 694 BC, he led a major expedition of his army and navy, the latter crewed by Phoenicians, against the Chaldean sea rovers in the Persian Gulf. One part of his fleet descended the Euphrates, while the other descended the Tigris part way then was hauled overland and launched into a canal to avoid arousing suspicion. After a near disaster due to the pirate-hunting navy's unfamiliarity with Persian Gulf tides and currents, Sennacherib made an offering to the god of the sea then led his forces ashore to victory. Once again, the destruction or capture of sea-roving bases proved to be an effective means of suppressing sea roving itself, although the method is not appropriate in all cases.[25]

The navy of Pharoah Necho II was active in both the Red Sea and Mediterranean circa 600 BC and almost certainly protecting Egyptian commerce from various sea rovers. Around the same time, Phocaeans were expanding both trade and colonies, even into Phoenician territory of the west, and took to the sea in warships in order to protect themselves. Doubtless most pirates left them alone. Hippas, son of Peisistratos the tyrant of Athens, hunted pirates circa 525 BC. Thucydides wrote that the Corinthians, grown wealthy by trade on land and sea, built a navy which was used to suppress piracy, while Herodotus claimed that Polycrates, the tyrant of Samos, "was the first of mere human birth who conceived the design of gaining the empire of the sea, and aspired to rule over Ionia and the islands." Such an empire would have required the suppression of pirates and other sea rovers.[26]

The common tactics of oared pirate versus sailing merchantman, and of oared pirate hunter versus oared pirate, changed very little, if at all, over the course of two thousand years. For much of the period, the galley was single banked (that is, it had only a single bank of oars), which limited its size, power, and speed. Warriors aboard ship fought predominantly with bow, pike, spear, shield, sword, and sling; there were probably no heavier shipboard weapons yet. However, four technological innovations set the course for significant changes in warfare at sea and marked the rise of organized professional navies, and thus of pirate hunters.

First, iron came of age circa 1000 BC. Now swords, spearheads, and armor could be made with a metal much stronger than bronze and which, in the case of cutting weapons, took a much better edge. Second, around 800 BC, the ram was invented. With its advent, the ship itself, strengthened to support this device, became itself a weapon, and as a result sophisticated ship and fleet tactics came into being. Organization and discipline in support of them were now vital. Maneuvering became even more important. Third, a narrow deck or platform was fitted amidships on many fighting ships, providing a platform from which marines or armed sailors could fight more effectively. The common version of this new vessel of ram and fighting deck was called a pentaconter, given its fifty oars. Two centuries later, the triaconter was developed, a swift fighting galley of thirty oars often used to chase and fight pirates. In battle, oarsmen were moved to a low row of benches amidships, protecting them. Now their muscle was necessary not merely to overtake another vessel or escape from it but also to breach an enemy hull. On a large scale at least, battles no longer had to be fought solely as pell-mell assaults of arrow flights and boarding actions; one ship could be sent to the bottom by the direct action of another without ever coming to hand-to-hand combat. Even so, boarding actions would remain an important form of naval warfare until the early nineteenth century, would be seen occasionally through World War II, and remain today as a staple of naval commando operations at sea.[27]

Last, with greater power needed for ramming, a means for adding oarsmen without overly lengthening the fighting galley—which would have weakened the vessel and also reduced its maneuverability—was necessary. The answer was found in adding an additional bank of oars above the first, probably between 700 and 600 BC.[28] The bireme, or two-banked galley, was followed by the trireme, or three-banked, which Thucydides credited to the Corinthians.[29] Aboard ancient vessels, each oar was manned by a single oarsman, and not as galleys often were during the Renaissance and later centuries, with multiple oarsmen to each oar.[30] With these changes, fighting ships grew more rakish and more powerful, although the open or "Homeric" galley remained in use by many rovers.

Unfortunately, we know far more about the ships themselves than we do about naval tactics of the period, much less about the men who made up the two or more millennia of the pirates and pirate hunters of antiquity.

THE CHARACTER OF THE ANCIENT ROVER

We can only speculate on the character of the ancient rover. Perhaps these men, many of whom were mariners, were similar to modern mariners. But mariners, although they share much in common with each other, are further identified by their specific occupations. The merchant seafarer is distinguished from the fisherman, for example, who in turn is distinguished from the navy man. Still, it is tempting to assume that ancient mariners, including pirates and pirate hunters, were similar in many ways to those of today, in spite of the paucity of direct evidence connecting the ancient seafarer with the modern. There is a more or less direct lineal progression, but this is no guarantee that nature and character have passed as well. We could argue that, because there are numerous similarities in character among mariners from the Middle Ages through the twenty-first century, ancient mariners were probably also much like mariners of later ages. After all, similar environments tend to attract and produce similar types. For much of history, seafarers engaged in extensive physical labor, were exposed to the elements of wind and water, committed themselves to the vagaries and unknowns of the sea, bonded as crews in a special environment, used a special language of ship and sea, and understood that to save themselves in a crisis, they must look to themselves.

However, we might also look elsewhere, beyond the commonalities of the sea over the centuries and the scraps of written and archaeological evidence of the life and character of the ancient mariner. There is an obvious ancient archetype who would have been immediately recognized in the Middle Ages, as well as in the twenty-first century, as the epitome or idealization of both pirate and pirate hunter, if not entirely of the common seafarer: Odysseus.

Homer's hero is no common seaman turned rover by dint of economics, oppression, opportunity, or adventure, but a prince among heroes, a leader among leaders who were born to a sea-roving lifestyle. Yet he fits what we might imagine the ideal rover to be—then, later, and today, for even the most common of pirates has always imagined himself a prince and believed himself a better man than most. Odysseus is aggressive and combative, believes in strength, and considers those not like him, including the weak, to be infe-rior. He has a need to prove himself to his companions. He is an individual with a strong ego yet understands teamwork and can, as necessary, subordi-nate his ego to the greater good—plunder, that is. He would rather rove and fight than stay at home and husband his land and family yet is not averse to personal wealth and luxury. In spite of his love of adventure, he is a devoted father when he is home, as the sailor in general has often been character-ized. He loves his wife, Penelope, but cheats on her during his long voyage, as sailors have for centuries been reputed to do in regard to their own wives, mistresses, and girlfriends—and a fair number of sailors did and probably still do deserve the reputation. For many, this virtue, or lack thereof, was and is part of the male sailor's panache, at least to everyone but his wife, mistress, or girlfriend.

Yet there is more to Odysseus's sea-roving character than a mere will-ingness to chase plunder and women and otherwise act like a sailor. In par-ticular, he is both courageous and cunning and holds the latter virtue to be of greatest value, for he knows that courage alone is rarely sufficient in itself. Whenever possible, he wins by his wits or guile, and not by the strength of direct attack. In many ways, he embodies the classic description of the swordsman or other warrior: "In Battle let Valour and Prudence go together, the Lyon's Courage with the Fox's Craft."[31] He knows well that if one cannot succeed by the lion's skin—by strength as did Heracles who wore the lion's pelt—he should do so by the fox's.[32] "Where the lion's skin will not reach, we must sew the fox's skin on to it."[33] Odysseus is not only a crafty bastard but also a born liar of the craftiest sort. He is a "sea story" raconteur who com-monly embellishes the truth without diminishing it, yet who can, as neces-sary to save his skin, salvage an enterprise, seduce a woman, or tell such lies as might deceive the gods themselves. That such liars are often found among sailors is no coincidence. As for warfare as an end, Odysseus does not make war solely for its own sake but also for glory and profit, the latter perhaps most of all. After all, why go to war if not to be rewarded with pillage and plunder in addition to the gory glory of the battlefield?

Odysseus is well-known for his deceptions during the siege of Troy and during his odyssey home. The brutal yet lifesaving trick he played on Poly-phemus the Cyclops comes to mind: Odysseus and his men blind the Cyclops in his sleep, then escape from his cave strapped to the bellies of his sheep. Odysseus himself deceives Polyphemus as to the identity of the man who has tricked and blinded him. More broadly, when Odysseus takes his revenge on Penelope's suitors, he shows the rover's martial virtues in full flower. In disguise, he makes a reconnaissance, deceives the suitors as to his identity and power, hides their weapons, and bolts their avenue of escape. When the time is right, he reveals his true identity and kills the suitors. All of these virtues (some of them flaws, some might say)—a roving yet loyal nature, a willingness to take risks yet not be rash, cunning combined with courage, not to mention a seafaring lifestyle—make Odysseus the sea rover's archetype, for these virtues are also those of the pirate and privateer, and very often of the pirate hunter as well. It is well to remember, however, that he is only the archetype. Then as now, many pirates were little more than opportunistic thieves on the sea, relying largely on the strength of their numbers or arms (or both) and on the speed of their vessels. Many of the rovers of early antiquity probably preyed solely on weak vessels and ran from the strong, as rovers often have done, and wisely so, leaving little opportunity for stratagem in combat against an equal or superior enemy.

The pirate and privateer, no matter their motivation, seek profit. In doing so, they naturally seek to minimize the expenditure of resources that detract from profit, thus their preference for weak merchantmen. Likewise does the pirate hunter seek to minimize the expenditure of resources. Often a private entity or a resource-strapped navy, flotilla, or single vessel, pirate hunters have had to make the most effective use of their resources. Pirates and privateers, after all, are typically difficult to locate and engage. Like Odysseus, the rover must be cunning, for this minimizes the effort and resources required to capture the prey, and increases the likelihood of the pirate's survival. To trick the prey and take it by surprise, for example, makes it more likely the rover will both survive and succeed—after all, the rover wants to be able to spend his plunder. Cunning or trickery also reduces the chance that the prey will be significantly damaged or even lost. Likewise the pirate hunter's cunning is as important as his courage in capturing an elusive prey. This is not to suggest that the pirate hunter must be wrought from the same material as his prey. However, deception is the tactical and strategic fundamental and can be dispensed with only in the case of overwhelming power, and even then it is seldom wise to do so. And this the greatest of ancient pirate-hunting peoples knew well, for they had great experience in the use of power, deception, courage, and cunning, although one of them, the Romans, were not truly a sea people at all.[34]

4

Of Laurel Leaves and Pirate Princes

Pirate Hunting in the Mediterranean, 700 BC–AD 476

Before we turn to pirate hunting in this great age, a quotation from St. Augustine, writing of "How like kingdoms without justice are to robberies" in *The City of God*, bears repeating. Quoted almost to the point of cliché by philosophers, theorists, economists, historians, and clergy in support of social, political, economic, and religious views across the spectrum, it tells of a purported meeting between Alexander the Great and a captured pirate captain named in other texts as Dionides.[1] "For when that king had asked the man what he meant by keeping hostile possession of the sea, he answered with bold pride, 'What thou meanest by seizing the whole earth; but because I do it with a petty ship, I am called a robber, while thou who dost it with a great fleet art styled emperor.'"[2]

St. Augustine was repeating a story told by Cicero in *de Republica* five centuries earlier, although it may ultimately derive from Thucydides, the naval officer turned historian.[3] In his great opus, Thucydides commented on the growth of "tyrannies"—non-democratic governments—as a result of increased wealth, and he noted how some of these "tyrants" used their wealth to build navies and "put down piracy."[4] In other words, they violently eliminated the smaller competition.

The comparison of pirate and government as thieves of a kind has universal appeal, and it is easy to see how the ancient pirate, particularly with the rise of the great Greek and Roman empires that came to control the sea, might have felt now that his status was somewhat diminished. Even the small-time sea rover must have wondered if there were any real difference between his robberies and those of a king. Of course, a cynic might suggest that St. Augustine's pirate was merely using his wits as a defense by claiming to be

47

an equal in all but scale with Alexander. Similarly might a cynic suggest that Alexander's reply to the pirate may have been that "big fish eat little fish," as a medieval history of Alexander quotes him as saying after a dive underwater.[5]

The quotation is often used similarly today to explain, and sometimes justify, everything from anarchism to terrorism, not to mention theft—after all, some do wonder what is the crime in stealing from a thief?[6] On the other hand, some writers have taken different views. In *The Black Tulip*, Alexandre Dumas wrote, "'What difference is there between the figure of the conqueror and that of the pirate?' said the ancients. The difference only between the eagle and the vulture—serenity or restlessness."[7] One hopes that Dumas did not forget that eagles are also carrion eaters, at least part of the time.

St. Augustine, however, writing during the final days of the Roman Empire, was making the point that an *unjust* ruler is no more than a pirate and is a hypocrite for condemning him. St. Augustine was not justifying piracy. The pirate, romantic as he has been made out to be (and sometimes was), remains a thief. That governments may also be thieves does not alter this fact, although it is sometimes easier to sympathize with the pirate. Again, one person's tax collector is another's thief, and often the pirate was doing no more than an unjust emperor was: stealing from others by force of arms or by its threat. The argument that all governments are thieves is best discussed elsewhere, drink in hand.

OF PIRATES AND EMPIRES

We seldom realize, overwhelmed as we are by images of seventeenth and eighteenth century pirates of European and North African origin, that the reigns of the ancient pirates of the Mediterranean and beyond were far more diverse and longer-lived. The Mycenaean sea rovers, for example, reigned for more than three centuries, and their offspring were not eradicated until the nineteenth century. The Norsemen raided for several centuries, and the various Mediterranean corsairs of post-antiquity raided non-stop for almost fifteen hundred years. Even the relatively brief reign of the Cilician pirates lasted for a century and a half. These are but a few of many examples we have of sea roving's great ages. Compared to them, the mere seventy-five-year reign of the various "Golden Age" pirates originating in the New World seems almost insignificant.

We also often lack a sense of scale regarding these ancient pirates. In 302 BC, for example, a reported eight thousand pirate mercenaries—probably nowhere near the entire pirate population of the Mediterranean—joined

Demetrius during the Fourth Diadoch War, which was fought over control of part of Alexander the Great's empire.[8] Compare this to the two to four thousand buccaneers, filibusters, and pirates of the Caribbean who existed at any given time during their "Golden Age," or to the estimated one thousand to fifteen hundred modern Somali pirates. Part of the problem is that we simply do not know much about these ancient pirates. Indeed, we have far more information on the deeds of a handful of "Golden Age" pirate captains than we do of two entire millennia of ancient sea rovers.

From 700 to 65 BC, the Mediterranean was rife with piracy, and often with a relatively new form of sea roving, that of "privateering." Naval cruising and raiding were common as well. The latter varied from strategic to tactical to mere profitable reprisal, and at times to outright piracy. By 66 BC, piracy had lost its great hold on the Mediterranean when the last pirate empire was destroyed, leaving only small-time local sea thieves and raiders. In 27 BC, the *Pax Romana* came into being. Rome owned the Mediterranean.

In this chapter, I loosely define piracy as armed theft on or from the sea by both "common pirates" and sea-roving peoples, as opposed to state-authorized private or naval sea roving or raiding in times of war. The distinction is important, given that states during this period were growing more sophisticated and more powerful, and armies and navies were often no longer warlike tribes bonding together to fight a common enemy, but units specifically organized and trained for warfare in support of the state. Doubtless the pirate still did not see himself as an illegitimate thief at sea, but as a roving warrior taking what opportunity and tradition offered up to him. Alfred P. Rubin argues in *The Law of Piracy* that the Greek and Roman use of the word "pirate" (Greek *peiraton*, Latin *pirata*) did not originally impart the stigma of robbers (Latin *praedones*) or thieves (Latin *ladrones*), but of sea-raiding peoples whose thefts had been more or less legitimized, or at least understood or explained, by centuries of tradition. Only as empires grew—and with them their great sea trade—did sea roving become stigmatized as piracy as we understand it today: the practice of armed theft on or from the sea by "enemies of all mankind."[9]

In his *Histories*, Polybius describes the Illyrian sea-roving people as "not the enemies of this people or that, but the common enemies of all" because they attacked anyone and everyone solely for the purpose of plunder.[10] However, the Illyrians doubtless saw themselves as merely exercising their right to fish the sea and shore for slaves and other plunder—a roving form of warfare and expansion, in other words—but to the great empires they were an unacceptable intrusion deserving of outlawry. Again, the words of St. Augustine's pirate come to mind. This being said, it must be reiterated that to the victims of sea-roving attacks, the sea rover was a thief and often a murderer, no matter the color of his authority.

The empires and great kingdoms of this period depended on trade by sea to maintain their power, and smaller states depended on it to sustain both their quality of life and their survival via critical resources. Trade had expanded on an incredible scale and was the foundation of Mediterranean economies. All but the sea-roving peoples and pirates depended on seas free of piracy and other impediments. Naturally, given the number of great and petty states in the Mediterranean, the increasing sophistication of political and economic control, and the natural encroachment of one state onto the territory and trade of another, conflict was inevitable. As a result, opportunities for naval action great and small abounded: the Greeks defeated Xerxes's great Persian invasion in 480 BC, the first Peloponnesian War was fought from 461 to 445 BC, and the second, usually referred to as *the* Peloponnesian War, was fought from 431 to 404 BC. Later came the conquests of Alexander the Great and, after them, the wars fought over his empire, which largely collapsed after his death. The wars of Alexander and his various heirs were followed by the great, well-known wars and civil wars of the Romans. Numerous smaller wars and conflicts erupted during the period.

With this chaos of war came piratical opportunity. In the Peloponnesian War, for example, both pirates and "privateers" flourished, and navies engaged in commerce raiding: the capture or destruction of merchant vessels.[11] Pirate mercenaries often augmented armies and navies, and some states encouraged piracy as a means of economic expansion or to hinder competitor states. Navies, the bulwark against the pirate, had not only the task of patrolling for pirates and privateers, but also of defending cities, coastlines, and merchant fleets from enemy attack, engaging enemy fleets, blockading ports and coasts, and making descents (raids) on towns and villages both for supplies and for plunder. "Making descents from the fleet he ravaged certain places on the sea-coast, and captured Thronium and took hostages from it," wrote Thucydides of one of many such naval raiding expeditions.[12] Naval vessels frequently attacked the shipping of enemies and neutrals.[13]

Just as they are today, navies were heavily tasked and spread thin. Merchant vessels were unable to take to the sea without fear of attack and so had to arm themselves or seek naval protection or both. Crews and passengers traveled in fear, not only of their lives at Poseidon's often tempestuous hand, but of enslavement or murder at the hands of the various sea rovers and navies seeking riches by force of arms on the sea. Thucydides, for example, notes that the Lacadaemonians "butchered as enemies all whom they took on the sea, whether allies of Athens or neutrals."[14] Hostage-taking for ransom was a popular means of financial gain among both pirates and "privateers," but only rich captives were held for ransom—the poor were sold into slavery or murdered if inconvenient or unsuitable. As in the Mycenaean Age, human captives were still the most significant pirate plunder.

The mariners of this later age of antiquity—whether merchant seamen, pirate adventurers, or navy sailors—were not amateurs. The trade of handling a vessel at sea in peace or war had become a profession with highly specialized subtrades. Pericles, speaking of the enemy to the assembled Athenians, put it well: "Familiarity with the sea they will not find an easy acquisition . . . It must be kept in mind that seamanship, just like anything else, is a matter of art, and will not admit of being taken up occasionally as an occupation for times of leisure; on the contrary, it is so exacting as to leave leisure for nothing else."[15] Knowledge of the sea and skill in ship handling had increased to the point that even long-range exploration by sea was deemed possible and even pursued. The Phoenicians, for example, under commission from Pharaoh Necho II, reportedly sailed from the Red Sea around the Horn of Africa and back to Egypt through the Strait of Gibraltar circa 600 BC, a voyage that took three years.[16] Some scholars doubt whether the voyage actually occurred, but it was entirely possible given Phoenician maritime skill and technology.

Although navies dating to the Minoan had their origin in suppressing piracy and other forms sea roving and sea raiding (and surely also in engaging in such attacks), the growth of sophisticated political economies and associated states in the Hellenic Age provided competition and conflict on a large scale, requiring in turn that navies grow larger and more sophisticated in order to protect shipping lanes, defend the state from attack, or assault a neighboring state. Advances in technology, in particular in ship design and arms development, provided additional impetus to the advance of maritime art and science, piracy and pirate hunting included.

PIRACY AND SEA ROVING 500 BC–AD 476

It is easy to summarize the period at hand: petty piracy existed throughout it, large-scale piracy rose and fell as empires fell and rose, and privateering enjoyed its first of many heydays. Various cities, states, and peoples were

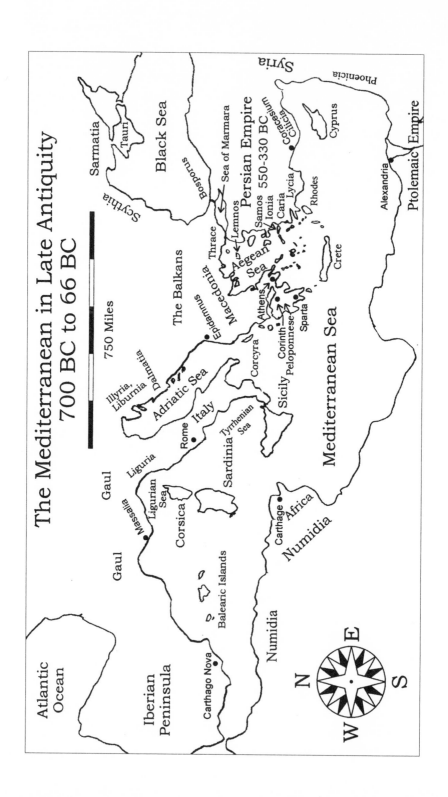

The Mediterranean in Late Antiquity
700 BC to 66 BC

750 Miles

Atlantic
Ocean

Iberian
Peninsula

Carthago Nova

Gaul

Gaul

Massalia

Liguria

Ligurian
Sea

Corsica

Balearic Islands

Sardinia

Rome

Italy

Tyrrhenian
Sea

Illyria,
Liburnia

Dalmatia

Adriatic Sea

The Balkans

Epidamnus

Macedonia

Thrace

Corcyra

Sicily

Corinth

Peloponnese

Sparta

Athens

Aegean
Sea

Lemnos

Sea of Marmara

Bosporus

Black Sea

Scythia

Sarmatia

Tauri

Samos

Ionia

Caria

Lycia

Rhodes

Crete

Persian Empire
550-330 BC

Coracesium

Cilicia

Cyprus

Syria

Phoenicia

Alexandria

Ptolemaic Empire

Mediterranean Sea

Carthage

Africa

Numidia

Numidia

N E S W

known for their sea roving: Lemnos, Samos, Liguria, Caria, and Illyria or Liburnia, for example, among many.[17] Certain locales were known as sea-rover haunts: Crete, Myonnesos, Halonnessos, Alopeconnesos, and Chalcis, among many.[18] The Tyrrhenian was long noted as a pirate sea, and historian Lionel Casson notes that the Tyrrhenian pirates were probably "Etruscans, Italians, Sardinians, and Greeks from southern Italy."[19] We cannot forget the Tauri and Sarmatians, Black Sea rovers who sometimes raided into the Mediterranean.[20] They were many, these sea rovers, in numbers and histories only hinted at in the written record.

Many were the great pirate captains as well, but few of their names have come down to us. Who now even recalls the names of two of the great "arch-pirates" of this age—Timocles, for example, and Ameinias?[21] Few even recall Queen Teuta of Illyria, who dispatched her vessels far and wide to plunder ship and shore of all.[22] Of particular note is the rise of mercenary sea rovers during this period, especially from the fourth century BC onward. In times of war, pirates often offered their services to the highest bidder. The Spartans and their allies during the Peloponnesian War used pirates to great effect, as did others in the decades that followed.[23] Dionysius I used them at the siege of Rhodes in 305 BC, although to less effect, for the siege failed.[24] Many of these rovers and pirates were little more than mercenaries known for their courage in battle, and some commanders reserved them specifically for use in desperate circumstances.[25]

In this often unregulated and calamitous period, sea rovers appear to have had little difficulty recruiting. Roving in its various forms offered the possibility of wealth for many, or at least of a better standard of living. Wine, women, and reasonable prospects were surely more easily had by the rover than by the peasant tilling the land, and sea roving was the basis of many local economies. Navies in this age were often plagued with a problem that would show up in Europe in the seventeenth and eighteenth centuries, that of navy seamen preferring privateering—and in antiquity, service also as piratical mercenaries—to naval service.[26] Although dismal economic circumstances are often associated with piracy—substantial poverty or economic turmoil on an ungoverned coast along which merchant shipping travels is one of several recipes for piracy—opportunity combined with tradition and a sense of adventure cannot be discounted as one of several motivations for many of these ancient rovers. Historian Henry A. Ormerod noted that "Greek love of adventure, as well as continued faction in the states, drove men abroad to serve as mercenaries . . . or . . . to become freebooters."[27] Sea roving was a longstanding tradition in the Mediterranean and would remain so for another two thousand years.

Sea roving remained composed primarily of raids on towns and villages ashore, as opposed to attacks on shipping at sea.[28] Although the latter were routinely practiced, they were subordinate to descents ashore in scale and profitability. A quick raid on an undefended population on or near the sea provided slaves, supplies, and various other plunder. And, as was pointed out in the discussion of the Homeric rovers, permanent habitations are fixed targets, thus the rover need not waste time lying in wait nor chasing. Towns were usually taken by surprise, either at dawn or by ruse. Polybius has left us with one ruse used, albeit unsuccessfully in the end, by Illyrian pirates: they sailed into the harbor of Epidamnus, "and, landing as if for the purpose of watering, lightly clad but with swords concealed in water-jars, they cut down the guards of the gate and at once possessed themselves of the gate-tower."[29]

However, there was one significant change to roving in this period, other than the addition of privateering: pirate empires developed from the riches to be had from the great trading empires. Again, it is a cycle that fed on itself: to grow, the state suppressed the pirate, who later reappeared to take advantage of the opportunity of new, greater wealth afforded by the state, which sometimes had grown into empire.

NEW NAVAL VESSELS AND TACTICS

The period was also one of great change in technology, including shipbuilding and naval weapons. By the fifth century BC, the three-banked trireme with a crew of roughly two hundred had replaced the two-banked penta-conter as the principal Mediterranean warship.[30] Built for heavy ramming, it was stouter than earlier fighting galleys. Built for speed with three banks of oarsmen, its upper works, which included an "outrigger" to support the third bank of oarsmen, sat higher above the water than those of earlier fighting galleys. Soon after came the quadrireme (four banks) and quinquereme (five banks); even far larger ships resulted from regional arms races.

The catapult was put to use at sea, launching not only various missiles but also combustibles. Fireships were used by the Romans.[31] In the latter years of the period, the Byzantine navy developed the siphon (essentially a flamethrower that shot Greek fire) for use at sea. Greek fire was a combustible mixture that even burned on water and was very difficult to extinguish. Portable "fighting towers" were added to the bow and stern of some ships. The Romans developed the *corvus* or raven, a boarding gangway or bridge with an iron spike on the end. Fireworks were developed, including what would later be called the firepot: "pitchers to be filled with pitch and tallow, and thrown into the enemy's vessels, when being broken by their weight, they spread the combustibles about, to serve as aliment for fire."[32] Hannibal reportedly "advised the king of Antioch to throw into the enemy's vessels vases filled with vipers, that the soldiers, disgusted, might shrink from the fight, and the seamen be impeded in their manoevres," and the "same was done, when his fleet began to retire, by Prusias."[33] Tactics varied according to navies; some preferred to ram, some to board. All were prepared to do either.[34]

The crews of these vessels were now professionals with a distinct officer class, plus specialist petty officers, marines, archers, and rowers. The number of armed men varied according to preferred tactics. The Athenian navy, for example, preferred to ram and so limited the number of marines. Other navies preferred boarding tactics, and their crews reflected this. Oarsmen were free men except in rare cases, but were usually recruited from the poorer classes. Slaves were considered too valuable to use as oarsmen, and probably too unreliable as well for a navy that required strict, motivated discipline.[35] These men were not oarsmen-warriors as had been the case during the Mycenaean Age, but citizen specialists whose sole purpose was to row. "The men were each to take their oar, cushion, and rowlock thong," wrote Thucydides.[36] Occasionally, non-citizen oarsmen were hired, but they were still free men.

As ships developed in size and complexity closer to the new millennium, their crews reflected this, particularly in the addition of more specialist officers and petty officers, some of whom would in later centuries be referred to as "sea artists." In addition to the usual crew of past centuries, a Rhodian quadrireme carried a doctor, specialist seamen to handle the rigging, an "oar binder" to tend the oars, and catapult operators, among others. However, these large vessels, which corresponded to the ships-of-the-line of later centuries, were unsuitable to engaging swift pirates unless they could be trapped in a harbor or cove.[37] No longer were the principal warship and the pirate craft one and the same.

This is not to suggest that the development of these capital ships did little to aid in the war against pirates. What did result from their development, and what would prove significant in the suppression of piracy, was organization. As naval discipline and order became more sophisticated in order to deal with these large, complex vessels and their tactics, these virtues passed to all naval vessels, leaving them manned with professional, highly disciplined crews, a distinct advantage in a direct engagement against a less disciplined crew, no matter how skilled or courageous. However, it should be noted that in certain tactical circumstances, the less-ordered, less-confining character of many pirate crews might have been an advantage. Rigid discipline, after all, is predictable and often inflexible. Further, numerical and technological superiority can breed complacence even among the disciplined and courageous, while desperation can often enhance innovation and courage. When Athenian admiral Phormio exhorted his fleet before battle with the Peloponnesians, he noted that, "An adversary numerically superior, like the one before us, comes into action trusting more to strength than to resolution; while he who voluntarily confronts tremendous odds must have very great internal resources to draw upon. For these reasons the Peloponnesians fear our irrational audacity more than they would ever have done a more commensurate preparation."[38] Such "irrational audacity" has often confounded discipline. The ideal, of course, is discipline and audacity conjoined.

STRATEGIES OF PIRATE HUNTING 500 BC–AD 476

Pirate hunting in this age had the problems of pirate hunting throughout all of antiquity, and for that matter, throughout much of history. Before conquest and empire gave governments access to naval bases across much of the Mediterranean, naval warfare was limited in its scope. War galleys could not handle stormy and had to keep close to shore. Nor could they carry sufficient supplies for a long campaign, and so naval forces were not only often camped ashore but also had to forage or plunder for supplies along the coast and in the hinterland. Even the manner of battle at sea required a camp or base ashore. Although fighting galleys often cruised under a single large sail, they did not go into battle under sail—warships needed to row swiftly and turn swiftly and tightly. A large mast and sail produced drag if rigged and took up space required for oarsmen if un-stepped and stowed on deck. Instead, the main mast and sail of a fighting galley was left ashore, and only a small mast and "boat sail" was retained to assist in battle, primarily in retreat.[39]

Naval forces alone often could not force pirates from their havens, for rover harbors were typically well-protected both by nature and by prepared weapons or fortifications. Ancient historian Livy described one noted pirate harbor into which Roman ships had chased a pirate flotilla:

Myonnesus is a promontory between Teos and Samos. It consists of a
hill rising from a pretty large base to a sharp top, in shape of an obelisk.
From the land, the access to it is by a narrow path; towards the sea it is
terminated by cliffs undermined by the waves, so that in some places the
superimpending rocks project beyond the vessels that lie at anchor. The
[Roman] ships not daring to approach lest they should be exposed to
the weapons of the pirates, who stood above the cliffs wasted the day to
no purpose. At length, a little before nightfall, they gave over the attempt
and retired.[40]

Such defended places had to be captured from land.

Further, although pirate havens might be easily located, pirates on the
sea were not. To travel into well-defended, hostile waters in order to hunt
pirates required not only time and patience, but also a significant force of
warships and soldiers or marines capable both of defeating an enemy at sea
and of defending itself against attack ashore. Anti-pirate patrols were thus
out of the question in all but local seas or colonial waters.[41] The problem was
ultimately one of economics: at what point did piracy become such a threat
to economy or security in general, or both, that it had to be eradicated?
Typically, it was the merchant class who pressured their rulers or assemblies
to take action against pirates, although at times invasions purportedly motivated by piracy appear to have been motivated as much by the desire for conquest.[42] The best solution (albeit an expensive one) to the problem of piracy
significant enough to threaten the state was not merely the destruction of
offending pirates, vessels, and bases, but the defeat or even conquest of the
offending people itself. Yet even in the case of the defeat of a sea-roving people, their piracies usually remained suppressed only as long as land and naval
forces of the conqueror were stationed in the region. The early Romans, for
example, defeated the Illyrian rovers twice, yet they continued to be a problem for another fifty years.[43]

Livy described the destruction of the Ligurians, the noted pirates of
northwest Italy (modern Genoa, Imperia, La Spezia, and Savona), and pointed out the desperate valor common to many sea-roving peoples: "The general . . . [noted] what a shame it was that a Roman army should be besieged
by Ligurians, people more properly styled robbers than a regular enemy. . . .
What the Spaniards, the Gauls, the Macedonians, or Carthaginians, never
dared to attempt, a Ligurian enemy dares: he marches up to the trenches
of a Roman camp, besieges and assaults it."[44] The Ligurians attacked the

Roman camp, but the Romans immediately counterattacked, surprising the attackers, for they had expected the Romans to fight from their fortified position. The Ligurians broke and ran. In disarray, they were easy prey for the highly disciplined legionnaires, as Livy described:[45] "About fifteen thousand of the Ligurians were killed, and two thousand five hundred taken. In three days after the whole state of the Inguanian Ligurians gave hostages and surrendered. The masters and crews of the ships which had been employed in piracies were carefully sought for and thrown in prison; and thirty-two ships of that description were taken by Caius Matienus on the Ligurian coast."[46]

The battle is also a reminder that "irrational audacity" is perfectly suitable to both disciplined conventional professionals and to irregulars and other unconventional forces.

There were many concerted efforts to suppress piracy from 500 to 67 BC, and many were successful. In some cases, treaties and economic inducements were combined with the threat of military force. Alliances against pirates and piratical states were common. Notably, Athens suppressed much of the piracy in the Mediterranean after her defeat of the Persian invasion, but the Peloponnesian wars undid all that Athens had gained against the scourge of piracy and other sea roving.[47] Clerk-turned-tyrant Dionysius I of Syracuse put his navy to use clearing the Tyrrhenian and Adriatic seas of pirates, and quite successfully.[48] Alexander the Great ordered his admiral Amphoterus to clear the seas of piracy, and the effort appears to have had good results, at least until Alexander's death.[49] Soon after, Rhodes, with only a small but highly trained navy, rose to power in part as a trading ally of Ptolemaic Egypt and in part as an independent broker of naval power, and effectively suppressed much local piracy.[50] The Roman navy and army likewise suppressed piracy, including the aforementioned Illyrians as well as the Cilicians.

Bribery in pursuit of pirate hunting was not out the question. Circa 300 BC, Lycus, one of Lysimachus's generals, bribed Andron, a pirate chief using Ephesus as a base, to turn the city over to him. Ephesus at that time was held by forces of Demetrius I, an enemy. Andron brought a number of Lycus's soldiers into the city disguised as prisoners but with swords beneath their robes. Once inside, the "prisoners" killed the city's sentinels and guards and signaled to Lycus and his army, who then captured the city. Andron and his pirates, per agreement, were paid and set free. Although the goal was the seizing of the town by an enemy, the taking of the town also denied pirates a local base.[51]

Prosecutions of corrupt officials who directly aided pirates, or enabled their depredations by weakening local defenses or otherwise failing in their duty, are also known. Cicero, for example, was the prosecutor in the trial of Gaius Verres, governor of Sicily, who, among his many crimes, aided and abetted pirates by embezzling funds intended for the navy and local defenses, taking pirate bribes, and letting pirates have free reign of the waters surrounding Rome's most vital breadbasket.[52]

Nonetheless, in spite of these successes, the age was known as much for the reigns of pirates great and small, and even of their encouragement, as it was for their suppression or eradication, until the Pax Romana.

THE TACTICS OF PIRATE HUNTING 500 BC–AD 476

To deal with attacks by pirates, privateers, or naval raiders ashore, defenders ashore employed tactics common almost to the present day. They kept a watch on the sea, and if a potential enemy were sighted, they lit warning fires that alerted inhabitants to flee within city gates or to the hills, and alerted warriors to arm. For example, wrote Livy, "In Spain there are several towers placed in high situations, which they employ both as watch-towers and as places of defense against pirates."[53] If a naval force were nearby, locals would alert it so that it could counterattack.

Other tactics were likewise unchanged. Defenders might attempt to repel the attackers as they came ashore; attack them as they plundered; attack their campsite, fortified or otherwise, if they made one; or attack the raiders' flank as they attacked the walls of the town, if the town were fortified. Thucydides described how a local Spartan commander, Brasidas, came to the defense of a town under attack by a fleet of fifty Athenian vessels that had been cruising about and ravaging the coast. "Hearing of the attack, he hurried with a hundred of heavy infantry to the assistance of the besieged, and dashing through the army of the Athenians, which was scattered over the country [probably plundering] and had its attention turned to the wall, threw himself into Methone. He lost a few men in making good his entrance, but saved the place."[54] Weapons and armor in this age were much improved, as were unit tactics such as the Greek phalanx, for example.

To deal tactically with the pirate at sea, a swift, light-but-sturdy vessel, capable of carrying sufficient soldiers or marines, was required. Pirates and other sea rovers of antiquity had long been the innovators of the search for speed at sea, producing light, swift vessels designed to overtake merchant sailing ships or rowing galleys and to escape from warships. The common pirate vessel of this period was the *myoparo*, a small, light, swift, open galley, little changed from the Homeric raiding galley of the Mycenaeans. With such vessels, piracy had to be practiced as it was during the Mycenaean Age: attack from close ambush or during a calm, for otherwise pirate oarsmen might exhaust themselves before they could capture their sailing merchant quarry, which in the right wind could make five knots. Pirates could, of course, use double or even triple-banked fighting galleys, but they still had the same problem: in the right winds, the quarry might out-sail them. What they needed was a fighting galley that could be rowed under sail.

And they found it in the *hemiolia*, or "one and a half." It could be used under sail and oar simultaneously (provided that the sea was accommodating), giving rovers the advantage when pursuing merchant ships or running from pirate hunters. The aft upper bank was arranged so that the crew could drop mast and sail and stow them as they prepared to board their prey. Rovers developed other suitable piratical vessels, including the *lembos* of the Illyrian or Liburnian pirates. It was a light, swift, highly maneuverable vessel, and was soon adopted by the Macedonian navy. The Illyrians later developed the *liburnian*, a similar swift, light vessel eventually adopted by the Roman navy.[55]

Tactics in the use of these vessels were sometimes unconventional, especially when opposed to conventional warships. The Illyrian rovers, for example, defeated an Achaean relief force off Corcyra by lashing their vessels together in groups of four and presenting them broadside to the attacking ships. When "the enemy's ships had charged and struck them and getting fixed in them, found themselves in difficulties, as in each case the four boats lashed together were hanging on to their beaks, they leapt on to the decks of the Achaean ships and overmastered them by their numbers. In this way they captured four quadriremes and sunk with all hands a quinquereme."[56] Some of the greater pirates also used conventional fighting ships at times, both to defend against naval attack as well as to attack small cities and states.

Swift pirate vessels inspired navies and naval architects to come up with solutions. Early on, Athens developed the *triaconter*, a thirty-oared fighting galley, to pursue pirates, among other tasks.[57] Circa 300 BC, Rhodes, realizing the need for an anti-pirate vessel swifter even than the hemiolia, took the pirate's own design a step further and developed the *triemiola*, a three-banked ship that could use sail and oar simultaneously. Rhodes used this swift vessel to help sweep the seas of pirates.[58]

Until the mid-nineteenth century AD, merchants, ship owners, and merchant crews accepted as the cost of doing business that their vessels must be armed in peacetime against pirates, in wartime against pirates, privateers, and cruising men-of war. This was well understood in antiquity, and perhaps the only real question was whether or not to spend the money to arm a vessel, and, if the decision were made to arm the vessel, how much to spend. As the technologies of ship and warfare changed, merchant vessels accommodated them. From at least the seventh century BC onward, some merchant ships—probably those designated for cargoes of great value—added a fighting deck or platform and carried armed men for protection. A design on a mid-seventh-century piece of pottery shows three warriors standing upon a raised fighting platform in preparation to receive an attack. All are armed with large shields painted with various devices, have spears at the ready, are wearing helmets, and typically would be wearing armor.[59] According to Pliny, describing Egyptian merchant voyages in the Red Sea, "companies of archers are carried on board the vessels, as those seas are greatly infested with pirates."[60] The same circumstance probably prevailed among merchant vessels carrying rich cargoes through Mediterranean pirate waters as well.

However, most merchant sailing vessels remained un-decked and lightly armed, able to defend themselves only against a small, lightly manned pirate vessel. On the one hand a typical merchant sailing vessel carried a small crew, and so could make little resistance to a well-manned pirate whose crew would number at least the number of oars it carried. On the other hand, the merchant trading galley, unlike the merchant sailing vessel, could row, although not nearly as swiftly as the pirate, given the trading galley's broad beam. Even if it did not carry a contingent of archers or marines, the larger crew of a merchant galley was still better able to put up a fight than the crew of a merchant sailing vessel, assuming, of course, they were willing. Nonetheless, armed or not, most merchantmen could only hope to escape by running from a well-armed pirate. Even the typical battle between a pirate and a merchant willing to defend itself would have been a running fight between archers once the vessels were in range, followed by a violent boarding action if the pirate overtook the merchant and its crew refused to submit. Poorly protected merchant vessels were commonly picked off one at a time as pirates came upon them in chase: "Then as each was last in flight, he was first in danger, for the pirates came upon the last ships first."[61] Cargoes were pillaged, common seamen enslaved, and captains ransomed—or sometimes killed.[62]

Convoys and escorts were used in antiquity to protect merchantmen, but it is difficult to gauge how common they were. There are references to them during the Peloponnesian War, for example, but, given that warships could carry only limited supplies and preferred not to stand far out to sea, convoys may have been prohibitively expensive on many merchant sailing voyages. Further, although it might seem that conventional warships were unsuitable to convoy duty, given the speed of the typical pirate vessel, they nonetheless had advantages, as Cicero pointed out: "[F]or that ship [a quadrireme] was large enough to have been a bulwark to the rest, and if it had been engaged in battle with the pirates, it would have looked like a city among those piratical galleys."[63] By late antiquity, the virtues of large ships as "castles" against smaller, lower rovers was well understood. Merchant vessels could rally around the warship, whose high fighting deck gave it an advantage in battle over low, open pirate ships. Providing the escorted merchant vessels kept close together, the tactic was viable. Still, the merchant vessel's best defense, other than sailing in convoy with warships, was to travel armed if possible, keep a good watch, and hope that naval vessels were doing their job and keeping the seas clear of the pirate menace.

And what might battle actually have been like in this period, between pirates and the pirate-hunter fleets intended to sweep them away? What might it have been like, not from the perspective of the armchair historian who ponders tiny model ships on large maps, but from the perspective of the men actually in battle? Thucydides provided a hint in his description is of a battle between the Athenian and Peloponnesian fleets, undoubtedly similar to many battles at sea during this period:

> When the wind came down, the enemy's ships were now in a narrow space, and what with the wind and the small craft dashing against them, at once fell into confusion: ship fell afoul of ship, while the crews were pushing them off with poles, and by their shouting, swearing, and struggling with one another, made captains' orders and boatswains' cries alike inaudible, and through being unable for want of practice to clear their oars in the rough water, prevented the vessels from obeying their helmsmen properly. At this moment Phormio gave the signal, and the Athenians attacked. Sinking first one of the Admirals, they then disabled all they came across, so that no one thought of resistance for the confusion, but fled.[64]

A battle against the Syracusians, fought in narrow confines which limited ramming, might even more resemble a fight between pirates and pirate hunters: "So long as a vessel was coming up to the charge the men on the decks rained darts and arrows and stones upon her; but once alongside, the heavy infantry tried to board each other's vessel, hand to hand."[65] Doubtless ended some of the large-scale battles between pirate hunters and pirates of this period as well.

ROME VERSUS THE ILLYRIAN AND CILICIAN PIRATES

In the second half of the third century BC, Queen Teuta ascended the Illyrian throne upon the death of her husband. Almost immediately, she authorized Illyrian vessels to plunder those of all other states and sent part of her fleet and army to plunder various shores as well, largely as part of an economy based on pillage, and probably as part of intended imperialist expansion as well. As such, her roving vessels can be considered both as privateers, in that they captured vessels belonging to territories over whom she wished to extend her influence, and also as pirates, in that they captured vessels of any nation. Polybius, from whose work most of this Illyrian history is taken, suggests she did this because she was a woman, and thus shortsighted; doubtless he would have had a different excuse for men who behaved in a similarly arrogant and foolish manner, of whom there were certainly many. The material success of a raid on Epirus inspired Teuta to seek additional conquests and perhaps made her even more arrogant as well. Visited eventually by Roman ambassadors who protested her privateering, such as it was, Teuta assured them that she "would see to it that Rome suffered no public wrong from Illyria, but that, as for private wrongs, it was contrary to the custom of the Illyrian kings to hinder their subjects from winning booty from the sea." The youngest of the Roman ambassadors warned her that Rome would force her "to mend the custom toward the Illyrians of their kings." Teuta, pirate queen and unaccustomed to such "inopportune frankness," had the ambassador assassinated.[66]

Rome by now saw itself as the principal power in the Mediterranean, and was therefore unwilling to let the insult go unpunished, not to mention that politically it would be foolish to permit a rival just across the Adriatic to expand. Equipping a force of 200 ships, 20,000 infantry, and 2,000 cavalry with which to chastise the pirate state, the nascent empire set forth while Illyria was busy attempting more conquests. With the aid of Demetrius of Pharos, Roman soldiers captured Corcyra (Corfu), followed by Epidamnus and Issa. The Roman navy made coastal conquests, although the Illyrians did hand the Romans a defeat at Nutria. Teuta fled, and Rome placed most of Illyria in Demetrius's hands. Teuta eventually sent a peace emissary and agreed to give up most of Illyria, pay tribute, and "not to sail beyond Lissus with more than two unarmed vessels [*lembi*]."[67]

Unfortunately, the Illyrian roving habit was hard to break, and in 220 BC, the Roman surrogate Demetrius sent ships on a plundering expedition to Greek shores in violation of the treaty. Rome once again retaliated by successfully attacking Illyria and gave support to Demetrius's successor. Even so, significant Illyrian sea roving would not end entirely for another fifty years, and it took Roman control over the interior of Illyria in the time of Caesar Augustus to largely eradicate it.[68]

Nor did the demise of the Illyrian pirates end the pirate menace in the Mediterranean. With the fall of the Selucid Empire in the late second century BC, Cilicia began to develop into a true pirate empire of the purest sort, unrivaled in antiquity, and perhaps in history. The region had long been known for its daring brigandage and the "military qualities" of its inhabitants; they adapted well to outright piracy.[69] Alliances—one with Mithridates IV of Athens, which gave the Cilicians two- and three-banked galleys, and possibly hemiolias, and another with Quintus Servilius, a rebel Roman general in Spain, for example—increased Cilician power. At their height in the first century BC, they had "diverse arsenals, or piratic harbours, as likewise watch-towers and beacons, all along the sea-coast; and fleets were received that were well manned with the finest mariners, and well served with the expertest pilots, and composed of swift sailing and light-built vessels adapted for their special purpose." Some vessels had gilded masts and purple sails, and Cilician pirates were renowned for their revelry. According to Plutarch, the Cilicians would even mock some Roman captives by feigning fear of them— and then put out a ship's ladder and force them overboard (probably part of the origin of the myth of the "Golden Age" practice of "walking the plank"). "Even at first, under a leader named Isidorus, they did not confine themselves to the neighbouring sea, but exercised their piracies between Crete and Cyrene, and between Achaia [Achaea] and the Malean Gulf, which from the spoils that they took there, they named the Golden Gulf."[70]

Part of the Roman Republic's problem with pirates stemmed from her policy that governors of dependent states be responsible for defending themselves against pirates.[71] Rome was also often distracted by her various wars. A centralized, standing navy with attached legionnaires might have served Rome far better than her practice of preparing expeditionary forces when governors could not control their districts—in other words, when it was already late in the game. Rome also tended to rely on her legions ashore to solve all problems, including those at sea. In short, Rome often neglected to effectively ensure freedom of the sea. Piracy, like terrorism, grows quietly, is often ignored in its early stages, and only receives attention when it is already well established. The time to destroy piracy is in its nascency.

In 100 BC, Marcus Antonius, grandfather of Mark Antony of Caesar and Cleopatra fame, had some success against the Cilician pirates. Although he and his forces did not conquer them, they did defeat some and established a base within the region.[72] But it was not enough. His son waged a three-year campaign against pirates, first at Spain and Crete, then at Cilicia, but the latter expedition was a disaster and the pirates were further empowered.[73] Better results were obtained by Publius Servilius, who led a highly successful campaign on land and sea, diminishing but not destroying them: "Publius Servilius was sent against them, who, though he worsted their light and nimble brigantines with his heavy and well-appointed ships of war, did not obtain a victory without much bloodshed. He was not, however, content with driving them from the sea, but sacked their strongest towns, stored with spoil that they had been long in collecting."[74]

Julius Caesar served briefly under Servilius in the Cilician campaign and was later captured by Cilician pirates who held him for ransom for almost forty days. Upon his release after the payment of a fifty talent ransom, Caesar, in a well-known story, put a flotilla together and pursued his captors. He had a natural talent for tactics and had learned his lessons under Servilius well:

> On the night succeeding the day on which he was ransomed by the public money of several states, (which, however, he managed so as to make the pirates give hostages to those states), he collected a squadron of private vessels hastily fitted out, and sailing to the place where the pirates were, dispersed part of their fleet, sunk part, took several of their ships and men, and then, delighted at the success of his nocturnal expedition, returned to his friends.[75]

When Proconsul Junius refused to put the prisoners to death, apparently preferring to sell them as slaves for his own profit, Caesar had them crucified, a punishment they had jokingly threatened him with while he was their prisoner. Reportedly as a demonstration of his humanity, he first had the pirates' throats slit so that they might not suffer.[76]

But it was a single man over the course of less than a single year, in 67 BC, who did what all before him were unable to do. Gnaeus Pompeii, commonly known to us as Pompey the Great, received from the Senate—and not without serious concern—the unlimited power to govern the seas within the Pillars of Hercules, as well the adjacent mainland for four hundred furlongs. He also had the power to levy however many soldiers and seamen he needed, could demand and receive whatever funds he needed, and had "sole and irresponsible sovereignty over all men" within his purview. He quickly put his power to use, for the Cilician pirates were not only a plague upon the seas but were also threatening the grain shipments on which Rome so desperately relied to feed herself. Pompey posted naval forces at the entrance to the Bosporus and at the Strait of Gibraltar so that none could escape, then divided the Mediterranean into thirteen parts, "allotting a squadron to each . . . and having thus dispersed his power into all quarters, and encompassed the pirates everywhere, they began to fall into has hands by whole shoals." The remainder fled to Cilicia.[77]

At Coracesium, they made their final stand at sea, "But they did nothing more than meet the first onset, for immediately afterwards, when they saw the beaks of our ships encircling them, they threw down their weapons and oars, and with a general clapping of hands, which was with them a sign of supplication, intreated for quarter."[78] Some retreated inland, where Pompey besieged and defeated them. Many victorious commanders might have behaved brutally toward defeated pirates, but Pompey was merciful. He resettled and retrained them, dispersing many across the Mediterranean and turning them into farmers. The entire campaign took three months and Pompey did not lose a single ship. "Never did we obtain a victory with so little bloodshed. Nor was any nation afterwards found so faithful to us."[79] Pompey proved what can be done where there is the both the will and the means. In a curious quirk of history, one of Pompey's assassins eighteen years later was Lucius Septimius, a military tribune who had served under him during his campaign against the Cilicians.

Although many of the Cilician pirates had been attacked and destroyed ashore, others were taken at sea. Ramming remained a principal naval tactic, but ultimately the Roman fight at sea was often decided by hand-to-hand combat. Rome was justifiably fond of her famed legions, and they and their tactics were used at sea as well as ashore. Roman legions were highly disciplined, trained, and professional, part of a war machine hitherto unseen in

Western history. The typical Roman soldier was armed with *gladius* (short sword), *scutum* (shield), *pugio* (dagger), and two *pila* (*pilum*, a short javelin or spear whose tip would bend after being thrown, so that it could not be thrown back), and was armored as well. Some carried a *hasta* (a long spear) instead of the two pila. Broad-bladed, the gladius inflicted wide, penetrating wounds to the chest and abdomen, many of which were probably immediately incapacitating, if not outright mortal. The pirate was probably similarly armed with armor, a short sword of some sort, shield, and spear. At sea among both pirates and pirate hunters, pikes would have been ready at hand and archers would have been carried in addition to soldiers. Spears and stones were commonly used at sea as well.

Fights between Roman and pirate flotillas were probably similar to other battles at sea in which heavier fighting galleys engaged lighter ships and craft, a perhaps typical example being the engagement between the forces of Decimus Brutus and those of the Massilians (of Massilia, modern Marseilles). According to Julius Caesar, the soldiers who manned the Roman vessels were "a special corps of men selected from all the legions for their courage." Besides the usual arms of the legionnaire, the Roman soldiers carried "hooks [*manus ferreas*] and grappling-irons [*harpagones*] and had supplied themselves with large quantities of javelins [*numero pilorum*], throwing-darts [*tragularum*] and other missiles [*telorum*]." Massilian tactics relied on "the speed of their ships and the skill of their steersmen"—maneuverability, in other words—and included large numbers of archers, several ships attacking a single vessel simultaneously, sailing "close alongside our ships [to] snap off the oars," attempts at surrounding the Roman fleet, and the use of numerous small craft (probably manned with archers) in addition to seventeen warships. Small, maneuverable craft could harass large, slower vessels as they attempted to engage other large warships. The Egyptians, for example, later used small vessels against the Romans at Alexandria, arming them with "fire-darts" and combustibles (*malleolis ignibusque*). The Romans, who could not ram the Massilians because Roman oarsmen were untested and Roman ships were not as maneuverable, grappled whenever they could, "boarding the enemy vessels and killing many Albici and herdsmen." The Albici were warriors of notable courage from the mountains. The Massilians also used herdsmen slaves, promising them their freedom if they were victorious, a tactic often used in future centuries. Against such an enemy, the Roman soldier preferred to come to close quarters, where Roman close combat martial skills could be put to best use.[80]

In his *Pharsalia*, Lucan described the battle:

Then, whatever ship tried the oaken sides of that of Brutus, conquered by her own blow, captured, she stuck fast to the one she had struck. But others both grappling-irons united and smooth chains, and they held themselves on by the oars [were broadside to broadside]; on the covered sea the warfare stood fixed to the same spot. No longer are the darts hurled from the shaken arms, nor do the wounds fall from afar by means of the hurled weapons; and hand meets hand. In a naval fight the sword effects the most. Each one stands upon the bulwark of his own ship, facing full the blows of the enemy; and none fall slain in their own vessels. The deep blood foams in the waves, and the tide is thickened with clotted gore. The ships, too, which the chains of iron thrown on board are dragging, the same do the dead bodies clogged together hinder from being united. Some, half-dead, fall in the vast deep, and drink of the sea mingled with their own blood. Some, adhering to life struggling with slowly-coming death, perish in the sudden wreck of the dismantled ships. Javelins, missing their aim, accomplish their slaughter in the sea, and whatever weapon falls, with its weight used to no purpose, finds a wound on being received in the midst of the waves.[81]

The nautical core of pirate hunting—the fight at sea—would remain largely unchanged for another millennium and a half. The bloody boarding action would predominate, and those who could best wield the sword would often carry the day.

With the destruction of the Cilicians, the pirate empires of antiquity were no more. Former pirates now often served as mercenaries or plied their trade on a small scale. Some served in the fleet of Sextus Pompeius, who was not only the youngest son of Pompey the Great, but also a Roman admiral, pirate hunter, and, by all accounts, a pirate under whom served some of the Cilicians his father had conquered. Piracy remained along the Dalmatian and Liburnian coasts, and attempts to subdue the adjacent regions were only partly successful. Nonetheless, piracy no longer flourished as it once had.[82]

But the Roman peace, which came at the price of the Roman Republic, could not last forever. Eventually, the Empire split into the Roman and Byzantine Empires, or Western and Eastern. As the Western Roman Empire began to decline, Rome was unable to effectively restrain her enemies on land or sea. In the West, Franks, Saxons, Britons, Picts, Scots, Frisians, Chauci and other Germanic tribes, as well as Scandinavians, roamed and raided. In the third century AD, sea-roving Goths, who "obtained their ships and learnt their seamanship largely from the piratical tribes of the Black Sea coasts," entered the Mediterranean. Two centuries later, Rome was sacked, first by the Visigoths, then by the Vandals, and was threatened by the Huns. Some of Rome's former European colonies were overrun by Germanic tribes. The Western Empire, based in Rome, collapsed.[83]

By the time the Western Empire fell, the entire range of pirate-hunting strategies and tactics had been explored, often successfully: convoys and escorts, patrols, armed merchantmen, and naval bases established in pirate or enemy waters were common practice. Various treaties, alliances, and other political maneuvering—including tribute, bribery, amnesty, and treachery—had been used. Taxes had been levied to support anti-piracy operations, and at times broad military authority had been granted in order to suppress or even destroy piracy. Attacks on individual pirates as well as on pirate fleets were common, as were raids on pirate bases, the destruction of pirate vessels and material, and even the capture of pirate bases. Innovative naval technology, including fighting vessels built for speed, was adapted to pirate hunting. Finally, conquest and colonization of entire sea-roving regions (often removing or enslaving large numbers of native inhabitants), and even conquest followed by resettlement that provided pirates and other rovers with a different, more peaceful, livelihood, had been used successfully.

But lessons are often forgotten; leaders are often ignorant, shortsighted, or cannot be made to listen; and people are often too busy with the momentary needs of survival or are too distracted by the comfortable mundane to predict the rise of enemies, no matter how obvious their likelihood. Sometimes there is simply no way of knowing, predicting, or remembering, and one may only react anew to a crisis. With the fall of the Western Empire, Western Europe slipped into a period of turmoil from which it was slow to emerge. In such an often chaotic, ungoverned, opportunistic state, it was only natural that the sea rover and pirate would emerge again on a large scale, making the seas unsafe for all, mandating the intervention once more of the pirate hunter.

5

The Scourge from the North

Standing Against the Norsemen, 780–1066

"Piracy: commerce without its folly-swaddles, just as God made it," might well have been the motto of the broad spectrum of medieval maritime venturers who preferred to take rather than trade—or more correctly, who often preferred to both take and trade, the former as much or more so as the latter.[1] With the collapse of the Western Roman Empire and the expansion of various peoples and tribes throughout Europe, the Levant, and North Africa, sea roving harkened back to its roots, returning in fine traditional form to take advantage of the opportunities offered by weak or non-existent navies, numerous distracted and competing states, and political turnover. Brigandage in general, both on land and sea, was rife, and brigands served variously as pirates, privateers, mercenaries, and insurgents, not to mention in their common capacity as bands of thieves ashore. Indeed, the brigantine, a later form of light sailing and rowing vessel deriving from the Middle Ages and often used for roving and raiding, takes its name from brigand.[2] From the Baltic to the Mediterranean and even beyond, pirates, privateers, quasi-navies, and sea-roving peoples put to sea for plunder, and in so doing helped create new states, shape history, and at times even provide sustenance for entire kingdoms. The effects of these rovers of the Middle Ages are felt even today, not only in the maritime world but in the world at large.

It is hardly surprising that with major political and economic transition or breakdown came both the need and opportunity for sea roving. As various peoples struggled not only to survive but also to assert themselves and take advantage of neighboring weakness, the redistribution of wealth by sea was a given. In spite of the popular tendency to refer to the Middle Ages as

71

the Dark Ages, trade and commerce by sea were active and stretched from the Baltic to the Levant and into the Black Sea, providing the foundation for significant sea roving both at sea and on land. Although raiding ashore remained significant and, among some rovers, was the predominant form of pillaging, attacks on shipping increased; many rovers began to attack shipping exclusively.

Broadly speaking, and certainly with exceptions, sea roving in the West during this period was divided by the Strait of Gibraltar. In the Mediterranean, Christian and Muslim empires competed violently for control of sea and shore, and in particular for trade routes, not to mention for control of religious expression. Sea rovers—piratical, privateering, and naval—were encouraged by both ideologies and took advantage of the situation to enrich themselves under the pretense, and sometimes even the sincere belief, of doing God's work or will. Beyond the Strait of Gibraltar in the northern waters, whose rovers are the subject of this and the following chapter, sea roving likewise took on these forms, as well as another, seldom seen in such piratical purity: a people whose culture and purpose—and indeed, its very soul—were derived from raiding from the sea.

THE NORSEMEN

"We fought with swords: we enjoyed the fight, when we sent the inhabitants of Helsing to the Hall of Odin. We sailed up the Vistula. Then the sword acquired spoils: the whole ocean was one wound: the earth grew red with reeking gore: the sword grinned at the coats of mail: the sword cleft the shields asunder."[3]

The lines encompass the idealized essence of Norse culture, whose peoples are commonly referred to today as the Vikings: a culture of wealth and renown by violence, honor via the bloody blade, and sword, ship, and sea as the means not only of greatness, but of eternal life as well. At the core of his culture, a Norseman won "wealth and honor" by daring to face "danger and tough single combats"—by daring to put himself to the test and "find out what fate has in store."[4] This twofold purpose is often repeated in Viking *Sagas* and lore: "He himself left with thirty ships and took to harrying Scotland and Ireland. And this course he pursued for three years, acquiring great wealth and fame."[5]

Beginning in the late eighth century, the various peoples known collectively as the Norsemen or Vikings—the Danes, Norwegians, and Swedes, and referred to also as Northmen, Ostmen, and pagans—began sailing south across the open waters and raiding wherever they might. As with the Mycenaeans, sea roving in the form of shore raids was the principal form of warfare for the Norsemen, one designed to cause economic harm to the enemy while simultaneously and immediately enriching the attacker. Even so, the Norsemen were also great traders, farmers, fishermen, explorers, and settlers (Iceland, Greenland, various Scottish islands, Ireland, England, Normandy, Russia, and even briefly as far as North America), yet, again like the Mycenaeans, they extolled the virtues of arms and pillage over those of commerce and husbandry.[6] The only real common ground in the Viking *Sagas* between commerce (which by all accounts was more profitable in the long run than raiding) and sea roving is that plundering violence was often attached to trading voyages and excellence in seamanship, whether in sailing a war-seeking longship or a trading *knarr*, was a virtue worthy of notice. Even the Icelandic *Sagas*, in which trading voyages often play a critical role, have a pervasive warlike mien.[7]

Some *Sagas* suggest that this expansion began when Norsemen sought to escape local tyranny or other political conflict.[8] Scholars suggest a growing Scandinavian population, a lack of land suitable for cultivation (possibly a response to the expanding Carolingian empire) and the development of the longship, an extraordinary class of swift, open, oared warship which carried a single sail and was highly seaworthy everywhere—in fiords, estuaries, and rivers, as well as in coastal waters and on the open ocean.[9] The latter circumstance may have been particularly compelling, given the human tendency to put tools of war and other violence to use. The sight alone of a Viking longship—arguably the epitome of functional beauty created by mankind—probably inspired many to put it to the test, just as the sight of the Viking sword certainly inspired many to pick it up and do more with it than test its balance and swing it a few times. A culture of pillaging warfare combined with the appropriate tools and opportunity is a sea-roving epoch just waiting to be achieved.

We do not know whether the longship was originally developed for long-range raiding and exploration, or if its extraordinary suitability for these adventures was realized soon after. It may be that, as is common with practical ideas and technology, its development had elements of both. Similarly, Viking culture was probably focused and developed even more toward raiding as the wealth and renown to be derived from it was revealed. But whatever its inspiration and origin, we do know that the Viking longship was put to very effective use for more than two centuries; need and means are indeed inspirational and, when coupled with daring, can take a person or a people far. Without doubt the final form of the longship, that of the *drakkar* or dragon ship, was intended to meet the requirements of long-range pillaging and invasion.

The Norse raiders were not the first to plunder the coasts of Atlantic Europe, nor were they the only ones to plunder during the "Viking Age." Frisians and Franks made occasional raids in the early Middle Ages, and the Angles and Saxons, who had made numerous plundering descents in late Roman times, invaded Britain in the mid-fifth century AD. The various competing kingdoms all made raids against each other, both before the coming of the Norsemen and during their heyday. In 1049, for example, thirty-six ships filled with Irish raiders entered the Severn River in England, joined the forces of the king of South Wales, and plundered the region.[10] However, the Norsemen plundered far more systematically and on a scale hitherto unknown in the northern waters. Many historians consider them to have been the best European warriors of the age, and certainly they often demonstrated their prowess. In 789, Norsemen made the first recorded raid on the coast of England, in 793, the first on the coast of Ireland, and in 799, the first on the coast of Aquitaine in the land of the Franks.[11]

The early Viking raids were exactly as described: raids, not conquests, although by necessary circumstance they were associated with both exploration and intelligence collection, which ultimately facilitated both conquest and colonization. Three decades into the ninth century, Viking raiding increased in quantity and severity, with Norwegians often raiding Ireland and Danes raiding England and western Europe. Settlement and colonization followed soon after.[12] Norsemen not only raided as far as the Mediterranean by sea and Russia by river but also raided among themselves according to local political circumstances.[13] Viking raiding and the defenses and counterattacks arrayed against it were often tinged with religious conflict between pagans (those who worshipped the Norse gods) and Christians.[14] As they settled lands to the west and south of their homelands, conflict among the dispersed and descendant Norse peoples was common and often taken as opportunity for plunder.

Norse roving was conducted primarily ashore in the form of quick raids, with a quite understandable preference for richer targets, although Norsemen did not restrict themselves to only the most lucrative. Villages and even farmhouses were routinely raided. The rise of Christianity in Ireland and England brought with it ecclesiastical wealth, typically centered on monasteries and the towns that grew up around them. The repeated sacking of Irish monasteries, wholesale slaughter of holy men and women, and enslavement of multitudes of native Irish by Viking raiders is recalled in Ireland even today, although many attacks on Irish monasteries were in fact conducted by Irish raiders.[15]

The brutality of Viking attacks, many of which were by all accounts literally bloodbaths, is well known and was recorded not only by the victims, but by the Norsemen themselves, strongly suggesting that victims' complaints and lamentations were not mere exaggeration or propaganda. Even allowing for poetic license, we read in *Egil's Saga*, "Let us go back to the farm and acquit ourselves like true warriors: kill everyone we can catch and take all the valuables we can carry." The saga continues: "They went to the farmhouse and stormed it, killing fifteen or sixteen men . . . . They took all the valuables and destroyed what they could not take with them. They drove the cattle down to the shore and slaughtered them, filled their boat, then proceeded on their way, rowing out through the sounds."[16] A far larger, quite possibly apocryphal raid is summed up simply in another saga, again by a Norse *skald* (bard): "When the Jómsvíkings entered the town they laid it waste almost completely. They killed many and plundered an immense amount of property, so that the townsmen had a sad awakening."[17] Apocryphal or not, the description more than adequately conveys the Norse attitude toward raiding. Notwithstanding the brutality of Norse raids, the period was well known for its extreme violence, including the murder of prisoners, among all peoples in raiding and general warfare.

The violence of Viking raids also lays bare the legal notion—once again, perhaps "legal fiction" or "hair-splitting" are better terms—that there is a difference between pillaging and killing done by the pirate, considered an enemy of all mankind, and by the sea rover or sea raider who has legitimate authority, if only in the eyes of his people. There can be no doubt that the victims of Viking raids saw their attackers as scum of the sea and worse—again, no matter the color of their purported authority. And often this authority was no more than that which comes from the edge or point of a sword, or, as it would a few centuries later be expressed, from the barrel of a gun. The sense of fear or terror, not to mention the fact of life-changing victimization, is not altered by the fact that some people then and now might consider these extraordinary acts of violence simply as lawful acts or even mere "facts of life."

Viking raiding itself was fairly simple, at least in the early decades, consisting of a quick attack and quick withdrawal. Pillaging, after all, was the object. Demonstrations of valor were important, but probably not at the expense of plunder; valiant reputation-earning single combats could be fought at home. Defenders and even noncombatants were often killed, women raped, buildings and fields burned, livestock butchered and carried away as provision, inhabitants often carried away for ransom or as slaves, and anything else of significant value plundered as well. The raids were typically supported by reconnaissance and intelligence gathering, with fishermen, as ever through the ages, a common source of information.[18] The longship facilitated raiding: it could cross open seas under sail or oar, enter shallow waters and be drawn ashore, and be rowed swiftly as required for attack, retreat, or egress.

Viking tactics on land were a combination of individual actions and heroics in the quest for honor and fame and highly effective group tactics against arrayed or fortified enemies. According to the *Sagas*, Viking raiding parties sometimes included *berserkers* (also written as *berserkurs* and *berserks*): Norsemen known for their strength, prowess with arms, and in particular an apparently psychotic "animal" or "beast-like" courage in battle, which may have been fortified by religious conviction, fanaticism, or even drugs or alcohol.[19] However, it is quite possible that the berserker was a literary creation, albeit one surely based on the reality of the enraged warrior who lived for battle, for such exist even today.

Norse arms included the sword, ax, spear, and bow. Armor consisted of a simple helmet (*never* horned) with some form of nose protection, and a mail shirt if the warrior could afford it. The sword, an object of veneration among the Norsemen, was expensive, well made, double edged, and used with a shield to defend against the adversary's sword and ax blows. The shield, round at first and as much as forty inches wide, also served as defense against spear, arrow, and stone. The Viking sword, primarily a cutting weapon, was described as very effective (assuming a skilled warrior wielded it, as with any sword), and modern analysis by students of historical swordplay supports this evaluation. It was not overlong, making it reasonably suitable for shipboard and close quarters use as well. However, the Viking ax—as finely designed and functional as the Viking sword—may have been more popular (certainly it was less costly) among these bloodthirsty warriors.

FIGHTING BACK AGAINST THE VIKINGS

Assuming the early targets of Viking raids had no warning and thus were unprepared for them, local inhabitants very quickly would have established a few basic security measures common throughout most of history. First, if they did not already have one, residents along coasts and rivers established a watch, supplemented ideally by an armed force capable of reacting to the threat. Even the Norse raiders maintained a coast watch, an obvious necessity in times of feudal strife and opportunism. In *Beowulf* are the Norse "Watchman, the Scylding set to guard / The water-cliffs" and the "Haven Guard" who identify and give warning of those who approach the shore.[20] How vigilant these coast watchers were is conjectural. Raids were often years apart, and vigilance is usually at its highest when an attack is highly likely, imminent, or in its immediate aftermath. Eventually, unless well disciplined, security tends to lapse into laxity, the distraction of comfort, and overconfidence—at least until the next raid.

Assuming an adequate, reasonably alert watch, if nothing else it could give warning in time enough for residents to retreat inland with their valuables, including livestock, either to a local castle or other fortification, or into hiding. Throughout history, this has been the foremost defense of those vulnerable to pillaging attack from the sea: to post a watch and, when warned, retreat immediately into hiding with whatever valuables can conveniently be carried. If there were a local armed force, it might have time to march to the sea before the Norse raiders landed. Often the sight of waiting men-at-arms was enough to deter an attack. As was the case in antiquity, defenders could attempt to repulse attackers as they came ashore, relieve a farmhouse or fortification under attack, counter-attack as raiders were distracted by pillage, and attack as raiders withdrew to their longships. But to do this required an adequate local force, or at least one within quick marching distance. Often there was none.

Invariably, fighting the Viking ashore meant either meeting him on open ground or forcing him to attack a castle or fortified house. Catapults and similar artillery (the trebuchet would come later) that could have been used to attack the invaders ashore or their longships as they made their way up rivers and estuaries, appear to have been unavailable at many of the places Vikings attacked. However, a coast watch, fortification, and what in modern terminology is called a "quick reaction force" are all essentially passive measures in that they are static: the enemy not only gets to make the first move, but also gets to decide when to make his move. In most cases, the defender can only react. Anticipation of an attack and action based on it require both experience and information in the form of intelligence. Even retaliatory attacks launched by land against raiders settled in England, for example, were slow, logistics intensive, and difficult to keep secret. This is not to suggest that there were not victories by land. In 915, Norse raiders entered the Severn, but "numerous bands from the neighbouring towns, suddenly fell on them. . . . The rest fled, and were driven by the Christians into an enclosure, where they were beset until they delivered hostages for their departure." Detachments of men were stationed on the "south side of the Severn, from Cornwall to the mouth of the river Avon, to prevent the pirates from ravaging those districts" for the Norsemen did indeed return. Most were slain or forced to withdraw.[21]

However, to truly turn the tide against the Viking raiders, a navy was mandatory. With a navy, defenders could become as mobile as their seaborne attackers. Warships could patrol headlands and promontories and engage attackers there or warn a village of an impending attack and summon reinforcements. Ships could ferry warriors to the site of a raid often more quickly than warriors could march overland, trap raiders in river or estuary, and pursue raiders by sea as they made their escape. Best of all, as Viking raiders began to invade and colonize foreign lands, the victims of their attacks could raid the Norsemen themselves.

Were we to name one man as the preeminent pirate hunter of the Viking Age, it should be Alfred the Great. Inheriting a kingdom plagued by attacks from Danish raiders across the sea as well as from those settling in England itself, he built a navy and raised levies to man it, justifiably making him the father of the English navy: "In the same year, the army of the pagans, settled in East-Anglia and Northumberland, carrying off booty along the sea-coasts, severely harassed the land of the West-Saxons, mostly in long and swift galleys, which themselves had made some years before. To oppose these other ships were made by Alfred's orders, twice as long, swifter and less shaky, so as to beat the above-named ships of the enemy in strength."[22] The galleys were longer than the Norse ships, "loftier," purportedly swifter, and better trimmed so they did not heel as much.[23] The emphasis appears to have been on size in order to support large numbers of armed men, for the significantly longer ships may have been less maneuverable and more difficult to manage in the narrow waters of rivers and estuaries where pagan raiders were likely to be trapped. Speed was necessary to overtake the Viking ships, and the higher sides provided both protection from Norse missiles and a higher vantage from which to engage in close battle.

Although it had its setbacks, Alfred's navy became a thorn in the Norsemen's sides. "When these [new ships] were sent out to sea, the king ordered them to take alive all they could and to slay the rest. Wherefore it came to pass that 20 ships of Danish pirates were taken alive in that same year; of whom some were slain, some brought alive to the king, and hanged on the gallows."[24]

Alfred's navy did more than merely patrol for Danish raiders: it made plundering raids ashore and plundered Viking ships as well. "In the same year Alfred, king of the Anglo-Saxons led his fleet, full of fighting men, out of Kent to the country of the East Angles, for the sake of plunder; and, when they had arrived at the mouth of the river Stour, immediately thirteen ships of the pagans [Danes, Norsemen] met them, prepared for battle; a fierce fight ensued and all the pagans, after a brave resistance, were slain; all the ships, with all their money, were taken."[25]

Over time, Alfred was able to gain the upper hand over the Viking invaders, for whom permanent settlement appears to have been their intention, although plunder was by no means forgotten. In 878, twelve years after the army had landed in England and after several years in which he employed a variety of tactics—including truce, retreat, guerrilla warfare, naval raids and warfare, open battle, siege warfare, and treaty—Alfred defeated part of the Norse invaders and regained control of Wessex. A year later, he gained some control over East Mercia when the Danes moved on. He was followed by other successful leaders who stood against the Norse incursions, including Edward the Elder and Athelstan.[26] The eventual and largely successful strategy was one of fortified boroughs combined with a navy that could "meet the raiders on even terms at sea"—if it could find the enemy on the sea.[27] Locating the sea raider there was difficult if not entirely impossible except for luck, and the navies of the period were not composed of vessels that cruised the open seas. The English navy, for example, was unable to halt large Norse invasions in the period 1010 to 1015 and again in 1066.[28]

On the other hand, piratical Viking raids do seem to have been significantly diminished by a central government supporting a system of national defense composed of both army and navy. That being said, it was not always easy to maintain such a strategy:

And when they [the Viking raiders] went to their ships, then ought the forces again to have gone out against them, until they should land; but the forces went home: and then they were eastwards, then were the forces kept westwards; and when they were southwards, then were our forces northwards. Then were all the witan [advisers] summoned to the king, and they were then to counsel how this land might be defended. But although something might be then counselled, it did not stand even one month: at last there was no chief who would assemble forces, but each fled as he best might.[29]

LONGSHIP WARFARE

All things martial are more difficult at sea. Even when land warfare has been emulated at sea, as it often was from antiquity until the seventeenth century, it was and remains complicated by the cramped conditions of an armed vessel, the vessel's rolling and pitching (and often by consequent sea-sickness), the lack of avenues of retreat, the very real likelihood of drowning, and the hazard of burning to death—again, there is often no place to go but into the grasping, often chilling, breath-stealing arms of the sea.

Based as it was on close combat between warriors, Norse naval warfare was no different. As pirate hunter closed on Viking raider, or vice versa, the vessels arrayed themselves for battle and maneuvered to best advantage, taking land, wind, and sea into consideration. Given that most of these battles necessarily were fought near land, often in fjords, rivers, or estuaries, both the shore and the shallows were a vital part of the martial seascape. If part of a larger force ran aground, for example, the remainder of its ships might be vulnerable to the smaller adversary. Depending on their size and armament, individual ships aground were often vulnerable to a more mobile adversary. "This being done, when the English wished to return to their companions which were near the Danish ships on the opposite shore, they were stranded; and the Danes seeing this, left their own ships and fought against the English who were in the three ships."[30] Likewise was the wind an important part of the martial seascape, for it could force a ship ashore, deny an avenue of escape for a ship which had lost most of its crew, and even diminish the range and effectiveness of flights of arrows.[31] Tide, current, and sea state were also tactical considerations. Also important was the twofold nature of the Norsemen as fighters on land and sea. In some cases, one or both parties might choose to fight ashore rather than at sea, depending on tactical conditions.[32]

In the case of pursuit—for example, when chasing a raider from shore to sea—the pursuer might put two men to an oar, if he had them.[33] And he very well might, given that in such circumstances, he could man his ship with as many men as it could carry. This would give him not only speed over his quarry, but an advantage in numbers as well when the ships came to grips.

In the simplest of tactics, a battle between two vessels or even two fleets began first with the by now probably ancient speech or exhortation of captain to crew or leader to warriors, as well as of battle orders.[34] The ships "set up their banners," then rowed into action, or in some cases lay waiting, even lashed together.[35] Norsemen aboard the longships were all warriors, and all worked the oars. As in the case of many of the ancient rovers, there was no stigma attached to the oar. Norse ships were not fitted with rams, nor did they carry heavy artillery such as catapults or ballistae (large mounted crossbows). Battles typically began at long range with flights of arrows, which would continue until the adversary was reduced in number or until most or all of the shafts were spent. As the range closed, warriors threw spears by hand and rocks by sling and by hand. The helmsman appears to have been a particularly enticing target, given that his attention was on ship-handling and not on defending himself, and that his death or injury could, briefly at least, leave the helm unattended.[36] One saga describes a single combat between two ships: "Vagn and his crew hurled such a volley of stones that Sigvaldi and his men could do nothing but protect themselves and were hard put to do even that. Then they lay broadside to broadside. And when Vagn and his crew ran out of stones they fell upon their opponents with sword blows, and Sigvaldi was obliged to order his ships to fall back to land for more stones."[37]

We know something of the "battle stations" of the Vikings at sea, and probably their adversaries were similarly arrayed. In *Egil's Saga*, King Harald put his most notable warriors in the prow of his ship and lined the gunwales with berserkers.[38] In the *Saga of the People of Laxardal*, the captain of a grounded longship attacked by the Irish ordered his men to man the sides such that they "stood so close together that their shields formed an unbroken row, with a spear point extending from the lower end of each shield." The captain stood in the bow in impressive martial array.[39] The shield formation was common and was probably a vital defense against the various missiles, as well as against boarding.[40] In many cases, men would also have been at the oars. Archers would probably have been in the stern, although if the sail were raised, it would have interfered with their forward aim.

As ships came close, battle continued at close quarters, each attempting to board or defend against boarding. Wall of shield might clash against wall of shield.[41] Ideally, arrows, rocks, and spears would have reduced the adversary sufficiently that boarders could clear the decks. Some *Sagas* report ships coming together bow to bow, facing each other, and others broadside to broadside. Some undoubtedly came together bow to stern, and others all ways in between, and, surely, whenever possible, two or more ships would attack a single longship. Grappling hooks were used as necessary.[42] In one *Saga*, King Olaf lay his ships behind some rocks hidden just beneath the surface, making it difficult for his enemy to come alongside.[43] Another *Saga* reports two men boarding at the prow and clearing the decks from there.[44] At first glance, this could appear to be mere heroics, or even literary license. However, the narrow prow would have limited the number of the enemy who could get to the boarders; defenders could only approach a few at a time. Ships may have often fought prow to prow as the best means of both offense and defense: "They fought at the bows, so that only the men on the bows could strike; the men on the forecastle thrust with spears and all who were farther off shot with light spears or javelins or war arrows. Some fought with stones or short stakes and those who were abaft [behind] the mast shot with the bow . . . they urged each other on with mutual cheering and there was one great hurra through all the ships." Likewise in this case was the ship cleared from the prow. Shouting and even trumpets were common, both being useful for fortifying the spirit in battle.[45]

The level of violence was doubtless as violent, or even more so, as that described in *Egil's Saga*:

> Egil darted his shield to block the spear . . . His own spear struck the middle of Onund's shield and sank in so deeply that it stuck there, making it heavy for Onund to hold. Then Egil quickly grabbed the hilt of his sword. Onund began to draw his sword, but had only pulled it half-way out of its sheath by the time Egil ran him through with his sword. Onund recoiled at the blow, but Egil drew his sword back swiftly and struck at Onund, almost chopping his head off.[46]

Boarding itself was no time for anything but overwhelming violence designed to cow or kill the enemy as quickly as possible, and to suppress any possibility of hesitation in the attacker. Bloody, slippery decks; dead and dying men; amputated limbs; the rolling of the ship; the close press of attackers and defenders swinging and thrusting weapons; men pushing, shoving, striking, stumbling, falling, shouting, and screaming; and the overwhelming wash of adrenaline and fear would have made the boarding of a longship in battle something akin to a scene from a modern horror film—except that it was real.[47] The aftermath may often have appeared to have been of isolated ships manned by the dead drifting on a sea of bodies and blood.

One tactic, generally reserved for large fleet actions among Vikings, was that of lashing ships together as fighting platforms. Typically, they were lashed broadside, stern to stern, so that the prows of the leaders' ships (usually longer) stood out as a sign of courage: "If the Long Serpent is to lie as much more ahead of the other ships as she is longer than them, we shall have hard work of it here on the forecastle."[48] In Olaf's flotilla of eleven ships, for example, he put his ship at the center, its bow protruding ahead of the others. On either side were the *Short Serpent* and the *Crane*, and then the rest of the ships were lashed, four on each side.[49] In one battle, Norsemen attacking longships lashed together attacked an outer ship first: "But Earl Eirik laid his ship side by side with the outermost of King Olaf's ships, thinned it of men, cut the cables, and let it drive. Then he laid alongside of the next, and fought until he had cleared it of men also."[50]

Occasionally, a student of Viking history will question whether Norsemen actually did secure their longships together in battle at sea and also debate how common battles at sea among the Vikings actually were. As for the latter, we do know that the Norsemen fought battles great and small at sea, not on the open seas but in protected waters inshore or in fjords or rivers. As for the former, the evidence from the Norse *Sagas* and runic inscriptions strongly supports the tactic, although it must be noted that the *Sagas* are literature, typically a combination of fact and fiction, and often written long after the events they recount.[51]

But the tactic was not limited to the Vikings. Fighting ships were sometimes secured together in battle in antiquity. We have already seen how the Liburnian pirates bound their galleys together in groups of four to defend against a ramming attack and to provide a fighting platform supporting enough warriors to overwhelm an attacker. There are accounts of galleys of the great Italian maritime cities being lashed together in battle to form a defensive platform, and of galleys chained together in the Sicilian wars of the late thirteenth century.[52] At the Battle of Sluys in 1340, the English reported that French ships were lashed together.[53] In the mid-seventeenth century, a Persian fleet attacked Cossack raiders, first securing their ships together by chains "so that they should keep their Body intire, lest the *Cossacks* should set upon any single Vessel." In this case, however, the Cossacks used their guns (cannon) to sink the outboard vessel, which drew the attached vessels into the abyss with it.[54] From the sixteenth to eighteenth centuries, and probably in centuries prior, a ship coming to the aid of a boarded ship (in other words, one with an enemy lashed alongside) would come alongside the friendly vessel, lash itself to it, and board over the friendly decks, creating a larger, stronger defensive platform.[55]

Most of all, though, the Viking tactic of lashing longships together made sense in fleet actions, especially if the adversary were stronger and the conditions were right.[56] In a random melee of individual combats between longships, the victor was probably often the fleet with the most ships and men, assuming all else was equal. But by lashing vessels together, a weaker enemy could deny a stronger enemy the ability to bring its entire strength to bear at one time. Further, the enemy was largely forced to attack at the broadside ends (the flanks, in other words) of the lashed ships. Warriors from the central ships could easily support attacks here or at any other point. Attacks on the bows of ships lashed together were possible, but boarding here would have been much more difficult, either bow to bows or broadside to bows, given that the defenders could attack the boarding vessel from the flanks. Any ships not lashed to the main body, however, must necessarily have been wary of being attacked and overwhelmed. Further, there were dangers in lashing ships together. Any significant sea state would have battered the ships together severely, and wind and current might push the platform of ships aground or into other hazards, unless anchored.

There are few accounts of Norse attacks on large ships and thus of how such ships defended themselves. In the *Orkneyinga Saga*, Norsemen who ventured into the Mediterranean came across a *dromon*, a form of war galley discussed further in chapter 7. The dromon the Norsemen discovered was actually a Saracen sea-roving galley: large, double banked, well armed, well manned, and with sides much higher than anything to which they were accustomed. Consulting about the ship they faced, they were told, "I think you will find it difficult to attack the Drómund in your long-ships, for you will hardly be able to reach their bulwarks with a boarding-pike, and they have probably brimstone and boiling pitch to pour under your feet and over your heads." The Norsemen attacked anyway in several longships, intending to come alongside where hopefully the Saracen missiles would fall beyond them. If the battle did not go their way, they could row swiftly away. "But when they came close under the Dromund, she was so high in the side that the Northmen were unable to use their weapons, and the others poured blazing brimstone and burning pitch over them"—but most of it missed the ships below. Most of the longships stood off, permitting their crews to attack with bow and arrow. This proved effective and kept the Saracens' attention from the longship still alongside. And this was a mistake, for the Vikings were hacking their way into the hull of the ship and soon enough boarded it, one group onto the lower deck, another onto the upper. They captured the ship, looted it, kept a few prisoners, and "All the rest they killed, and obtained great booty and many precious things." They burned the ship but had not searched it well: a great treasure was melted into the sea.[57]

Although Norse warfare superficially appears to have been based primarily on force against force, it was anything but. The Norsemen were not fools. Indeed, most who make their trade on the sea or in warfare are not fools, for fools seldom live long in these environments. Whether at sea or ashore, there was plenty of opportunity for bloody close combat, no matter the tactics or circumstances. There was no need to add to the hazards of combat by entering into it blindly. Deception—the foundation of tactics— was widely practiced by the Norsemen and their adversaries. Treachery, ambush, and cunning were common ashore, according to the *Sagas*, and where possible were common at sea as well.[58] In the *Saga of the Jómsvíkings*, King Harald sent ships to ambush an enemy who suspected no harm. The adversary was caught by surprise with his awnings up (tarps set up on deck when not underway). Harald's men cut the awnings down, dropping them onto the unsuspecting men, making them easy prey.[59] In the *Saga of Ref the Sly*, Ref escaped from a pursuer by suddenly dropping his sail and only pretending to row. His enemy, unable to slow down quickly, slipped alongside, whereupon one of Ref's crew "cut through all their stays, the sail went overboard with all its rigging and at that moment the ship seemed likely to capsize." Ref and his men escaped, but not before Ref pinned the enemy commander to the freeboard with a spear.[60] Odysseus would have been right at home.

THE END OF THE VIKINGS

Sea fights notwithstanding, the defeats of the Vikings were typically to be found on dry land, raiding party against armed defenders or army against army. The great Viking naval actions were largely fought among the Scandinavians themselves in their own waters.[61]

Historically, perhaps the greatest of Viking defeats came at the hand of an English king descended from the Norsemen themselves. In 1066, Harald Hardrada of Norway invaded England at York with two hundred ships and several thousand warriors. Harold Godwinson, king of England, responded with a rapidly assembled army and a fast forced march to surprise Hardrada at Stamford Bridge. The English defeated the invasion force; Hardrada died in battle.[62] A few months later, another descendent of the Norsemen, William of Normandy (of the land of the Norsemen, in other words), brought an army across the English Channel in ships much resembling those of his northern kin. At Hastings he defeated Harold, largely marking the end of the Viking Age. But the Vikings did not disappear per se. Rather, they evolved into regional peoples, not only Scandinavian waters but also in the areas they settled. In the south, their descendents built defensible kingdoms in Normandy, England, and elsewhere, and with these kingdoms rose trade and trading fleets. In the north, trade replaced raiding as a way of life. What was once a reality subordinated to the culture of war became the culture itself. Trade, and with it the invariably associated political, social, and economic conflict, began to reign in the northern seas, notwithstanding the chivalric arms and armor of nobles and princes.

And where there is trade at sea and insecurity ashore, there will inevitably and invariably be piracy. The descendents of the Vikings, and many others as well, would keep up the traditions of sea-going trade and thievery—the latter of which would leave pirate hunters hard pressed and travelers at sea in fear for their lives, and for very good reason.

6

A Sea Roving Free-for-All

Pirate Hunting in the Northern Seas, 1066–1492

Although medieval sea roving in the northern seas is popularly considered to have been largely Viking, it was anything but. The Norsemen hold the record in scale and in fame (and infamy) during the Middle Ages, but sea roving in general was a popular trade among the many various mariners and brigands, and even at times among noblemen. As used in reference to sea robbers, the word *rover* was common by the mid-fifteenth century and dates at least to the late fourteenth century, if not earlier.[1] Sea roving in a variety of forms grew significantly after the Viking Age, and it is likely that every European seaport during the Middle Ages at some point hosted pirates, not to mention privateers and naval surrogates. By the mid- to late-Middle Ages, much of the period's piracy and most of its privateering was centered on the major ports. Both were viable trades not only in times of almost constant open warfare, private warfare, and "*petite guerre*," but in times of peace as well, and merchant seamen had the requisite vessels and skill in seamanship.

MEDIEVAL PIRATES AND PIRACIES

No region lacked its own pirates: England, Scotland, Ireland, the Spanish kingdoms, Brittany, Normandy, Zeeland, Holland, and the Baltic states all produced thousands. Some pirates sailed under foreign flags—French pirates under Scottish commissions or pretended Spanish nationality, for example—in order to engage in piracy under the guise of legitimacy, while simultaneously carrying on a form of surrogate warfare in what was ostensibly peacetime.[2]

Merchant seamen were often pirates, unlawfully attacking both the vessels of competing foreign kingdoms as well as those of competing national

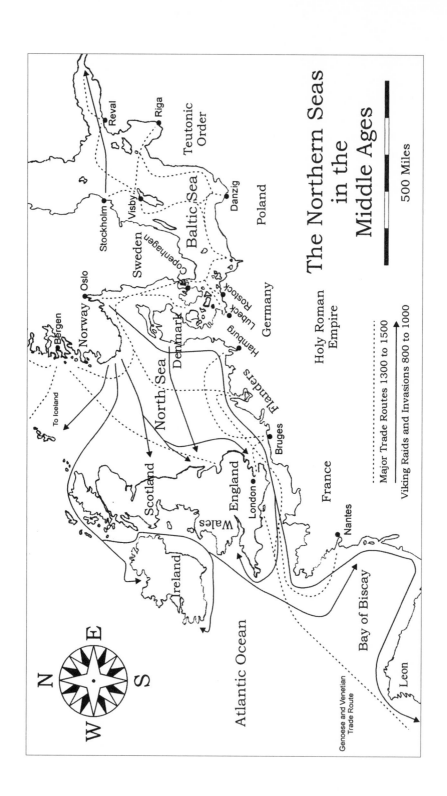

The Northern Seas
in the
Middle Ages

500 Miles

Reval
Riga
Teutonic
Order
Danzig
Poland
Baltic Sea
Stockholm
Visby
Sweden
Copenhagen
Oslo
Norway
Rostock
Lübeck
Germany
Hamburg
Holy Roman
Empire
Denmark
Flanders
North Sea
Bergen
To Iceland
Scotland
England
London
Bruges
Wales
France
Ireland
Nantes
Bay of Biscay
Atlantic Ocean
Leon

---- Major Trade Routes 1300 to 1500
→ Viking Raids and Invasions 800 to 1000

Genoese and Venetian
Trade Route

ports. Mariners of the Cinque Ports (originally Sandwich, Dover, Hythe, Romney, and Hastings, to which were added Winchelsea and Rye), for example, once threatened retaliation against the men who had aided in the capture of Cinque Ports pirates. The pirates had captured not foreign vessels, which might be overlooked, but some belonging to competing ports in Cornwall. The crown intervened, ordering the Cinque Ports to take no further action.[3]

Piracy conducted by brigands and outlaws located in various remote, often fortified haunts was also well represented. John of Newport, for example, made the Isle of Wight his base and was known for attacking English shipping and "morthering the kingis people and hus frendis, castying them owte of har vessellis into the See as thei have be comyng to the port of Hamptom."[4]

Pirate vessels operated individually, in flotillas, and at times even in fleets. They cruised for prizes, lay in wait for them off headlands, shipping routes, and outside of ports, and attacked them in port. In 1436, eight English balingers (oared sailing vessels) and barges "arrayed for war" captured the *Seynt Nunne* in a Brittany port, for example.[5] Deception was undoubtedly common. In 1441, three merchant ships en route to London anchored near Yarmouth on the Isle of Wight, "through fear of enemies on the sea." A "balinger of Plymmouth, whereof John Cornyssh is master, arrived at the same port with thirty-six armed persons therein, who had friendly communication with the said merchants; and the said Cornyssh persuaded them that they could safely sail to London, whereupon they put out with the balinger, which forthwith attacked them and took one of the three ships."[6]

As in most ages, sea roving in this period was not limited to the lower and middle classes. A number of noblemen—and even noblewomen—took to piracy during the various English rebellions and civil wars in the Middle Ages, the turmoil providing both opportunity and a pretense of legitimacy. In some cases, this piracy might be better regarded as a form of privateering, or as a sea-going tool of rebellion or civil war, although often it appears to have been primarily the seizing of a profitable opportunity under the pretenses of tactical necessity, patriotism, or feudal loyalty.

What we would today term conventional privateering was common in the northern seas, both during rebellions within kingdoms and during wars between kingdoms. The period was fraught with wars and warfare: the Plantagenet wars and civil wars, the Saintonge War, the Barons' Wars, the Scottish Wars of Independence, the Hundred Years' War, the Wars of the Roses, the Dutch-Hanseatic War, and the Anglo-Hanseatic War are but a few among many. The first mention of "letters of marque and reprisal"—in other words, of a privateering commission—in England dates to 1293, although according to R. G. Marsden, such written authorizations without doubt existed earlier.[7] The term *letters of marque and reprisal* was not always used, and sometimes a privateering commission was referred to simply as a license.[8] By the fourteenth century, privateering was fairly well-regulated in most kingdoms. Letters of marque and reprisal were also issued for reasons other than warfare, for example to recover losses sustained at the hands of the people of another state or kingdom, in violation of law or custom.[9]

The letters are often surprisingly broad. Those issued to John de Waghen in 1414 permitted him to recover the debt owed him by a single Leyden merchant by attacking *any* Leyden vessel.[10] Typically, these licenses required the holder to respect "the safe conducts granted hitherto"—in other words, to attack only those vessels not granted safe conduct by the crown.[11] In some cases, and perhaps in many, piratically inclined privateers and reprisal-makers simply took the safe conducts and "threw them overboard."[12] Such broad authorizations contributed not only to the already strained relations between kingdoms, but also to piracy by authorizing it under color of the law, not to mention by providing the opportunity for abuse.

The merchant fleets were perfectly suited to this armed mayhem on the sea. The Cinque Ports, for example, had a royal mandate to provide ships and men for the defense of Britain and often sent ships both as part of naval expeditions and on privateering cruises. In 1242, Henry III of England sent "orders to the masters of the Cinque Ports to injure, in every possible way, the traders and others belonging to the French kingdom who should be travelling by sea. These men, at once fulfilling the commands of the king, indulged, like pirates, in pillage and rapine, cruelly exceeding the bounds prescribed by the king, in their greediness for gain; for they despoiled of their property even the English and their neighbours and those known to them, when returning from their pilgrimage, paying no regard to relationship or kindred, and some of the French they cruelly put to death," according to one thirteenth-century historian.[13] The Cinque Ports privateers had orders not to harm churches or Englishmen and to deliver up one fifth of their plunder to the king. In essence, Henry III had temporarily replaced his navy with privateers, given he was by all accounts "unable to summon a levy from the maritime districts." The treasury was empty and he could not afford to maintain his navy.[14]

VESSELS, ARMS, AND FIGHTING SEAMEN

Improvements to vessels from 1066 to 1492 affected not only the merchant trade, but also sea roving, pirate hunting, and naval warfare in general. Ships built on the model of the longship or knarr lacked the necessary cargo-carrying capacity, and from them new forms developed. As ships grew larger, the sail became vital for propulsion; rowing was too inefficient and too expensive. In the northern waters of the mid- to late-Middle Ages, sailing vessels were used primarily for shipping, military transport, and fleet actions in naval warfare and were now often completely decked over, with temporary or permanent fighting towers (called *castles*) fore and aft, and a platform known as a *fighting top* on the mast.[15] The early ships were double-ended with a curved stem and stern, as well as a steering oar on the starboard or "steering board" side, and were obviously descended from the longship or knarr.[16]

In the fourteenth century, the cog, descended from these descendants of the Scandinavian longships but with its stern modified to accept a rudder, became both the common merchant ship and, when pressed into service and fitted with castles and a fighting top, the common warship and often a pirate and pirate-hunting ship as well. In 1275, a pirate fleet consisting of fourteen Zeeland cogs attacked several London merchant vessels, for example.[17] The cog was broad abeam with a deep hull and mostly straight keel, often had straight stem and stern posts, was usually single-masted until the fifteenth century (like all northern medieval ships), and began to resemble, more or less, what most of us have come to expect an "age of sail" ship to look like, including a figurehead developed from the "dragon head" at the bow of the old longship, although many vessels had no such ornamentation. By the late fourteenth century, the *hulk*, a large flat-bottomed double-ended ship, and the *carrack*, a large, heavily timbered ship built both for the merchant trade and for war, had largely replaced the cog.[18] Although they were excellent cargo carriers, none of these ships were particularly swift or maneuverable.

Raiding, privateering, and pirate hunting, however, were often conducted from galleys descended ultimately from the Norse longships, although it is possible there was some Mediterranean influence on their design. These galleys of the "narrow seas," North Sea, and Baltic had to be strongly built in order to survive the notoriously rough waters. As with most warships prior to the early modern period, details of the fighting galley used in northern waters are sparse and are still debated by maritime historians.

In general, the northern fighting galley of the thirteenth century was "double-ended with a curved stem aft" and forward with no ram or spur and had a single mast with a large square sail, a fighting top, a small fighting castle both fore and aft, hurdles running fore and aft between the castles for protection of the rowers, and perhaps eighty to one hundred twenty oars.[19] Some appear to have had outriggers for the oarsmen. A period source states that some of these galleys were "peaked with iron"—fitted with rams or spurs, that is, although this may be a mistake on the part of the chronicler.[20] "Long ships" used as a coast guard and "galliases" are also noted.[21] A century or two later, the term *galley* is rarely mentioned in English documents. Letters of marque and reprisal issued in 1404 to Henry Pay instead list "ships, barges, and balingers" as the means to "do all hurt he can to our open enemies, as well for their destruction as for the safe guarding and defence of our faithful lieges, and for the safety of our realm."[22]

The English *barge* was a type of galley, often manned with eighty men or more and typically weighing fifty to one hundred tons, although much larger barges existed. A few barges may have had up to eighty oars, but forty to fifty were common. The barge also carried a mast and square sail and was seaworthy under both oar and sail. Some barges had two decks, a castle bow and stern, and cabins. An English *balinger* or "balynser" (Spanish *ballenere*), whose name and probably hull design derive from whaling, was a similar vessel of much the same, or sometimes smaller, tonnage, and notably shallow-drafted and low-sided. One maritime historian has described it as a clinker-built square rigged ship that could use oars.[23] The balinger was probably lighter than the barge: it had roughly the same number of oars (forty to fifty, sometimes fewer) but typically had a smaller crew, roughly one per oar. It may have been longer, with a narrower beam, shallower draft, and sharper lines. Like the barge, the balinger had a single mast and sail and was likewise seaworthy. It was occasionally referred to as a small barge, and also as a balinger of war to distinguish it from those deployed on merchant passages.

The balinger constructed to accompany Henry V's great but unused *Gracedieu* in the early fifteenth century weighed eighty tons and had a single mast and yard, a sail with four bonnets, a bowsprit, a cock-boat, a pump, two anchors, thirty-eight oars, and a crew of fifty-nine. The barge associated with the *Gracedieu* was only twenty tons greater but carried forty-eight oars and three anchors. (It could be that by this time, barge was the term for the larger of a ship's accompanying vessels, balinger the smaller.) Both the barge and the balinger probably had small fighting castles fore and aft, and one fighting top or "topcastle" (and possibly as many as three) on the mast. Oars were used in calms and as necessary in battle. The speed of these vessels under oar is unknown, but it was probably similar to that of other single and double-banked galleys. Barges and balingers were common naval, pirate, privateer, and pirate-hunting vessels of the northern waters and were often manned for conventional naval warfare and pirate hunting with both sailors and soldiers.[24]

The West Highlands of Scotland had its own form of the galley, the *birlinn*. Light and fast, the birlinn, or West Highland galley, used a rudder rather than a steering oar, although it was otherwise very similar to the ships of the Norsemen. The galleys of Irish pirates may have been similar. Last, the *pinnace* or "spinace" of twenty to thirty men, probably a small light vessel or large boat for sailing and rowing, was a common vessel used for a variety of tasks, including warfare.[25]

Both ships and galley variants were used for naval warfare and attacks on enemy shipping. However, the hybrid oar and sail vessels such as galleys, barges, balingers, and pinnaces were by far the most suitable for coastal raiding and attacks on merchant vessels. In conventional naval combat, the galley and similar vessels were at a disadvantage due to their low freeboard relative to the tall castles of a warship well manned with men-at-arms, but such disadvantages disappeared when attacking the relatively small crew of a merchant ship or running up a river to attack a town. By the end of the period, however, the sailing vessel reigned in the northern seas. Even so, the ability to row was retained among many of the small sailing vessels used for sea roving and pirate hunting for another three or more centuries.

These agile roving vessels were typically described as "armed and arrayed in manner of war."[26] Pikes, lances, javelins, halberds (a combination battle-ax and pike), and other polearms were common, as were the other conventional arms and armor of the period, including sword and shield, particularly among the professional soldiery. The many variants of the "knightly sword" were common among knights who went as soldiers to sea, as probably were the "transitional swords" (a modern term) of the late fifteenth century. Falchions—short, heavy curved cutting swords—were common and suitable for boarding actions in the confines of a ship. Indeed, the medieval falchion is a likely forbearer of the cutlass.[27] The baselard (a form of long dagger) and the common period "short sword" of the soldier would have been typical as well. Axes, both long and short-handled, were probably common, both for fighting and damage control.

Longer-range armament consisted primarily of the bow and, from the latter thirteenth century, the crossbow. The bow was highly accurate and had a high rate of fire but required great skill to use effectively, which in turn was based on years of training. The crossbow required much less skill and training but was also less accurate and had a much slower rate of fire. Some large crossbows were mounted shipboard on pedestals, and, in the Mediterranean at least, some large vessels carried small catapults called sea-mangonels or onagers. Stones remained common projectiles, often thrown by hand from the tops, and spears, lances, and javelins remained in use, both as projectile weapons and as arms of close combat. Pots of unslaked lime (calcium oxide: quicklime, burnt lime) were sometimes used to burn and blind the enemy. To be safe to the user, unslaked lime had to be launched from windward. A highly caustic substance, calcium oxide causes chemical and thermal burns to skin, eyes, and lungs when combined with water, even in slight amounts such as perspiration or common skin moisture.[28] The use of lime at sea was noted by Leo VI circa AD 900 in his *Tactica* and was probably in use long before this. Today, we would consider it as chemical warfare. Various fireworks (combustible devices) were used to burn the enemy's ship and crew.[29]

With the introduction of gunpowder, fireworks became even more common. These fireworks included firepots whose contents could be as simple as gunpowder intended to burn men or as complex as viscous combustibles intended to set fire to the enemy vessel.[30] In the early fifteenth century, the gun, or cannon as it would be known ashore, became common at sea. Breech-loaded, it was made of wrought iron and fired stone shot. Smaller pieces called serpentines were mounted on the "gun wales" or castle rails, while larger pieces called bombards were mounted on deck and fired over the gunwale.[31] Gunports would come later.[32] Aboard most pirate, privateer, and merchant vessels, this artillery was of a smaller caliber, if it were carried at all. Firearms—referred to as hand culverins and hand bombards—were in use at sea from at least the mid-fifteenth century and may have been used at sea a century earlier.[33]

Arms noted as being issued specifically to balingers and similar craft include plate armor, lances, bows and sheaves or arrows, and crossbow bolts called quarrels (and, one would thus expect, crossbows). Twenty bows, strings, and sheaves of arrows are listed for the *Valentine*, the intended consort barge of the *Gracedieu*.[34] Without doubt other arms were carried aboard, probably as the personal property or issue of soldiers and sailors. Records of merchant armament are sparse, but a thirteenth-century inventory evaluated and published in the late nineteenth century is instructive. Although it describes the stores of a Mediterranean merchant vessel of 1294, ships in the northern seas were probably similarly armed. Among the two officers and twelve crew, there were three crossbows: two of wood belonging to the captain or *padrone,* the third, of Damascened steel, to the other officer. No other projectile devices are noted. Everyone was armed and armored identically: a cuirass (*coracia*) of some sort, a quilted jack worn beneath the cuirass, a small gorget (*gorzarina*) to protect the throat, a metal helmet, an iron gauntlet for the right hand, a shield or buckler of unspecified material, and an iron lance. The captain's cuirass was covered with red silk, and he had a skull cap as well.[35] In many cases, some or all members of a merchant crew probably owned or were issued a short sword or ax, and all would have carried a utility or multipurpose knife and quite possibly a dagger. Period illustrations of sea battles typically show armored knights and soldiers in battle at sea, but for the merchant sailor, full armor was prohibitively expensive.

The men who handled these arms were by now distinguished into two sorts: mariners and soldiers. The soldier was typically a professional man-at-arms, the mariner a professional man of the sea for whom seamanship was necessarily a priority. Often the mariner had experience in four capacities: merchant seaman, naval conscript, privateer, and pirate. A balinger being outfitted in 1442 "to resist the king's enemies" was to be manned with "thirty fencible men" arrested (impressed) for the purpose, indicating that mariners did not constitute the greater part of the complement.[36] A privateering license of 1436 for William Berkyng, owner of the fifty-ton balinger *Goodyere* of London, lists the apparently typical complement as "master, mariners, men at arms, [and] archers."[37] Fighting oarsmen need not be seamen, or at least not all of them, and oarsmen at this time were still free men and were expected to fight as well. Like those of later centuries, medieval sea rovers probably recruited sailors both as mariners and as fighters, men-at-arms as boarders, and archers for the obvious. Even so, many naval and sea-roving crews in the late Middle Ages may often have been composed largely of seamen who did their own fighting: the *Blacke Booke of the Admiralty* (*Liber Niger Admiralitatis*) notes "to know likewise by good and lawfull inquests . . . how many *fighting marriners* are in the realme"[38] (author's italics).

Of the seaman himself there is only minimal information as compared to later centuries. However, from Chaucer's description in *The Canterbury Tales,* the seaman seems to have been what we would expect. Dressed in a knee-length frock of coarse cloth, he carried a knife hanging from a cord around his neck, was burned brown by the sun, drank wine heavily and often (Bordeaux, stolen stealthily from the merchant's own cargo), and understood the complexity of the maritime art, including navigation, tides, currents, harbors and havens, and the various dangers of the sea. Most important to us, though, are the following lines: "Nice conscience was a thing he never kept. / If that he fought and gained the upper hand, / By water he sent them home to every land." Chaucer's sailor was, at least when circumstance or opportunity warranted, a pirate. As for the passengers and crew of his quarry, he either killed and dumped them into the sea or tossed them overboard alive and watched them drown.[39]

The written record of the Middle Ages is filled with instances supporting this characterization. In 1403, in one of many sea battles of the period, a Breton fleet defeated an English privateering fleet and reportedly took two thousand prisoners. In an all-too-common act, "the greater part of the prisoners were thrown overboard and drowned, but some escaped by promising punctual payment of their ransom."[40] This may well be the point at which the English word *pirate*, which in the early Middle Ages merely referred to a sea-going fighter or rover, began to take on its modern "murdering scum of the sea" connotation. As in antiquity, travelers beseeched that their vessel be spared the double hazard of the sea: "[T]hat the billows may not overwhelm it, nor cruel pirates seize upon it."[41]

THE NAVAL MEN-OF-WAR

Navies and coast guards were the readily apparent immediate response, if not solution, to sea roving in the Middle Ages, just as they are today. In 1120, the Archbishop of Santiago created the Armada de Galicia to defend Spain against attacks by Moorish corsairs, and in 1205, more than one hundred naval galleys were stationed in England, Wales, and Ireland to defend against attack, primarily from piratical raiders such as those described by Florence of Worcester: "Pirates from Zealand and Holland, making a piratical descent in the neighbourhood of Yarmouth and Dunwich, plundered all that fell in their way, butchered the people, and carried off some ships with their cargos."[42] Unfortunately, due to their small size, the long coastlines they were expected to protect, and the financial inability to maintain them, navies and coast guards were often ineffective without augmentation, and even then often failed to significantly suppress sea roving. Many were composed almost entirely of hired or "arrested" vessels and men. Vessels and armed men were typically conscripted into government service in order to suppress pirates and serve otherwise in a naval capacity.[43] Ports were often recruited to provide ships and men to defend against maritime attack. Merchant ships and crews were also recruited to harass foreign commerce. Attacks on enemy commerce could help bring the conflict to an end, which would in turn result in the suppression of enemy privateering, or at least this was the theory then and for centuries afterward.

NONVIOLENT ANTI-PIRACY

Treaties and trade agreements defining piracy and its redress were a fairly common means of attempting to redress piracy, but they were often breached. Cooperative organizations such as the Cinque Ports were common. The Hanseatic League was founded in the thirteenth century in part as a means of defending Baltic merchant trade against pirates.[44] More locally, the crown might order ports to ensure that their mariners did not attack incoming shipping, given that common mariners were also often common pirates, and their prize goods were typically carried into their home ports.[45] In extreme cases, foreign vessels might be prohibited from trade. When English pirates got out of hand in the northern waters in the years surrounding 1400, the Baltic was briefly closed in retaliation.[46]

Suppressing one's own pirates was a viable but difficult means of diminishing the number of retaliatory roving and coastal raids. By the late fifteenth century, security was sometimes required to aid in suppressing privateers' common urge to engage in occasional piracy.[47] However, other privateering licenses provided that "should any offence [piracy] be done to the king's friends only those by whom such offence be done shall answer for it, not the balinger nor her owner or victuallers [suppliers, especially of food]," probably further encouraging piracy.[48] Proclamations against piracy sometimes required merchant ships to give security before sailing in order to ensure their good behavior at sea, although the temptation of lucre many times greater than the security must surely have been tempting.[49] Similarly, English seaports were at times required to give surety for the "good behavior of their own ships," and in at least one case, this provision was incorporated into a treaty with France.[50]

Proclamations against harboring pirates or receiving their goods were common, as were laws governing the restitution of goods taken by pirates.[51] The *Rolle of Olayron* (Laws of Oleron) of the late Middle Ages provided that in the case of shipwreck, "[Y]f they be pirates, pillagers, or sea-rovers, or

Turks, or others opposed to and enemies of our Holy Catholic Faith, every one may take from suche manner of men as from dogs, and may strip them and despoil them of theyr goodes without any punishment."[52] However, given the number of complaints of piracy in the mid- to late-Middle Ages, the anti-piracy methods of surety, restitution, and confiscation do not seem to have been particularly effective, although in many cases, piracy was actually encouraged by the crown or by local government or both, or at least both turned blind eyes toward it. Traditional enemies—England and France in particular—often had little reason to object to piracies committed one against the other.

At the criminal level, investigations into piracy were routine by the fifteenth century, with warrants typically issued for the local sheriff to locate and seize the captured vessel and goods, as well as to seize the men who had stolen them.[53] Local pirates were pursued both at sea and ashore by local law enforcement: "[They] followed on the sea with their ships certain pirates, who with their ship had put into the port of Fawie [Foway] and there killed a mariner . . . and committed thefts and other crimes on sea as on land." In this case, the malefactors were captured and delivered to the "king's prison." Some resisted capture and were killed.[54]

Although many pirates were prosecuted and often hanged upon conviction, many were granted amnesty in return for service to the crown at sea. Some successfully petitioned to be pardoned on the basis of having equipped a ship of war for the king.[55] Privateers who seized cargos illegally were typically held in custody, their vessels and any cargo impounded, until they made restitution.[56] Special courts were sometimes set up to deal with captured pirates; the Cinque Ports were granted a "commission of oyer and terminer" in 1289 to try pirates, for example.[57] In England at least, the law of piracy was still developing, especially in regard to jurisdiction, and pirates were tried variously under both the common law and the maritime law.[58]

There were other nonviolent means of reining in pirates. The Count of Brittany's piracies, detailed below, were curtailed by the "king of France, at the request of the king of England . . . under a threat of disinheritance."[59] Some pirates and privateers were little more than mercenaries, and governments sometimes bribed or otherwise recruited them en masse to change allegiance. For some, allegiance was strictly a business arrangement easily managed in times of rapidly shifting alliances, not to mention wars and civil wars.

MERCHANT DEFENSES

Merchant vessels were usually armed sufficiently to repel small attacks and attackers. Naval convoys of merchant fleets were now common, and individual ships were often convoyed as well. In 1437, one barge and two balingers convoyed the merchant ship *Marie* to Zeeland and were ordered to "keep the sea for a month after her arrival to fight the king's enemies." Any booty they took was theirs, less the shares due the "admiral of England and the warden of the Cinque Ports."[60] One suspects that the month at sea, doubtless a temptation to piracy beyond any legitimate privateering, helped pay for the escort. Balingers and barges were also used to carry cargo. On the one hand, such arrangements would have been expensive if a full complement were carried, but on the other hand, a large crew could defend the vessel from pirates, might be able to make a faster voyage, and might also plunder other vessels. In one fashion or another, merchant owners were expected to defray the expense of defending the merchant fleet and coastline from pirates and other marauders. For example, at one time the customs duty on wine imported to England went to pay for convoy service, less any profit the convoy vessels made from their own trade or prizes.[61]

ANTI-PIRATE REPRISALS

Retaliatory attacks were common. Some were legitimate, but others appear to have been mere pretense for piracy. After the aforementioned English attacks on French shipping in 1242, the French responded in kind, fortifying their ports against attack and sending their own privateers to sea with orders "not to spare the persons or goods" of the English.[62] In this they appear to have been quite successful, not only thrice repulsing the English rovers, but also engaging in similar piracy themselves. "Moreover, to crown our troubles, the inhabitants of the confines of Normandy, those who guard the more distant shores, together with the pirates of Wissant [Ushant] and Calais, will scarcely let us, even to a small extent, look after our fishing. Pirates, also, guarding the deep sea in galleys, do not even permit travellers to return to their own country."[63] The Cinque Ports rovers were broken financially, and the king could spare them no aid; a truce soon followed.[64] It is likely that the actual response of French seamen was focused as much on tit-for-tat war on commerce as on attacking the attackers, given that commerce raiding was more profitable than naval warfare.

Even with the truce, the situation did not get much better: "But the count of Brittany, a crafty and wily man, pretended to be ignorant of all these things [the treaty between England to France], and after the manner of pirates vigilantly applied himself to plunder and rapine on the sea with his galleys and other vessels, unwilling to come to the shore, lest a royal mandate should restrain his wicked and mischievous expeditions."[65] Often, privateers on both sides grew fat from the proceeds of theft on the high seas, some of it legitimized by war, some it frankly unlawful and merely the result of opportunity seized in the chaos of war. These unlawful excesses would remain a problem until the nineteenth century.

Reprisals were not limited to commerce at sea. Again, one of the best means of dealing with the sea rover has been to attack his shore bases; he and his crew might be captured or killed, and even if he were not, his base of operations might be so damaged or compromised that he must move elsewhere or commit extra resources to defending it in the future. With luck, his vessels might be captured or destroyed as well. Severe damage combined with the obvious threat of a return visit might even discourage him temporarily or, with luck, permanently.

In the late fourteenth and early fifteenth centuries, England's most successful privateer and patriot pirate was Henry Pay. Often operating under a legitimate commission, he also practiced piracy in times ostensibly of peace between England and France and could be considered a pirate hunter in that he made lucrative raids, again ostensibly, in reprisal for French and Spanish piracies. According to Gutierre Díaz de Gámez (biographer and comrade-in-arms of Pero Niño, the noted Spanish pirate), pirate hunter, and contemporary of the English pirate, Pay attacked and captured French and Spanish vessels indiscriminately, successfully raided Flanders, captured many ships and *barques* along the Castilian coast, burned Gijon and Finisterre in France, stole the crucifix of the church of Sainte-Marie de Finisterre, and held many prisoners for ransom.[66]

In 1404, Pay was captured by a better-manned Norman vessel after a desperate boarding action. The French bound their prisoners, "told them to prepare for death," then, due to the heat, took off their helmets and gauntlets, and some of them even their armor, and went below to plunder. Pay and his surviving crew freed themselves from their bonds, surprised and killed their captors who remained on deck, and, with the dead men's arms, killed those below. From there they met with an allied vessel, hoisted French colors, and sailed into the Seine, where the French took them for a French ship with an English prize. Pay and his company plundered and burned a fair number of French vessels then returned home.[67] It is not without reason that the

Spanish considered England to be a nation of pirates, although such accusations were frankly hypocritical. Again, it is important to remember that in this period, as in many in history, the distinction between pirate, privateer, legitimate naval officer, and pirate hunter was tenuous at best. Often they were indistinguishable.

In 1405, a joint Spanish-French expedition was prepared against the English, largely in reprisal for English pirate attacks in what was technically a time of peace between kingdoms. In fact, piracy was largely tolerated, at least when it was in the national interest. The Spanish commander, Pero Niño, was an experienced corsair, having commanded pirate-hunting expeditions against Spanish pirates in the western Mediterranean, Moorish corsairs in the Levant, and Barbary corsairs in North Africa. Although his primary mission was to protect merchant shipping, he joined his three Mediterranean galleys to two belonging to French corsair Charles de Savoisy and headed for the English coast. At Cornwall, the punitive pillaging expedition captured nineteen fishing boats, interrogated their crews, then drowned the hapless men. From there the expedition attacked and plundered Shouta (East Looe) in spite of a "brave resistance," killing many residents, burning the town, and carrying away two merchant vessels. The attackers attempted a raid on Falmouth but were put off by the sight of a large body of armed men, then made largely unsuccessful attacks on Saltash (Plymouth) and the Isle of Portland. At the latter, Pero Niño reportedly refused to burn the houses of the inhabitants because he did not wish to make war on the poor.[68]

These attacks provide some details of defenses ashore. At Shouta, the pillaging pirate hunters were attacked with stones (probably from catapults or trebuchets) and flights of arrows on both sides of the channel as they departed, and at Saltash, they were similarly attacked from the fortified walls of the town. At Portland, they were dispersed by a large number of archers who were landed on the island.[69] England was by now garrisoned, with often substantial forces within marching distance. In 1385, for example, "those able and willing to go to the sea-coast in defense of the realm and City" were to be paid "12 pence for men-at-arms properly arrayed and 6 pence for archers." Price gouging by arms providers—we would call them defense contractors today—was apparently common: "that no armourer, bowyer [bow maker], or "fleccher" [arrow maker] enhance the price of his wares in consequence of this proclamation."[70]

However, the final object of these pillaging pirate hunters, either as originally intended or as a target of opportunity (the latter, Díaz de Gámez suggests), was Poole, home of Henry Pay who was himself apparently absent, fortunately or unfortunately. Here the Spanish landed, the French refusing due to a disagreement on tactics. They burned a storehouse after a stiff resistance and carried off a variety of arms and naval stores. The English soon counter-attacked with archers and various men-at-arms. The English bow was pitted against the Spanish crossbow and began to give the English the upper hand. Seeing his countrymen in danger, Pero Niño landed with the remainder of his men as reinforcements, followed by the French. The battle was brutal. An account of one of Pero Niño's later combats is probably similar to this combat:

> There were struck very fair blows with the lance wherewith many were hit on both sides and some even overthrown. Leaving the lances they grasped axes and swords and engaged in a rough mellay [melee]. There might you have seen helmets torn from breastplates, and arm and leg pieces stripped off from some, and axes and swords fall from the hands of others; some come to grips one with the other or take to their daggers; some fall to the ground, others rise again, and blood flowing abundantly in many places.[71]

Poole fell, and with it one of Henry Pay's brothers. After plundering and burning the town, then making a brief venture inland and a desultory visit to the Isle of Wight, the raiders returned across the channel.[72]

Land warfare in the suppression of sea roving was not limited to reprisal. Conquest of a raiding state, or at least its defeat and surrender, could obviously suppress state-sanctioned piracy. Large-scale piracy or privateering deriving from rebellion was typically quelled by capturing the major instigators or the rebellious regions or both. Prince Edward—later King Edward I, known as Longshanks—led efforts that suppressed rebellion in Dover and among the Cinque Ports during the unrest caused by fractious nobles—the Barons' Revolt—from 1264 to 1267. Land warfare, not naval, was the key. Suppressing rebellion in these areas effectively suppressed large-scale piracy as well, and "by this conduct, great tranquility was spread over that sea,"[73] at least for a time.

Attacks on bases ashore were also a viable anti-pirate tactic not only in the case of notorious foreign pirates and privateers like Henry Pay, but also in the case of local renegade pirates holed up in island retreats. Small-scale sea-going brigands and their gangs were often tracked down and taken ashore by force or by "treachery"—what we would today refer to as raids or arrests based on good intelligence and appropriate deception. Sir William de Marish (also known as William Marsh), a knight accused of treason in 1242, made Lundy Island in the Bristol Channel his headquarters, and from there indulged "in plunder and rapine" along the nearby coast. Sea-going nobles attempted to capture him, but, realizing his position was largely impregnable, they advised the king "that the said William and his followers could not be seized unless by treachery, [and] they told the king that they must act, not forcibly, but prudently," which they did. Sir William was captured—he was building a galley with which to further his piracies—and forthwith hanged, disemboweled, quartered, and displayed. The eighteen accomplices captured with him were dragged through London by horses and then hanged.[74]

However, in many cases of both small-scale local pirates and large-scale pirates and privateers, the most effective means of their destruction was to capture or kill them at sea.

PIRATE VERSUS PIRATE HUNTER AT SEA

Several graphic accounts of actions at sea were written in the Middle Ages, but most are associated with conventional naval warfare, such as it was. The typical naval action consisted of a fleet of cogs or other ships pitted against a similar fleet. The battle began at long range with archers and flights of arrows, then with crossbows and quarrels and often lances or javelins as the range closed, and soon followed with attempts at boarding, with men-at-arms battering away at each other in brutal, bloody combat, with sword, ax, lance, or poniard (a slender-bladed dagger) in hand. Thankfully for our subject, one of these actions actually did involve a notorious thirteenth century pirate and mercenary, Eustace the Monk. Eustace, a Fleming by birth, had indeed been a monk, but his sea-going proclivities of arms and plunder did nothing to endear him to the Church, much less his reported repudiation of his vows in order to lay claim to his deceased and childless brothers' estates. Eustace began as a common pirate and was known as such by 1206, if not earlier. From here he graduated to a combination of piracy and occasionally dubious service under King John, whom he served until he transferred allegiance to France in 1211. In 1216, he commanded the French fleet of six hundred vessels and eighty cogs that carried the French prince Louis to England to join the rebel English barons who had offered him the crown.[75]

After Louis' defeat in 1217, Eustace commanded a smaller fleet intended to rescue the prince. He was intercepted by an even smaller but more agile

English fleet commanded by Hubert de Burgh, William Marshall, and Philip d'Aubigny. The fleet included Cinque Ports vessels whose captains and crews reportedly preferred to meet Eustace at sea, where they stood a better chance against him, rather than ashore. According to chronicler Matthew of Paris, the fight began at long range:

> Philip de Albiney [d'Aubigny] with his cross-bow men and archers sending their missiles amongst the French, soon caused great slaughter . . . they also threw hot lime-dust on the sea, which, being borne by the wind, blinded the eyes of the French. A severe engagement took place between the fleets, but that of the French, who were not well skilled in naval warfare, was soon defeated; for the crews were struck down by the weapons and arrows of the English sailors, who were used to naval fights, pierced them with their javelins and arrows, or cut them down with swords and lances, whilst others bored holes in their ships' bottoms and sank them.[76]

Of particular note is that the English "threw grappling-irons and made them fast to their own vessels, and boarding them with their axes, they cut away the rigging supporting the mast and yards, and, the expending sail falling, the French were caught like birds in a net." Reportedly, some of the French knights threw themselves into the sea rather than be captured. Eustace was discovered hiding in the hold. He attempted to bribe his captors, to no avail: he was beheaded.[77]

A well-known period illustration of a sea battle between cogs, taken from a Psalter circa 1330, shows archers in the stern of the attacking ship and men-at-arms at the "fore castle" (thus the modern term, *forecastle* or *fo'c'sle*). Aboard the attacked ship, defenders engage in hand-to-hand combat in an attempt to repel the boarding.[78] Another period illustration, this one of the battle itself and taken from the *Chronicle* of Matthew of Paris, shows men-at-arms on the stern of the attacking vessel throwing pots of unslaked lime via slings with long wood handles and also shooting them from bows.[79] Slings are an excellent method of hurling objects. Bows would seem less so, yet "we threw small bottles full of lime, made to be shot from a bow."[80] A grappling hook secures attacker to attacked, and men-at-arms and seamen armed with sword and ax dispatch the enemy.

The tactic of cutting down rigging and sails was not new, nor was the use of the weather gage, which gave advantage to light projectile weapons such as arrows, quarrels, and, in this case, unslaked lime. Perhaps the most innovative aspect of the battle was, as naval historian Susan Rose has pointed out, that it hinged on seamanship and not simply on the melee between ships and men-at-arms.[81] Thus the likely victor may have been the adversary who best sailed and maneuvered. As for the statement that some French vessels were sunk by galleys beaked with rams, one naval historian has made the reasonable suggestion that if any French ships sank as a result of enemy action, they were probably bilged as English ships struck them as they came alongside to board, and not sunk by rams.[82] Mediterranean-style galleys with "boarding spurs," some of which were iron tipped, were largely unknown in medieval England, although they were seen occasionally among the French and Spanish in the northern seas.

This action was in many ways indistinguishable from other large-scale naval actions of the period. There were, however, smaller, more common pirate-hunting actions. At one end of the spectrum are small-fleet actions against the fleets or flotillas of classic pirate brethren, so to speak—against those whose primary purpose was piracy and who operated in gangs held together by bonds of common experience and common purpose. One of the most significant of these pirate brethren was the *Vitalienbrüder* or Victual Brotherhood, a relatively short-lived band operating in the Baltic and North Sea in the late fourteenth century. Like many pirates, the *Vitalienbrüder* had its origin in privateering, having been recruited and supported as privateers by the duchy of Mecklenburg (whose ports, Rostock and Wismar, were part of the Hanseatic League) in a dispute with Denmark in the late fourteenth century.

The Brotherhood attacked not only Danish shipping, but Hanseatic shipping as well. So effective were these rovers, among whom at first were Mecklenburg noblemen, that by 1392, trade in the Baltic had nearly ceased. A 1395 treaty removed the pirates' privateering pretense, and so, from their base at Visby in Gotland, they began a piratical rampage in the Baltic. In 1398, Konrad von Jungingen and an army of four thousand or more destroyed the Brotherhood's base, slaughtered many of the pirates, and forced the remainder from the Baltic. The Brotherhood now had no choice but to make their attacks in the North Sea. Two years later, a Hanseatic fleet under the command of Hermann Lange and Nikolaus Schoke attacked and destroyed the remaining *Vitalienbrüder.* Unfortunately, we know nothing of the actual battle itself.[83] In a related curiosity, a spiked skull believed to be that of one of the *Vitalienbrüder* leaders, Klaus Störtebeker (Klaus "Tip Up the Mug"), was stolen in January 2010 from the Hamburg History Museum.[84]

In similar pirate-hunting fashion, a French fleet of thirty vessels and twelve hundred men engaged "the English, who had a large fleet at sea on the look-out for merchantmen like pirates" in 1403, defeating them after a three-hour battle, reportedly taking two thousand prisoners and capturing "forty vessels with sails, and a carrack."[85] But again, the details are absent. In 1489, Scottish admiral Sir Andrew Wood, with only two vessels at his command, captured a flotilla of five piratical English ships sent to support Scottish rebels and raid Scottish shipping. Later ambushed by a retaliatory English squadron of three vessels commanded by noted privateer Stephen Bull, he captured them all. (King James freed the English captain, who was soon captured by the Spanish in 1492.) The battle was fought at longer range with cannon, then the vessels came to grips with knights, pikemen, and crossbowmen all in close combat; the fighting lasted until evening. The vessels parted then began fighting again the next morning to a large audience of spectators on the shore.[86] Alas, once more the details on tactics are lacking.

Fortunately for us, though, Díaz de Gámez once more comes to the rescue, providing some of the more exacting details we need on the fight at sea between pirates or privateers and their hunters on a somewhat smaller scale. A year after his pillaging voyage along the English coast, Pero Niño set sail with his galleys and three French balingers for the North Sea coast of England, having intelligence that the Cornish and Southern coasts were now too well watched, thanks to his recent escapades. In the English channel, he ran into a flotilla of English vessels, all manned for war. Summoning a council, Pero Niño decided to attack. The wind was calm, providing his galleys with ideal conditions. He ordered wine to his oarsmen to fortify their hearts, for they seldom drank wine at sea, and when they did, they drank little. He ordered his soldiers and sailors to arm.[87]

The English flotilla likewise arrayed itself for battle and made all the sail it could. The largest balingers took their post at the front of the formation in a line and parallel to each other with their bows facing forward the enemy. In the rear were two large ships and a German cog. In the center were the smaller balingers, and a few other small balingers maneuvered variously about. The English ships put out their colors at their sterns and arrayed their fighting men, armed with bows and lances, on deck.[88]

The Spanish attacked with a fierce onslaught of "arrows, darts, bolts and stones." Pero Niño ordered his vessels to row close enough to use quarrels "dressed with tar" in order to burn the English sails, but not all obeyed, fearing to close with the English. Whatever the circumstances, the quarrels failed to set any of the English vessels afire. Next, Pero Niño sent a fireboat filled with tar toward the English, pushing it along with a spar, but the English fended it off with their lances. The wind rose, but Pero Niño and the crew of his galley were too busy fighting to notice. The other Spanish galleys, however, did notice. With their comparatively low freeboard, the galleys were vulnerable to heavily armed and manned sailing ships, unless they could maneuver, which they could not do if they were caught up in close battle. As long as there were a wind, a ship could easily sail alongside a galley caught up in close battle and rain projectiles onto it or even board it. The galleys thus turned and ran, as indeed Pero Niño's officers advised him to do. Instead, he continued to fight.[89]

By now Pero Niño was under attack from two balingers—one port, one starboard—apparently intending to keep him engaged until the ships came up. Díaz de Gámez stated that had the balingers approached closer they would indeed have been able to prevent the escape of Niño's galley, but the vessel's vigorous defense via "bolts and with flights of arrows and darts" kept the English at bay. However, with the approach of the other English vessels, Pero Niño's galley was in danger of eventually being overwhelmed. But his allies had not deserted him—French balingers came swiftly to his aid, intercepting two English balingers that intended to block the escape of Pero Niño's galley. The leading French balinger rammed one of the pursuing English at the prow, breaking its bowsprit.[90]

Now to leeward, Pero Niño's flotilla retreated to the French coast, the English following. There, Niño invited the English flotilla to continue the battle, but it declined the invitation, probably, as Díaz de Gámez notes, because the wind was now light and the water shallow. The sailing ships would not be able to maneuver to their advantage.[91]

According to Díaz de Gámez, the English flotilla was commanded by Henry Pay and, they later learned to their despair, was conveying Princess Philippa, daughter of Henry IV, to Denmark to marry the king. But if this was in fact the flotilla Pero Niño engaged, it was commanded by Admiral of Merchants Nicholas Blackburn and not Henry Pay. Second in command was John Brandon, an English pirate and privateer with vast experience in the North Sea. Above all, the engagement exemplifies the difficulty distinguishing between pirates, privateers, naval vessels, merchant seamen, and pirate hunters during the Middle Ages, as well as distinguishing between privateering, naval warfare, pirate hunting, and piracy.[92]

MERCHANTMAN VERSUS PIRATE

Last and certainly the most common of fights against rovers at sea were those of merchant versus pirate. This is ultimately the critical juncture, for if merchant vessels were able to adequately defend themselves against sea-roving attacks, there would be no need for pirate hunting, other than defenses ashore. Unfortunately, we once more have little information on actual tactics used during these attacks. "Closed quarters"—fighting from behind barricaded decks and bulkheads—probably developed in this period, and with it the boarding ax, or at least its name. Ships which were completely decked over, and particularly those with a raised forecastle, could be fortified against attackers, who must then hack their way into the cabins or holds while braving an onslaught of projectiles. Unfortunately, the evidence for this tactic in this period is little more than conjecture. Recalling the merchant armament listed earlier and assuming it was typical, we can be assured that most fights probably ended quickly, with the pirate or privateer as victor due to their overwhelming numbers and arms. In many cases, merchant vessels with small crews probably surrendered immediately, although this is only a surmise. Given that merchant crews were often thrown overboard after capture, many may have chosen instead to fight to the end, knowing it might be their only chance at survival.

However, the 1491 petition of French privateer and pirate hunter Jehan Maulpetit (Jean Maupetit) provides a peek at a fight at sea between two ships, one of them possibly a merchantman, and also at some apparent duplicity as well. At the very least, the petition gives us a brief look at a combat between two ships, from long range to boarding. Maupetit, a pirate-hunting privateer and probably at times a pirate as well, claimed to have taken to the sea as a corsair out of a concern for Breton, English, and Spanish piracies. In the case of a Spanish ship he attacked, he claimed to have taken arms against it out of belief that the Spaniard, who may have come near merely to hail the French vessel, in fact intended to attack. To support his claim of legitimate reprisal (which may have been a merely pro forma pretense that fooled no one), Maupetit maintained that a Spanish ship had recently captured a French vessel and murdered her captain and most of her crew, and therefore the Spanish ship before him might well be a pirate, perhaps even *the* pirate.[93]

The fight began when the Spaniard came near. Fearing the ship might be a rover, or so the petitioner claimed, he quickly saw to it that "all of the crew were in arms and a great multitude of artillery and arrows [or bolts] was fired." Many were killed and wounded on both sides before the boarding took place. The fight on deck was vicious, and Maupetit has provided us with a snapshot, assuming he has been truthful: "There was even one of these Spaniards who fought against the quartermaster . . . he thrust his dagger at him and would have lanced him through, but the petitioner [Maupetit], seeing this, thrust his sword into the Spaniard's belly, of which he died."[94]

This brief sea fight—one of many hundreds of thousands, most of which were never recorded—came at the end of the Middle Ages as a new form of naval warfare was developing. But before we move on to the pirate hunting of the sixteenth century and beyond, we must first pass the Strait of Gibraltar and head into the Mediterranean to take a look at a region where sea roving in the Middle Ages was as complex and widespread, or even more so given the conflicting and often hypocritical intersection of religious conflict and mercenary greed, as that of the northern seas we are leaving.

Mediterranean piracy of the period might be best introduced with the exhortation of a passenger upon his realization that his vessel was about to be attacked by a corsair. Probably something similar was spoken by many mariners and passengers of both the Christian and Muslim religions at the approach of a corsair, who often belonged to the competing faith: "O Lord God, we shall be taken and slaughtered."[95] In fact, in the Mediterranean, they were often more likely to be enslaved, notwithstanding common faith-based throat-slitting.

7

Of Faith, Galleys, and Greed

Defeating the Mediterranean Corsairs, 476–1492

"But what can be more dreadful than a fight at sea? What more savage, where such various fates await the combatants? Some are tortured by the burning of the flames; some falling overboard are swallowed in the waves; others wounded perish by the enemy's weapons," noted a chronicler of the Third Crusade when describing a Mediterranean sea fight.[1]

A century later, Jean Froissart wrote much the same thing of a fight in the northern seas: "This battle was right fierce and terrible; for the battles on the sea are more dangerous and fiercer than the battles by land: for on the sea there is no reculing [drawing back] nor fleeing; there is no remedy but to fight and to abide fortune and every man to shew his prowess."[2]

Fierce battles are not uncommon on land or sea in any age. In any fight, fear rears its head and is then suppressed, channeled, augmented, given free reign, or takes control, according to the unique circumstances of each man in each moment. At times, this combination is melded into a complex variety of other factors and leads to extraordinary actions. However, many writers—many of whom were veterans of sea combats—have noted exactly what the chroniclers did: the nature of the sea itself has often made men fight more fiercely. In the Middle Ages, the loss of one's vessel often meant death, as did capture at sea, thus the motivation to fight as fiercely as possible. But sea combats in the medieval Mediterranean had an added element that may have helped induce extreme violence: the bigotry of Holy War.

OF FAITH AND GREED, AND GREED AS FAITH

The medieval Mediterranean retained the ancient tradition of sea roving as an accepted means of economic gain. Roving was not "rediscovered" as a lucrative profession, nor was it significantly altered. Mediterranean geography was unchanged, providing the necessary physical environment; sea-going trade was extensive, providing the sine qua non; and the political environment continued to be complex and varied, providing the opportunity for exploitation. Naval warfare remained composed as much of commerce raiding and pillaging ashore as of conventional fleet actions. Sea rovers raided as they always had: "The Pyrats [corsairs], who landed day and night in several parts, pillaged the Cities, burnt the Houses, massacred and carried away many of the Christians."[3] Repeat the quotation, substituting "Moors" for "Christians," and the picture is complete.

With a warning that transitions in history often go unnoticed at the time of their occurrence, we can divide Mediterranean sea roving in the Middle Ages into three eras: the early Byzantine Empire and Muslim conquests, the Holy Wars, and the late Middle Ages. Throughout the period, the Mediterranean was infested with privateers and naval commerce raiders, as well as pirates whose depredations had the tacit approval not only of their home kingdoms or city states, but also of those who benefited from the pirate's raiding and plundering. The pirate in service solely for himself—in essence, a sea-going brigand—was also common. As in the northern seas, many mariners served variously in the quintuple capacity of merchant seamen, naval seamen, privateer, pirate, and pirate hunter.

Similarly, many navies were composed all or in part of hired or "arrested" ships and men, and often the privateer served as a quasi-naval vessel and pirate hunter as well, its duties at times going beyond profitable commerce raiding at sea and looting ashore. Again, the privateer, quasi-naval commerce raider, and pirate hunter were often indistinguishable. The common Mediterranean term for these legitimate or at least state-sanctioned rovers was *corsair*, a word which derives ultimately from the Latin *cursus*, meaning to run, pursue, or "course." The term is often taken today as a synonym for pirate, given the common tendency to refer to any sea rover as a pirate, especially one whose primary purpose is not privateering in support of a war with another nation, but privateering as an end in itself.

In 527 AD, control of the Byzantine Empire fell to the hands of the emperor Justinian. Much of the Mediterranean at this time was controlled by Vandals, Ostragoths, and Visigoths, and to counter them, Justinian built a powerful navy. With it, in combination with an army commanded by his famous general, Belisarius, he retook control of much of the coastline, and thus to a large degree much of the sea itself. In doing so, he created a "restored Roman Empire" in the Levant, or Eastern Mediterranean. (Many scholars divide the historical Mediterranean culturally and economically into east and west.) Persia was the great competitor at first, but in the mid-seventh century, a new force emerged in the Mediterranean, one that took both to sea-going trade and to sea roving: the Arab-Muslims. According to historian George Hourani, "When the first Muslims reached the coasts all round them, some of them displayed a tendency to go raiding across the sea. This was but an extension of the immemorial pagan practice of *ghazw* [raiding] in the desert; one rode a ship (*rakaba markab*) as one rode a camel, either for commerce or for spoil."[4] Arab expansion, which included Crete, parts of Northern Italy and the French coast, Sicily, and North Africa, extended even as far as the Spanish kingdoms, much of which they conquered. The Abbasid Caliphate reigned early on, followed by the increasing power of Berbers and Turks. Besides the typical economic conflict between sea-going empires (not to mention the inevitably associated piracy and privateering), the conflict very quickly turned religious. Byzantium lost its dominion over the Mediterranean. Subsequent competition and warfare, which would run for more than a thousand years, consisted of wars over trade and trade routes, wars of conquest, and wars over religion, often one and the same.[5]

The rise of powerful merchant city-states coincided in the middle era with the economic and religious conflict between empires and gave rise to a complex international politics, with the usual strange bedfellows. In the Muslim Mediterranean, the Fatimid Caliphate reigned over much of the region until the late-twelfth century, followed by the Mamluks in Egypt and Syria. The Christian kingdoms of Europe mounted nine Crusades to the Holy Land, from 1095 to 1272. Conflict between the two Catholic faiths— Latin Christianity or Catholicism under the Roman Pope, and Byzantine Christianity, known today as the Orthodox Church—grew, and the Byzantine Empire developed into a separate culture, isolated from the culture and Christianity of the west. On the one hand, Christian states were ostensibly united by their faith and with the Byzantine Empire against the various Muslim states and empires. Yet on the other hand, in what amounts to an ancient history retold many times, Christian states also simultaneously made war on each other. For example, in 1204, Venice and the Crusaders brutally sacked Constantinople, the capital of the Byzantine Empire, for example. A notable and long-running Mediterranean Christian conflict over trade was fought among Pisa, Genoa, and Venice, with Venice reigning in the end as a great Mediterranean power responsible for much of the trade and naval development in the region, and whose income was based both on trade and on sea roving. But there were many other long-running maritime conflicts.

The final era ranged from the fourteenth to the late fifteenth century. The Crusades to the Holy Land were over. The Byzantine Empire was fragmented, and when Constantinople fell to the Ottoman Empire in 1453, it effectively ended. Christian Spain was busy expelling the Moors until 1492, when the *reconquista* was complete. Uskok piracy—the latest form of Liburnian and Dalmatian sea roving—was on the rise in the Adriatic. Christian European states fought with each other, with the smaller Muslim states, and with the Mamluk, early Ottoman, and Byzantine Empires. Likewise did Muslim states still make war on each other, on Christian states, and against both the Muslim and Byzantine empires. Christian Mediterranean traders now routinely ventured as far as the Baltic, and Turkish and Moorish corsairs and pirates ventured beyond the Strait of Gibraltar. Christian traded with Muslim, and vice versa. The various city-states, kingdoms, and empires were constantly at war or peace with one or another, creating complex circumstances such that, for example, "two Venetian galleys, laden with merchandise for Saracen merchants" would be arrested by the Christian Knights of Rhodes.[6]

In such circumstances, piracy and privateering flourished, taking advantage of the many public and private wars, declared and undeclared. The tactics of sea roving remained much as they always had been: galley based and consisting of swift attacks on merchant ships and swift plundering, slave-taking raids on coastal towns. Voyages were fraught with danger from pirates and corsairs. During the various Crusades, for example, the voyage to and from the Holy Land was hazardous for man-at-arms, pilgrim, and merchant alike. The route had been commonly infested with pirates for more than two thousand years, and the Crusades offered an extraordinary increase in sea travel, and thus an increase in pirates. Piracy, after all, has a strong opportunistic side. Chronicler Roger of Hovedon's description of the king of France's return from Acre with fourteen galleys notes pirates at the "River Winke," also called the Port of the Pisans (that is, of Pisa) because "Pisan pirates often frequent the harbour. The king captured four pirate galleys, but the pirates had fled into the hills." He further noted of Karkois that no one lived within the old city walls out of fear of pirates, and he also pointed out that many Greek islands were deserted for the same reason. Certain sites were noted as places where pirates often lay in wait for passing ships.[7]

Similar descriptions are found throughout the entire period across the entire expanse of the enclosed sea. The ancient lairs typically remained corsair or pirate haunts, and hardly an island in the Mediterranean was not associated with rovers at some point. Greece, Italy, and Dalmatia continued as sea-roving centers, and with rise of Arab navies, North African ports became centers as well. The Spanish kingdoms, both Muslim and Christian, did not lack for corsairs, nor did the French. During the Crusades, the problem was compounded by deserters turning pirate: a "body of deserters from the Franks, who had been put in possession of several barks, with the view of despoiling the Christians by sea, had landed in the island of Cyprus on a certain feast-day. A great number of the inhabitants were in the church, which was close to the sea-shore. The pirates took part in this service, and then threw themselves on the congregation . . . They had taken great store of treasure and twenty-seven women. They say that each of the men engaged in the adventure received four thousand pieces of silver."[8]

Men-at-arms and sailors also deserted to the opposing faith as sea-roving renegades:

A great number of deserters had come over to us, driven by want of food to leave the Frank camp. These men said to the Sultan: "If you will supply us with ships and smaller craft, we will protect you against the enemy by sea, and we will share our booty in equal parts with the Moslems." The Sultan gave them a bark . . . they then fell in with some merchantmen, whose cargos consisted chiefly of ingots of silver and silversmith's work for the enemy's camp. They boarded these ships and succeeded in capturing them after a sharp fight.[9]

The plunder and prisoners were brought before Saladin, who took nothing for himself. The Muslim chronicler notes that the "Moslems rejoiced to see how God had inflicted a defeat on the enemy by means of their own men."[10]

Any vessel at sea and any town on the coast was subject to attack by a variety of rogues and renegades. Perhaps the words of Saladin's chronicler best explain the justification of sea roving in the Mediterranean:

The rain fell, the sea was tossed to and fro, and the *waves were like mountains* . . . This was the first time that I had ever seen the sea, and such was the impression it made upon me that if anyone had said, 'Go but one mile upon the sea, and I will make you master of the world,' I should have refused to go. I looked upon those who go to sea to earn a few pieces of gold or silver as mad, and I endorsed the opinion of the doctors who have declared that one cannot accept the evidence of a man who is travelling on the ocean.[11]

If one must go to sea, one might as well make it worth the distress and ever-present dangers.

The religious warfare of the region was bound to affect the nature of naval warfare, including sea roving and pirate hunting. Descriptions of sea fights are often colored by religious propaganda, particularly during the Crusades. In one instance, upon seeing a Turkish galley approach with eighty corsairs aboard, most of the fourteen aboard the small vessel being chased bemoaned their likely fate. But not all of them:

> Ivo de Vipont said, "Why do ye of little faith fear those whom you shall soon see dead?" And when the enemy's galley appeared by force of rowing to be on the point striking the vessel with its beak, Ivo leapt into it and began to cut down the Turks who pressed upon him, with the axe he carried in his hand. His companions, when they saw his work prosper, gaining heart, leapt into the galley also, and either beheaded whomsoever they found, or led them away captive. Thus these men triumphed who placed their hope in God.[12]

Although faith can often be inspiring, one doubts that it is sufficient enough that fourteen men can defeat eighty armed, probably veteran corsairs in close combat with swords and axes. Still, similar accounts exist from all ages.

Worse was the slaughter or enslavement of the victims of pirates and corsairs, often justified in the name of religion. The capture of English knights and men-at-arms by Saracens is described by John, Lord of Joinville: "On the opposite shore were immense numbers of our vessels that the Saracens had taken, which we feared to approach; for we plainly saw the murdering their crews, and throwing the dead bodies into the water and carrying away the trunks and arms they had thus gained."[13] Those who were not killed immediately were not guaranteed survival, for survivors were often killed if wounded or ill, as has been the practice in many cultures throughout history, including the Viking:

> In like manner did they deal with the other prisoners; for as they were drawn out of the hold of the galleys wherein they had been confined,

there were Saracens purposely posted, who on seeing any one weak or ill, killed him and threw him into the water . . . I told them, through the interpretation of my Saracen, that they were doing very wrong, and contrary to the commands of Saladin the pagan who had declared it unlawful to put to death any one to whom they had given salt and bread. They made answer, that they were destroying men of no use, for that they were too ill with their disorders to do any service.[14]

Such brutality was by no means confined to Muslim corsairs. "Having drawn the captured galley on shore, they gave it up to be plundered by both sexes who came to meet them. On this our women, dragging the Turks by the hair, after treating them shamefully and cutting their throats in a disgraceful manner, beheaded them. And the weaker the hand to strike, so much the more lengthened was the punishment inflicted; for they used knives, not swords, for cutting off their heads."[15] The objection seems to be that women were doing the killing, and inefficiently at that. Men, the chronicler probably reasoned, should be killed by men, even if as prisoners, even if by throat slitting, beheading, or being cast overboard to drown. Certainly the Christian knights and other men-at-arms had no problem with putting Muslim prisoners to death: "[A]nd thus the vessel . . . began to sink. When the Turks saw it, they leapt into the sea to die, and our men killed some of them and drowned the rest."[16]

In 876, Pope John VIII, the "true founder of the Pontifical navy" as one historian described him, led his fleet against a fleet of "Saracen pirates," capturing eighteen vessels and freeing six hundred Christian captives. Christian forgiveness notwithstanding, John VIII sometimes had Saracen pirate captives put to death.[17] The Christian order of the Knights Hospitaller, also referred to as the Knights of Rhodes and from the sixteenth century on as the Knights of Malta, served as pirate hunters, addressing their efforts primarily toward the Ottoman corsairs, although they would pursue any real pirate of any faith. The rescue of Christian prisoners and slaves from Moslem corsairs and cities was considered a noble and notable duty, yet these Christian knights and other Christian privateering pirate hunters had no qualms about enslaving captured Muslims, profiting from plunder and slavery. All was said to have been done in the name of God or of God and king or state, but it is difficult for a cynic to suppress the notion that these dutiful Christians were motivated not by the Christian faith, but by greed as faith. The corsairs and pirate hunters of the Ottoman empire and Muslim city-states of North

Africa were no better, plundering ships and enslaving Christians in the name of Allah. No matter the political or economic causes of any Mediterranean conflict, if it were between Christian and Muslim, it was couched in terms of religion, of infidels and non-believers, which in turn was used to justify much of the profit from plunder, including the pretense of pirate hunting as a means of what often amounted to little more than outright piracy. There is a pervasive sense that religion was used to justify sea roving that would have been undertaken anyway.

All this being said, historians have noted that the extreme violence of many medieval Mediterranean conflicts, including sea fights, was not only apparent between Christian and Muslim, but between Christian and Christian, and between Muslim and Muslim as well, from the level of competing kingdoms all the way down to competing city-states and ports.[18] Faith seemed to have little effect on diminishing greed or the level of violence it inspired. Faith was, however, noteworthy for inspiring revenge. In 1182, a fleet of Christian corsairs sank a ship filled with Muslim pilgrims, an act which was sacreligious in Muslim eyes. A fleet of Saracen corsairs tracked the fleet down and captured all of the galleys. All prisoners were beheaded.[19]

Perhaps most important to note in this description of sea roving in this period is not only its universal appeal, but also its equality in its choice of victims, in spite of religious, ethnic, and nationalistic bias: both Christian and Muslim sea rovers had no qualms about attacking vessels and towns of their own faiths and did so routinely. Profit was profit, after all, and plunder the path to it. Any excuse would serve.

GALLEYS, SHIPS, ARMS, AND MEN

Throughout the period, the galley was the principal sea-roving and pirate-hunting vessel. It worked well in the Mediterranean, given the commonly calm seas from late March through early October. Tides are insignificant, winds and currents are constant, and safe havens and shores are plentiful. In many places, galleys could be drawn easily ashore, permitting them to hug the coastline as they made their voyages. Unfortunately, this also made one of the most difficult aspects of piracy—finding the prey—fairly simple. The pirate need only lie in wait, hidden, at suitable locations along the common and highly predictable merchant routes.[20]

The usual early Byzantine warship was the dromon. It was a light, swift oared craft, probably with two masts and two square sails intended for passages, not battle. By the ninth century, the sails were probably lateen (triangular or "Latin"), possibly invented by Arab mariners and certainly propagated by them.[21] The dromon, which might have been able to make more than six knots under oars, was used not only by the Byzantine Empire, but also by the Ostragoths and, after the mid-seventh century, by Muslim corsairs as well.[22] Procopius, the early Byzantine historian, described them as "single-banked ships covered by decks, in order that the men rowing them might if possible not be exposed to the bolts of the enemy. Such boats are called 'dromones' [runners] by those of the present time; for they are able to attain great speed."[23] The dromon had high bulwarks to help protect the oarsmen, and oars were thrust through oar-ports. By the tenth century, the dromon had developed into a large double-banked warship. A variety of lighter oared vessels now took the place of the early light dromons as sea-roving craft.[24]

During the period of the Holy Wars, galleys were both single and double banked. Single-banked galleys were short, "easily turned, and light for running to and fro; they are better for throwing fire." Double-banked galleys were "long and graceful, not high out of water, and [had] a piece of wood at the prow, which is commonly called the spur; with which the enemy's ships are struck and pierced."[25] The waterline ram had long since given way to the spur or boarding prow, sometimes tipped with iron. Corsairs and pirates favored light single-banked galleys, often called *sagittas* or *saetias*, typically rigged with a single mast, lateen sail, and boarding spur.[26] Doubtless many common small craft of all peoples were also used as corsair and pirate craft.

The final period saw several significant changes in both warships and merchant vessels. First, circa 1300, the seating of oarsmen changed to a form termed *alla sensile* (in the simple fashion). Instead of being seated at different levels, oarsmen were now clustered in twos or threes to a bench on each side of the galley. The benches were angled such that each oarsman, although seated next to another, could pull a separate oar. The system required coordinated crews but permitted a lower, less top-heavy, more seaworthy vessel.[27] Second, Venice introduced the merchant galley, or *galia grosa*, as a viable long-range trading vessel. Until this time, most shipping was handled by sailing vessels. However, merchant galleys had the advantage, due to their oars and large crews, of speed and defense and were suitable to Mediterranean conditions. For a while at least, the merchant galley provided a safe, secure form of transport for both cargo and passengers.[28]

Third was the development of the true square-rigged sailing ship. Although the lateen was and would remain the common working sail of the

Mediterranean, shipbuilders of the region recognized the potential virtues of the cog and hulk and from them developed the three-masted square-rigged ship or *nao* (which included the carrack form) by adding two more masts, perhaps a topsail on the mainmast, and a lateen mizzen sail. Due to its extraordinary versatility and seaworthiness, this ship was soon re-adopted, as it were, in the northern seas. By the end of the period, the three-masted square-rigged ship had largely replaced the galley as both warship and merchantman. If well-armed and sufficiently manned, it was for the most part impervious to the galley, or at least to a single galley, given its stout construction and high sides.[29] The carrack in particular was developed both as a merchantman capable of defending against pirates, and as a warship. With its high forecastle and stern-castle—the former higher than the latter—a large crew could literally rain death upon attackers in galleys. The caravel (a fifteenth century lateen or lateen and square-rigged sailing vessel of two or three masts) was also favored by merchants, pirates and, probably, pirate hunters.[30]

Vessel armament was similar to that of the northern seas, with a handful of exceptions. The waterline ram had long disappeared, replaced first by a stout wooden spur located well above the waterline, which was used to penetrate galley outriggers and upper works when boarding and provide a platform for boarding. By the end of the period, the spur had become a long narrow spear-like projection. Great guns (cannon) were introduced into the Mediterranean as well, but it would not be until the fifteenth century that they became an effective weapon aboard galleys and sailing ships. The galley was a poor gun platform, and its great guns were typically mounted at the bow and stern and aimed forward and astern. Aboard larger vessels, sea-mangonels (a form of catapult) and ballistae (large pedestal-mounted crossbows) were common, and some vessels had "wicker work" mounted on their sides to defend against stones.[31]

But perhaps the most effective ship's armament prior to the advent of the naval gun was Greek fire. It could be fired through a pressurized siphon often fitted at the bow of fighting galleys, launched from sea-mangonels and similar artillery, or thrown as a grenade. Arrows and crossbow bolts would help keep crews from fighting the fires caused by the mixture.[32] "That kind of fire with a detestable stench and livid flames consumes both flint and steel; it cannot be extinguished by water, but is subdued by the sprinkling of sand, and put out by pouring vinegar on it."[33] Ships likely to be attacked by Greek fire might rig themselves with heavy felt, "skins, iron plates, and baled wool," and have barrels of vinegar standing by.[34]

A powerful naval weapon, Greek fire was used by Byzantine against Muslim in the early years, and by Muslim against Christian during some of the Crusades. The secret of Greek fire apparently never made it beyond the Strait of Gibraltar, and even the crew of a defeated or sinking Muslim ship would destroy the composition rather than permit it to fall into the enemy's hands: "When the pagans [Muslims] found that they were beginning to sink, they threw their arms into the sea, and breaking the vessels, poured forth the Greek fire, and leaving the ship, leaped naked into the sea; on which some of the king's galley-men slew some of them, and took many alive."[35]

To clear the decks prior to boarding, the bow and crossbow (including a heavy crossbow called an arbalest) were common, as were lances, javelins, and stones thrown by hand and from slings. Pots of unslaked lime were common as well, as were various fireworks or combustibles, including caltrops (spiked wooden balls) covered with combustibles and set on fire.[36] Liquid soap and boiling oil were cast on enemy decks at times.[37] The oil could also be cast on the water near an enemy ship, then be set afire as ships drifted down upon it.[38] Greek fire was poured into small pots and thrown by hand or fired from bows. There are references to pots of venomous snakes still being used as a form of grenade, but how common such a device was, assuming it were actually used, is unknown. A great Saracen ship in 1191 reportedly had "on board a large quantity of Greek fire, in bottles, and two hundred most deadly serpents for the destruction of Christians." There is, however, no mention that the serpents were used in the battle that followed, and, given that the ship sank, it is unknown how the chronicler knew for certain what was aboard unless from one of the few survivors.[39]

Individual arms and armor among the Christian states were similar to those found in the northern seas. Among Italian oarsmen, it was common for those inboard to be armed with swords and half-pikes, and those outboard with bows and slings.[40] Shields, javelins, lances, maces, helmets, mail or lamellar armor, and the bow were common among Muslim forces on land and sea.[41] Most single- and double-edged Muslim swords appear to have been straight until roughly 1400, when the use of curved swords descended from those of Central Asia became common, although curved swords had been in use to some degree for two or three centuries prior.

Throughout most of the period, fighting galley crews were similar to those aboard the Byzantine dromons: "all rowers as well as fighting men;

for there was not a single superfluous man among them."[42] Oarsmen had to be able to fight, both in defense of the galley in case they were boarded, and to aid in overwhelming an adversary. Many, but apparently not all, merchant crews traveled armed; their armament was described in the previous chapter. Italian merchant crews in particular were known for traveling well armed, although those of the Byzantines and Muslims often did not. Like many of their counterparts in the northern seas, armed merchant seamen easily made the transition from merchant sailor to naval seaman, privateer, and pirate.[43]

DEFEATING THE CORSAIR ON LAND

The common strategy was the same as in antiquity: "to build upon the Coast at such & such distances, several Forts and Towers to hinder the landing of Pyrats."[44] This amounted largely to fortifications at the city and harbor itself, outlying fortifications, and galleys for additional defense as well as for raiding in retaliation.[45] Harbors were often protected by a chain at the entrance and fortifications where most useful: "When it is necessary, a chain is stretched from one tower to the other, inside which the galleys and boats take refuge, in time of war. Between the town and the tower of Roldan there is a castle with high towers, battlements, and turrets, and a wall surrounds the whole, to guard the city."[46] In the Byzantine period, Arabs built a series of watchtowers from Alexandria to the Atlantic Ocean and manned them with a warrior class both to keep watch and act as a defense force.[47] Such defenses cost a great deal of money, which had to be raised somehow. The Grand Master of Rhodes raised it by ordering knights who held their positions by virtue of "favour," as opposed to purchase, to donate their first year's revenues.[48] Sea-roving plunder was a source as well, as were tribute, customs duties, and taxes.

If a town had no defense or an inadequate one, residents usually retreated inland if they had time, taking their valuables with them. Attacks on towns ranged from quick small raids to major amphibious operations and sieges conducted by a large fleet and army. As it had been for the previous two thousand years, sacking or even conquering the home port or ports of corsairs or pirates was a viable means of suppressing sea roving.

On a smaller scale, corsairs and pirates could be captured or destroyed in small numbers when they came ashore for water, provisions, or reconnaissance. This was a particularly vulnerable time, for the shore parties tended to be relatively small. "The custom of these Moors is to prepare ambuscades in secret places; wherefore many Christians, not knowing how to protect themselves, have fallen into misadventure." A common means to draw a shore party into a trap was to attack, then pretend to retreat, luring the party into an ambush. To counter this, shore parties tended to be heavily armed, with members devoted solely to defense. Any nearby heights were commanded, if there were enough personnel.[49]

THE OTHER USUAL MEANS
Again, the means and methods were little different from those of the northern seas. Treaties were common between states and typically contained prohibitions against piracy and raiding:

> After some conferences between the Saracens and the Grand Master, the Ratification was made: and the principal Articles of the Treaty were, that the Order should not set forth any Ships or Vessels to annoy either by Land or Sea the Subjects of the Soldan [Sultan]. That should not permit them to joyn or assist with Souldiers, Pilots, or Guides, any forreign Rovers against the Soldan's interest. On the other side, that the Soldan should attempt nothing of prejudice of the Knights: and that if they were assail'd by their enemies, the Soldan should be oblig'd to assist and them defend them.[50]

The treaty went on to define the waiver of duties when sailing to the Holy Land through the Sultan's Egyptian waters, the requirement to permit freed Christian slaves to sail home, and the requirement to exchange Christian slaves for Moorish slaves.[51] Tribute and duties, typically set down in treaties and sometimes extortionate, were a common means not only of income, but also of financing defenses and of weakening adversaries.[52]

On the naval side, convoys were common among all seafaring cities, kingdoms, and empires, and were probably the most effective means of protecting merchant shipping. High-value cargoes such as gold were sometimes transported by warships.[53] Much Muslim trade consisted of seasonal convoys coordinated with great caravans ashore, and many merchant routes and convoys were planned to avoid common pirate haunts.[54] Naval flotillas were stationed abroad whenever possible, better enabling the protection of merchant vessels and trade routes.[55] Sea roving still inspired the creation of navies and corsair brethren. The Armada de Galicia was founded around 1120 to counter attacks by Muslim raiders, and the *Hermandad de las Marismas* was founded to counter and retaliate against French and English pirates.[56]

There were some means for recovering vessels and goods, or at least their value, lost to pirates and corsairs. Genoa and other Italian states introduced maritime insurance, for example.[57] If vessels were captured under a foreign flag, owners or their government could appeal to the foreign state for assistance. Similarly, if sea rovers carried ships and goods into foreign ports, owners or their government could appeal to the government to seize the ships, goods, and crews, but this was typically a long and often unsuccessful process. There were successes, however. In 1457, Genoese merchants "spoiled" the cargo of a Bristol merchant vessel trading in the Mediterranean. When her owner, Bristol mayor Robert Sturmys, complained to the English government, all Genoese merchants in London were jailed until his loss was made good.[58]

When all else failed, reprisals, both by capturing ships at sea and by plundering coastal towns, were the usual method of dealing both with pirates and with corsairs who plundered "as if open War had been declar'd," when in fact it had not: "Thereupon the Grand Master order'd his Galleys to cruize along the coasts of Syria and Egypt, and to make all the havock they could upon a faithless Barbarian."[59] As to punishments, piracy was punishable by death, and even legitimate sea roving commonly was as well if a corsair were captured by his enemy. However, it seems that most sea rovers accepted this as the risk they must run. What was the difference between being broken on the wheel or beheaded after trial for piracy when one was almost as likely to be slaughtered at sea for engaging in legitimate privateering or naval warfare?

PIRATE HUNTING AT SEA

Anti-piracy actions took the form not only of combats between pirate hunter and pirate, and of merchantman and pirate, but also of naval fleet actions designed to punish adversaries and ultimately restrict them at sea and ashore. At first glance, the typical sea fight in the medieval Mediterranean appears little different from its neighbor in the northern seas. Most consisted of flights of missiles at long range, followed by attempts at boarding. In two major engagements, we see the tactics of cutting down rigging and sails, and of fireships, but these were not new.[60] There were, however, two critical differences in naval combat between the Mediterranean and northern seas. First was the use in some circumstances of Greek fire prior to the development of the naval gun. Second was the use of the spur or boarding prow. Galleys would row at full speed in order to run the prow over or through the rails and outriggers, easing the entry of men onto the deck.[61]

A sea fight described by Roger de Hovedon between Muslim corsairs and Christian galleys at the siege of Acre in 1189 provides a good example of the middle period and was probably typical of the fierce fights between the various corsairs, transports, heavily armed merchant vessels, and warships of the Mediterranean. Fleets and flotillas arranged themselves as the situation dictated, or at least as commanders interpreted the situation. The crescent was still a popular defensive formation, with the strongest ships at the tips or horns. Even Christian fleets would use the formation, in spite of its symbolic connotation of Islam. A calm sea was ideal for Mediterranean warfare, based as it was on galleys: "The sea was perfectly calm and tranquil, as if it favoured the battle, and the rippling wave impeded neither the shock of the attacking ship, nor the stroke of the oars."[62]

As the fleets, or even merely two ships, approached, they would sound their trumpets, launch various missiles—arrows, bolts, javelins, and stones—according to range, "implore Divine assistance, and ply their oars strenuously, and dash at the enemy's ships with their beaks." Ships rammed, were rammed, or came alongside each other, entangling their oars. Galleys grappled and the fight was carried on hand-to-hand. "[T]hey fire the decks with burning oil, which is vulgarly called Greek fire." Men burned, drowned, died by cut and thrust, crushing blows, and penetrating missiles.[63]

"One galley, unskillfully managed by our men, exposed its flank to the foe; and being set on fire, received the Turks as they boarded her on all sides." Oarsmen fell or leapt into the sea, but the men-at-arms, who either could not swim or would have drowned in their armor, fought back desperately and, "trusting in the Lord's valour," overcame their enemy and captured the galley. Meanwhile, corsairs boarded another galley. On the upper deck, the corsairs attempted to row the vessel in one direction, while the oarsmen below tried to row toward safety. Eventually, the crew and men-at-arms overthrew the boarders and survived to tell the tale.[64]

A small sea fight prior to the capture of Damietta, Egypt, considered to be a Saracen pirate stronghold, was similar. Upon the arrival of the Christian fleet, several galleys surged forth to survey the enemy. They quickly found their retreat cut off and so were forced to engage. According to the Christian chronicler, "We therefore shot against them fiery darts and stones from our sea-mangonels, which were prepared to cast five or six stones together from a great distance; and we threw small bottles full of lime, made to be shot from a bow, or small sticks like arrows, against the enemies. Our darts therefore pierced the bodies of their pirates and their stuff, whilst the stones crushed them, and the lime flying out of the broken bottles blinded them. Three of their galleys therefore were at once destroyed, and some of the pirates were saved from being drowned, and made prisoners . . . The men whom we took were put to exquisite tortures, and made to confess the truth."[65]

The difficulty of galleys fighting a large, well-armed, well-manned ship is demonstrated in a description of a sea fight during the Crusades. Several Christian galleys filled with knights and other men-at-arms attempted to attack a large Saracen ship, but they were repeatedly repulsed by the advantage of the vessel's high sides and large armed crew: "It was defended by a guard of warriors, who kept throwing darts at them. Our men, therefore, relished not the darts, nor the great height of the ship, for it was enough to strive against a foe on equal ground, whereas a dart thrown from above always tells upon those below, since its iron point fall downwards." Of those who managed to board the ship, the Saracens "cut them to pieces as they came on board, and lopping off the head of this one, and the hands of that, and the arms of another, cast their bodies into the sea." The attackers bound the rudder with rope, but this did nothing to affect the vessel's stout fortification-like defense. Finally, according to the Christian chronicler, the galleys rammed the ship repeatedly with their spurs and eventually sank it.[66] According to the Muslim chronicler, however, the ship's captain, seeing all was lost, ordered it sunk.[67] Sea fights of the later period were much similar, with the exception of the lack of Greek fire and the addition of various forms of cannon and small arms. Sailing vessels now played a more prominent role, particularly the caravel and carrack. As usual, most descriptions are evocative but lack tactical detail:

> The Christians [aboard a large merchant ship] prepare themselves for a fight. The twenty Galleys surround the Vessel, and thunder upon her on every side . . . However, some that were best mann'd fetch'd her up by the strength of their oars; and having grappl'd her, a whole throng of Barbarians endeavour'd to enter upon all her quarters. But the Spanish

and Italians kept their ground with so much resolution, that after a bloody Fight of three hours, the Turks were constrain'd to give way.[68]

THE KNIGHT AS PIRATE HUNTER

Many corsairs and sea warriors of the Middle Ages came from the nobility, although certainly they were not the majority. Most fighting seamen and sea-going men-at-arms were "common men" (a poor term for those who venture their lives upon the sea), but the quest for gold and glory led many knights to the sea. They typically had a social need for "honorable" deeds and glory, a practical need for money, and the contacts to help authorize and finance their plundering and pirate-hunting ventures. Often the two ventures were combined.

The Knights of Rhodes, as the Knights Hospitaller who settled on the island came to be called, were well known for their pirate hunting, and for their privateering and raiding as well. From their commanding position on Rhodes, they were positioned not only to chase pirates, but also to be chased by them. Besides their engaging in their privateering slave trade, the Knights tended to their martial duties of protecting trade and traveler and punishing the unlicensed pirate: "[N]or had the Subjects [of Rhodes] any thing more to fear, but only the Rapines of certain Pirats that infested their Coasts; the most famous was Don Diego Ordonna, a Spaniard by Nation, a person bold and daring, of a savage humour, and bestial valour, more barbarous than the Infidels, cruising all Coasts with an Armed Caravel, and acknowledging no Right but Force, nor any God but Interest."[69]

The pirate was so bold as to take two Venetian ships within sight of Rhodes itself, and Rhodian ships feared to venture to sea. "And knowing that Ferdinand and Isabel, who were then subduing the Moors, did not allow a Castilian Pirate to be so vexatious to the Christians," Pierre d'Aubusson, Grand Master of Rhodes, sent one of his knights, Raymond Thivian, with a galley and another warship, each manned with "stout Knights; who coming up with this Pirate, pli'd him so warmly, that he was constrained to yield after a vigorous resistance." Ordonna was chained hand and foot, carried to Rhodes, and "broken alive upon the Wheel." The punishment was brutal: the executioner tied the condemned to a cross or wheel, then slowly and repeatedly broke the long bones with a hammer or iron rod. If the victim did not die of this trauma, the executioner would then put him to death with blows to the chest and stomach or by strangling. Ordonna's goods were distributed to his merchant victims.[70]

Gutierre Díaz de Gámez again provides detailed accounts of pirate hunting, this time in the Mediterranean. Don Pero Niño, perhaps the ideal in reality of late medieval Spanish chivalry and a foreshadowing of the conquistador ideal, was tasked in 1404 with punishing "powerful Corsairs, of Castillian birth, who went in the seas of the Levant, plundering men of Castille as well as foreigners." The expedition was to be outfitted secretly with the "best mariners," "sturdy oarsmen, brought up to the sea and stout of heart," the "best crossbowmen," and also "quartermasters and rowers, both for the forward and backward stroke, the best that there were." Pero Niño also recruited thirty men-at-arms of noble birth, including his cousin. The king provided him with excellent galleys and arms, as well as gold and silver for the voyage itself.[71]

The expedition set sail, passed east through the Strait of Gibraltar, then along the coast of Spain, making stops along the way. From there it passed into the open sea in search of Moorish ships, for the search for Spanish pirates did not mean that Pero Niño had to forego plundering. The expedition took on water on the Barbary coast, then returned to Cartagena where Pero Niño received word of a Spanish pirate, Gonzalez de Moranza, who lived at Naples but was at present cruising off the coast of Aragon. The trail soon led to the waters off Marseilles. The expedition sighted Moranza's two galleys and gave chase. Seeing that the pirate crews were arming themselves as if to fight, Pero Niño ordered his crews to arm. But it was a trick—the pirates had merely been passing arms and armor to the oarsmen, who in fact remained unarmed. "Now any man of understanding will see that an unarmed man moves more swiftly than an armed man, and that he is the freer to row; and that similarly a galley whose crew is in arms on the deck will be much hampered in giving chase or being chased." Even so, Pero Niño's galleys put forth all their effort and soon came within crossbow range, at which point "the quarrels sped from one ship to another."[72]

At this time, another galley, "in which came knights of great estate," appeared from the port. Pero Niño prepared to do battle with all three galleys and exhorted his men: "Let not a single one of you be taken prisoner, for he who is captured will not escape death for that. With the help of God and by His justice shall they be beaten, for they are robbers and evil doers: they shall not endure before us." But the battle never got underway. The pirate galleys retreated into the harbor, and a brigantine carrying an envoy came out to meet Pero Niño—the pirates "were there under the safeguard of the Pope," who was visiting Marseilles.[73]

Pero Niño lost these pirates but located others. In Alghero, Italy, he found three, but the "captain who held the city on behalf of the King of Aragon . . . earnestly begged the captain on behalf of the King of Aragon to leave these Corsairs in peace." And so he was forced to do, for the town was prepared to help defend them. In Orestano, he captured a pirate galley that had just taken a merchantman from Seville. Afterward, having word that Tunisian corsairs were on the loose, he set out secretly for the Tunisian coast, to seek both the corsairs and Moorish merchant carracks. For ten days they lay in wait, showing no light at night nor even lighting a fire for cooking, day or night. Tiring of the wait, they rowed silently into the harbor of Tunis and surprised a Tunisian galley, capturing it after a fight. From her crew they learned of a great Tunisian galleass (a hybrid galley-ship) in the harbor. Unfortunately, the crew of a Genoese carrack heard the fight and, thinking it was being attacked, sounded the alarm. The galleass attempted to flee into the river, Pero Niño's galleys in swift pursuit. Coming up on her stern, Niño leaped across and boarded the vessel, his boarding party behind him. To his great peril, the vessels separated at that moment, leaving him alone.[74]

According to his chronicler, Pero Niño fought like a lion, at one point even wounding and capturing the galleass's commander. But the Moors would not surrender even under these circumstances. Díaz de Gámez writes that Pero Niño, knowing he had only himself and God to rely upon, drove the Moors to their prow, at which point his crew boarded and came to his aid. To their credit, neither Pero Niño nor his chronicler disparaged the courage of their adversaries: "There, on the prow, he found himself face to face with a Moorish knight, of whom he had much to tell later, and he swore that this Moor struck him so hard on the head with his sword, that his knees bent beneath the blow."[75]

In spite of the bloody daring and valor of the Spaniards, they lost their prize in the end. Moors on horseback rode into the water to engage the Spanish galleys. Others ran into the water and tried to drag Pero Niño's galley ashore. So many lined the shore that "an arrow could not have been loosed among them without finding a mark." Around the vessels, the water "was all red with blood." In the end, the Spaniards had to abandon the galleass, for it was aground. Lacking the men to man her without weakening the other galleys, they looted the galley prize they had captured previously and then burned it. Upon their return to Cartagena, Pero Niño shared the spoils with his men, of which "it satisfied them all."[76]

THE PIRATE COLUMBUS

Merchants routinely traded from the northern seas into the Mediterranean and vice versa. For the Mediterranean trader, passing the Strait of Gibraltar was no reason to consider himself safe from pirates and other rovers, as the last chapter demonstrated. But it was not only the rovers of the northern seas he had to worry about, but those from the Mediterranean as well. In a way, the merchant vessel was the ultimate pirate hunter, for his was both the first and last line of defense. Wherever he sailed in the Middle Ages, he was in danger not only of the sea, but also of the sea rover.

In 1485, four galleys set sail from Venice to trade with England and Flanders, probably stopping first at Messina, Palermo, Majorca, and Cadiz. These "Flanders galleys" were well-armed. Assuming they were armed similarly to other Flanders galleys of the late fifteenth and early sixteenth centuries, each had twenty to "30 good arbalast men," four of whom may have been young noblemen armed with two crossbows, a *pede* and a *molineto*. The cross-bowmen would have been "licensed on the archery ground for the Flanders galleys." Firearms may have been substituted for a few of the bows. Well over two hundred men would have been aboard each galley, including 171 free oarsmen, plus officers, artisans, and various "footmen." Captain and crew were all well paid, and the voyage was well regulated—the 1517 instructions to the flotilla's commander included 125 regulations, 107 clauses, and thirty-four supplementary regulations, for example. The galleys were loaded with expensive trade goods and money.[77]

On August 22, they ran into trouble. Six or seven armed ships and balingers flying the flag of France and commanded by Nicolo Griego, known variously as Colombo, "*fio de Colombo corsaro*" (son of Columbus) and "*Colombo el Mozo*" (Columbus Junior), and described as "*corsaro genovese*," fell in with them at night off Cape St. Vincent. A month earlier, an intelligence report about a possible attack had already been sent to London and Bruges, and Venetian ships there were ordered to accompany the galleys, but to no avail. The galleys were on their own. At dawn the pirates attacked; the battle lasted for twenty hours. More than one hundred members of the galleys' crews were killed, including Lorenzo Michiel, master of one galley, and Giacomo Dolfin, master of another, "besides other noblemen." Three hundred were wounded. Colombo captured all four galleys and carried them into Lisbon. The loss to the state of Venice was estimated at two hundred thousand ducats. As for the attackers, they were arguably not pirates, for they had a commission authorized on the basis that the Venetian Republic was under an interdict from Pope Sixtus IV.[78]

Three years later, the galleys had better luck. Three English ships approached the galleys, claiming to be friends, but the suspicious galley commander, perhaps recalling events three years prior, "blew his whistle" and sent his men to quarters. The Venetians killed eighteen Englishmen, but even so the pirates pursued them into "Hampton harbour." The galley commander remonstrated to the king of England, "who sent the Bishop of Winchester to say he was not to fear, as those [English] who had been killed must bear their own loss, and that a pot of wine would settle the matter."[79]

The violent juncture of greed, faith, trade, opportunism, and sea roving did not end with the Middle Ages. A letter written by the Doge of Venice, Agostino Barbarigo, in 1491 to Giacomo Venier, captain of the Flanders galleys, best describes the unchanged nature of Mediterranean pirate hunting at the end of the era: "[They] have our orders not only to extirpate pirates but to defend the Christian religion."[80] Likewise were the orders of Muslim pirate hunters as well. In a year, the seeds of an even broader conflict would begin to emerge, one that would provide great opportunity for sea rovers and great need for pirate hunters. It would manifest itself among Christians fighting over a New World stumbled across by another Columbus, whose son claimed his father was with Columbus the *corsaro genovese* when he captured the Flanders galleys.[81]

8

Spanish Galleons and Portuguese Carracks

Plunderers Fighting Plunderers, 1492–1654

On October 12, 1492, Christopher Columbus, seeking a western route to the Indies, landed in the Caribbean and staked a Spanish claim to lands hitherto—for all practical purposes at least—unknown to Europe. Supporters consider him a great explorer who discovered a new world and changed history forever, and for the better. Detractors consider him worse than the pirates he is said to have sailed with in his youth, a man who immediately set in motion the conquest and decimation by arms, enslavement, and disease of the native peoples of two continents.

He was quickly followed by numerous expeditions of conquest commanded by adventurers and fortune hunters. With these *conquistadores* came representatives of the Catholic religious orders—a volatile combination of greed and god, some would say. Native Americans, and later Africans, were quickly exploited in the name of the Lord in the quest for gold. Merely a few decades after Columbus landed in the Americas, a new Christian religion emerged in Europe, adding fuel to the fire of faith and greed that had begun in the Mediterranean.

What Spain sought and soon found was wealth, much of it in the form of gold and, especially, silver. Immediately, the lure of precious metals—not to mention sugar, dyes and dyewoods, medicinal plants, tobacco, hides, chocolate, various foods and flavorings (such as ginger, vanilla, and allspice), and soon enough African slaves—drew sea-roving adventurers, legitimate and illegitimate, to the Spanish Main. Although exploration and conquest in the name of God and King was claimed to be the purpose, in practice it often resembled sea roving: "[W]e purchased three ships . . . the third, a bark, [we] bought on credit from the Governor, Diego Velásquez, on the condition that

133

all us soldiers should go in the three vessels to some islands lying between Cuba and Honduras . . . and make war on the natives and load the vessels with Indians, as slaves, with which to pay him for his bark."[1] Although these adventurers declined this offer, it nonetheless characterized much of Spain's behavior in the New World.

The Portuguese were the first Europeans to follow the Spanish there, but they came to trade—in 1494, the line of demarcation between Spanish and Portuguese interests was moved west, and in 1500, the Portuguese landed in Brazil on their way to the East Indies. By 1504, French rovers were off the coast of Brazil. The first to strike significantly was Jean Fleury—a Florentine in the service of France—off the Azores in 1522. These islands were the danger zones for returning Spanish and Portuguese treasure ships, given their proximity to Europe. Fleury, whom some claim was Giovanni da Verrazzano, was captured and hanged in 1523. Nonetheless, he was followed by other French pirates and corsairs who, when their attacks were not justified by a state of war, justified them by claiming a share in the wealth Spain had discovered. In 1528, the first known attack on Spanish interests in the New World was recorded. In 1540, the English entered the Caribbean contest, and in the early seventeenth century came the Dutch. Francis Drake, called Draque by the Spanish, awakened the Spanish with highly successful attacks in the Caribbean and South Sea. He was followed by numerous other English adventurers, including Thomas Cavendish, Richard Hawkins, and Walter Raleigh. The attacks would only increase, and by the first half of the seventeenth century, the English, French, and Dutch had established small colonies in the New World, all of which served as bases for sea roving against the Spanish and Portuguese there.[2]

A third of the way around the world in the other direction from the Iberian Peninsula were the East Indies, originally called simply the Indies but now necessarily distinguished from the colonial dominion to the west. The source of valuable spices, silk, saltpeter, and many other goods, the Indies already had long-established trade routes from the Red Sea and Persian Gulf to China. The East was opened to European seaborne trade by the discovery of the route around the Cape of Good Hope by Vasco de Gama in 1497, and by 1515, Portugal had an established trade route to India. England made its first, albeit unsuccessful, combination foray of trade and piracy into the East Indies in 1591, and in 1594, the Dutch formed the Netherlands' first East India trading company. Other countries followed, as did sea rovers and interloping traders, not to mention wars over the trade, particularly between the Netherlands and Portugal beginning in the early seventeenth century. Neither Spain nor Portugal would be able to keep either Indies to themselves. Both had to act quickly, vigilantly, decisively, and repeatedly to protect the wealth they had begun squandering almost immediately in their quite understandable arrogance.

PROTECTING WEALTH IN TRANSIT

When Columbus first crossed the Atlantic, his vessels were a small carrack and two caravels. A century later, the galleon, a ship with cleaner, "galley like" lines and a lower forecastle and stern works than a carrack, and whose forecastle was now lower than the "stern castle," had become the preeminent man-of-war as well as an important merchantman. It sailed better and maneuvered better than the carrack, and in particular was a better gun platform. In the early seventeenth century, it would be replaced by the frigate, a ship of even cleaner lines, lower upper-works, and better handling characteristics. This new ship was based on the light Mediterranean "frigates," which used both sail and oar.

An intermediate form between the galleon and frigate was the *galizabra*, or "treasure frigate," introduced in the late sixteenth century as a lighter, more maneuverable treasure ship, the better to defend against treasure-hunting rovers. The carrack was retained by Portugal, or at least its name was, and soon considered a lumbering castle on the sea, easily out-maneuvered by Spanish galleons and English "race-built" galleons of the sixteenth century and the frigates of the seventeenth. Both the carrack and the galleon made effective treasure ships in the early years: they were large, could carry a great deal of cargo and defenders, and made an imposing figure. To pursue them—and indeed, to pursue the pirates who pursued them—swifter, cleaner-lined vessels mounted with great guns were needed: race-built galleons, flyboats, pinnaces, and frigates, for example. Many retained oars as auxiliary propulsion.

Like changes in ship design, changes in gunnery affected both sea roving and pirate hunting. Great guns developed from the wrought iron bombard into the cast form we are all familiar with, first from bronze in the sixteenth century, then iron. Reportedly in 1501, the first gunports were cut into the side of a ship, below the main or upper deck. They made the ship a more effective gunnery platform, and new carriages were designed to take advantage of them. Sledge carriages and land carriages were used at first, but by the mid- to late-sixteenth century, an effective "bed" carriage, with

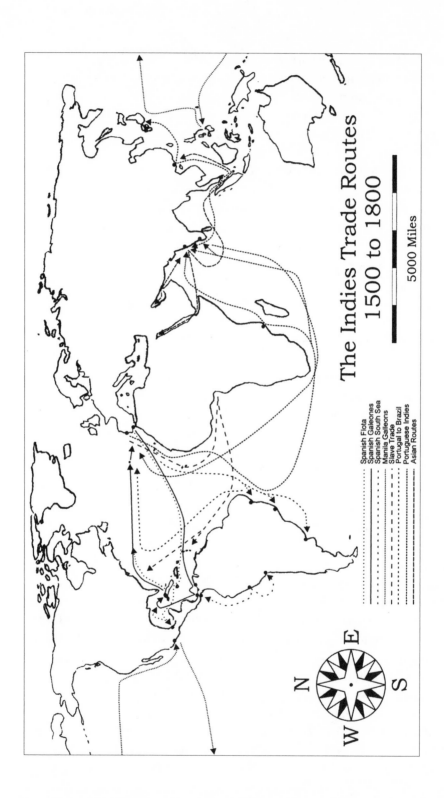

The Indies Trade Routes
1500 to 1800

5000 Miles

Spanish Flota
Spanish Galeones
Spanish South Sea
Manila Galleons
Slave Trade
Portugal to Brazil
Portuguese Indies
Asian Routes

N
E
S
W

small wheels called trucks, was in use in many nations, although period and archaeological sources note that the Spanish often used sledge carriages and land carriages on their ships until the seventeenth century.[3] The period from 1492 to 1588 was a critical period not only in the development of the ship as a gunnery platform, but also in its tactics. Both would affect the nature of the treasure ship, albeit more slowly than one might have expected.[4]

The routes followed by the treasure ships were fairly simple but filled with hazards of man and sea. On the West Indies route, or *carrera de Indias*, the fleets of galleons or frigates and other ships (*naos, urcas*) sailed from Spain to the Azores to the Caribbean via the trade winds, passing through the Lesser Antilles, and then to the various ports as necessary, with the final destinations of San Juan de Ulloa (Veracruz) and Havana. From Havana, the route passed north along the Florida coast and further until it met the North Atlantic westerlies, then across the Atlantic to the Azores and Spain.

Portugal maintained a trade route to Brazil, south from Portugal, often with stops for slaves on the African coast, then across the Atlantic. Its shipping was typically composed of caravels under two hundred tons. To the East Indies was the Portuguese *carreira da Índia*, which worked its way variously along the Azores, Madeiras, Canaries, and Cape Verdes, south around the Cape of Good Hope, then north and west as necessary to the various factories and East Indian trading ports and back again. The trip typically took six to eight months one way and was undertaken primarily by carracks, most at least of 400 or more tons; many were over 1,200 tons, and some were as large as 2,000.

Spain also had two Pacific trade routes. Along the coast of South America, the route carried silver from Potosí via the port of Arica, then passed north to Lima and Callao, then on to Panama. Goods from Spain were carried in the opposite direction. The *carrera de Filipinas* circled from Manila across the Pacific, south along the Pacific coast of North America and on to Acapulco, then back across the Pacific via Guam to Manila. Spain left the Manila route unprotected except for the size and armament of the Manila galleon (occasionally there were two), and the coastal South American route was similarly unprotected, given Spain's belief that it was protected by its location.

The Atlantic route of Spanish New World trade was protected by a convoyed fleet from the early sixteenth century, originally "on account of the Pirates that infested the Coast of Andalusia and Algarve, lying in wait for the Ships homeward bound." The convoys, small at first, evolved into two treasure fleets, the *Flota* and the *Galeones*, each having different routes and somewhat different purposes in the Caribbean. The sailing of the treasure fleets was often delayed by war or piratical incursion. The Portuguese route to the Indies was unprotected by convoy until the mid-seventeenth century, although in the Indies were two small fleets, the Armado do Norte and the Armado do Sol or Armado do Malavar, "the one against the *Arabs*, the other against the *Malabars*."[5] Merchantmen in the East Indies also had to contend with rovers from Indonesia, China, and Japan. The caravels trading to Brazil were unprotected by convoy or local armada.[6]

The treasure fleets were fairly secure against attack by anything but a large enemy fleet, but such attacks were not unknown: "At Cartagena we heard a report of three small sail of ships of Hollanders waiting for the galleons," wrote Thomas Gage of events in 1637.[7] Transit on the open sea was reasonably safe from attack by rovers, given the difficulty of locating the prey there, not to mention the poor strategy and economics of attempting such an attack. However, stragglers and small flotillas near land, separated from a fleet by weather or inattention, were often picked off by rovers. Even ships on the outskirts of fleets were vulnerable at times, depending on wind and the location of men-of-war: "Having got the wind of us, they singled out a ship of ours . . . Suddenly giving her a whole broadside and receiving a reply of only two guns, they made her yield, without any hope of help from so proud and mighty a fleet, for that she was somewhat far straggled from the rest of the ships."[8] Local merchantmen and ships trading independently or that had separated from the fleets were also vulnerable. Rovers were well aware that loitering off the Azores was often highly lucrative, for it was the intersection of the West and East Indies trade routes. After having encountered and lost a Portuguese East Indies carrack, a small English squadron waited around "Corvo and Flores for some West Indian purchase," for example.[9] And not even the treasure fleets always made it there and back again safely. In 1596, a combined English and Dutch fleet captured the Flota in Cadiz harbor, and in 1628, Dutchman Piet Heyn captured the Flota at sea. Both captures caused financial disaster for Spain.[10]

Both the Spanish and Portuguese routes were obvious and almost immediately well known, making it easy for rovers to lie in wait. For Spain, the problem was further compounded by the predictability of the New World treasure fleets. Not only were their routes and timings well known and for the most part invariable, but security surrounding the knowledge of their movement was understandably poor, given the state of communication in the period and the obvious and generally lengthy presence of treasure ships once they made port after a long voyage. In the Caribbean and Spanish South Sea (the Pacific coast of the Americas), any required details of when and where were easily gleaned by rovers by force or threat of force—and sometimes by outright cooperation, often based on illicit trade—from local inhabitants. The mule trains and trade fairs were just as predictable. Spain's only real remedy was to bolster defenses at sea and ashore. Until the rovers' home nations established bases in the Caribbean, local reprisal was not an option.

ARMS AND ARMOR

Ships were primarily armed with a combination of great guns and *pedreros* or *pierriers*, also known as swivels. The early guns, often breech-loaded, were little more effective than those of the fifteenth century, but with the introduction of muzzle-loading cast brass and iron guns in the early sixteenth century, ordnance became a truly effective weapon. By the latter part of the sixteenth century, great guns had most of the form and function they would retain until the early nineteenth century. Swivels, typically breech-loaded at this time, were not only useful on the rails for repelling boarders, but also from loopholes in bulkheads after an enemy had boarded. Stone shot was still in use in the late sixteenth century but was much less prevalent than iron round shot. "Crosse barres and chaine-shot" were common, typically fired into the rigging, yards, and sails. Cases of "small shott, joyned two and two together, with peeces of wyer, of five or sixe inches long" were also used to damage rigging, and bags and cases of musket balls, iron scrap, and sharp stones were commonly used against men in the open, fired both from great guns and swivels. In the first half of the sixteenth century, gunners would remove the chambers from guns after firing, then take them below deck for reloading. In an emergency, guns were loaded with loose powder from a "*barril de pólvora* [keg of powder] . . . on the poop, lashed to the mast" and covered with a "damp cloth." By the second half of the sixteenth century, naval guns were loaded with cartridges, for the dangers of loading via ladles and loose powder in action, above or below deck, were well understood. Cartridges were also much more efficient.[11]

Ships still had supplementary defensive and offensive weapons. "Sherehooks," pikebolts in the wales (sharp bolts protruding from the wales), "and other engines of antiquitie" were still in use, but by the late sixteenth century, "Many I know have left the use of them."[12] According to John Smith, sherehooks, which attached to the ends of yards and would cut the sails and rigging of a ship coming alongside, grew out of favor because they were heavy, could break yards, and also had a tendency to cut one's own rigging.[13] A drawing of a Spanish *galizabra* or "treasure frigate" made by an English spy in the late sixteenth century shows sherehooks at the ends of the lower yard-arms. The ship is armed with culverins (eighteen pounders) on the lower deck, demi-culverins (nine pounders) on the upper deck, and falcons (three pounders) on the quarterdeck and forecastle. (See figure 6.) The ship has three tiers of bow and stern chasers, and a note indicates that the prow would be manned with musketeers.[14] Another period drawing of a Spanish treasure ship shows *arquebuceros* and *mosqueteros* stationed in the waist, in the tops, at the prow, and on the stern gallery.[15]

Boarding nets were common, as were "close fights," which consisted of "waist cloths which hang round about the ship to hide men from being seen . . . also any bulkhead afore and abaft out of which they may use murderers [swivel guns] or small shot, or generally any place wherein men may cover themselves and yet use their arms, are called *close fights*."[16] Gratings between the foremast and mainmast were also referred to as part of the close fights.[17] Some ships had barricades fitted with wheels so that they could be moved where they were needed. Close fights might be made of anything at hand, particularly aboard merchant vessels, whose cargo—hides, for example— could be put to good use as barricades.[18] In the early sixteenth century, the Spanish used bedding to protect both the rails and the tops and set up a "shield wall" at the gunwale in the waist.[19] "Race-built" ships were considered vulnerable due to their lower sides and rails, and such protection was considered necessary, although it was often limited to the common "waist cloths" of simple painted canvas designed to hide, not protect, the crew in action.[20]

Both gratings and boarding nets or "nettings" were commonly defeated by using grapnels or the kedge anchor to tear them away, but true closed quarters were more difficult to defeat, requiring a thorough battering or an aggressive boarding whose nature was something akin to the breaching of a fortification during a siege. Smith believed that "there is no such dangerous Service ashore, as a resolved resolute Fight at sea" against a ship fitted with closed quarters or close fights.[21] However, according to Sir Richard Hawkins, the Spanish used "few close fights or fire-workes," although in many cases it is obvious they did.[22]

Various fireworks were common. Some were grenades of a variety of sorts—cast iron, "fire pots" or clay pots, and glass bottles—filled with gunpowder and designed to burn the enemy or smoke him out, and to a lesser degree to injure him with what was fairly weak fragmentation. Some were designed to produce a suffocating smoke, while others were designed to burn the enemy and his vessel.[23] Unslaked lime was still used as a common grenade in the first half of the sixteenth century, but it seems to have gone out of favor by its end.[24] The fire-pike (*trompa de fuego*) was a pike fitted with a bottle of burning combustibles, used both ashore and aboard ship. At sea, it was used to light the rigging, sails, and anything else convenient on the enemy's ship as it came alongside, although it must have been a danger to the user's vessel as well.[25] According to Richard Hawkins, "Arrows of fire, to bee shott out of slur-bowes" (crossbows with barrels like those of firearms) were effective. Sir Henry Mainwaring, master mariner and former pirate, lists fire-works as being "fire-pots, fire-balls, fire-pikes, trunks, brass-balls, arrows with firework, and the like" in the early seventeenth century.[26] "Brasse balles of ar-tificiall fire" were also fired from slur-bows, according to Hawkins.[27] Powder chests—small explosive mines placed on deck to injure boarders—probably came into use in the late sixteenth century and were common by the early seventeenth. Mounted on decks and in various outboard locations on the hull, they were "sprung"—exploded—as the enemy boarded.

Stones were still a common weapon, but now limited to those cast from the tops, although Hawkins in the late sixteenth century suggests they were not as common as they once were, and by the early seventeenth century they seem to have gone largely out of use (although Smith mentions them in 1626), replaced by musketeers and swivel guns in the tops.[28] Handheld sick-les were used, at least by the Spanish, in the early sixteenth century to cut rigging and sails.[29] "Darts" or "harpoons" were used by both Spaniard and Englishman and could not only impale men but also cut rigging and sails.[30] The Spanish often manned a boat with men, muskets, shields, crossbows, axes, wedges, and augers to attack the enemy, in particular to wedge the rud-der or drill holes in the hull. The boat was kept, manned, on the side of the ship opposite the engagement until it could be employed.[31]

Personal arms included a cutting sword (often short), target or other shield, bow and arrow (with both "great sheaf arrows" and "fine roving shafts"), crossbow, musket or *mosquet* (a heavy matchlock musket), *arquebuce* (a light matchlock musket, also called a hackbut), fowling piece (a musket used for hunting, probably a wheel lock), pistol (again, probably a wheel lock), "caliver" (a short-barreled musket), lance and javelin (both thrown by hand), partisan (a polearm with a broad blade), short pike, ax, and dagger.[32] Pikes were typically greased or "tallowed" at the far end to prevent the enemy from grasping them.[33] The rapier became a common sword in the period, particularly among gentlemen and noblemen. Among the Spanish, any man with a pretense to being a gentleman carried one. Typically, it was used with a companion dagger or "poniard" but was not the ideal battlefield weapon. Muskets fired not only lead balls, but also "hail shot" (roughly the size of modern buckshot), small shot connected with wire (musket ball halves connected by wire that would unwind when fired; it was used to cut rigging and sails), "quartered shot" (musket balls cut in quarters or eighths), "poysoned bullets," and, among the English in the late sixteenth century at least, small arrows which according to Hawkins would penetrate bulwark planking. The arrows had to be loaded on top of a wooden tompion or plug, but Hawkins kept this fact from his Spanish captors.[34]

The use of armor, both of "proof" (armor that would stop a musket or pistol ball) and "light corseletts," continued through the sixteenth century, although English seamen seem to have avoided using it, even when available, except for officers.[35] By the late sixteenth and early seventeenth century, its use at sea was under considerable debate, and many fighting seamen, including their officers, considered it useless, given its weight and the now prevalent use of firearms, although others, such as Hawkins, found it essential[36]: "For besides, that the sleightest armour secureth the parts of a man's body, which it covereth, from pike, sword, and all hand weapons, it likewise giveth boldnesse and courage: a man armed, giveth a greater and a waightier blow, then a man unarmed; he standeth faster, and with greater difficultie is to be overthrowne."[37]

The Spanish were more fond of it, or at least their soldiers and perhaps their gunners were, using corselet, a mail shirt worn over the clothing, or a "jackette [a "jack" or armored coat], at least a buffe-jerkin [heavy leather jerkin], or a privie coate [a mail shirt worn under normal clothing]." Spanish seamen themselves "were unarmed," though.[38]

By the mid-seventeenth century, armor had largely disappeared from use at sea, although the corselet was occasionally recommended for use by captains past the mid-eighteenth century.[39] Arguably another form of armor, albeit a false one which Hawkins railed against, was "to drinke themselves drunke." As he put it, "the pott continually walking, infused desperate and foolish hardiness in many, who blinded with the fume of the liquor, considered not of any danger, but thus and thus would stand at hazard."[40]

The tactics of engagement were changing as well, particularly as the combination of ship and gun design improved, making the ship an effective gun platform. Spanish crews consisted of seamen, gunners, and soldiers:

seaman managed the ship, gunners the guns, and soldiers their arms. The system reflected land warfare and retained a strong preference for boarding actions, although this began to change in the late sixteenth century.[41]

GALLEON AND CARRACK VERSUS ROVER

For the local trader in the New World, defense against a large number of well-armed pirates was virtually impossible. Lightly armed and manned, its best defense was to run, hoping to survive until darkness increased the chances of escape. Deliberately running itself ashore was also viable. A ship run ashore was more difficult to capture than one at sea, and rovers were often unable, due to limited space in the hold, to salvage the entire cargo even if abandoned. Rovers might even leave a merchantman grounded ashore alone, considering it not worth the trouble or too dangerous should an enemy man-of-war come upon them. Otherwise, small trading vessels had little recourse against pirates. Francis Drake had no noted problems with most of the common merchantmen he encountered, for example, on his voyage that began as a raid on the Spain's New World possessions in 1577 and ended three years later with a circumnavigation. The merchantmen wisely yielded to him.[42] The results of other adventurers to the New World were similar.

Treasure ships, however, stood a much better chance, even when separated from the fleet. The galleons, galizabras, and hulks or *urcas* of the New World trade were well-armed and fairly high-sided as compared to some of the developing swift ship designs, including the English "race-built" galleons, and could easily be turned into floating fortresses. One could argue that the large carracks were by definition floating fortresses.

In 1587, in the South Sea, an English squadron under Thomas Cavendish attacked the 700-ton Manila galleon *Santa Ana*, apparently not armed with great guns, or at least without them mounted. As a Spanish account put it, "He found her (that sea being pacific) without a sword."[43] A member of Cavendish's crew described the battle:

> Now, as we were ready on their ship's side to enter her being not past 50 or 60 men at the uttermost in our ship, we perceived that the captain of the said ship had made fights fore and after, and laid their sails close on the poop, their midship, and forecastle, and having not one man to be seen, stood close under their fights, with lances, javelins, rapiers, and targets, and an innumerable sort of great stones, which they threw over-

board upon our heads and into our ship so fast, and being so many of them, that they put us off the ship again with the loss of two of our men, which were slain, and with the hurting of four or five.[44]

Cavendish stood off, and instead of attempting to carry the galleon by boarding, "gave them a fresh encounter with our great ordnance and also with our small shot, raking them through and through, to the killing and maiming of many of their men."[45] To rake was to fire fore-and-aft and especially stern-to-bow, for the stern was the weakest point on a ship's hull; shot would travel the length of the ship and do their most damage. Cavendish attacked a third time, encouraging his men with trumpets and probably diminishing the spirits of his adversary as well after the battering they had just taken. The battle lasted for five or six hours until the Spanish struck. Cavendish looted then burned the ship. He put the crew and passengers ashore, except, according to a Spanish account, for a priest whom he hanged.[46] The state religion of England was no longer Catholicism, and religious extremism colored many things.

The attack was successful by virtue of the combination of gunnery, seamanship, and a ship that could be handled well, but not valor in boarding, for which the Spanish were well prepared to defend against. After 1588 and the failed Armada expedition against England, Spain began to adapt to these tactics and even adopt them. For closed quarters to work against a ship capable of managing its guns well, the defender either had to have a significantly larger and stronger hull that could resist the battering of relatively weak guns, or had to maneuver and use its guns to batter the attacker, forcing it to either break off the attack or come to grips where the defender then had the advantage, particularly if it had a large, well-armed crew. For the boarder, getting close enough to board was itself hazardous if the adversary's ship were well-handled and its guns were large and well-served. Unfortunately, many ships, particularly after long voyages, often had many of their guns "struck below" (stowed in the hold) and their decks so "lumbered" and "pestered" that it was difficult to manage the guns even if they were mounted. The merchant ship as "castle" now also had to be an effective mobile gun platform if it wanted to defeat a significant adversary. A large ship with a large number of defenders alone was no longer a guarantee against pirates.[47]

The Spanish should have already learned their lesson regarding arming their ships in the South Sea. In 1587, after receiving intelligence about her, Francis Drake and his *Golden Hinde* found and fought the treasure ship *Nuestra Señora de la Concepción,* called by her crew the *Cacafuego* (*Shit Fire* or *Fire Shitter*). "It fortuned that *John Drake* going up into the top, descried her about three of the clocke, and about sixe of the clocke we came to her and boorded her, and shotte at her three peeces of ordnance, and strake downe her misen, and being entered, we found in her great riches." Her name notwithstanding, the treasure ship was not only unable to repel Drake's small man-of-war, but apparently unable to put up much of a fight. When Drake released the pilot and boy he had captured aboard the *Cacafuego,* the boy "sayd thus unto our Generall: Captaine, our ship shall be called no more the *Cacafuego,* but the *Cacaplata* [*Shit Silver* or *Silver Shitter*], and your shippe shall bee called the *Cacafuego*: which pretie speech of the pilots boy ministred matter of laughter to us, both then and long after." Spain unfortunately assumed that her trade in the South Sea was secure from sea rovers and foreign traders. She was to be proved wrong many times, and each time she had forgotten or ignored the lessons taught her by rovers like Drake.[48]

In the North Sea, the lesson may have already been brought home to Spain, and perhaps to Portugal as well. Unfortunately, the lumbering Portuguese carracks of the East India trade lacked the maneuverability to play their often light armament to best effect. In 1592, an English squadron battered the *Madre de Dios* of sixteen hundred tons, thirty-two pieces of brass ordnance, and six or seven hundred crew and passengers for three hours, raking her as they could. The Portuguese beat off one boarding attempt, but not a second. Boarded by three ships and a hundred men, she struck. Her cargo was of immense value and contained spices, drugs, silks, calicos, pearls, elephant teeth (ivory), Chinese porcelain, and much more. The English did not come off unscathed. One vessel had her foremast shot by the board, and another had to stop a leak made by a shot at her waterline by a "cannon perier" (*pierrier,* a breech-loading swivel gun).[49]

In 1593, three English "tall ships" encountered and engaged the East Indies carrack *Cinque Llagas,* whose name novelist Rafael Sabatini would later appropriate in Spanish form (*Cinco Llagas*) for the captured Spanish frigate his pirate hero, Captain Blood, re-christened as his flagship *Arabella.* After an initial engagement by the *Sampson* in which her captain was wounded in the first broadside, the attack was put off until morning. Then, according to plan, the English intended to give her "three bouts [broadsides] with our great ordnance, and so should clap her aboard." They then fired their broadsides (actually more than planned), then all three laid the carrack aboard.

The *May Flower*'s captain was slain immediately, and the vessel fell astern of the *Cinque Llagas* and was damaged as she did. The captain of the *Exchange* was shot through both legs at the same time, one of which he would lose. The carrack's crew, firing from behind "Barricadoes," beat off the attempt. The English ships, still alongside, fired their great guns as high as they could, and one of the English guns set the carrack's beak-head afire. The English ships were barely able to disentangle themselves, one of them only after fire burned the carrack's sails and rigging entangling it. In spite of the now prevalent use of ordnance, its use was often not as extensive as we might expect, and boarding was still considered a principal means of overcoming an adversary. The *Sampson* fired only seven broadsides for a total of forty-nine shot at distance, and only twenty-four shot while grappled. More broadsides would probably have helped, but the English seemed in a hurry to board.[50]

Barring all else, a treasure ship could be run aground and, if necessary, burned to prevent capture. The same flotilla that captured the *Madre de Dios* lost the carrack *Santa Cruz* when her crew ran her aground and set her afire. The English came ashore, dispersed the crew, and salvaged what they could.[51] In 1597, a carrack's crew ran her aground under similar circumstances. Boats took off crew, passengers, and what money and goods they could, then burned her. Spanish treasure ships are reported to have done the same when necessary.[52] In spite of the size and armament of most treasure ships, armed convoy remained their best defense.

AGGRESSIVE MEASURES

Retaliation against New World sea-roving bases might have been out of the question in the early years, but reprisals against sea and shore targets in the Old World were not, nor were attacks on the rovers themselves. Ashore, the tactics were largely the same as they had been for millennia: oppose rovers as they landed; defend the place attacked; counterattack with a force dispatched for the purpose when rovers attacked a defended place; ambush rovers as they withdrew; and chase and attack them as they sailed away. The treasure fleets occasionally served to defend cities from attack. On a smuggling voyage, John Hawkins was attacked and battered at San Juan de Ulloa when the Flota arrived while he was there, for example.[53] From the mid-sixteenth century onwards, Spain found its New World cities vulnerable. Jacques Sores sacked Havana in 1556 and Drake sacked Nombre de Dios in 1572, only two of the many successful attacks of the period and of the many more to come.

According to Spanish surveyor Baptista Antonio in 1587, often the problem was the local mentality. Describing Panama and the region surrounding it, he noted, "And forasmuch as the most part of these people are marchants, they will not fight, but onely keepe their owne persons in safetie, and save their goods; as it hath bene sene heretofore in other places of these Indies."[54] John Steinbeck took the sentiment a step farther in his novel *Cup of Gold*: "These were the merchants, keenly decisive when there was a farm to be wrested by law from its owner, or when the price of food was raised for outland colonists, but fearful and cowardly when steel was rattling about on steel."[55]

Until the coming of the Armada de Barlovento in the Caribbean and of similar but smaller armadas later in the South Sea, Spain was typically ill-prepared in the New World to immediately pursue the attackers of her ships and towns, and often to pursue them at all. The nature of the Caribbean did not help, with its hazards to navigation, numerous small islands and coves, and immense coastline to guard and patrol. Even so, Spain managed well enough at times, in spite of Spanish bureaucracy and lack of preparation. Certainly, despite the merchant character that came to afflict New Spain, she had plenty of valiant men ready to put to sea in order to defend her possessions, as well as to seek out and punish those who deigned to plunder her seas and shores.

In the mid-sixteenth century, Menéndez de Avilés began a program of improving the defenses of the Spanish New World. He proposed fortifying the principal harbors in Spain, the creation of squadrons to patrol the Caribbean, the creation of a flotilla to patrol between the Azores and Spain, the fortification of Florida, and the use of powerful men-of-war to escort the treasure fleets and even serve as treasure ships. Early efforts proved effective and were subsidized by New Spain, but subsequent efforts lagged—warfare tugged on finances. De Avilés was responsible for the capture of more than fifty pirate, privateer, and interloper vessels during his tenure, but the Caribbean remained vulnerable, and the development of local squadrons lagged. In 1582, two galleys were sent to Santo Domingo to patrol for pirates and interlopers, but one was lost aground and the other to mutiny. In 1596, a proposal was made to establish an *armadillo* (an armed vessel or flotilla) for the Caribbean to replace the expensive and often ineffective galleys, but the proposal lapsed, as did others until 1635. Even then, the Armada de Barlovento would not appear in the Caribbean until the 1640s, and its effectiveness would be limited by a lack of funding and its existence short-lived until the 1660s.[56]

More common, and often far more effective, was the fitting out of local *armadillos* to pursue attackers. Prior to the establishment of English, French, and Dutch colonies in the New World, it was reasonable to expect that attackers would remain in the area, attacking other vessels or places, provisioning, and possibly careening. This was particularly true in the South Sea, where the voyage home in either direction was long and difficult. Upon the discovery of sea rovers, Spanish authorities would typically place an embargo on local shipping until the raiders were destroyed or escaped. They would dispatch runners overland and swift vessels by sea to order vessels to remain in harbor, towns to prepare for attack, and *armadillos* to arm. In the case of the Caribbean, raiders might or might not be long gone before a force was dispatched. In the South Sea, however, rovers would invariably work their way up the long coastline, knowing it was poorly defended. In this case, the time it took to recruit a force and send it to sea was not usually in vain.

In 1594, upon news that Sir Richard Hawkins and his ship the *Dainty*, whose painted arms at the stern were "a negress with gilt ornaments," had entered the South Sea, the viceroy of Peru named Don Beltran de Castro y de la Cueva to command an *armadillo* to seek out and destroy the English rovers. Working night and day, de Castro fitted out three ships in eight days, a time so short it was considered "almost incredible." Sixty brass guns were divided between the two greater ships, the *Capitana* and the *Almiranta*. A third was mounted with four. According to a period Spanish account, three hundred men manned the ships, with a handful or two of young gentlemen volunteers added. According to Hawkins, the Spanish ships were manned with "thirteene hundred men and boyes, little more or lesse, and those of the choise of Peru." In either case, Hawkins and his seventy-five men and boys were substantially outnumbered.[57]

The *armadillo* found Hawkins and attacked. Hawkins was taken off-guard immediately (a circumstance he quite professionally relates for the benefit of others in his place) at the first exchange by two circumstances. First, the leading Spanish ship slipped to leeward and fired its broadside instead of keeping the weather gage (sailing between the wind and the enemy), as would be expected. This was not intended as a tactical surprise, although it indeed was one. Rather, the leading Spaniard was heeling in the wind and its leeward guns, much too long for proper service aboard a ship that size, could not be elevated enough to fire. By slipping to leeward, the heeling of the ship pointed the windward guns up where they could be used effectively.

Second was the lack of appropriate preparation of his guns. Cartridges were not made up, thus the guns had to be loaded, at least at first, with loose powder and ladles, a very dangerous practice. Worse, many guns were improperly loaded at the first encounter when it was most vital that every gun serve its purpose. Hawkins accepted full responsibility both for not having inspected his guns and for not having monitored his gunner.[58] (A ship's gunner was responsible for overseeing a ship's ordnance.)

The "fight continued so hott on both sides, that the artillery and muskets never ceased playing." According to Hawkins, the two great Spanish ships intended to board him, one on his broadside, the other alongside its comrade to support him. But the "captaine of the vice-admirall being more hardy than considerate," boarded too soon, before his consort was in place. The English battered the ship considerably, clearing the enemy decks with musketfire and fireworks, until the other Spaniard came up and "laid him abourd, and entred a hundredth of his men, and so cleared themselves of us."[59]

The battle continued for three days, a tactical engagement of great guns and small arms, each side battering the other continually. During the fight, Hawkins received six wounds. According to the Spanish, he received his two most serious (one in the neck and the other through the arm) from gunshots when he tried to seize the Spanish ensign with a bowline. The *Dainty*'s captain—Hawkins was the admiral or "General"—was knocked down after an exchange of blows during the Spanish boarding attempt, when he "opposed the entry of [Juan de] Torres [Portugal] with a shield and sword." The Spanish commander quickly abandoned any further attempt at traditional early-sixteenth century tactics: "If our ship is bigger and more strongly manned, even if with less artillery, she should close after the first broadside, or even before, if she can. She should grapple the enemy, so as not to let the latter fire often."[60] Musketry played a greater role, and probably at greater range, than in the past. In the early sixteenth century, musket and crossbow fire was reserved for close range and when boarding.[61]

The Spanish ships dogged the Englishmen relentlessly; Hawkins, sorely wounded, was unable to manage the fight as he might have, either to seize victory when they shot away one of the Spaniard's mainmasts, or to break off the engagement and escape. He wrote that "our sayles being torne, our mastes all perished, our pumpes rent and shot to peeces, and our shippe with fourteen shott under water and seven or eight foot of water in hold; many of our men being slaine, and the most part of them which remained sore hurt

. . . our best course was to surrender ourselves before our shippe sunke." And so they did, although the Spanish account claims the *Dainty* was captured by boarding. In either case, gunnery ultimately decided the action.[62]

The Englishmen had a commission to attack the Spanish and so were spared hanging or strangling as pirates, even though some of the Spanish referred to them as such. Some of the Spaniards also objected to such fair treatment, for the English rovers "were Lutherans; and for that cause, the faith which was given to us, was not to be kept or performed."[63] Hanging and other methods of putting captured pirates out of Spain's misery were not limited to small numbers of "pirates" in far-flung regions. In 1582, after the defeat of a French force at sea by a Spanish armada, "Eighty gentlemen and 313 soldiers and sailors, taken prisoners, were beheaded and strangled in cold blood by order of Santa Cruz, five days after the fight."[64] It was clear that the men were fighting recognizably and honorably on behalf of France, but, lacking a legitimate privateering commission or proof of one, the Spanish commander elected to put the men to death, an act considered barbarous even by many Spanish officers. Sir Richard Hawkins pointed out that although England would not prosecute its own rovers for attacking Spain in times of war, even if they lacked a commission, the Spanish behaved contrarily, punishing their own for attacking the English without a license, or so they claimed.[65]

There were other means of capturing a rover at sea. Treachery could work. According to Richard Hakluyt, after the seventy-ton English ship *Dog* captured three Spanish ships in the Gulf of Mexico, it espied, pursued, and engaged a Spanish man-of-war for three days. The Spanish eventually put out a flag of truce and asked for a parley. They met aboard the English vessel then invited the English over to theirs. There they "suddenly assaulted our men, and with a dagger stabbing the English pilot to the heart, slew him. Others were served with the like sauce; only William Mace the Master (and two others) notwithstanding all the prepared traps of the enemy, leaped overboard into the sea, and so came safe to his own ship."[66]

Treachery notwithstanding, a fight between men-of-war tended to go to the larger, better-armed, and better-manned ship, assuming it was well handled—that is, to the ship with the most guns, particularly if they were bigger guns than the adversary's. The rule, however, did not apply in the case of a small rover and a large merchantman, unless the merchantman were very well armed and manned.[67] In this case, small arms and boarding would continue to be a primary tactic, best defeated by great guns and closed quarters.

The combination of guns; swift, maneuverable ships; and seamanship was now vital in the hunt for pirates and privateers, or at least the well-armed ones. No longer would a swift vessel with a large boarding party alone suffice.

The victory against Hawkins set the tone and tactics for subsequent Spanish actions against the incursions of pirates and privateers. "All Peru rejoiced at this victory, and that the enemies of the holy faith should have been captured in that sea, a thing which had never before happened."[68] Although it would happen again in both seas, it was no sign of overall victory to come, but the converse, for the great modern "Golden Age" of piracy in the Caribbean and beyond was about to begin.

9

Of Blind Eyes and Opportunity

An Introduction to the "Golden Age," 1655–1725

"About the twenty-first, captain Munroe [Moreau], who had a commission from Jamaica, turned pirate, and took the English merchant ships bound thither; after whom captain Ensom, in the Swallow ketch, was sent out, who met with him, fought him, killed many, and took the rest of his men, being thirteen, who were brought by him to Jamaica, and there condemned and hanged," wrote Colonel William Beeston in 1665.[1]

This attack on pirates epitomized the ideal of pirate hunting in the age of sail: sending a naval, hired, or private man-of-war against a specific pirate, then finding and destroying him. It also epitomized some of the problems with pirate hunting, for the Frenchman Moreau had but recently been a "privateer" for the English. In other words, he had recently committed piracy under the guise of legitimacy, then abandoned pretense for reality. But before we look at pirate hunters and their tactics in this era, we need to review the sea rovers they sought, including a brief history, description, and some of our misconceptions of these rovers, for they are a principal influence on our modern Western understanding of piracy and pirate hunting.

The oft-named "Golden Age" of New World sea roving began with an English military expedition to the Caribbean in 1655, part of Oliver Cromwell's "Western Design" against the Spanish colonies in the Americas. Commanded at sea by Admiral William Penn and ashore by General Robert Venables, the secret adventure was intended to permanently relieve the Spanish of the burden of governing one of their great colonies. Penn and Venables chose Hispaniola as the best prospect and landed an army of seven thousand or more troops roughly seven leagues from Santo Domingo, unopposed. From this point onward, however, the invasion was a disaster. A participant best summed it up: "Friday the 4th of May the ships weighed from before the towne, and we set saile, having lost of our armie about 1000 men, and 2 or 3000 thousand armes in 20 dayes. And the armie having scarce 2000 healthful men amongst them to doe service. The losse which the enemie susteined wee conceive not to have been above 40 men in all." But the expedition's failure cannot be entirely attributed to Penn and Venables, for much of the army was unskilled in arms, inadequately equipped, and poorly victualled."[2]

Although the invasion of Hispaniola was an embarrassing failure, Penn and Venables salvaged the expedition by invading Jamaica, whose name was taken from the Arawak word *xaymaca*, meaning a place "of many springs." In short order, the English conquered the island, except for a small but significant number of slaves and soldiers in the hinterland, who would wage a guerrilla war for several years after.

THE PIRATES OF THE CARIBBEAN

So began four generations of the pirates of the Caribbean, often termed the "Golden Age of Piracy." Almost immediately, the conquerors of Jamaica began pillaging Spanish cities, using the harbor town of Port Royal as their base. In 1655, Santa Marta was the first to be sacked. The early expeditions were actually combined operations of the English navy and army, and they validated the effectiveness of previous sea-roving attacks on Spanish towns. In the words of one participating English naval officer, "Must say he thinks 'this kind of marooning cruizing West India trade of plundering and burning of towns, though it hath been long practised in these parts, yet is not honorable for a princely navy, neither was it, I think, the work designed, though perhaps it may be tolerated at present.'"[3] Although the English navy might have disdained such warfare, one of its officers, Capt. Christopher Myngs, led the way. He had no problem finding volunteers. Soldiers, tired of drilling and working the soil, were eager for the chance at plunder.

By 1658, the English had begun commissioning French and English privateers to attack the Spanish, and soon an effective if precarious alliance of English buccaneers and French filibusters was terrorizing Caribbean waters and Spanish coastlines. The Spanish retaliated with their own form of piracy under pretense of legitimacy, attacking not only buccaneers and filibusters, but also legitimate English and French merchantmen. The latter were usually more profitable, not to mention less combative.

The first generation of this Golden Age lasted roughly twenty years (from 1655 until the early 1670s) and was characterized by the sacking of numerous Spanish towns and cities, many of them described in the various editions of Alexandre Exquemelin's *The Buccaneers of America*. It was the era of, among many notable others, Christopher Myngs, John Morris, Robert Searles, Bernard Speirdyke, Morris Williams, "Garrett Garretson *alias* Rocky*" (the famous Roc Brasiliano who even swam with sharks and killed them with daggers), Bartholomew Portuguese, Diego the Mulatto, Willem Blauveldt (called Blewfield by the English), Edward Mansfield, the psychotic butcher Jean David Nau (called L'Ollonois), and Henry Morgan.[4] In general, this buccaneering resembled Mycenaean sea roving. Under pretenses of war or reprisal and often with legitimate commissions (if often stretched beyond their actual terms), "privateers" sacked dozens of Spanish towns, following the precedent of the conquest of Jamaica and the early raids of Captain Myngs. The raids brought financial gain to the colonies of Jamaica and Saint-Domingue, further weakened the Spanish New World empire, caused reprisals that harmed English and French commerce, and were generally conducted purely for profit, although there was a strategic aspect in the damage caused to Spanish holdings. The principal bases of piracy and privateering were the island of Tortuga off the north coast of Hispaniola, and Port Royal at Jamaica.

The second generation began soon after the sack of Panama in 1671 by an army of buccaneers, filibusters, hunters, and miscellaneous volunteers commanded by Henry Morgan, and lasted until 1688. Many of these new commanders had served under Morgan or another of the famous early buccaneers and filibusters. Tortuga was replaced as a pirate haven by Petit Goave, and Port Royal began to decline as a pirate base. In particular, the period is noteworthy for the first serious attempts at suppressing the buccaneers and filibusters, who often referred to themselves as "privateers" but never as pirates. In the previous decade, authorities had made a few largely ineffectual attempts to suppress "privateering," for the trade antagonized Spain and thus interfered with a potentially enormous trade in slaves and goods.[5] In the 1670s and 1680s, as trade with Spain grew, attempts at suppression increased in both magnitude and government resolve, and by the late 1680s, English buccaneers found refuge primarily with the French at Petit Goave. Notable commanders of this period included Bartholomew Sharp, Richard Sawkins, Edmond Cook, the sieur de Grammont, Nicolas Van Horn, Captain Yanky, Captain Le Sage, Thomas Paine, and Laurens de Graff. Spain had its own set of privateers and pirates who often made reprisals against the English and French: Pedro de Castro, Juan Corso, and Blas Miguel were notable among them. The period is also noteworthy for the rise of pirates who began to routinely attack vessels other than those of the Spanish. In particular, there was one who made no pretense of being a "privateer" or of hiding behind pretense of legitimacy, and who indeed called himself a pirate: Jean Hamlin, who may be considered the archetype of the last of these four generations of pirates of the Caribbean.

From 1689 to 1697, European nations were at war, followed soon again from 1701 to 1713. During this third generation, many buccaneers and filibusters turned legitimate as privateers and sometimes even as commanders of troops ashore. For those who did not care for government service, piracy was tempting, and the Red Sea and the Guinea coast of Africa were primary hunting grounds. Often these pirates were financed in the New World colonies; New York was a common source of pirate venture capital. Pirates established bases on Madagascar and at New Providence in the Caribbean. This was the age of Thomas Tew, William Kidd, and Henry Every, among others.

The Treaty of Utrecht ended the War of the Spanish Succession in 1713. The age of the buccaneer and filibuster had passed. Spain was no longer the great target. Easier pickings were to be had among the English, French, Dutch, and Portuguese merchantmen. With thousands of displaced privateer seamen, a lack of protection for merchant shipping, and thousands of miles of unprotected coastline in which to hide, the age of the true pirates of the Caribbean—the pirates who owed little or no allegiance to anyone or anything but their comrades and the sea—was born. They had havens at Madagascar, New Providence, and, to some degree, the Guinea coast. They were characterized as much by their flamboyance as by their deeds, glorified in literature by Charles Johnson's popular history, and permitted an almost free rein by a weak naval presence. They forcibly recruited men, often refused to let crew members leave the company before a cruise was ended (contrary to the practice in previous generations), and in general had a gang-like mentality. They devastated merchant shipping and the slave trade in the Caribbean and along the coasts of North America, Brazil, and Guinea. They took nearly all of their prizes without a fight, rarely engaged men-of-war deliberately, sacked few places and none of any significance, and lasted less than a decade. From these men, and from a few women as well, has descended most of our popular images of the pirate. Theirs are names we know well, among them Blackbeard, Bartholomew Roberts, and Calico Jack Rackam.

MEN AND MOTIVATION

Early on, all sorts flocked to the "privateer's" trade: former Cromwellian sol-diers, French *boucaniers*, renegade deserters from the armies and navies of various nations, common seamen, transported criminals, slaves, and former slaves were among the many.[6] The famous French *boucaniers*—the cattle and pig hunters of Saint-Domingue—typically led a dual existence of hunter and occasional filibuster, and many who began as hunters or their servants ended as filibusters. The English soldiers left at Jamaica after the conquest, "being poor, and wanting conveniencies to settle, they gladly embraced this oppor-tunity."[7] Many had become hunters on the *boucanier* model, and their shoot-ing skill would have been just as valuable as that of the French hunters.

Former indentured servants—some of whom were undoubtedly tricked into their indentures, as well as those who ran away from their servitude— were common among the Caribbean rovers.[8] Transported English Monmouth rebels and Scottish "Covenanter" rebels were probably among the Caribbean sea-rover ranks. Almost certainly some of the "English, Scotch, or Irish pi-rates, prisoners in the Dorchester gaol, to be forthwith sent to Barbadoes, Bermuda, or some other of the English plantations in America" continued their trade in the New World.[9] In 1668, convicted criminals being transport-ed to Barbados for four years' indenture "in the latitude of 23 degrees they killed the master and surgeon, and put six others in the boat with some pro-visions, since which they have been upon the coast of Hispaniola and Cuba, and given chase to our privateers, and much damaged one of them."[10] Irish renegades fled to the Spanish rovers, whose ranks were often predominantly mulatto and mestizo. Among the pirates of the last generation of the Golden Age, seamen and runaway indentured servants were the most common. War was over, maritime wages had dropped, and men needed adequate employ-ment.[11] Overall, the economic motive—the purpose of profit by plunder— predominated. One suspects that many of these men would not have turned to piracy, or would not have stayed with it long, if they had had better eco-nomic opportunities.

Even so, there were also legitimate cases of revenge as motive for piracy, at least in part. Pirate captain Edmund Cook first took to piracy partly out of revenge for the seizure of his ship, the pink *Virgin*, in 1673 by Capt. Philip Fitzgerald, an Irish renegade who said he served Spain because "his coun-trymen were ill-used by the English 24 years ago, and he should never be satisfied with English blood, but could drink it as freely as water when he was adry."[12] Paul Abney, Bartholomew Sharp's lieutenant aboard the frigate

Josiah in 1685, may have been inspired to piracy in part out of revenge, or at least frustration. In 1679, Don Antonio Quintana, admiral of the Armada de Barlovento, seized his vessel and its cargo of cacao. When Abney produced a pass from Governor Carlisle of Jamaica, the admiral reportedly "wiped his breech with it and threw it at him again." The Spanish ambassador, Don Pedro Ronquillos, later denied that Quintana had seized any such vessel. Soon after, Abney went as pilot aboard the HMS *Hunter*—which had been ordered to take a potentially profitable break from the ship's duties of pirate hunting and restoring English prisoners from Cartagena—to locate a Spanish wreck on the Abrojos reef in order to "fish" for her silver. Unfortunately, he could not find the wreck or perhaps thought the better of it and chose to keep its location a secret until he could later benefit from it, and so was jailed by the governor.[13] Abney soon turned to piracy or "privateering," if he had not already. There are numerous other similar examples. Some of the Anglo-American pirates of the early eighteenth century claimed, in the words of the aforementioned Captain Davis, that "their reasons for going a pirating were to revenge themselves on base merchants and cruel commanders of ships" although the cruelty of the pirates was typically far greater.[14]

However, Sir Henry Morgan, the buccaneer knighted and appointed lieutenant governor of Jamaica, best described the principal reasons men went to sea for piracy: "Their [the pirates'] numbers are increased by the necessitous and unfortunate, and they are encouraged by the security of the Spaniards and their pusillanimity under all their plenty. Nothing can be more fatal to the prosperity of the Colony than the temptingly alluring boldness and success of the privateers [pirates], which draws off white servants and all men of unfortunate or desperate condition."[15]

Given that these Caribbean pirates, privateers, buccaneers, and filibusters are the principal source of most people's perception and image of the pirate today, we need to briefly evaluate other several popular, related perceptions of these rovers: they were colorblind men with multi-racial crews who often freed slaves and took them into their crews; they were democratic sea-going "Robin Hoods" who were sympathetic to their fellow seamen of the merchant fleet; they became pirates out of a sense of rebellion against unfair government and social conditions; and that they influenced the development of Western democracy and even founded pirate utopias where slaves were freed and all men lived as equals. The evaluation of these perceptions and myths, and the debunking of some of them, is in itself, after all, a form of pirate hunting.

PIRACY, RACE, AND SLAVERY

The first three generations of buccaneers, filibusters, pirates, and privateers who originated from Port Royal and Petit Goave were predominantly white. Even so, these crews usually had significant numbers of both enslaved and free blacks, mulattos, mestizos (persons of mixed European and Native American ancestry), and Native Americans among them. Mulattos and mestizos made up the greater part of Spanish pirate and privateer crews, and blacks were well represented.[16] Mulatto captains were known both as privateers or pirates, depending on the point of view, sailing for and against Spain. Throughout the Golden Age, individual slaves were occasionally freed by all European nations in the Caribbean on account of courage in action or sometimes for simple loyalty over time. He "proved very true, and killed 2 of the Spaniards charging us, [and so] he obtained his freedome," wrote an English officer in 1655 of a slave originally captured by the Spanish from the English.[17]

Capt. Richard Sawkins, an English buccaneer, freed a black slave whose heroism had probably earned him that freedom and ultimately caused his death at Arica when, surrounded by Spaniards, he refused to surrender.[18] Most Caribbean colonizers armed slaves in time of war: "The French negroes also came all armed, being promised each man a white wife and freedom, as well as plunder," wrote an Englishman of the fight for St. Christopher's (St. Kitts) in 1668.[19] Spanish militia was largely made up of both enslaved and free blacks and mulattos who constituted the most effective and feared element of the Spanish New World military, often earning their freedom as such. Many of them were hunters: "Thes goe by the name of Cow killers, and inded it is thayer trad, for thay liue by killing of Cattille for the hides and talow: Thes are those that doth doue all the mischefe [i.e. fight effectively against the English], and hear are Negors and Molatos which are thayer slaves: to thes thay did proclaim fredom if they would fight."[20]

By the end of the "Golden Age," blacks were well represented among many of the infamous Anglo-American pirates, perhaps in part because these pirates of European origin recognized a kinship with them, and perhaps also because recruits were hard to find, and many slaves were ready and willing to shed their shackles for the freedom and vengeance to be found in sea roving. Nonetheless, the general idea that these pirates freed many slaves, and that they did so out of a sense of egalitarianism or social rebellion, has far less merit than it is sometimes granted. During the first three periods of the Golden Age, slaves were a significant source of plunder and profit, and only occasionally were they brought as free men into pirate or buccaneer crews. Pirates captured and traded thousands of slaves during this time.[21] Even the Anglo-American pirates of the final period trafficked in slaves when they could and often treated them as brutally as any slaver at sea or slave owner ashore. Howell Davis, for example, gave a sloop filled with 140 slaves as a present to a Dutchman whose ship he had captured after a long fight, and the pirates who captured William Snelgrave offered to give him "as many of the best slaves as would fill the ship" to sell in the free port of St. Thomas.[22] Bartholomew Roberts attacked "Calabar negroes" after they refused to trade with him, and he burned a ship with eighty slaves chained aboard—unshackling them turned out to be too time consuming.[23]

In general, there was a hypocritical duality in the treatment of African slaves and former slaves by pirates. Those who had been elevated to the status of pirate were treated, as far as we know, as equals, but we do not know to how many this privilege was extended, relative to the number of slaves who passed through pirate hands. The pirate La Bouse's crew of sixty-four was half black, for example, and a third of the men aboard Bartholomew Roberts's *Royal Fortune* when it was captured were Africans who had been originally purchased as slaves by slave ships.[24] Further, their status among the pirates is difficult to determine from the record. Blacks in Roberts's crew were not tried for piracy when captured, for example, but were treated as slaves, although many of them had indeed "lived a long time in this piratical way."[25] Certainly, slaves not entered into pirate crews were treated by pirates as slaves or as otherwise inferior. To be fair, pirates appear to have considered most people to be their inferiors, and their double standard in the treatment of blacks has a parallel in their treatment of white seamen. It is also important to note that the treatment of former African slaves who had been entered as crew members was far more egalitarian than the treatment of slaves and former slaves at the hands of most white members of colonial societies, and far more egalitarian than even that of whites in common society.

PIRATE DEMOCRACY

Another common perception, based on assumptions of "one man one vote" (captains appear to typically have had two votes) and "one man one share" (with a few exceptions) among the Golden Age pirates, was that theirs were democratic societies. And indeed they were, in many ways far exceeding even our own modern democracies in equality and other notions of fairness. On the other hand, these pirate communities were not communal in the sense of communistic, as some occasionally propose based on the concept of everyone sharing equally. This is not to suggest that there never were such. Livy described the Liparian pirates of antiquity as having "the custom of the state to make a general division of all booty acquired, as if piracy were the public act of government," and piracy historian Ormerod noted their "communistic organization."[26] But such communal societies, of which we have little knowledge, are so rarely recorded as to be the exception. The Golden Age pirates had no intention of bringing everyone up or down to the same level—as levelers to pull the nobleman from his horse or pedestal, so to speak—or to otherwise create a world where all men were equal. Rather, they intended to elevate themselves above most men, using democracy and theft as the mechanism. The Golden Age pirate considered himself (and, on occasion, herself) the equal of most any man and superior to most. Each considered himself a leader and the equal of any other pirate, or, as chronicler Charles Johnson put it, "every man being, in his own imagination, a captain, a prince or a king."[27] Among such men, democracy was without doubt the most viable form of government, but it was not new among sea rovers.[28]

Although pirate articles invariably provided for medical treatment and disability compensation paid for from the plunder before any other distribution was made—again, not a new concept—plunder was otherwise not considered a community possession except as the pot of everyone's shares, which was typically quickly divided, each man doing with his as he pleased.[29] Pirates valued their largely equal shares in plunder and were scrupulous about the division of booty, a process whereby plunder became personal property, and occasionally, when invested, real property. Pirates did not intend to redistribute wealth, except to take from others for their own limited benefit and more or less live as princes, however briefly. Nor was the concept of equal shares new. Shares, probably largely equal among most roving crews of the past, are noted as far back as Odysseus.[30] Among the Viking *Sagas* are references to "agreement that anything of value they obtained would be divided equally among them," and the *Vitalienbrüder* were also referred to as the *Likedeelers*, a term which means equal sharers.[31]

What these rovers were after was plunder as the means to freedom and freedom as the means to plunder. Some rovers even grew wealthy. More probably would have but for the tendency to go on a drinking, gambling, whoring, and general spending spree after a successful cruise. Captains who owned their ships (often they were awarded to them by the articles) during the first three generations could grow very wealthy indeed, for they were allotted shares based on the size of their ship: ten for a small one of one hundred tons or so, for example, and thirty for a large one of four hundred tons or so, a process that was frankly capitalistic.[32] One might even argue that their political philosophy was a form of social democracy combined with aggressive laissez-faire economics. These buccaneers, filibusters, and pirates were indeed democratic, but theirs was not a democracy which intended that all men should be equal, or even that the members of their broader society should be equal. Their notion of equality extended no further than themselves, and their depredations harmed not only wealthy merchants, but also the middle and working classes, including indentured servants, slaves, and the poor, except for the rovers themselves.

PIRATES AS REBELS

In regard to the idea that many of the New World pirates of the late seventeenth and early eighteenth centuries were rebelling against unfair government or social conditions, the most popular supporting model or theory sees piracy as the natural reaction to the exploitation of common sailors by corporate overlords (merchant owners) and their minions (captains and officers)—a form of class warfare, in other words. Pirates, harmed and offended by an unjust political and economic system, vent their spleen upon their oppressors, or at least upon the symbols of their oppression. And for many common seamen, life was brutal, and without doubt some seamen were inspired to rebel. However, this argument fails to note the complexity and multiplicity of piratical and sea-roving motivation in the seventeenth and eighteenth centuries.[33] Further, it also forgets that word and deed are often two very different things. One may describe a thief as a rebel, or a thief may even describe himself as a rebel, but if his only purpose is to steal for private purpose, he remains a thief, even if reasonably and sympathetically excused. Sea rovers in general did not take from the rich to give to the poor, except that the poor were the rovers themselves. Charity begins at home, after all. Rather than considering pirates as having rebelled in a political sense against adverse social and political conditions, we might better view many of them as having fled such adversity or seized an illicit or semi-licit opportunity to improve their condition. Their rebellion was invariably economic, not political, although it must be noted that political rebellion is often economic at its core.

Rebellion as a motive for sea roving—beyond the simple rebellion of taking to the sea or to another hazardous profession for whatever reason—is typically over-emphasized or even inserted by some writers and scholars. We forget that throughout history, many forms of sea roving were considered lawful and appropriate professions for those with the spirit of adventure, need, or greed (or all three). Privateers by definition have had the law on their side. Among sea-roving peoples, plundering has been the social norm. Governments have often turned blind eyes to pirates, given their usefulness. Pirates themselves have often dismissed their legal or moral lapses as justifiable, as did reformed pirate Sir Henry Mainwaring, who suggested his piracy was "*Pulchrum Scelus*" or "honorable crime."[34] His is an almost viable argument, and certainly an appealing one, given that most of us would agree that one man's tax collector is often another man's thief.

This being said, rebellion is indeed a fact of sea roving, although not of rebellion intended to overthrow society, but to spurn it. All mariners who have gone voluntarily to sea—whether merchant seaman, fisherman, whaler, navy tar, pirate, or privateer—have had one thing in common throughout history, besides the sea: a rejection, great or small, of common society. In other words, all are to some degree rebels. For all, no matter their voluntarily reason for doing so, whether personal, spiritual, or economic, the rebellion of taking to the sea has granted a sense of independence. It was and remains today a rejection of the common intrusive indiscipline of shore-based society, a rejection of the apparent loss of personality among the masses, a rejection of the lubber's mundane. However, for the majority of sea rovers then and now, rebellion is at best an excuse and not the ultimate reason for their depredations. Sea roving was and is a livelihood and usually a lifestyle as well, but the sentiment of need or greed, of plunder seeking, predominates. This sentiment is repeated in many journals of sea rovers of all sorts, as well as in many of those who observed them firsthand.

While there are actual elements of social and economic rebellion in piracy, as there are in all marginal lifestyles (and often in mind in conventional lifestyles), again they seem as much of an excuse as they do a reason. Many early eighteenth century pirate captains, for example, seem to have been thugs and opportunists rather than oppressed seamen rebelling against abuse and an unfair economic system. Novelists and Hollywood filmmakers have often promoted the image of the pirate as a rebel toppling unfair regimes. In *Swashbuckler*, for example, pirates help overthrow a corrupt island government, and in *Pirates of the Caribbean: At World's End*, pirates band together to overthrow the evil East India Company.[35] Unfortunately, these and similar films and novels, not to mention the wishful thinking of a few historians, do not reflect reality.

In a factual instance of rebel rhetoric among pirates, a few Caribbean buccaneers in 1687 "confessed" to a shipwrecked doctor who had been transported for rebellion "that they were rebels too," supporters in spirit of the Protestant Duke of Monmouth's rebellion against the Catholic King James. But such words came easily to men thousands of miles away from a failed rebellion fought not over social conditions, but over paternity, royal succession, and especially religion, as an early-eighteenth-century pirate points out: "[H]e did not care who they chose captain so it was not a papist; for against them he had conceived an irreconcilable hatred, for that his father had been a sufferer in Monmouth's rebellion."[36] Such buccaneers and pirates had no intention of actually overthrowing any government or society and were soon "at the main continent, where they hauled up their piraguas [large canoes propelled by oars and sails], and stayed there about a fortnight, waiting to seize some Spanish vessel that might come that way."[37] From these buccaneers was Rafael Sabatini probably inspired to depict his fictional Captain Blood as a rebel pirate, further popularizing the false image of the pirate as a social rebel seeking political reform in the face of tyranny or avenging his unjust treatment at the hands of a tyrant.[38]

To better illustrate the reality of political rebellion among pirates of the Golden Age, a brief look at the only significant uprising in which these pirates were involved is in order. The tale begins in 1685 when King James II revoked Bermuda's private charter and installed a royal governor, Col. Richard Cony. The colonists—accustomed to self-rule and inspired by the recent failed Monmouth rebellion in England, by a book entitled *The Liberty of the Subjects of England*, and to a lesser degree by the prior removal of the governor of New Providence—quickly opposed Cony. Their rhetoric was seditious, arrogant, and quite democratic. "[T]his is what [we] had long expected, slavery," said one rebel. An observer noted, "[T]hey esteem all Government to bee Slavery but what is of their own establishing."[39]

Accustomed for years to making their own rules, the imposition of formal English government must have come as a shock. Almost immediately, many Bermuda colonists—"a mutinous, turbulent, hypocritical people, wholly averse to kingly government," according to Captain St. Loe of the HMS *Dartmouth*—thwarted the rule of their governor and even attempted to depose him. The governor's major "crime" was that he attempted to collect duties on tobacco and whale oil, required bonds of merchants and whalers in case they failed to pay duty on their goods, required vessels to properly clear port prior to departure, demanded that captains produce cockets (documents proving that goods had cleared customs), and reserved the King's lands to the Crown. Beyond this, the colonists also accused their governor of requiring unlawful oaths and forcing tavern owners to pay unlawful license fees, and they vilified him with accusations of swearing, cursing, and killing a widow's hog. Bermudans saw all of this as an infringement upon their rights, clearly did not approve of legitimate government cutting into private profit, and felt that their own local government was quite capable of managing Bermudan affairs. Many of their complaints are reminiscent of later revolutions: "That no man may be deprived of his property without legal trial," and "That no man be imprisoned without crime or advice of counsel."[40]

In late 1685, notorious buccaneer captain Bartholomew Sharp, claiming to be in need of provisions and holding a dubious commission from Sir William Stapleton to "take and apprehend savage Indians and pirates," arrived in command of the *Josiah*, a frigate of ten great guns (cannon), eight "patararos" (swivel cannon), and one hundred men. Also aboard were "a few Indians" taken as slaves during the recent sack of Campeche "which he offered for sale" in order "to supply their [his crew's] wants, for they were poor," of whom thirty—probably the entire cargo—were sold.[41] Contrary to the popular image of the pirate as an enemy of tyranny, Sharp was happy to offer his services to Governor Cony, who quickly retained him for assistance and security against the rebels. Soon after, the pirate Edward Conaway (or Conway) arrived from New Providence in command of the *Prosperous* and joined Sharp as a steadfast supporter of the royal government against the rebels. The recalcitrant local population was soon intimidated by the more than one hundred veteran pirates. Sharp and Conaway recovered two forts from the rebels, and Sharp imprisoned one of the ringleaders aboard his small frigate, among other services rendered to the royal governor. In turn, Sharp and Conaway were accused of strong-arming those who disagreed with Cony and supporting a corrupt, unfair government. The rebels tried to bribe Sharp —"the people have offered him large sums to desert me," wrote Cony—and even drafted charges against him, but he remained both loyal and nonplussed. Indeed, one of the complaints the rebels later made against Cony was that he "has entertained Bartholomew Sharpe, a pirate."[42]

And the pirate played his cards well, writing to the English Secretary of State, the Earl of Sunderland: "[T]here is rebellion against the King in all these Islands, and that the people will not believe that any king but

Monmouth is living."[43] Sharp was a well-known, picaresque, and by now infamous English pirate who had raided in the Caribbean, had crossed the Isthmus of Darien and raided the Spanish in the South Sea, had been tried and acquitted in England of piracy in the South Sea, and was now being sought by the governor of Nevis on charges of having committed piracy both at Campeche and in the act of capturing the frigate *Resolution*, which he had taken from the pirate Henley and renamed *Josiah*.[44] Sharp was undoubtedly trying to curry favor in Bermuda, having seen the opportunity after he arrived to sell slaves. "He is very zealous for the King's service," wrote Cony.[45] Upon arriving at Bermuda, Captain St. Loe arrested Sharp in spite of Governor Cony's protests and carried him to Nevis, via New England and Barbados, where he stood trial for piracy. Sharp was acquitted for the second time.[46]

Sharp's was not the only instance of pirates, who are indeed in many ways rebels, refusing to join rebellion against tyranny, or at least against perceived tyranny. Perhaps the most famous instance is that of Spartacus, the escaped slave and gladiator who led a rebellion against Rome from 73 to 71 BC but was betrayed by Cilician pirates after they agreed to sail him and two thousand men to Sicily, where he hoped to kindle a slave revolt. "But after the pirates had struck a bargain with him, and received his gifts [payment], they deceived him and sailed away."[47]

Again, the well-documented reality of plunder as ultimate purpose throughout the history of sea roving overshadows any underlying motivation. For every instance of documented rhetoric of revenge and rebellion, there are many more of plunder as purpose: crime for profit is not usually an overt act of political rebellion or revenge. Among many examples, one buccaneer, a contemporary of the Monmouth-supporting pirates just mentioned, noted "our hungry appetite for gold and riches," while a pirate contemporary of Captain Davis stated, "I, as I believe most of the company, came here to get money, but not to kill, except in fight, and not in cold blood, or for private revenge."[48] Even the modern Somali pirates, whose attacks a spokesman once tried to excuse by claiming they were necessary "to protect the country's sea resources from illicit exploitation by foreign vessels," are not part of a political movement or government but are solely interested in profit from plunder or ransom, notwithstanding the fact that some of their plunder goes to their warlord or militia leader.[49]

All of the pirates, buccaneers, and filibusters of the "Golden Age" were, as noted earlier, democratically organized, and one can argue that this was at least in part the result of rebellion against existing social and political conditions. Some rovers, perhaps many, were no doubt rebelling against unfair government and associated social conditions, but, all rhetoric aside, their rebellion went no further than theft on the sea and along its shores. At best, we might consider their rebellion as the seizing of the opportunity of sea roving in order to escape harsh or unfair conditions. Political rebellion that was intended to improve social conditions and change government was nurtured ashore primarily among poor settlers, small freeholders, religious separatists, and various merchants who were putting down their roots, raising families, and cultivating community beyond mere bands of sea robbers. These men and women were the true rebels of the New World. Even the common seaman, often noted as being a rabble-rousing rebel, had far greater influence in issues of government than did the pirate, who was by definition an outcast. The Americas were a crucible of political rebellion in the seventeenth century, eventually leading to the American Revolution of the late eighteenth century and other American revolutions afterward.

THE MYTH OF PIRATE UTOPIAS

In its ultimate form, rebellion rejects or destroys the status quo and builds anew. The most popularly cited instance of such social rebellion and rhetoric among pirates is that of the French captain Misson and his colony of Libertalia, founded with the Italian priest Caraccioli and the English pirate captain Thomas Tew in Madagascar in the late seventeenth century. Charles Johnson described the colony as an ideal democratic community that made war on the commerce of the state, freed slaves, spared prisoners, and lived in utopian harmony. Plundering, however, was not forsaken.

Unfortunately for romantic revolutionaries and revisionists, there is no evidence that Misson or his colony ever existed, nor that Captain Tew, who did exist, was associated with any such colony. Misson, Caraccioli, and Libertalia are doubtless the invention of Charles Johnson, who, inspired by some of the actual independent pirate settlements at Madagascar, adapted rebellious pirate rhetoric to front for a broader theme of social rebellion and reform. Caraccioli was the well-known name of several prominent Italians, including a famous priest who preached in Rome in the fifteenth century and is the object of a brief comical story in the well-known "*Mery Tales*," a book noted even by Shakespeare. In the tale, the priest shouts "Phy on S. Peter! phy on St. Paul!" and spits to the left and right in protest of the "great pompe, noise, and ruffiying" of the cardinal and his bishops.[50] This "rebellious" Caraccioli may well be Johnson's inspiration. As for Misson's origin, there was a pirate captain named William Mason (also given as Masson) who commanded the *Jacob*, originally a privateer outfitted in New York and commissioned by Jacob Leisler. He visited Madagascar in the late seventeenth century, attacked ships in the Red Sea, and was associated with Tew and other pirates, but he was an Englishman and there is no record of him establishing a colony.[51]

Johnson's inspiration of both Misson's name (probably in combination with Captain Mason's name) and his colony was quite likely the purported memoir of Jaques Massé, actually written by freethinker Simon Tyssot de Patot. In these *Voyages et Avantures*, Massé travels to the Indian Ocean, visits Madagascar, and is shipwrecked at Australia, where he and another survivor discover an anti-European utopia where all men are equal, all are atheists, and all live in harmony.[52] In fact, the actual pirate settlements at Madagascar were established not only as a way for some pirates to "live like princes" while they continued the trade of piracy, but also as a way of avoiding capture, prosecution, and hanging—but not as freethinking democratic utopias. Some of these pirate settlements were attacked and destroyed by native inhabitants.[53] Pirates and other sea rovers did function as rebellious independent societies in the form of pirate crews and even as "communities" ashore, but in all cases their purpose of plunder by force of arms never wavered.

To go to sea voluntarily is itself an act of rebellion, and to go for the purpose of plunder is often an extraordinary statement of rebellion. One need not infer beyond this to revolution or utopia, except to note that sea roving is both the pirate's act of revolution and often his utopia as well. And it was this that governments and merchants were eventually determined to destroy in the Caribbean and beyond.

10

The Real Pirates of the Caribbean

Pirate Hunting in the "Golden Age," 1655–1725

"As *Roberts* the Pyrate, by the bold Sweep made in August, had struck a Pannick into the Traders, we were several times in our late Cruise alarmed with Stories of their being again to Windward; which kept us *Plying*, till others contradicting such Report, and considered with the rashness of the Attempt, returned us to our Rendezvous in Cape Corso Road, where we had scarce well arrived, before Mr. Phips received intelligence by two or three Canoos dispatched to him, of Vessels chased and taken by them a few Leagues off, committing great Cruelties . . . The Conclusion of our Advices, was to follow them to *Whydah* . . . We missed them however by 24 hours, but following quickly to Cape *Lopez*, luckily fixed the limits of their Navigation."[1] The English navy had run the pirates to ground.

Unfortunately, the pursuit of pirates by men-of-war was more often than not hampered by circumstances beyond the control of naval commanders and their crews. "That you get two or three small light frigates, that can go into shoal water, and can follow the enemies *barqua luengos*, to cruize to and from the island, to prevent the many depredations and robberies daily committed about the coasts of this island," instructed the Council and Assembly of Jamaica to the agent for Jamaica in 1693.[2] Conversely, New York governor Lord Bellomont complained in 1699 that, "If I had a 4th-rate ship here and a 5th-rate at N. York I would undertake to secure all the coast . . . especially if the Captains were honest fighting fellows, for I would keep them constantly cruizing all the season of the year that ships can live on this coast. A 4th-rate would terrify the pirates exceedingly; many of their ships are a match for a 5th-rate."[3] (Light frigates were usually sixth rates, smaller than fourth and fifth rates.) After nearly four decades of piracies against Jamaican shipping, pirate hunting still often lacked hunters and vessels appropriate to local circumstances. In large part, pirates, by no means invulnerable, had the odds stacked in their favor, for colonial anti-piracy operations were typically inadequate.[4]

Broadly speaking, pirate hunting in the Caribbean, along the east coast of North America, the west coast of Africa, and in the Indian Ocean and environs was constrained by several more or less constant issues. From 1655 through the 1670s, the large number of Caribbean rovers gave local governments and naval vessels pause. "The calling in the privateers [buccaneers and filibusters] will be but a remote and hazardous expedient, and can never be effectually done without five or six men-of-war," yet "all the privateers, both English and French . . . shall have at all times as much liberty of this port [Port Royal, Jamaica] as ever they had, and that they may be with abundance of safety come hither."[5] Sir Thomas Modyford, an early governor of Jamaica, put it plainly: "[H]e has an account of no less than 1,500 lusty fellows abroad, who if made desperate by any act of injustice or oppression, may miserably infest this place. . . . Therefore he has hit it right that unless Tortudas [Tortuga] be reduced, and a fleet of frigates to awe them, they must be 'tempored' with."[6] Spain in the New World was overwhelmed by the depredations of these variously lawful and unlawful rovers, and France and England were unable to take effective steps against their piracies; they needed buccaneers and filibusters as a defense against Spain and, for that matter, against each other.

The official promotion of sea roving against Spain, combined with lukewarm attempts at pirate hunting, set a tradition of plundering that would take decades to break. Early on, French and English governors issued commissions against Spain. Even after England quit promoting Caribbean "privateering," French governors continued to issue commissions against Spain, both on pretense of reprisal should their vessels and crews be attacked while hunting or fishing, and on pretense of damage already done them.[7] In wartime, many buccaneers, filibusters, and even pirates were thankfully in the service of the state, for local naval assets had little time for pirate hunting. Both during and for a decade or two after King William's War (1688–1697), the French government still supported filibusters as a defensive force and as active contributors to local economies.[8]

Even when proscribed, Caribbean rovers often had strong support among some local government officials and merchants, and pirates in the early eighteenth century often received similar, albeit more circumspect, support. "I have seen one captain Prince, who is said to be a proclaimed pirate, with others said to be privateers, leading each his woman by the said earl [of Carlisle] as he sat in his coach viewing affairs," deposed one witness in 1680.[9] Another provided a trenchant indictment from the same period: "And this deponent verily believeth, by what he hath heard and seen, if the said earl and sir Henry Morgan had at several times shut their doors they might have catched most of the chief pirates and privateers in their houses."[10] Such encouragement made the job of pirate hunting more difficult than it already was, and was not limited to isolated instances of a few corrupt officials. "That you discover to the lords the great dishonour done to their majesties, and the inconveniencies that happen to the rest of their majesties plantations, by New England, New-York, Carolina, Providence, &c. entertaining and encouraging pirates; whereby all profligate fellows flock thither, to be encouraged and fitted out for the Red and South Seas, where they daily commit piracies and murders," wrote the Council and Assembly of Jamaica in the late seventeenth century.[11]

The environment aided the rover as well. With its tortuous coastlines, numerous islands, treacherous navigation, and many shoals and shallows, the Caribbean was a perfect place for the sea rover to lay in ambush, escape, and hide. The east coast of North America offered similar protection along its sparsely settled coastal regions, bays, and inlets, and both regions provided ports receptive to plundered goods and silver. To the east, the west coast of Africa was poorly protected, and the Indian Ocean and East Indies were so large and so far flung that tracking rovers was almost pointless.

Worst of all for the pirate hunter was the quality of the rovers themselves, particularly as compared to their prey. In the first three generations, pirate hunters had to contend with rovers who were veterans of numerous bloody combats at sea and ashore. Only during the fourth generation did the level of experience in warfare, especially land warfare, appear to diminish among Caribbean sea rovers, at least as compared to the first three generations. On the other hand, pirates generally had good intelligence of naval movement, typically had swift and often shallow-drafted vessels, and were often on the move. They knew the region as well as or better than their pirate-hunting adversaries did. Their organization was flexible and adaptable. If pressed, pirates could shift into other trades such as logwood cutting, the "sloop trade" or smuggling, and turtle fishing in the Caribbean, or into the maritime community in general, then reappear later. Because their primary purpose was plunder, they avoided confrontation with naval forces unless the ships were carrying treasure (as Spanish men-of-war often were), the pirates significantly outmatched them (which was seldom the case), or they had no choice. They attacked either as guerrillas or as conventional forces as the situation demanded. Because their goal was plunder, they could attack when and often where they chose.

CHANGES IN SMALL-SCALE WARFARE AT SEA

By the early seventeenth century, the frigate had begun to replace other ship types, and by the mid- to late-seventeenth century had replaced them. This was not the frigate we are all familiar with from C. S. Forester's *Hornblower* series and similar novels. That frigate was a class of light warship used for cruising and scouting, among other missions. In the seventeenth century, however, the frigate was a broad term for the general type of man-of-war, sleeker and lower than the galleon, of almost any size and armament. Typically, it retained the raised quarterdeck and forecastle, and sometimes a poop as well, and had at least one deck that ran the full length of the ship. Smaller frigates, often classified as sixth rates in the English navy, were light, fast, reasonably well armed with ten to twenty great guns and usually a number of swivels, and often carried oars, sometimes referred to as sweeps, for rowing. Originally developed as a privateer, by all accounts in the Netherlands, then further developed as a cruiser against pirates and privateers, the light frigate was put to good use by pirates, privateers, and various pirate hunters, including naval cruisers. In the seventeenth and early eighteenth centuries, a small number of "galley frigates" were developed by several nations. Rather than placing the oars between gunports, and thus between guns, these ships had an entire deck devoted to oars, with few if any great guns mounted here. The noted HMS *Charles Galley* and HMS *James Galley* of the seventeenth century, Captain Kidd's *Adventure Galley*, and a class of early-eighteenth-century English sixth rates of the HMS *Blandford* type (including the pirate hunter HMS *Greyhound*) were all galley frigates. Other ships were used as rovers and pirate hunters as well. The fluyt or *urca* was a common merchantman occasionally used as a warship, and some round-bellied merchantmen were converted for use by pirates or pirate hunters.[12]

More often, though, rovers used smaller vessels, typically swift, weatherly (did not drift off course as much as other vessels), shallow drafted, and often fore-and-aft rigged. Rovers needed speed for overtaking their prey, shallow draft, and, preferably, a fore-and-aft rig to escape from their hunters. For these purposes, the Caribbean sea rover used the dugout canoe; the *pira-*

gua or *periagua*, a larger version of the canoe and capable of both sail and oar; the *tartana* or tarteen, a lateen-rigged one- or two-mast vessel; various two-mast vessels such as the brigantine; the *barcalonga*, a swift oared vessel carrying one or two lug sails, and the *barque longue*, a similar French vessel; and the sloop, a swift single-mast fore-and-aft-rigged vessel with two or three headsails.[13] The characteristically shallow draft of these vessels drove some local Caribbean governors to build various forms of "half-galleys" or "periagers"—large oared vessels with one or two masts, a large complement of men, and often mounted with a great gun in the bow and swivels along the rails—in order to pursue rovers in shoal waters. The "half-galley" or large "periager," if well armed and manned, seemed the obvious solution to the nuisance of easily rowed, shallow-drafted sea-roving vessels. An English half-galley almost captured Spanish *guarda costa* and pirate Juan Corso, who often himself used piraguas or half-galleys for his roving.[14] The light frigate was also suitable for tracking and attacking similar and smaller pirate vessels, including half-galleys, but when pirates graduated to larger vessels, fourth and fifth rates were needed to engage them.[15] Unfortunately, no matter the vessel used, the pirates had to be found first.

Naval gunnery had worked the kinks out of cast brass and iron muzzle-loading and reached a form of gun and carriage that would last, with a few changes, until the advent of the large pivot-mounted guns of the nineteenth century. As mentioned earlier, gun carriages of this period were invariably "bed" carriages on wheels called "trucks"; the "truck and axle" carriage, in which axles replaced the solid bed, would not become common until the mid-eighteenth century. By the latter half of the seventeenth century, guns were typically reloaded inboard, although there were a few exceptions to this practice, most notably among the Spanish in the South Sea, who loaded their guns outboard from platforms, leaving the loaders vulnerable to musketry and case shot.[16] A period account of an encounter in 1686 with five pirate ships noted that "their men lading their great guns wth out board (as is ye custom of these West India Gunn^r Pyrates) were cut of as fast as they appeared to doe their duty, and this was ye reason they fired but few great guns when they bore down on us for wch wee are beholden unto o^r small firearmes."[17] This does not suggest that gunners stood on outboard platforms and loaded as William Dampier scornfully reported some South Sea Spaniards did (if pirate gunners did this, he would not have disdained the Spanish for doing it), but rather that they probably loaded with their ports open. The reason these French pirates, reportedly from the Caribbean, loaded this way is unknown.[18]

Guns were loaded with powder cartridges and a variety of shot similar to that noted in chapter 8, primed with loose powder, and fired with a "slow match" attached to a linstock. The need for great guns was now well understood, and even the crew that intended to retreat to closed quarters understood that effective gunnery was a necessary part of this tactic, if only to delay the enemy while closed quarters were prepared and inflict damage upon him as he boarded. Swivel guns, both breech- and muzzle-loading, were common, and in some cases numbered as many or more as the great guns.[19]

Just as important to the rover was the flintlock musket, often of a very long-barreled, club-butted form referred to as a "buccaneer gun" or *fusil boucanier*. This weapon, not the cutlass or pistol, was the principal arm of the Caribbean rover (with the possible exception of the early eighteenth century pirate), and for that matter, of sea rovers in general at this time. Its principal virtues were its ease and speed of loading and its lack of a match to give away one's position at night by its burning end, or day or night by its smell. The buccaneer gun was believed to have had a longer range as well. However, among the Spanish, the matchlock musket in both light (*arcabuce*) and heavy (*mosquet*) forms remained the principal long arm for most of the period. Musketry had become a significant part of the naval action between ships and was often the principal tactic of rovers who lacked great guns. Given that vessels often engaged with great guns at "half-musket shot" (roughly 350 to 400 feet), this was within the effective range of a musket, making it an excellent associated weapon and tactic.[20]

Boarding remained a viable tactic. It was popular among rovers, for it spared the prize and was often necessary for the pirate hunters' success. Boarding arms remained much the same as in the previous century. The cutlass, a fairly heavy short-bladed sword with a straight or slightly curved blade, was now the common blade at sea, although others were used as well, including the rapier among the Spanish and Portuguese. Pistols, now typically flintlocks or miquelet locks, were more effective than in the past and were a principal boarding arm. Notably, the early eighteenth century Anglo-American pirates displayed them from lengths of silk hung from the neck, giving the impression that they were their principal arms. And perhaps they were, given that nearly all of their targets were typically weak merchantmen who seldom put up a fight. Boarding pikes were still in use, primarily as a defensive weapon. The blunderbuss—a short-barreled "scattergun"—was common, but as a defensive weapon against boarders. The boarding ax was an offensive weapon, intended primarily to breach closed quarters by cutting holes in the deck, into which grenades and other fireworks would be thrown to burn, kill, and flush out the adversary. It also served as a directly offensive weapon as well—for splitting skulls, that is, and otherwise inflicting serious injury—in boarding actions. The fire-pike, crossbow, and similar sixteenth-century arms had disappeared by the mid-seventeenth century, although the fire-pike was still mentioned in some seventeenth-century gunnery manuals based on earlier editions.[21]

Grenades and fireworks remained much as they had been. They ranged from cast iron grenades to clay pots filled with gunpowder and sometimes with an iron grenade inside as well. Firepots intended to set fire to ships were still in use. "Stinkpots"—incendiaries that produced a suffocating smoke and stench—were common as well, in particular when flushing defenders from closed quarters. Powder chests were routinely used by merchantmen in self-defense. Some ships, Spanish ones in particular, hoisted barrels or jars of powder, with lighted matches attached, to the ends of the lower yard-arms, intending to drop them on the deck of an enemy as it came alongside. Boarding nets remained common, and the fight from "closed quarters" reached a sophisticated level.[22]

NAVY VERSUS PIRATE

In the best of circumstances, finding pirates was not easy. Naval vessels were limited in number, typically over tasked, and quite often under manned, under funded, under provisioned, and in ill repair. Some commanders were more interested in lining their pockets via trade in slaves and other goods than in pirate hunting and preferred to stay in port unless a voyage could be tied to personal profit.[23] "Capᵗ Georg lyes here in harbour twould be more for the Service of the Country that he were out Cruising upon the Coasts: but that is the Presidents busines," complained colonial agent Edward Randolph about a man-of-war's inactivity.[24] Many naval commanders were known for their high-handedness and often refused to submit to the wishes of local governors. A 1693 document instructed the Jamaica agent to ensure that "what frigates are sent hither may be under the direction and command of the governor residing here, and no other person in America, otherwise their majesties service will be obstructed for want of a good correspondence and fit directions."[25]

On a strictly tactical level, many of the vessels sent to protect against pirates and other rovers were inappropriate. Fourth- and fifth-rate ships were simply too large to venture into shallow waters and too slow to overtake a sloop or swift light frigate. However, they were necessary to deal with the larger pirate ships, some of which mounted thirty or more great guns. Pirate victims and hunters were quick to recognize the need for appropriate vessels to deal with the Caribbean rover and his wide-ranging offspring, but governments were often slow to provide them. Even so, naval vessels had some notable successes against pirates.

In general, naval vessels were arrayed against pirates either as part of a flotilla that patrolled for pirates and reacted to their presence as necessary or stationed as a coast guard both to deter pirates and to pursue them. The former was largely a Spanish practice and existed primarily in the form of the Armada de Barlovento, while the latter was common among all nations. Patrolling, however, was often a futile exercise unless tied to the comings and goings of merchantmen, as Charles Johnson advised in the early eighteenth century, complaining of the failure of English men-of-war to do so: "Therefore, I say, if the men-of-war take the same track, the Pirates must unavoidably fall into their mouths or be frighted away, for where the game is, there will the vermin be."[26] But the areas to be patrolled were large. In the case of the Armada de Barlovento, its established route was predictable, and thus it was easily avoided unless it changed its route or its timing: "The Privateers keep out of their way, having always Intelligence where they are."[27] In the case of guard ships, many were too slow, too deep drafted, or not in condition to set sail immediately. However, patrolling based on good intelligence could be productive. The sack of Veracruz by filibusters and buccaneers in 1683 spurred the Armada de Barlovento into retaliatory action, for example. Over the course of a deliberate, focused cruise, the Armada captured six purported pirate vessels and 110 purported pirates.[28]

There were two primary means of locating and attacking pirates. First was to find and attack them at sea, an easy proposition only in novels and motion pictures. The open sea was too large and was not in fact even considered as a place to seek pirates, or anyone else for that matter. Coastal routes, common routes among the islands, and common landfalls were better pickings, especially when matched with the sailings of merchantmen, but searches were often fruitless without good intelligence. The fact remained that the second means of locating and attacking pirates—catching them at anchor or while careening—was far more effective and far more common.

1. The construction of the *Argo*, the first named pirate hunting ship. Athena, the patron goddess, is on the left; Typhis, the pilot, is in the center; and Argo, the shipwright, is on the right. The *Argo* was a fifty-oared "Homeric" galley. (Photograph by Marie-Lan Nguyen of a Roman bas-relief in the Townley Collection, British Museum.)

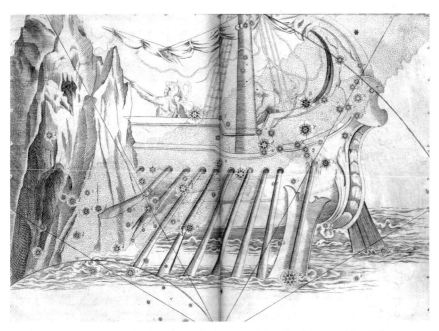

2. The enormous constellation *Argo Navis*, named for the famous ship of Jason and Argo. Today, it has been broken into four: *Carina*, *Puppis*, *Vela*, and *Pyxis* (*Keel, Poop, Sail*, and *Compass*). *Volans* and *Columba* (*Flying Fish* and *Dove*) are associated with the ship. (From Bayer's *Uranometria*, 1661. US Naval Observatory image.)

3. The defeat of the invading Sea Peoples by the forces of Ramses III in the 12th century BC, from a bas-relief at Medinet Habu. The illustration probably accurately depicts what must have been the organized chaos of close battle at sea in this period. (From George Rawlinson's *Ancient Egypt*, 1902.)

4. Assyrian warship circa 700 BC, probably manned by Phoenicians. Sennacherib used these biremes in an attack on sea-roving peoples in the Persian Gulf. Note the ram at the bow and the shields arranged for protection. (Photograph of a bas-relief in the British Museum.)

5. Francis Drake's *Golden Hinde* engaging the largely unarmed Spanish treasure ship *Nuestra Señora de la Concepción*, known by her crew as *Cacafuego* (*Shitfire*), in the unprotected South Sea. Overconfidence is a common flaw in any defense. (From a published engraving by Levinus Hulsius, 1626.)

6. Sketch by an English spy of a Spanish "*gallizabra*" designed to transport treasure. Defensive measures include a half-dozen bow and stern chasers each and sickles at the yard arms for cutting enemy rigging. A note indicates that musketeers were placed at the ship's beak. (From a plate in *Drake and the Tudor Navy* by Julian S. Corbett, 1898, of an original 16th century drawing.)

7. Buccaneers attacking a Spanish town in the late seventeenth century. The plate illustrates many of the common weapons and tactics, as well as the chaos of pirates attempting to storm the walls of a town. (From Esquemelin's *De Americaensche Zee-Roovers*, 1678.)

8. The Castillo de San Marcos at St. Augustine, Florida. Fortifications were a typical, if not always successful, means of defending against sea rovers. Filibuster captain Nicolas Brigaut was put to death here in 1686; his crew had been killed at nearby Matanzas. (National Parks Service photograph.)

9. Henry Morgan attacking the Armada de Barlovento at Lake Maracaibo in 1669 after it trapped him there. The Armada, which suffered significant losses during the engagement, was tasked with protecting Spanish shipping and cities in the Caribbean. (From Esquemelin's *Buccaneers of America*, 1684. Image from a 1911 edition.)

10. A seventeenth-century ship on fire. Although not a contemporary illustration, the painting conveys a good sense of the advantages of a large vessel with high sides over a small vessel. ("The Burning Ship" by Howard Pyle in *Collier's Magazine*, 1904.)

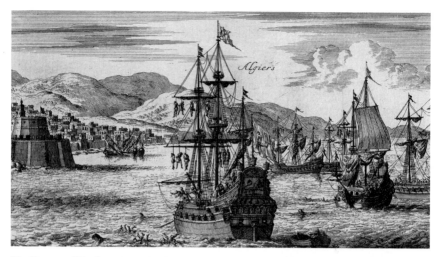

11. Captured Barbary corsairs hanged from the yardarm or bound and thrown into the sea alive at Algiers on the order of Admiral "Moy" Lambert, commander of a Dutch flotilla in 1624, in response to the pasha's refusal to sign a new treaty and release ships and prisoners. (From an illustration by Jan Luyken in *Historie van Barbaryen en des Zelfs zee-roovers* by Père Pierre Dan, 1684.)

12. The young U.S. Navy bombards Tripoli during the war with the Barbary corsairs. Attacking sea rover bases was a common tactic. (From a Currier and Ives print circa 1846. Library of Congress.)

13. The burning of the captured USS *Philadelphia* in Tripoli harbor by a U.S. Navy personnel under the command of Stephen Decatur. The action would be termed as a special operation today. (Engraving by John b. Guerrazzi, 1805. Library of Congress.)

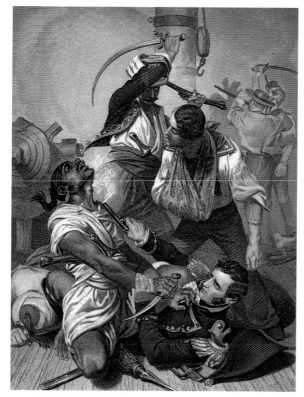

14. Stephen Decatur and members of his crew in hand-to-hand combat with Barbary corsairs. (From an oft-published engraving, after a painting by Alonzo Chappel. This late-nineteenth-century copy was taken from *Our Country* by Felix O. C. Darley. Author's collection.)

15. HMS *Opossum* and a fleet of Chinese junks rendezvous in preparation for an attack on Chinese pirates. Note the difference in naval technology; the local vessels are sail powered, while the British vessel is steam powered and uses modern artillery. (From a drawing in the *Illustrated London News*, 1865. Author's collection.)

16. Boats from the HMS *Medea* attacking Chinese pirate junks at anchor. Using boats to attack anchored vessels, either by surprise or by outright assault, was a common tactic in the age of sail and remains one today. (From a drawing in the *Illustrated London News*, 1849. Author's collection.)

17. Boats of the HMS *Racehorse* in hot pursuit under sail and oar of Chinese pirates. Attacks by small craft on larger armed craft typically require large numbers of attackers and overwhelming firepower, even if from small arms. (From a drawing in the *Illustrated London News*, 1855. Author's collection.)

18. Malay "pirates" chasing an armed boat from the pirate hunting *Royalist*. Pirate hunters were not only predators, but at times prey. (From a drawing in the *Illustrated London News*, 1868. Author's collection.)

19. Destruction of the Confederate privateer *Petrel* by the frigate USS *St. Lawrence* in 1861. The *Petrel* was sunk on her first day out of harbor. Engagements between vessels propelled solely by sail or by sail and oar were in their final days. (From an engraving by R. Hinshelwood after a painting by Paul Manzoni. Library of Congress.)

20. The engagement off Cherbourg, France, between the sloop-of-war USS *Kearsarge* and the commerce raider CSS *Alabama* in 1864. The *Kearsarge* sank the *Alabama.* Note the relatively long range and the use of steam alone for propulsion in the battle. (From a popular 19th century illustration, this copy from an 1887 history book. Author's collection.)

21. Boats from the HMS *Vigilant* burn Arab "war dhows" belonging to a local chief accused of piracy in the Persian Gulf in 1868. The gunboats in the illustration—*Clyde* and *Hugh Rose* of the Bombay Marine—had destroyed a local fort belonging to the accused pirate chief. (From an illustration in the *Illustrated London News*, November 28, 1868. Author's collection.)

22. A "Q-ship" or "mystery ship" destroys a U-boat during World War I after decoying it to the surface. (Reproduction of a drawing by Charles Pears, published 1918. Library of Congress.)

23. World War I U.S. Navy recruiting poster intended to evoke outrage over unrestricted submarine warfare and its effect on non-combatants. The comparison of submarine warfare to piracy was in many ways understandable. (Autolithograph by F. Brangwyn, A.R.A., for the U.S. Navy. Library of Congress.)

24. Coast guard cutter *Spencer* depth charging German *U-175* in 1943. The U-boat was forced to the surface, but the submarine sank before a boarding team was able recover its code machine and other intelligence. (U.S. Coast Guard photograph by Jack January, USCGR.)

25. Law enforcement maritime tactical operations team. Its missions include ship-boarding and hostage rescue. Similar forces are called upon to deal with piracy in much of the world. The rigid inflatable boat (RIB) and helicopter are typical means of insertion and ingress. (Photograph courtesy of the Lee County, Florida Sheriff's Department.)

26. Members of a law enforcement ship-boarding team climbing a containership amidships. The photograph illustrates the difficulty and danger for both pirates and anti-pirate forces in boarding a large vessel anywhere but at the stern. (Photograph courtesy of the Lee County, Florida Sheriff's Department.)

27. Somali pirates in the Gulf of Aden captured by a helicopter and VBSS (Visit, Board, Search, and Seizure) teams from the guided-missile cruiser USS *Vella Gulf*. (U.S. Navy photograph by MC2 Jason R. Zalasky, USN.)

28. The destroyer USS *Bainbridge* with cargo ship *Maersk Alabama*'s lifeboat in tow after the rescue of Capt. Richard Phillips. The amphibious assault ship USS *Boxer* is in the background. (U.S. Marine Corps photograph by Lance Cpl. Megan E. Sindelar, USMC.)

29. Suspected Somali pirates with a now-less-than-threatening mien. Compare with the adjacent Howard Pyle painting. The pirates are under the control of a USS *Gettysburg*/U.S. Coast Guard boarding team. (U.S. Navy photograph by MC1 Eric L. Beauregard, USN.)

30. Howard Pyle's illustration of captured pirates looking less than fierce. Compare with the photograph of captured suspected Somali pirates. ("Scene in the Town Jail" by Howard Pyle, in *Harper's Weekly*, December 16, 1893.)

31. Samuel Tully and John Dalton hanged for piracy and murder in 1812. Hanging was a common end for many pirates, but in fact, only Tully was hanged. Dalton was pardoned and is said to have become a preacher afterward. (From a broadside published in Boston in 1812. Library of Congress.)

32. Tonkin "pirate" about to be beheaded in Vietnam in the late nineteenth century. The term pirate was used not only for Chinese and Vietnamese pirates in the region, but also for local brigands and anti-French insurgents. (From *Nature's Wonderland* by J. Sterling Kingsley, 1893. Author's collection.)

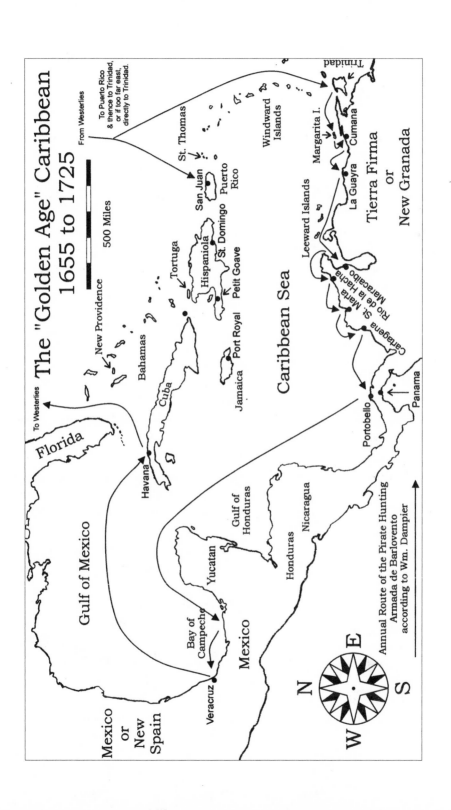

The "Golden Age" Caribbean
1655 to 1725

500 Miles

From Westerlies

To Puerto Rico
& thence to Trinidad,
or if too far east,
directly to Trinidad.

St. Thomas

San Juan   Puerto Rico

Tortuga

Hispaniola   St. Domingo

Petit Goave

New Providence

Bahamas

Cuba

Port Royal

Jamaica

Caribbean Sea

Windward Islands

Leeward Islands

Margarita I.

La Guayra   Cumana

Trinidad

Tierra Firma
or
New Granada

Cartagena   St. Maria

Rio de la Hacha

Maracaibo

Havana

To Westerlies

Florida

Gulf of Mexico

Mexico
or
New Spain

Bay of Campeche

Yucatan

Gulf of Honduras

Honduras

Nicaragua

Mexico

Veracruz

Portobello

Panama

N   E
W   S

Annual Route of the Pirate Hunting
Armada de Barlovento
according to Wm. Dampier

A third means—attacking their haunts or ports—was used on occasion, and sometimes even effectively. However, no matter how the pirate hunter intended to track down and destroy his prey, he needed intelligence regarding pirate locations or anticipated destinations, the speed to overtake the pirate (or at least to arrive at his location before he absconded), the men and arms to overwhelm him, and capable commanders to apply the appropriate leadership and tactics.

Once a pirate was located on the water, the first and most obvious tactic was to engage him. Although pirate successes against men-of-war are typically played up in popular histories, successes against English and French forces consisted primarily of escapes, and early-eighteenth-century pirates who engaged these forces were typically, although not always, defeated. Buccaneers and filibusters did have some notable successes against powerful Spanish men-of-war, but these men were veterans of numerous combats against well-defended towns and vessels, the latter including conventional men-of-war as well as local *armadillos*. They had been bloodied in battle, not only against amateurs but against professionals. But even they lost some of these battles.

Although fights at sea sometimes began with a rover lying by and waiting to engage a man-of-war, or even by chasing the man-of-war (usually by mistake), the pirate typically ran from confrontation with a stoutly manned and armed adversary, although there were notable exceptions. Often it was a running fight, the pirate attempting to escape the hunter. In 1723, two pirate sloops, the *Fancy* and the *Ranger* (commanded by pirates Edward Low and Charles Harris), gave chase to the HMS *Greyhound*, a twenty-gun galley-frigate. The *Greyhound* permitted the pirates to chase for two hours, ensuring that they would believe they had a merchantman on the run and were not about to "catch a Tartar." In the words of Charles Johnson, "The *Greyhound* . . . [then] stood towards the two sloops . . . both which hoisted their piratical colours and fired each a gun. When the *Greyhound* came within musket shot she hauled up her mainsail and clapped close upon a wind, to keep the Pirates from running to leeward, and then engaged. But when the rogues found who they had to deal with, they edged away under the man-of-war's stern and the *Greyhound* standing after them, they made a running fight for about two hours."[29]

The wind dying, the sloops got out their oars—but so did the *Greyhound*, which then closed on the pirates. "The Pirates hauled upon a wind to receive the man-of-war, and the fight was immediately renewed with a brisk fire on both sides, till the *Ranger's* mainyard was shot down. And the *Greyhound* pressing close upon the disabled ship, Low, in the other, thought fit to bear away and leave his consort a sacrifice to his enemy." Low was a notorious pirate, murderer, and violent abuser of innocent seamen, and by abandoning his consort proved himself the coward such men often are. Harris and his crew were captured and twenty-five were hanged. Low was eventually marooned by his crew, escaped to commit a few more piracies, and was finally set adrift in a small boat or sloop by his mutinous new crew after he murdered one of them while the man slept. He was soon taken up by a French vessel, tried, and hanged, although as late as 1726 there were inaccurate reports that he was still alive.[30]

The subject of engagement between two vessels is far too complex to describe adequately here. Suffice it that vessels usually either fought broadside to broadside, more or less slugging it out, or maneuvered to best advantage, ideally hoping to rake the adversary fore and aft, particularly stern to bow to cause the most damage to the enemy's vessel and men. Often the more powerful vessel would lie by or sail before the wind, battering the weaker vessel as it came within range.[31] But every fight was different, and the man-of-war did not always have the advantage. In 1699, the frigate *Essex Prize* of sixteen guns and seventy men engaged the pirate James, commanding the *Alexander* of twenty-six or more guns and 150 men, for "four hours and the frigate having lost 40 men was forced to bear away."[32] Of note is that the crew of the frigate, outnumbered two to one and outgunned three to two, managed to engage their enemy for four hours before withdrawing. The *Alexander*, formerly known as the *Providence Galley* or "Providence frigate," had once been commanded by pirate hunter William Rhett, who lost it to the pirate Hynde after "a very generous defence, but was outdone and taken by the said Pirate." Captain James succeeded to command after the crew mutinied.[33]

Many pirates ended their careers in battles far less glorious than the popular image would have it. Bartholomew Roberts, for example, is a popular figure among many fans and scholars of piracy due to his characteristic flair, his piratical accomplishments, and Charles Johnson's embellished prose. Roberts wore crimson damask clothing and a gold chain around his neck, drank tea, and captured more than four hundred vessels, all apparently merchantmen except for two small French coast guards and, reportedly, one stout man-of-war, and nearly all without a fight. He was not without his faults, though, even among pirates: one of his crew—despite a sword wound from Roberts—once "threw him over a gun and beat him handsomely" after he learned Roberts had killed a friend; he once foolishly set sail in an unprovisioned sloop in chase of a brigantine, and which he and his crew almost died of dehydration; and "in the latter part of his reign" his crew grew mutinous, for he "had run counter to in every project that opposed his own opinion."[34]

Similarly, his engagement with the HMS *Swallow* was anticlimactic at best. The *Swallow* located Roberts's consort, the *Ranger*, first. As the fifty-gun man-of-war approached, the pirate sallied forth to engage her, thinking her a slaver. After an engagement of an hour and a half, the *Ranger* struck, having suffered only twenty-six killed and wounded out of a crew of 123. A few of the crewmen reportedly tried to blow up the ship with a small amount of powder after surrender, but to no avail. Two days later, the *Swallow* found Roberts and his *Royal Fortune* of forty guns and 152 men. The man-of-war hoisted a French ensign until Roberts came within "Pistol Shot," then gave the pirate a broadside. Roberts's ship returned the compliment and ran. His crew, "drunk, passively courageous, unfit for service," surrendered after three hours of "a running Fight, while only our chace Guns could play upon them, and struck presently when our Broadside reached, without the least Damage done to us," even though the pirates had lost only three of their more than 150. Roberts was killed by a grapeshot to the throat. The *Royal Fortune*'s mizzen-topmast and mainmast were shot "by the board"—shot down, that is. Notwithstanding the popular image of the courage and fighting prowess of the early-eighteenth-century Anglo-American pirates, the *Swallow*'s surgeon, John Atkins, summed it thus: "[U]p went the black Flag, and down their Courage." In spite of their oaths to blow up their ship rather than be captured, none did, although it is said that a few tried. Charles Johnson pointed out rather caustically that there was nothing to prevent the pirates from taking their own lives, if indeed they were so inclined. Only two pirates are on record as having killed themselves to avoid capture in this period. Each shot himself in the head with a pistol.[35]

Pirates at anchor could be attacked with great guns or, if they could not be approached within effective range of great guns, with ship's boats. Careening was an ideal time to catch a pirate, for his ship could be destroyed. Capturing the pirate crew would require an expedition ashore, however, which in turn required a fairly large force. The best documented example is the surprise of Joseph Bannister's *Golden Fleece* of thirty-six guns and Pierre Lagarde's small frigate *La Chevale* while careening at Port Samana on Hispaniola in 1687. Both men were pirates, Banister somewhat of a novice albeit a quick study, Lagarde a well-known filibuster and pirate. Bannister was best known for escaping Port Royal under a cannonade from the port's stout fortifications and for picking up the filibuster DuChesne ("Duchean") at Jamaica after the English captured his ship.[36] Having intelligence that the vessels were being careened, a process that could take from several days to several weeks, Governor Hender Molesworth of Jamaica dispatched the sixth-rate frigates *Falcon* and *Drake*. "Now they [the pirates] having hal'd ashore their guns on the island, and fortyfied themselves, they obstinatly fier at His Majestie's frigets without shewing any colours. And soe they continued for two days together with all boldness imaginable, in which time the Faulcon and Drake continued fiering at Banister's ship with the cannons, by which means they tore hir all to pieces, and uterly stopped hir forever putting to sea again."[37]

Bannister and Lagarde had built two batteries (one of six guns, the other of ten guns) yet were unable to deter the frigates, which anchored, set up "springs" to bring their broadsides to bear, and pounded the pirates from "musket shot" range, roughly seven to eight hundred feet.[38] The action left the frigates unable to engage any other pirates until they returned to port: "In the action against Banister Captains Sprag [Spragge] and Talbot spent nearly all their powder. Sprag had only one round left and Talbot not more than eight or nine."[39] Neither pirate captain was captured during the engagement, unfortunately, and even after their ships were destroyed, their crews fired muskets as parting, if desultory, shots. Bannister was soon pursued relentlessly to the Mosquito Coast, where Moskito Indians turned him over, leaving him "and three of his consorts hanging at his [Captain Spragge's] yard-arm, a spectacle of great satisfaction to all good people and of terror to the favourers of pirates, the manner of his punishment being that which will most discourage others, which was the reason why I empowered Captain Spragge to inflict it."[40]

Other pirates were captured or killed in this manner of attacking them where they could not flee. Blackbeard and his crew, for example, were trapped and attacked after boarding in Okracoke Inlet by a party under Lt. Robert Maynard. Notwithstanding Blackbeard and crew's reputation as terrifying fighters, fifteen of them (eleven in Maynard's account) were unable to defeat an attacking party composed of thirteen naval seamen and officers whose vessel Blackbeard boarded.[41] Blackbeard was killed and decapitated, his head preserved as a prize and warning. But pirate hunters were not always successful when they had put their adversaries between "the sword and the wall," as the Spanish proverb goes. Roughly half a century earlier, the Armada de Barlovento trapped Henry Morgan and his buccaneer flotilla at Maracaibo. This was the first encounter of the Armada against the rovers it was intended to combat, but the result was the escape of Morgan, the destruction of three ships of the armada, and the loss of more than 130 Spanish sailors and soldiers. It was more than an embarrassing defeat for the Spanish: it was a disaster.[42]

Men-of-war attacked pirate bases as well, although the heavily fortified Spanish cites, often used as bases by Spanish pirates, were not attacked in retaliation for piracy, even if attackers claimed otherwise. However, the French considered destroying Santiago de Cuba in retaliation for the piracies of Spanish *guarda costa* Juan Corso and also used Corso as an excuse to issue commissions against the Spanish.[43] English attacks on pirate bases were intended to either destroy their vessels and small fortifications or, in the case of Governor Woodes Rogers and New Providence Island, permanently occupy it and thus prevent its use by pirates. Spanish attacks on the English and French roving bases, as well as on small colonies and habitations which might provide support for rovers, were typically brutal plundering assaults, although the same was true of sea rover attacks on Spanish possessions. From the mid- to late-seventeenth century, the Spanish attacked the sea rover bases of Old Providence and New Providence, Tortuga, and Petit Goave, the small nests at Anguilla, Tortola, Samana, and Vieques, and the logwood cutting camps at Campeche. Often these attacks were made not by Spanish men-of-war but by privateers or *guardas costas*. Except in the case of Governor Rogers's occupation of New Providence, attacks on Caribbean sea-roving bases, logwood camps, and interloping habitations did little if anything to stem piratical depredations.

GUARDAS COSTAS AND PRIVATE MEN-OF-WAR
Most nations posted coast guards where pirates and interlopers were known to frequent, for example Campeche, the mouth of the Rio Santa Maria where buccaneers and filibusters usually went to make their way across the Isthmus of Darien, along the slave coast of Africa, and so on.[44] Spanish coast guards in the Golden Age were typically locally commissioned ships, although the coast guards of most nations were men-of-war. Local privateers were also commissioned as pirate hunters, although in the case of New World Spain, their mission was not merely privateering in time of war and pirate hunting at all times, but also intercepting interloping traders of other nations. Spain had a somewhat uncomfortable history with her privateers. Until the discovery of the New World, Spanish privateers, who were usually pirate hunters as

well, were often Vizcayans (Basques), well known for their maritime prowess, particularly that of warfare. As descendants of practitioners of guerrilla warfare against the Moors, they carried this mindset with them upon the sea. In 1498, Spain prohibited privateering but renewed it in 1521 as a "defensive instrument," although its view toward privateering in the Caribbean remained jaundiced.[45] Even after the startling increase in attacks on the towns and vessels of New World Spain in the mid-seventeenth century, it took Spain until 1674 to authorize the commissioning of New World privateers to attack pirates and interlopers, although in fact they had been authorized locally the year before, and perhaps before that.[46] Immediately, they constructed large well-armed, well-manned piraguas and used them most effectively on the coast of Campeche against interloping traders and logwood cutters.[47]

In 1666, Flemish investors sought to send privateers to the Caribbean to deal with buccaneers and filibusters, as did Vizcayan investors in 1669, but the crown refused, fearing they would smuggle goods and money back into Spain.[48] A period source notes that the "consequences of such a Toleration appearing to be no less mischievous than the evil they were to obviate."[49] Still, there are references to "Old Spain" privateers authorized as early as 1670 "against the English and French, and not to give quarter to any Jamaicans, or French that belong to Tortuga," for example.[50] In 1685, filibusters having sacked Veracruz and committed other depredations, Spain authorized the Armada de Vizcaínos, an armadillo of four ships, to attack pirates in the Caribbean, and so they did, even engaging the famous Laurens de Graff at one point.[51] But pirates were not the only prey they engaged.

And this was the problem. Pirate hunting was seldom profitable, and the Caribbean rovers usually fought vigorously when attacked and were known for their victories over Spanish men-of-war. Much easier pickings were to be had by attacking logwood cutters and interloping merchantmen, and indeed, this was part of the Spanish privateer's primary mission. And here the profit lay. But it was only a short leap to the assumption that all English, French, and even Dutch merchant vessels were interlopers, and thus to the practice of attacking under any pretense. Local Spanish privateers, *guardas costas*, and Vizcayan privateers attacked innocent shipping. "I have daily complaints of the Biscayans, who take all ships that they can overcome, carry them into Spanish ports, use the men barbarously, and at best make them slaves," wrote Jamaica governor Christopher Monck in 1688.[52] An English petition of 1678 claimed that England "by computation has lately lost 1,000 English mariners, in all probability murdered by the Spaniards at sea, for seventy sail of merchants are lately missing."[53]

But from the Spanish point of view, this was entirely understandable, even laudable; they were simply doing what was being done to them. But in the long run, it probably increased piracy against Spanish vessels and possessions, for it provided an excuse for men to take to privateering and piracy, and for English and French governors to support them. English efforts to have Spanish governors restrain their privateers and *guardas costas* were typically in vain, understandable when considering the Spanish point of view, in which their privateers were enforcing a ban on trading with Spanish colonies, preempting possible attacks, retaliating against previous attacks, and occasionally actually capturing pirates.

None of the foregoing is intended to suggest that Spanish *guardas costas* and privateers did not attack pirates or, in time of war, privateers. They did, often successfully. Many had a reputation for brutality, rivaling that of the worst English, French, and Dutch rovers. One brief example of Spanish pirate hunting deeds and bravado may suffice, that of the commander of the frigate *San Pedro y La Fama* in 1670:

> I, Captain Manuel Rivero Pardal, to the chief of the squadron of privateers in Jamaica. I am he who this year have done that which follows. I went on shore at the Caimanos, and burnt 20 houses, and fought with Captain Ary, and took from him a catch [ketch] laden with provisions and a canoe. And I am he who took Capt. Baines, and did carry the prize to Carthagena, and now am arrived to this coast, and have burnt it. And I come to seek General Morgan, with two ships of 20 guns, and having seen this, I crave he would come out upon the coast and seek me, that he might see the valour of the Spaniards. And because I had no time I did not come to the mouth of Port Royal to speak by word of mouth in the name of my King, whom God preserve.[54]

Local privateers and hired ships were often fitted out on short notice against rovers, with varying results:

> [The merchantman] was unfortunately taken by one Thompson a notorious pyrate within sight of Port Royal, and none of H.M. ships of war being then in harbour, the freighters and owners of that ship made application to me, to commission two sloops, which were then lying in har-

bour ready to sail, to goe in quest of the said pyrate, they promising at the same time part of whatever was recovered, as a reward beyond what H.M. had been pleased to promise in his Royal proclamation, to such who wou'd goe out in the said sloops on that service; I did thereupon grant two Commissions to the said vessels to continue in force for the space of two months, and no longer, and gave the Commanders thereof propper instructions, and took the usual security on like occasions for the due observance of them: and they were soon man'd and sayl'd the 26th Dec. in pursuit of the pyrate. But at the South West part of this Island they mett wth. two vessels, one of which upon their approach hoisted a blagg Flag at the topmasthead, and then the engagement began, the other proved to be a sloop the pyrate had lately taken: one of our vessels after an obstinate dispute was boarded and overcome by the pyrate, who threw vast numbers of powder flasks granado shells and stinkpots into her which killed and wounded several, and made others jump overboard, seventeen of which our other vessell took up, who inform'd them of the strength of the pyrate which so disheartned the men on board ye other vessell, the pyrate having a superior force, that they made the best of their way back to Port Royal. The pyrate by information proves to be a vessell from Trinidado on Cuba with 150 banditti of all nations.[55]

Local pirate hunters had the problems of volunteer crews who may or may not have had any real idea of what they were getting into and vessels whose armament was often inadequate against a pirate of significant force. Like many of the Spanish *armadillos*, they were often manned and fitted out in haste. Still, there were positive results. In 1689, the sloop *Mary*, commanded by Capt. Samuel Pease and commissioned by the government of Massachusetts, set sail with a crew of twenty to engage the pirates Pound and Hawkins. Thomas Pound was a former privateer and pirate hunter recently turned pirate, whose piracies to date were small time and largely limited to the theft of arms and provisions, there being little else of value aboard their prey. Not long before, Pound had commanded the *Mary* and before that had served as pilot on a privateering and pirate hunting cruise aboard the HMS *Rose*. Thomas Hawkins, though, deserted the expedition. One historian has suggested that "this piracy was sort of a miscarried political coup d'etat" associated with local political turmoil. However, given the testimony that Pound, Hawkins, and crew intended to sail for the West Indies; the crew was composed of local pirates as well as forced men; and Pound had engaged in the piracy of provisioning typical of the start of a roving voyage, Pound's purpose was almost certainly piratical, not political.[56]

Having intelligence that the pirates lay at Tarpaulin Cove, Massachusetts, the *Mary* steered her course accordingly, found Pound's vessel, and engaged it. "[A]fter we were all ready we espied a Sloop ahead of us, we made what Saile we could, and quickley came so neere, that we put out our Kings Jack, and o[r] Sloop Sailing so very well we quickly came within Shot, and o[r] Capt[n] ordered a great Gun to be fired thwart her fore foot, on that a man of theirs presently carryed up a Red flagg to the top of their maine mast." The *Mary*'s captain ordered the pirate to surrender, an order that was promptly declined. "Cap[t] Pounds standing on the quarter deck with his naked sword in his hand flourishing, said, come aboard, you Doggs, and I will strike you presently or words to y[t] purpose his men standing by him with their Guns in their hands on the Deck."

The engagement began, both sides firing quickly and repeatedly:

We still fired at them, and they at us as fast as they could loade & fire, after a little space we saw Pounds was shot, and gone off the deck. . . . wee many times called to them, telling them if they would yield to us we would give them good quarter, they utterly refusing to have it, saying ai yee dogs we will give you quarter[.] By and by, we still continued o[r] fight, having two of our men more wounded, at last our Capt[n] was much wounded, so that he went off the deck. The Lieu[t] quickly after ordered us to get all ready to board them which was readily done, wee layd them on bord presently, and at o[r] Entrance we found such of them that were not much wounded very resolute, but discharging o[r] Guns at them, we forthwith went to club it wth them and were forced to knock them downe with the but end of our muskets at last we queld them, killing foure, and wounding twelve, two remaining pretty well.[57]

Captain Pease, "shot in the Arme, and in the Side, and in the thigh," died of his wounds, but the pirates survived their wounds long enough to be tried for piracy and murder. Pound had been shot in the side and arm and had "Severall bones Taken oute." One of his crew had been shot through the jaw and similarly lost some bone. Another had "7 holes in his Arme," another was shot through the ear and "oute his Eye & Lost it," another through both legs, and others variously through the hand, arm, or head. Most of the pirates were tried, convicted, and sentenced to be hanged. Judge Samuel Sewall and the Rev. Cotton Mather, both of whom would soon play an ugly role in the Salem witch trials, visited and prayed with them. However, not long after their conviction, most had their sentences commuted, the Massachusetts elite showing a mercy toward those convicted of piracy they would not display two years later toward those convicted of witchcraft. But then, Massachusetts had a long history of favoritism toward pirates, the Puritan faith tending to take precedence over everything but business, which pirates contributed to handsomely. Both Hawkins and Pound were soon aboard the HMS *Rose* and took part in an engagement with a French privateer. Hawkins was killed in the action.[58]

In a manner similar to the destruction of Blackbeard, Col. William Rhett and a force of volunteers trapped and captured dilettante pirate and Barbadian planter Stede Bonnet and his crew after a brisk engagement of five hours, at which point "they stood for the Pirate to give the finishing stroke, and designed to go directly aboard him, which he prevented by sending a flag of truce." Bonnet surrendered, and he and his surviving crew were jailed. He soon escaped but was recaptured and hanged, along with most of his crew. Rhett had better luck this time than he had two decades earlier when he engaged the pirate Hynde.[59]

Of course, the best known instance of sending a privateer to hunt pirates, although in terms of success one of the most insignificant, is that of Capt. William Kidd and his commission to seek French merchantmen as well as Anglo-American pirates in the Indian Ocean and environs. Most readers know the basic story. Kidd was commissioned by a group of Whig investors and politicians to hunt pirates but failed to find any. He captured a merchantman but let it go free, believing its capture would not have held up in a prize court. His crew grew mutinous over the release of the ship, as well as over the lack of prizes in general, and Kidd killed his insubordinate gunner with a wooden bucket. Subsequently, Kidd and his crew attacked some merchant vessels and plundered others, including the Armenian merchant ship *Quedah Merchant*, a rich prize commanded by an English captain. Kidd believed the ship's French passes—documents instructing French privateers and men-of-war not to plunder it—made it a legitimate prize. Soon after, most of his crew deserted to the noted pirate Robert Culliford. Kidd returned to New England and was arrested, sent to England, tried, convicted of murder and three counts of piracy, and hanged—twice, actually, in the last circumstance, for the rope broke the first time. As a pirate hunter, Kidd was a complete failure.[60]

Apologists for Kidd consider him a scapegoat for Whig politicians, private investors in the voyage, and East India traders, and indeed there is little doubt he was. The French passes that might have acquitted him on two charges of piracy disappeared before the trial. Unfortunately, the passes would not have helped him on the charge of murder, although there is a viable argument that the charge should have been manslaughter, of which he was certainly guilty, if not of murder. Further, there is little doubt that Kidd did attempt piracy and probably committed it as well, although privateers often got away with such borderline excesses in pursuit of plunder. The real question is whether he would have been hanged had there not been extraordinary political pressure to make an example of him. In the seventeenth and eighteenth centuries, many in England were hanged for far less while others, although they did far worse, were not.[61]

It is easy to accuse Kidd of poor leadership, and there are strong indications that he was indeed a poor commander on this voyage. But his circumstances were difficult, perhaps even impossible. Any crew, other than one under the strict discipline of a man-of-war, might have been tempted to turn pirate halfway around the world aboard a heavily armed warship amidst a sea of treasure on a largely unprofitable cruise in a region known for notoriously successful piracy. Kidd's voyage held a lesson: do not send your own private men-of-war to hunt your own pirates, except in local waters where you can rein them in. Privateers were well known for their excesses, and privateering was considered by many to be but thinly cloaked piracy. Pirate-hunting privateers worked for the Spanish in the New World, for the pirates they sought were nearly always their enemies, political or religious. Many were *perros ingles* (English dogs), and *Luteranos* (Lutherans; Protestants, that is) at that. But there were notoriously routine excesses among them as well. Just as egregious, or more so, were the excesses of the Biscayners sent from Spain to the New World to check piracy. English colonial privateers were often successful against local pirates, but in this case, the privateers were usually commissioned in response to an immediate local threat. Their purpose was duty and defense, not profit by plunder. In nearly every case, where the ultimate purpose was profit, sending a private man-of-war to deal with a pirate led to excesses ranging from criminal abuse of authority to outright piracy.

SETTING A THIEF TO CATCH A THIEF

Kidd was a former privateer commissioned as a privateer and pirate hunter, not a former pirate commissioned as one, which was actually a popular notion of pirate hunting. The English, for example, recruited buccaneer John Coxon to clear out English logwood cutters, many of them buccaneers, and later commissioned him to recruit the pirate Jan Willems, called Yanky, to hunt the pirate Jean Hamlin. The latter mission failed: Yanky did not accept the offer and Hamlin was never captured. The English later recruited Captain Jeremiah Conway, a buccaneer, to capture Coxon when he turned to piracy again, but he failed. The English even briefly entertained an overture by famous filibuster Laurens de Graff, but the French soon rescinded their repression of their filibusters and the Dutch rover remained in the service of France. Often the results of sending a pirate to hunt a pirate were about as one might expect: Captain Morris (Morrice), a noted buccaneer who commanded the frigate *Lilly*, "pretended to be sent against [the pirate] Yellows . . . yet never attempted to pursue him . . . but has laden his frigate with logwood."[62]

The Spanish typically welcomed foreign rovers into their service, first requiring them to become Catholics in accordance with Spanish law. These foreign rovers knew the ways of the English buccaneers, French filibusters, and Dutch freebooters, and so could be of great service. Dutch rovers Jan Erasmus Reyning and his lieutenant, Jelles de Lecat (called Yellows by the English), went into Spanish service when attacks on the Spanish were proscribed after the sack of Panama. Yellows captured a large number of English logwood cutters and Dutch and English trading vessels at Campeche. Together, Yellows, Reyning, the renegade Irishman Philip Fitzgerald, and several Spanish *guardas costas* captured more than forty English and Dutch ships at Campeche. Reyning ("John Erasmus" in English accounts) had been originally dispatched by the English as a pirate hunter to bring Yellows in, for Yellows had been using Reyning's ship to attack the Spanish. Instead, Reyning joined Yellows, and the two became renegades, at least from the English point of view.[63]

From this same point of view, one of the most notorious renegade pirate hunters, perhaps second only to Yellows, was John Beare. Originally commissioned by the governor of Nevis to hunt pirates and "Indians" (Caribs), he captured a purported Spanish pirate while hunting for the Spaniards who had sacked Tortola, then subsequently attacked some English vessels. Proclaimed as a pirate, he took his girlfriend, the "daughter of a rum-punch-woman of Port Royal" whom he would keep on his ship dressed in "man's apparel," and fled to Havana, where he accepted Spanish service and married his "strumpet," pretending she was the daughter of a noblewoman. Immediately, he began plundering English shipping and soon attacked Anguilla but was driven off. When the English allied with the Spanish during King William's War, Beare fled to the French at Petit Goave, accepted a commission, and continued to raid the English.[64] Overall, these renegades were ineffective as pirate hunters, for most of them spent more time plundering merchantmen than hunting pirates.

MERCHANTMAN VERSUS PIRATE

We must pity the poor merchant crewman of this period, for unless his was a stout ship with a large brave crew—and sometimes not even then—he was the most vulnerable of men at sea. All other vessels were fairly well protected, although not invulnerable, either by their size and armament or by the fleet they sailed with. Convoy had proved an effective method of protecting treasure fleets from pirates. In the case of the Spanish treasure fleets, no pirate of the period 1655 to 1725 ever captured either of them, or part of them, or even a single one of their treasure ships when sailing in convoy. For that matter, across the entire expanse of the seas, these rovers captured only a handful of ships, at best, that could truly be considered treasure ships. Unfortunately, Spanish ships that sailed independently of the fleets, whether local merchantmen or *navios de registro* ("registry" ships) that had permission to sail from Spain to the New World and back alone, were not so well protected, nor were the common merchantmen of other nations. The crews of these common merchantmen made up the majority of merchant seamen.

A merchantmen had only three choices if a rover "come up with the Chace": "fight, run a shore or surrender."[65] Most simply surrendered. Merchant crews were not paid enough to take the hard knocks of a fight with rovers who typically outnumbered, outsailed, and often outgunned them. Many feared retaliation if they fought back and lost.

The black flag or so-called "Jolly Roger"—not in use by Caribbean-associated pirates until after the end of Queen Anne's War (1703–1713)—was intended to inspire fear sufficient for surrender under reasonable quarter (if not always actually given), and typically did. Its usual device of a skull and crossed bones or similar symbols was not original among these pirates, having been used in fifteenth-century warfare and perhaps earlier, although it may have been designed independently by Golden Age rovers in a fashion akin to parallel evolution.[66] Barbary corsairs were known to use the symbol also, and as a pirate symbol, it may have originated with them. The device of "skull and bones" was a common one, displayed on everything from tomb-stones to memorial rings and watches, for example, as a reminder that life is fleeting, although displayed to an enemy it meant this more pointedly: "Your life will end if you don't surrender."[67] From the early seventeenth century under Gustavus Adolphus, the Pomeranian Cavalry of Sweden wore a skull and bones device in their fur caps, and a small gold skull and bones charm, believed to have belonged to a cavalry officer, was even recovered from the wreck of the Swedish man-of-war *Kronan*, which sank in action in 1676.[68] The earliest known use of the skull and crossed bones by Golden Age rovers is noted in a filibuster journal describing an attack on Acaponeta, Mexico, on December 6, 1688. It described a "red banner with a death's head above and two bones crossed below the head, in white, in the middle of the red" being raised in place of the white flag of France after they noticed Native Americans allied with the Spanish lying in ambush for them.[69] It is unknown whether these filibusters ever flew this flag at sea, but they were probably prepared to, if necessary, in the manner of the red banner described below.

A bit of prose from 1702 described Charon's banner on the River Styx, anticipating the black pirate flag: "There are no Men of War belonging to this River; nay, there's no Vessel but mine, no variety of Ensigns or Colours. Deaths Head and Marrow Bones, is the only Flag in a Sable Field."[70] Catalans defending Barcelona against a Franco-Spanish army in 1714 fought under a black flag with a death's head and defiantly placed it in a breach in the city's walls after repulsing an attack.[71] The black flag began to appear routinely as a "Golden Age" pirate banner in 1716.[72] Statements that it appeared in 1704 as the pirate John Quelch's flag incorrectly attribute the description of the pirate Harris's flag; Quelch did not fly a black flag, leaving 1700 as the earliest instance of the "Golden Age" pirate's black banner.[73] In 1723, the Boston *News-Letter* reported that Harris's crew referred to their flag as Old Roger; Johnson's *General History of the Pirates* noted that Bartholomew Roberts's crew referred to theirs as Jolly Roger in 1722; and a published let-ter by Capt. Richard Hawkins noted that the pirate Spriggs and his crew re-ferred to theirs also as Jolly Roger in 1724.[74] All three flags depicted a "Death" or "Anatomy"—both are terms for a full skeleton—and other devices, but not a skull and crossed bones. Roberts's flag also had the figure of a man holding a flaming sword. Spriggs's and Harris's flags were identical to Edward Low's, all having sailed together at times, and thus all three may have referred to their own flag as the Jolly Roger. Other pirates may have used the names as well, but from as few as two references has Jolly Roger become the common name for the black pirate flag of death's head and crossed bones.

We can probably thank *Treasure Island* as well for the term's popularity. Old Roger was a term for the devil, and Jolly Roger may derive from this, but almost certainly not from "*Joli Rouge*," of which there are no period references. Nor is there evidence to support fanciful theories that state that "Jolly Roger" derives from "Ali Raja" or the Medieval Knights Templar—wishful thinking does not count as evidence. Jolly Roger was also the main character in a popular song at the time—"Twangdillo" or "Jolly Roger Twangdillo"—whose lyrics describe a rich, lusty farmer working his way through a pack of female suitors, and whose name is probably related to period slang.[75] As early as 1714, and probably much earlier, "roger" was a term for a man's "yard" or penis, and "to roger" was to "bull or lie with a woman," purportedly because bulls were often named Roger.[76] Symbols often have multiple origins and multiple meanings. The black pirate flag may have been a combination symbol of "death, the devil, and domination," with a bit of gallows and sexual humor thrown in for good measure. After all, the language and image of domination is often sexual, and men in hazardous professions typically have a dark sense of humor. Put bluntly, pirates hoisting the grinning Jolly Roger were sending this message: "Surrender or be screwed."[77]

Throughout the period, if the prey did not strike (lower its colors and topsails in submission when threatened—whether by a warning shot, a verbal demand, a waved sword, or the black flag—the rover often hoisted the red flag or "bloody red banner," also known as the "*sans-quartier*" (no quarter) and "*pavillon de combat*" (battle flag), to indicate that no quarter would be given. The red flag was not invented by the Golden Age pirates but long preceded them and was often used by pirates, privateers, and some men-of-war, the latter most often in the sixteenth and seventeenth centuries. In 1721, one pirate hoisted the red flag first, then the black, after variously having shown white (French) then black colors: "The pirates immediately drew up in a line, struck their red, and hoisted a black flag, with a death's head in the centre, a powder horn over it, and two bones a-cross underneath."[78] Pirates, although not terrorists—terrorism requires a political or "public" motive, not a private one—had no qualms about inspiring abject fear, otherwise known as terror, as a means of easy victory.

The concept of the ship as a floating castle, with the crew retreating to closed quarters against a determined adversary, remained among merchantmen. The captain's apprentice on the East Indiaman *Bauden* in 1686 described a pirate attack near the Madeira Islands that was thwarted by closed quarters:

> [A]nd about eight or nine in the morning she came under our stern, ranging up our starboard quarter. Then our capt. ask'd, Where he was bound? He answer'd, Aboard us, the drummer beating a point of war. The captain told him, Win her, and have her. He thereupon boarded us and four or five hours, cutting our poop and ensign-staff; and his shot cut many of our shrouds. Our ship beig very much pester'd, we play'd but three or four guns; yet we beat his gunnel in, and made him put off, and lie upon the careen . . . So by the brave courage of our captain and men the pirate was forc'd to leave us.[79]

At nearly the same time and not far to the south was a similar engagement, and this time we have the pirate's account, one so similar that it might have been of the same fight (we certainly wish it had been):

> A degree south of the line we encountered a large English ship of fifty or sixty guns which was sailing to the East Indies. We boarded her, and were five or six glasses [two and a half or three hours] on her deck. They were entrenched in their closed quarters fore and aft. Among us they killed, as many on their deck as on ours, thirty-eight men, and the majority of the rest were wounded. We were obliged to cut the cable [holding the ships together] and retire with the disgrace of our desire to undertake this enterprise.[80]

But closed quarters were not always successful. Father Jean Baptiste Labat, who closely observed filibusters, described how capable they were at defeating closed quarters, particularly if merchant crews failed to implement them strictly and vigorously.[81] A Honduras ship or "Hulke"—an urca of seven hundred or more tons, often with a consort—was captured at least four times by buccaneers in spite of its high bulwarks, closed quarters, and the shower of grenades and other fireworks typically rained down upon attackers.[82] Again, the effective use of great guns was usually necessary to the success of closed quarters. Unfortunately, unless a merchantman could also sustain adequate small arms fire, as well as effectively use grenades and powder chests, pirates would be able to breach the closed quarters and attack the defenders within.

All too often, though, merchantmen refused to fight even when it was the best recourse. Fear, too, often reigned, and many vessels were unprepared for a real fight. A merchant commander needed not only a crew capable of following orders and handling arms, but also had to be able to lead the crew by the example of confidence, courage, ship-handling ability, and fighting skill. He needed to be able to inspire and encourage by word and deed. Many pirate vessels were small, with small crews and light armament, and could be withstood if the crew were willing and the captain stout and brave. Even strong roving vessels might be defended against, or at least outrun until nightfall when the prospects for escape increased. Merchant captain Edward Barlow of the thirty-six gun *Scepter*, whose excellent journal of seafaring life in the late seventeenth century was not published until the twentieth century, drove off Kidd and his *Adventure Galley* of thirty guns by putting on a brave show and being ready to back it up:

> And seeing the pirate come as near as he intended to come, being almost abreast of us, we presently hoisted our colours and let fly two or three guns at him well shotted . . . We fired at him as long as he was anything near, and judged did hit him with some of our shot . . . But having no mind to engage, as we drew near him he made sail again from us, doing so twice' and seeing us still follow him, at last set all his sails and away he went.[83]

In October 1686—a banner year for Caribbean pirate attacks among the east Atlantic islands—five French pirate ships attacked the English merchantman *Caesar* in the Azores. Using gunnery to great effect, the *Caesar* kept the pirates, "Ships of Burthern" which "could not have lesse than between 20 & 30 gunns each and [which were] full of men," at bay for five hours, after which the pirates "began to beare away to amend and repaier ye damage recieved from us." The *Caesar* escaped.[84]

An eighteenth-century manual of tactics for the merchantman had words for the merchant captain and crew who might doubt whether to fight or not:

> And when a Merchant Ship cannot otherwise well discharge herself, the Necessity of Fighting is evident; for no Man is so devoid of Reason as not to know, that it is his peculiar Interest to defend his Property, unless he will toil and labour for others, and like the Sheep patiently endure the Shearing of his Fleece. And it is certainly far more tolerable as

well as reputable to perish like the Bee in the Hive, than by a cowardly
Submission part with the Honey to every Drone, and consequently left to
starve for want of that he has been working for.[85]

In the case of pirates, a merchantman might be fighting for the lives of
its crew as well.

Unfortunately, once a crew had surrendered, submissiveness and cooperation were the best strategies to minimize injury to crews and even to a
vessel and goods that rovers had no need for. Some captured crews did occasionally rise up successfully against their captors, and sometimes, if rovers
did not plan on keeping the prize vessel, a merchant crew might try to cheat
them by hiding valuables, money in particular, or at least not providing information as to its existence. In 1681, buccaneers in the South Sea captured
the *Santo Rosario* with 670 pigs of silver aboard—a fortune. The buccaneers
"thought [it] was silver, found to the contrary," and left it behind. Only "one
was brought away to make Bullets; part of which we gave to a *Bristol* Man, being about a third part of a Pigg, when we came to Antego, and he sold it at
Bristol for 75 *l.* Sterl., for it was silver."[86]

PRIVATE MONEY AND DEVIOUS COMPLICITY

Then and now, the merchant's typical solution to a problem is to throw someone else's money at it. Governments are the first choice of funding, but when
they cannot provide all that private business needs, business must turn to
itself for solutions or, as some suggest, be silent. All merchant shipping companies prior to the mid-nineteenth century understood that they had to arm
their vessels, for it was impossible, except in the case of convoyed treasure
fleets, to protect the majority. In one instance, Spanish merchants in the
South Sea, fed up with three series of piratical incursions in less than a decade, pooled their funds and established the Armada del Nuestra Señora de
Guía in 1687.[87] Unfortunately, by this time, the major piratical incursions
were over, to be replaced by those of privateers two decades later.

The merchant had a few tricks up his sleeve as well. Spanish merchants
often bought stolen goods from rovers, and during attacks (and sometimes
even when surrendering), tried to negotiate terms that might be less costly,
both in terms of the direct loss of money, valuables, and goods, and of the destruction of property. Treachery was an occasional recourse, merchants and
local officials agreeing to ransom a town, then delaying until pirates could
be attacked. After all, even Cicero pointed out that "Tis no deceit to recede

from it [a promise to a pirate], tho' he had given his Oath for the performance: for we are not to look upon *Pirates* as *Open* and *Lawful* Enemies: but as the Common *Adversaries* of *Mankind*. For they are a sort of men with whom we ought to have neither *Faith*, nor *Oath* in common."[88] The consequences of failure, however, were often severe and could include the burning of the town, the beheading of prisoners, or both.

As in the case of the *Santo Rosario* silver, cheating pirates out of goods was another option, albeit a dangerous one if the merchant got caught. In 1679, John Coxon plundered the warehouses at Lake Izabal, southwest of the Bay of Amatique, Guatemala, of their indigo. As his crew was loading the chests, "a *Spanish* Gentleman, their Prisoner, knowing that there was a great deal more than they could carry away, desired them to take only such as belonged to the Merchants, (whose Marks he undertook to shew them) and to spare such as had the same Mark with those in that great Pile they were then entring upon; because, he said, those Chests belonged to the Ship-Captains, who following the Seas, as themselves did, he hoped they would . . . rather spare their Goods than the Merchants." Coxon complied, only to regret it later when they discovered that of the few "Ship-Captain" chests they did bring were filled with annatto, a more expensive red dye.[89]

At least one historian has argued that some pirate raids on small ports and towns were often "stylized" or "collusive," in that "defense was limited, damage contained, and honor satisfied," all in order that pirates might "milk, not kill, the cow" of minor Spanish ports.[90] If this was in fact the case, it was probably due more to the desire of rovers to limit their losses and waste as little time as possible over a petty target, and not specifically to preserve the cow, so to speak. Pirates generally treated small merchantmen in a similar manner, quickly plundering them and often letting them go. They simply were not worth any great effort or risk. Given the general rapacity of sea rovers, not to mention the tendency of many of them to live in the moment and pay little attention to the future, it is unlikely that they intended to preserve small ports so they could be attacked again. However, it is probably a given that small towns made a superficial and even "collusive" defense at best, if any, followed by an immediate surrender and cooperation in order to limit damage. It was in their best interest to do so.

DEFENDING AGAINST PIRATE ARMIES

Suffice it to say that Spanish forces in the New World were often poorly armed, had too few professional soldiers among them and even fewer combat veterans, and were typically unprepared for attack. Their most successful strategies were to defend from fortification (whether a stout castle or a simple barricade), attack from ambush, or both. Open battle was fraught with complications.

First, Spanish forces in the New World were not composed of well-armed, highly trained regulars, but primarily of a core of professionals backed by militias and volunteers of various armament and abilities. Perhaps the best Spanish soldier in the New World was the *lancero* or spearman, often an enslaved or free mulatto or black working man, armed with a long lance with which he was extraordinarily adept. But such men and associated tactics worked best from ambush in the field, not from fortification except at the moment of storming where their lances and spears could be used to advantage, and certainly not in open combat where sea-rover musketry would destroy them at long range. Second, open battle required a disciplined force capable of loading and firing effective volleys under duress. Volunteers and militias were generally poorly prepared to do this, much less to deal with an enemy who fired from cover and kept up a constant fire consisting of aimed shots at individual targets. Against fortifications, pirate tactics consisted primarily of engaging with accurate musket fire to suppress the enemy's fire, approaching under cover of fire to clear the ramparts or barricades with grenades, and closing and engaging the enemy first with musketry then hand-to-hand with pistol and cutlass. Spanish defenses against this tactic consisted primarily of great guns, muskets, and grenades and firepots. Occasionally, Native Americans armed with bow and arrow augmented Spanish forces.[91]

Some towns kept a constant armed watch, particularly the larger seaports. Even the French and English typically did so, largely out of concern for reprisals for peacetime piracies and for surprise attacks should war begin. For example, Dr. Hans Sloane noted that "One from *Tortuga* and *Petit-Guaves* [filibuster headquarters], told me that at this last place the *French* have about Thirty inhabitants keeping always good Guard for fear of the *Spaniards*."[92]

A journal entry from 1663 reveals the typical details of Spanish preparations when forewarned:

> This Mitchell also brought news that the Spaniards in Campeche had timely notice of the English designing on them from St. Jago; to prevent which they had sent their wives, children, and goods, to Merida, an inland town twenty leagues from Campeche; that they had 1500 men in

the town to oppose their landing, and had unrigged all the ships in the harbour, that they might not carry them away, and had hauled them on shore, and landed their guns on batteries; had sent one ship to windward and another to leeward, to give advice that no ships might come thither, and set watches along the sea coasts, to give intelligence of their approach.[93]

It was the best approach under the circumstances, but often it was not nearly enough. The effectiveness of pirate tactics, as well as the ineffectiveness or weaknesses, of Spanish defenses is proved by the dozens of cities, towns, and farms sacked by buccaneers and filibusters from 1655 to 1688.

COMPREHENSIVE MEANS

When all else failed, amnesty was a common inducement to pirates to end their illegitimate careers, although recidivism appears to have been fairly high. Inevitably and necessarily, amnesties were combined with other pirate-hunting methods, including naval engagement and the trial and hanging of captured pirates, for governments were unable to provide economic inducements sufficient to overshadow the potential booty to be gained from piracy. "[N]otwithstanding the proclamation, captain Morris Williams brought in a great prize with logwood, indigo, and silver, and several privateers went out," noted one seventeenth-century observer.[94] Some proclamations indirectly encouraged piracy: "[A]nd also a proclamation against the English cutting of any more logwood at [left blank] or the Bay of Campeche."[95]

Driving men out of occupations that were often a substitute for piracy merely exchanged one problem for another. Measures that were only partly effective—making piracy more difficult but failing to provide a lawful outlet for those inclined "go on the account"—encouraged pirates to venture into other regions—the South Sea and the Red Sea, for example. Rewards—land for example—were proposed at times, as were rewards for the capture of pirates, but neither seems to have done anything to diminish piracy. Nor did the occasional prosecution of officials and merchants complicit in piracy. Pressure from naval pursuit and the potential of trial and hanging, combined with amnesty for those willing to abandon the trade and denial of markets for stolen goods (difficult anywhere, anytime), worked best, particularly when there were other trades pirates could be induced or driven into, such as smuggling, local trading, logwood cutting, and turtle fishing. Perhaps the best effort came in 1718 with the appointment of former privateer Woodes Rogers as governor of the Bahamas, and thus of New Providence, with amnesty in one hand, deadly force in the other. Still, it would take seven years to suppress the Anglo-American pirates.

Many of the first generation of Caribbean Golden Age sea rovers retired after the sack of Panama, and many of the second shifted into government service or into piracy during the third and had moved on or passed away by the fourth. Of those who began their careers in the third, they shifted into privateering then piracy, if they were still around and had not found another trade, in the fourth.

For this last generation of the Golden Age rovers, they had nowhere to go as pirates. Men-of-war were dispatched against them, often successfully. Many of the more notorious pirate captains were captured and hanged along with their crews or were killed in battle. Association with pirates was proscribed, and finding buyers for pirate goods became difficult. The luster of piracy tarnished quickly for many in the face of reality, and many pirates grew weary and accepted amnesties or slipped quietly back into the mainstream. Perhaps most debilitating of all, there were no free ports to support them as St. Thomas had done late in the last century, nor were pirate efforts at establishing their own bases viable. New Providence was lost. The Madagascar pirate habitations were too distant and subject to their own problems, not the least of which was isolation and hostile inhabitants. The growth of colonies, combined with associated control of sea and shore, ensured that *significant* local pirate bases would not survive. Sea rovers must have bases of some sort for economic support and physical protection, and without them, piracy is doomed to fail. A few former pirates settled in various isolated locales, such as the Mosquito Coast and near Darien, but these were not sea-roving communities. In all, the lifestyle could not and did not sustain itself for long. The buccaneers and filibusters lasted forty to fifty years owing to enabling governments, but the true pirates of the black flag who followed in their wake lasted not even a decade.

But Caribbean piracy did not end here. It remained a serious risk to navigation until roughly 1830, although never again did it achieve anywhere near the level of the "Golden Age." Operating primarily from Cuba, Florida, and, at one point, Louisiana bayous, this piratical progeny was largely suppressed by naval and coast guard action; naval pirate-hunting tactics and merchantman defensive tactics remained unchanged.[96] With the exception of Jean Lafitte, none of these latter-day rovers ever matched the Golden Age rovers in renown, and none, not even Lafitte, in piratical accomplishment.[97] For the pirate hunter, perhaps this was in some ways a disappointment, given that the hunter is measured by his prey. But for the merchant captain, crew, and owners, it was without doubt a blessing.

11

From the Mediterranean
to the North Sea

The War Against Pirates and Corsairs, 1493–1830

In 1571, the struggle between the Ottoman Empire and several Christian maritime states and kingdoms—particularly those of the Holy League of Venice, the Vatican, and Spain—came to a head at the Battle of Lepanto, the last of the great naval engagements of galley versus galley. The Christian fleet was victorious. Given that sea roving—the trade of the corsair—had since antiquity been a significant form of naval warfare in the Mediterranean, it might be reasoned that the defeat of one half of the great corsairing enterprise would diminish sea roving in this region long abused by sea-going thieves, slavers, and murderers. But it did nothing of the sort. The Christian victory was a defensive one and left the corsairs of both sides in place. The Mediterranean remained politically and geographically ideal for sea roving and slave raiding, as it had been in the days before Lepanto when the brilliant Kheir-el-Din Barbarossa reigned supreme as both corsair and admiral—when to be a corsair was to be a prince, if only aboard one's own vessel.[1]

The region was dominated throughout the period by greed, political expansion and skullduggery, religious conflict, xenophobia, regionalism, nationalism, racism, and slavery, all of which bled into the sea and thus into sea roving. Yet paradoxically, probably due to trade, there was also a great mixing of peoples and transfer of knowledge. Hypocrisy, a not uncommon practice where there is ideological difference of opinion, was rampant. European Christians, for example, typically condemned Muslim slaves even though enslaved Africans and Native Americans. Busily expanding trade empires in the Mediterranean and across the seas, Europeans also condemned North Africans as mere thieves: "*Barbary* Corsairs being born Pirates, and not able to subsist by any other Means, it was the *Christians* Business to be always on

201

their Guard, even in Time of Peace," noted one observer, and another noted succinctly how "Pyracy indeed being their principall trade."[2]

But Christian pirates and privateers likewise wrought havoc on merchantmen of all states and faiths in peace as well as war, and Christians were ready to condemn other Christians as pirates: "I declared that I could not abide their Ambassador nor the whole race; for they are a pack of thieves and pirates, and ruin this country," noted Lorenzo Bernardo, the Venetian ambassador to Constantinople in a letter to the Doge regarding the English.[3] But Christians were not the only faith engaging in violent rivalry among its various peoples. In the early sixteenth century, North Africa was raided by Turkish corsairs and soldiers, many of them professional soldiers known as Janissaries; Aroudj Barbarossa, brother of Kheir-el-Din, sacked Muslim Algiers in 1516, for example.[4] The Muslim Turks were engaged in their own empire building.

In northern waters, mariners had to contend with conflict driven by nationalistic competition, plus Christian pirates and at times even Muslim corsairs. In the Mediterranean, the situation for mariners was similar but often far worse. One might have expected the Christian-Muslim conflict to have predominated, but in fact, Christian against Christian conflicts were just as severe.

In 1595, Richard Haselton was captured by Algerian corsairs, the fear of every Christian sea traveler coming true. He was beaten when captured, was sold into slavery, and spent five years as a galley slave but escaped when his galley wrecked. He fled to local Christians and soon was taken aboard a Genoese galley. But instead of liberation, he found himself reviled as a "Lutheran" and was sent to Majorca to face the Holy Spanish Inquisition. The issue of his arrest was both political and religious. When he asked why he was being held, he was told, "because the King hath wars with the Queen of England." He was imprisoned for a year, escaped, was captured, variously tortured (including by waterboard), escaped again, was recaptured by the Algerians and sent back to work as a galley slave, and was eventually ransomed with the help of an English merchant. His descriptions of his imprisonments and interrogations are filled with extreme religious rhetoric, as is the abusive language of his Christian captors. His Muslim captors seemed content to offer him freedom if he would convert and beat him when he was intractable or tried to escape.[5] By the seventeenth century, much of the conflict between Muslim kingdoms had settled down, and by the early eighteenth century, the overt religious conflict between Christians had likewise settled down—

but not the religious, political, and economic conflicts between Christian and Muslim, nor the political and economic conflicts between Christian and Christian.

Trade with the Mediterranean and between the Mediterranean and northern waters was extensive and as complex as it is today. Of English shipping alone in the first half of the sixteenth century, "Neither did our merchants onely employ their owne English shipping before mentioned, but sundry strangers also: as namely, Candiots, Raguseans, Sicilians, Genouezes, Venetian galliasses, Spanish and Portugale ships."[6] The English, like every other European nation doing business in the Mediterranean, did "traffique with Jewes, Turkes, and other forreiners," in cities ranging from Sicily to Cyprus, from Barutti to Tripoli.[7] Exports from the Mediterranean were many: "Silks, Chamlets, Rubarbe, Malmesies, Muskadels and other wines, sweete oyles, cotton wooll, Turkie carpets, Galles, Pepper, Cinamom, and some other spices, &c."[8] With such trade—added to the political and religious conflict of the period; the dozens of ports piratically inclined by virtue of tradition, means, and opportunity; and the thousands of underpaid mariners—piracy was certain, and thus also pirate hunting.

OF PIRATES AND CORSAIRS

England's long history of piracy from its own ports did not end until the seventeenth century. War with Spain was over in the early years of the century, and England had an enormous number of naval seaman and privateers left unemployed. Many turned pirate or renegade corsair. English Old World piracy was briefly in the midst of another Golden Age, rivaling that of the fifteenth century. John Smith, famous in the history of the founding of Jamestown, Virginia, the first English colony to survive in America, was once captured by a French pirate and served aboard involuntarily, "to manage their fights against the Spaniards, and bee a Prisoner when they tooke any English."[9] Smith described well the reasons for English seamen turning to piracy:

> After the death of our most gracious Queene Elizabeth, of blessed memory, our Royall King James, who from his infancie had reigned in peace with all Nations; had no imployment for those men of warre, so that those that were rich rested with that they had; those that were poore and had nothing but from hand to mouth, turned Pirats; some, because they became sleighted of those for whom they had got much wealth; some, for

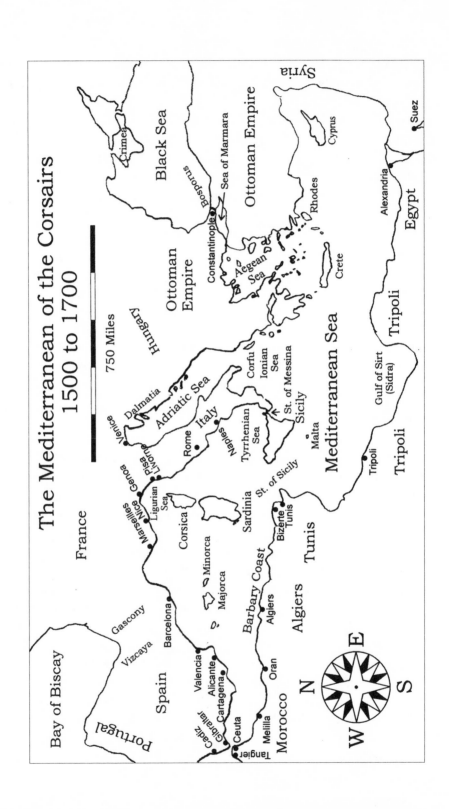

that they could not get their due; some, that had lived bravely, would not abase themselves to poverty; some vainly, only to get a name; others for revenge, covetousnesse, or as ill; and as they found themselves more and more oppressed, their passions increasing with discontent, made them turne Pirats.[10]

Irish pirates constantly threatened English and other shipping during the late seventeenth century, the most famous of them being Grace O'Malley, the Irish "Pirate Queen" renowned in history, legend, literature, and even a recent Broadway musical. English pirates often sought refuge in Irish ports. From the Baltic to the Strait of Gibraltar, pirates and privateers took to sea from every maritime nation and city-state. The waters just beyond the Strait of Gibraltar and off Cape Saint Vincent were "swarming with pirates" hoping to capture merchantmen of the northern seas, Mediterranean, New World, and East Indies.[11]

According to the popular notion, the pirates of the Mediterranean were slave-raiding Muslim corsairs called "Barbary pirates." (The term *corsair* refers to one who "cruises" or "crosses" for plunder, typically legally.) The statement is wrong on three counts. First, Christian corsairs (especially Spaniards, Italians, and the Knights of Malta) also raided for slaves into the seventeenth century. Second, Muslim rovers, commonly known in the West as Barbary pirates and almost universally considered by Christians to be pirates, were in nearly all cases not pirates at all but privateers. "[I]n their Company sailed also a small Algierman of 14 Guns, pitifully manned wth about 40 Moors he hath been out of Algier these two yeares, and all his Slaves being escaped from him, dares not returne, so resolves to turne Pyrat, and take every Vessell . . . she can master," wrote Thomas Baker, English ambassador to Tripoli in the late seventeenth century.[12] In other words, a Barbary corsair, like any other sea rover, was a pirate only if he sought prizes without a commission. Barbary corsairs were typically authorized by their pashas to attack nations with whom they were at war. Put more simply, nations who did not pay tribute—who did not make blackmail payments, in other words— were attacked, had their vessels and towns plundered, and crews, passengers, and coastal residents enslaved, many for years or even for life if no one could negotiate and pay a ransom. Third, the term *Barbary corsairs* refers only to corsairs sailing from North Africa, whether Turk or Moor. Many Muslim corsairs were "Turkish"—originated in Ottoman Empire in the Levant, that is— although the term *Turk* was often applied to any Muslim corsair, especially in the seventeenth century. Many Turkish corsairs were crewed not only by Turks, but also by a mix of Georgians, Cretans, Greeks, Genoese, Dalmatians, Albanians and other Balkans, and others, including slaves of any sort.[13]

Englishmen and other foreigners often served among the Barbary corsairs, some as renegades, some as slaves. In the early seventeenth century, the ratio of Muslim corsairs to renegade Englishmen was roughly "150 Turks to 20 English, yet the English in their persons are well used and duly paid their shares."[14] Many corsairs were commanded by renegades. Of the twelve corsair vessels listed in Tripoli in 1679, six were commanded by "Turks," one by a "Moor," and five by "Renegadoes"—four Greeks and one Frenchman.[15] In the early seventeenth century, there were several noted English renegades serving the Barbary corsairs.

Mariner slaves—especially gunners and those with experience as captains, masters, and mates—were aggressively recruited: "One of the guardians told me if I would turn Turk I might be captain of the ship," wrote Edward Coxere in the mid-seventeenth century.[16] Slaves served as oarsmen aboard galleys and did much of the common manual labor of the corsair ships. They even had their own slave petty officers; a slave boatswain aboard a corsair would have a "Turks' boatswain" over him, for example.[17] Although English renegades often served among Barbary corsairs, they were far better known among Muslims as Christian pirates who attacked Muslim merchantmen. Indeed, in the late sixteenth and early seventeenth centuries, the English were known along the Barbary coast as pirates, and the North African Muslims were known as "Barbary pirates" in England.[18]

Not to be forgotten were the Cossack pirates: "[B]etweene 70. and 80. boats of the Cossacks, with fifty men apeece, Rowers and Souldiers (watching their opportunitie of the Captaine Bassas being ingaged in Tartary) entred the Bospherus about breake of day, where dividing themselves, they sackt and burnt almost all the villages and houses of pleasure on both sides the River."[19] Also in the Black Sea were Circassian, Mingrellian, and Georgian pirates.

The principal North African corsair ports were Salé, Algiers, and Tunis, to which Tripoli was added (Tripoli was actually occupied by Spain from 1510 to 1523 and by the Knights Hospitaller from 1523 to 1551); there were many minor corsair ports. Ostensibly part of the Ottoman Empire after the sixteenth century, most of these ports were, for all practical purposes, independent."[20] Early in the seventeenth century, English pirates used Mamora (Mehedia), Morocco, as their base. For much of the period, corsairs also sailed from Ottoman ports in the Levant, Greece and the Greek islands, the Italian maritime city-states, Spain, and Malta. European pirates and privateers sailed from every North Atlantic nation from the Baltic to the Strait of Gibraltar, but by the eighteenth century, many of their numbers had been reduced, and many of their traditional ports were denied to them.

VESSELS AND ARMS

For millennia, the galley in one form or another exemplified piracy and privateering in the Mediterranean, but by the end of the sixteenth century, it was obsolescent except for one or two maritime niches. As a merchant vessel, it had been in decline since the early sixteenth century. Sailing vessels handled better and could carry larger cargoes. Skilled oarsmen had become difficult to find, and in the mid-fifteenth century, vagrants and criminals, followed soon by slaves, were harnessed to the oar. This in turn changed the form of rowing once again to *di scaloccio*, the placement of several oarsmen to a single oar, for this was an easier means of rowing with unskilled oarsmen, and it gave great power to each oar.[21] Even so, the oars of light corsair raiding vessels were usually manned by the corsairs themselves.

After the battle of Lepanto, the galley as pirate vessel remained in limited use in the Mediterranean, primarily for attacking small or lightly armed coastal merchantmen or larger becalmed merchantmen and making swift raids against small targets. In a pinch it could be run ashore, permitting its crew to make a quick raid or escape inland from an attacker. The Maltese corsairs used galleys for slaves raids on the Barbary coast and even attacked Barbary corsairs and shipping with them throughout the seventeenth century.[22] But the galley was too slow compared to many of the sailing vessels that had been developed, and it could not handle heavy seas. As a Venetian put it in 1588, "light galleys like ours are not built for ocean navigation."[23]

Further, as already noted, the galley made a very poor gun platform. Most galleys, when armed with guns, mounted one or two, and sometimes as many as five, in the bow as chase guns and mounted light swivels on the rails. As long as there was enough wind to maneuver with, a sailing ship armed with only a single tier of great guns and a crew large enough to man them could easily make short work of a galley, destroying its oars and slaughtering its oarsmen, even though they were galley slaves, typically of the same faith as those maiming and killing them. In 1628, the *Sampson* of London valiantly fought off four Maltese galleys, one of them mounted with a twenty-five-pound demi-cannon in the bow.[24] Even in a chase in light airs, a sailing ship could move several guns to its stern and "play" the guns severely on the chasing galley. Sail was now the dominant means of propulsion and speed at sea. Still, vestiges of the galley survived in the many small vessels and even light frigates that carried oars as auxiliary propulsion, and the galleass, a hybrid vessel of galley and ship, was a brief attempt at improving the galley's sea-going qualities.

What both the pirate and pirate hunter required foremost was speed. In the case of small pirate vessels, speed and the ability to sail close to the wind were often the only requirements. Larger vessels required speed as well as some ability to mount great guns. The now-traditional three-masted square-rigged ship was common among rovers and pirate hunters, given its speed, handling characteristics, ability to handle heavy seas, and capacity to mount batteries of great guns. It became just as common in the Mediterranean among both Europeans and, by 1606, among "Turks" as well in its various forms, including the galleon, frigate, pinnace, pink, and fluyt. Barbary corsairs used captured European ships and also built their own on European lines.[25] In the early seventeenth century, the small pink, *praam*, and flyboat of 180 to 200 tons were common among the pirates in the northern seas.[26]

In the late sixteenth century, the English and other northern rovers introduced the *bertone* (a swift, maneuverable sailing vessel) into the Mediterranean, where it quickly became the small vessel of choice among rovers.[27] The Mediterranean "frigate," whose lines probably inspired the frigate type of ship that superseded the galleon, was a swift, small vessel propelled by both sail and oar. Called a brigantine and sometimes a half-galley by the Europeans, it was common from the seventeenth through the nineteenth centuries and never had more than fourteen pairs of oars: "A small Briganteene [a half-galley] of this place [Tripoli] went a Christian-stealing" wrote Thomas Baker in 1680, and Henry Teonge noted a brigantine of twenty-three oars at Malta in 1676.[28] The settee or saetia, a typically two-masted vessel rigged with "settee" sails, was a common sea-roving vessel, as was the carvel, a small to moderate size lateen-rigged vessel often carrying oars as well. Half-galleys of forty or so oars were used much as they were in the Caribbean. Beginning in the late seventeenth century, the *polacre*, a ship of mixed square and fore-and-aft sails with a beaked prow, became common, and in the eighteenth century the *xebec*, a swift fore-and-aft-rigged vessel with a single tier of great guns, was introduced as a corsair.

Of the thirteen vessels listed as the Tripoli corsair fleet in 1679, nine were ships of force ranging from sixteen to forty-two guns plus swivels; two were smaller vessels of an unidentified type of six guns plus swivels; one was a settee of six guns plus swivels, and one a half-galley armed with a chase gun and sixteen "brasse bases" (swivels).[29] In general, ships grew larger and somewhat swifter from the beginning of the period to the end. Bow and stern castles turned into lower forecastles, quarterdecks, and poop decks, and by the early eighteenth century, many ships were flush-decked, called "galley-built." Lines typically grew cleaner, and speed began to become an important consideration even in merchant shipping.

In gunnery, the most significant changes beyond the early eighteenth century were the effectiveness of training among the crews of men-of-war, the general increase in the size of guns, and the development of the carronade in the late eighteenth century. The carronade (a short-barreled, short-range naval gun of large caliber) was devastating at close range and permitted smaller vessels to carry a powerful armament. A late-seventeenth century sixth rate (a light frigate) might have carried a combination of fourteen to twenty minions and sakers (cannon that fired three pound and five and quarter pound shot, respectively); an early-eighteenth-century sixth rate might have been armed entirely with twenty six-pounders; and a mid- to late-eighteenth-century frigate might have been armed with thirty-eight guns, including eighteen-pounders on the gundeck and nine-pounders above. The U.S. heavy frigates of the early nineteenth century—such as the famous USS *Constitution*, which is still afloat as a commissioned U.S. warship, were as well armed as fourth rates of other nations, with fifty or more guns: twenty-four-pounders on the gundeck and thirty-two-pound carronades on the upper deck. It was an admirable ship type, capable of the speed and maneuverability of a frigate with the firepower of a lesser ship of the line.

Most important to tactics, though, was not the development of speed at sea or the increase in the size of naval guns, but the professionalism of navies. By the mid-eighteenth century, age-of-sail navies were manned by a largely professional officer corps, petty officers, and, in part, seamen (many were often pressed landsmen), and by the Napoleonic Age had reached a level of professionalism that would be familiar to modern navy crews, although the corresponding brutal discipline would not.

The arms of the pirate and pirate hunter were those already described in chapters 8 and 10, with one noteworthy difference: the curved swords used among the Muslim corsairs. A variety of such swords were common, ranging from the scimitar, in both long- and short-bladed versions, to the *nimcha*. The strongly curved scimitar, descended from the Persian *shamshir* and ultimately from the curved Mongol swords, was a highly effective cutting sword, although the curve of its blade made it a less effective weapon for thrusting, requiring that it be "hooked." Making a sword for both cut and thrust is always a compromise; the ideal thrusting sword is invariably a less than ideal cutting sword and vice versa. Curved swords cut easily, especially from broad, swinging strokes; straight blades must be drawn across or through the target. The author of one period account describes the swords of the "Turkish pirates" as "sabels [sabers], which we call falchions, some with hatchets, and some with half-pikes."[30] He later refers to "scimitars" instead of sabers and still later refers to "scimitars, falchions, half-pikes, and other weapons." The "falchion" was probably either a short-bladed scimitar, of which examples exist, or any short curved sword. The various curved Muslim swords or the falchion (which may derive from them) may well be the forbears of or inspiration for the European cutlass. By the late eighteenth century, however, many cutlasses were straight-bladed.[31]

Firearms remained largely unchanged. The matchlock musket had been entirely replaced among Europeans by the flintlock by the end of the first quarter of the eighteenth century. Sea muskets grew shorter from the mid-eighteenth century; long barrels were no longer believed to have greater range. Armor was still in use among many Mediterranean rovers and pirate hunters at sea and ashore in the early seventeenth century, although some commanders ordered their men to abandon it "so that they should be able to fight more agilely."[32]

MERCHANTMAN VERSUS CORSAIR

Pirate and corsair tactics of the early sixteenth century were, with the exception of galley tactics, identical to those of the Caribbean and the New World and were largely unchanged until the coming of steam, and even then, not much changed. The principal difference in galley tactics from previous periods was the mounting of one or two great guns in the bow, which were used as chase pieces. But with the coming of the sailing ship and effective gunnery, the galley lost its effectiveness except in certain circumstances.

Former pirate Sir Henry Mainwaring described the common pirate tactics of the early seventeenth century, which would remain common in the Mediterranean and environs until the end of the age of sail:

> In their working they usually do thus: a little before day they take in all
> their sails, and lie a-hull, till they can make what ships are about them;

and accordingly direct their course, so as they may seem to such ships as they see to be Merchantmen bound upon their course. If they be a fleet, then they disperse themselves a little before day, some league or thereabouts asunder, and seeing no ships do most commonly clap close by a wind to seem as Plyers [vessels working their way to windward]. If any ships stand in after them, they heave out all the sail they can make, and hang out drags to hinder their going, that so the other that stand with them might imagine they were afraid and yet they shall fetch them up.[33]

Boarding was the principal tactic for capturing prey, preferably without a broadside and with musketry to suppress the small arms and great guns. Running was the invariable tactic against a pirate hunter, unless the pirate or corsair were stoutly manned and armed, which many were.[34]

Given the amount of trade and the number of rovers within and around the Strait of Gibraltar, merchantmen were bound to sooner or later run across pirates and corsairs. The *Dolphin* of London—a merchantman of 280 tons, nineteen great guns, and nine swivels—fought off five "Turks' Men of War and a Sattee [settee]" in 1617, proving how well some merchant crews could fight. The English renegade Walsingham attacked first and boarded the *Dolphin*. This engagement lasted two hours as the Turks tried to tear up the deck planking and cast grenades and firepots within, "but we having a murtherer [a small swivel gun] in the round house kept the larboard side clear: whilst our other men with the ordnance and muskets played upon their ships . . . .at last we shot them quite through and through, and they likewise us."[35]

The corsair stood off to mend its leaks. The English renegade Kelley came up next, and then another ship, and "So they laid us aboard, one on the starboard quarter, and the other on the larboard." The enemy "performed much manhood, and many dangerous hazards. Amongst which, there was one of their company that desperately went up into our maintop to fetch down our flag; which being spied by the Steward of our ship, he presently shot him with his musket that he fell headlong into the sea, leaving the flag behind him." Throughout the time the enemy was aboard the merchantman, the merchant crew fired into their hulls, so that they too were forced to stand off and repair their leaks. Finally came two more of the renegade Kelley's ships, and again the *Dolphin* was boarded. The Turks in their own language shouted for the English to "Yield yourselves!" "Yield yourselves!" while promising that the English "would be well used" and would have part of their goods back. The merchantman refused to surrender. Soon a fire broke out aboard the merchantman, and the corsairs, fearing it would spread to them, cut themselves loose. The *Dolphin*'s crew put out the fire and escaped. The attacking ships ranged from 250 to 300 tons, twenty-two to thirty-five guns, and 200 to 250 men. Three of their commanders were renegade Englishmen.[36]

Many merchant crews fought valiantly against "Turkish pirates," fearing enslavement, as did "Moorish merchantmen" against Christian corsairs, yet in the same period, both in the Old World and the New, many merchantmen appear to have been far more likely to surrender to pirates than to privateers or corsairs, perhaps because they feared fatal reprisal in the former case. In the Mediterranean, slave-raiding corsairs might beat the captured mariner but seldom killed him, for he had value as a slave. By the sixteenth century, the wholesale slaughter of prisoners at sea appears to have been largely condemned, and was commonly practiced only by and against pirates, including against privateers unfortunate enough not to have borne a commission. In some cases, Muslim corsairs offered to spare ships and crews from capture and enslavement if they offered up their goods, as noted earlier. This was done for practical reasons: "for by that means the common sort of Mariners are not so willing to fight for the Merchant goods."[37] Piracy and privateering, after all, are about profit foremost. Fighting was to be done only when necessary.

PIRATE HUNTING

Broadly speaking, pirate hunting in these regions and in this age was much as it was in other areas during this period, with one particular exception: extortionate tribute. Typically, tribute was considered less expensive than going to war, particularly in an age when states were often at war, treasuries were often depleted by campaigns, and violent suppression of North African roving was invariably short lived. Even so, tribute was often only partly effective. Mainwaring, for example, refers to the "unequal terms we hold with those of Tunis and Algiers, for although we have Merchants, Factors, Ledgers, there, and a free trade with them, yet at Sea they will take our Merchants; only if they do not fight, they will not make slaves of them, nor keep their Ships, but only their goods they will."[38] Similarly, "The Ship's Equipage were fifty-two Men, and in Condition to have made a good Defense; but they too far confided in the Sincerity of those on board a *Tripoline* Rover they met with, who, according to Stipulations, treated them as Friends, with abundance of Civility, yet finally seized and conducted them all to *Tripoly*."[39]

One of the difficulties in finding an end to the North African corsairs was that of Machiavellian politics among Christian states. Sir William
Monson pointed out in the early seventeenth century that the solution to
Barbary privateering would probably take years and needed to be a multi-
lateral one. Further, all affected European maritime cities should fund the
necessary expeditions.[40] Yet the governments of some Christian nations did
not want to do away with the Barbary corsairs. Rather, they wanted to prevent
attacks on their own shipping, but not necessarily on those of their economic
competitors. Barbary attacks on competitor shipping were a viable means of
damaging a foreign economy without having to do it oneself, and especially
without being blamed directly or indirectly for it. North African corsairs
were convenient surrogates and typically needed no prompting, although
it was given at times. "We are detained in this port by the fear of the fleet
of the King of Algiers; in addition to his twenty-two galleys there is reason
to suppose that Murad Rays is also out with twelve; and that they intend in
conjunction to capture the money which is being sent to Italy. The King of
France is accused of having suggested this operation to the King of Algiers,
in order to annoy the King of Spain. The mischief the Algerines are doing is
terrible; and if Spain is harried by the English to the west, it suffers no less
from Algerines upon the east," wrote the Venetian ambassador to Spain to
the Doge of Venice in 1589.[41]

This attitude, or political tactic if you will, was seen into the early nineteenth century. Politics of another nature made outright piracy difficult to
suppress in the sixteenth and early seventeenth centuries: pirates had a variety of ports to choose from. Driven from English waters, for example, a pirate
could enter service in "Leghorn" (Livorno) or Ville-Franche.[42] The historical record is filled with complaints of pirates of one nation or maritime city
hiding under the aegis of another: "the Grand Duke of Tuscany has lately
bought two Bertoni [a type of vessel used by pirates], and has sent them out
as corsairs flying the English flag . . . Everyone was trying to hide his own
misdeeds under the cloak of those English Bertoni."[43]

Retaliation against the "pirates" and corsairs of other states—some of
it sincere, some of it mere pretense—was common among all the major sea-
going peoples who traded in the Mediterranean. In 1586, the English ambassador to Constantinople complained that "owing to secret orders from
here (by which he meant from the Capadun Pasha), the Turkish officials in
Barbary not only refuse obedience to the Sultan's orders for the liberation of
English vessels and subjects captured by those galleys, but have actually com-

mitted fresh depredations. The Capadun answered that, on the contrary, English ships, while feigning amity, seized Turkish ships on the plea that they were common pirates, and that they deserved to be chastized."[44] Such retaliation appears to have done little if anything to diminish piratical attacks, although it did help line the pockets of roving captains, crews, and their investors.

Treachery was as ever a good way to capture pirates. In 1610, "Neill M'Cloyde of the Lewis" captured a "greatte ship" and its crew of pirates:

> This English Captaine wanting men, desyred some supplies from Neill, and he willinglie yielded to it. Neill is feasted aboorde of him, and will not be so unthankful, bot will repay him with a banket on land. The Captain and his company for most pairt being all invited, whatever theire faire wes, the desert was soure. Whether it wes that they refused to pay their reckneing, or that Neill held thame to be hereticks, and so thought thame not worthie to be keipt promiss to, for Neill is thoght to be of the Romishe faithe . . . By the reporte of the Messenger which comes from Neil, it is affirmed, that the pirate had that same intention against Neill, bot the other hes tane the first start.[45]

The letter writer points out that the "caise is altered when the broken hielanders are becom the persecutors of pirattes."[46] Scottish Highlanders were long known, before and after, as reivers—that is, as thieving raiders.

Former pirate Henry Mainwaring had his own ideas about pirate hunting and provided them to King James I of England, along with an analysis of why men turned pirate, how they practiced piracy, and where they practiced it and provisioned for it. It was an astounding piece of anti-piracy intelligence and tactical analysis, and proved Mainwaring's pardon was worth the trouble. As for ridding England of the pirate and corsair menace, Mainwaring first recommended that English seamen who might be pirates be required to provide security against their good behavior or be imprisoned. Irish seamen should be required to remain ten to twelve miles inland from the coast. "Next, to take away their hopes and encouragements, our Highness must put on a constant immutable resolution never to grant any Pardon, and for those that are or may be taken, to put them all to death, or make slaves of them."[47]

Third, he proposed that English ships be plain, good sailors, shallow drafted, and of "reasonable good force" so that they could stand against pirate and corsair attacks. Next, he proposed that men-of-war and small "advice" vessels (small, light, swift vessels, often small frigates) with oars be sent against the Algerian and Tunisian corsairs, and that captured "Turks" be sold into Spanish slavery. Last, he suggested means of "disappointing of them in Ireland, which I hold the most material of all; being that this is as the great earth for foxes, which being stopped, they are easily hunted to death." He recommended posting men-of-war at various locations in Ireland, each attended by a "Penecho Carvel" (a seaworthy carvel from Peniche, swift under sail and oar). The carvel, in harbor, would upon receiving word of pirates set sail to advise the larger man-of-war. He also suggested that the commanders of pirate hunters be forbidden any correspondence with pirates, on pain of severe penalty, in order to prevent collusion.[48]

Of course, some of these proposals were impractical or unlikely to be implemented due to politics and bureaucracy. It is curious to note Mainwaring's opposition to pardons for pirates, given that he was himself a pardoned pirate, but then, as a former pirate, he had insight into the problem others did not. Mainwaring may have recognized the recidivism prevalent among pirates. Further, while some pirates would accept an offer of amnesty, or pardon, others would stand "aloof," as has ever been the case.[49] Those who would not accept amnesty or pardon had to be driven into hiding or driven to ground and killed or captured. Given the complex politics and geography of the Mediterranean, this was impossible in all cases, as it had been for the previous three millennia. It was difficult enough in England and Ireland until the early seventeenth century.

There were other anti-piracy proposals. John Smith had a solution to English piracy, one repeated in later decades and centuries in various forms by other commentators: "I could wish Merchants, Gentlemen, and all setters forth of ships, not to be sparing of a competent pay, nor true payment; for neither Souldiers nor Sea-men can live without meanes, but necessity will force them to steale; and when they are once entered into that trade, they are hardly reclaimed." Smith went on to make a plea—perhaps sincere, perhaps an advertisement, perhaps both—that "Sea-men and Souldiers" who had turned pirate and were now regarded as "the scumme of the world," should "regaine therefore your wonted reputations, and endevour rather to adventure to those faire plantations of our English Nation; which however in the beginning were scorned and contemned, yet now you see how many rich and gallant people come from thence, who went thither as poore as any Souldier or Sailer, and gets more in one yeare, than you by Piracie in seven."[50] But the life of a poor planter was hard, and although many of England's poor did become wealthy, or at least comfortable, in the New World, far many more did not. The idea of finding an alternate occupation for pirates was an excellent one, but as was ever the case (and still is the case), selling the idea to pirates, as well as the implementing the idea in its bedeviled details, was difficult.

THE PIRATE HUNTERS

Henry Mainwaring pointed out that there is as much difference "betwixt hunting with a Lime-hound [bloodhound] in a string, and a kennel of dogs that run loose, as is betwixt a single combat, and a battle of two Armies."[51] In other words, the commander of a fleet might not be best at commanding a ship in single action and vice versa. Commanders needed to be chosen based on the needs of the situation. For pirate hunting, captains capable of engaging in single combat with a pirate or corsair, and willing to do so, were mandatory. They must be "such Commanders as know how to work and command like a man-of-war, where to find [the pirates], how to draw himself to them, as also have a Commission joined with a ready wit and judgment, to do sometimes that upon the occasion for which he can have no direction or rule, which thing is only mastered by experience."[52]

Alonso de Contreras, a Spaniard, was one such commander. Born in 1582, he knifed and killed a classmate out of spite when he was twelve. For this he was exiled, after which he became first a soldier then a corsair, occasionally a pirate hunter, and eventually a Knight of Malta. Lope de Vega, the famous and extraordinarily prolific Spanish playwright, also a Knight of Malta, even dedicated a play, *El Rey Sin Reyno* (*The King Without a Kingdom*), to him.[53] Contreras was typical of the sixteenth- and early-seventeenth-century corsairs; he served his nation by robbing its enemies, both political and religious. In his case, he attacked for profit the enemies of Spain, Malta, and the Holy Church and considered it a sacred duty to fight not only Muslims, but pirates in general: "I was quite justified in attacking Christians, as we were duty bound to fight pirates, Christian or otherwise." A pirate, of course, was a rover who lacked a commission, no matter that all else was identical between the pirate and corsair.

Being advised by the residents of a small Greek port that pirates had kidnapped their priest, Contreras set about to rescue him. "The Christians were certainly pirates," he noted, "sailing without commission, and they were sacrilegious. They robbed Moor and Christian alike." He quickly tracked down the pirate vessel and captured it without a fight. This was often more difficult than it might seem, for small-scale pirates could be difficult to locate; some would even sink their piratical vessels and take their plunder to shore in boats and disappear into the local population.[54] Contreras marooned the pirate captain naked, with no provisions, on a small island, leaving him "to expiate his sin by dying of hunger."[55] (Marooning was obviously not invented by the pirates of the Caribbean.)

Contreras had much experience against the Barbary corsairs, and his description of one of his early fights aboard a Maltese corsair galleon engaging a Turkish corsair was probably typical. The Maltese corsairs, many of whom were led by Knights of Malta, had a reputation as intrepid fighters against the Muslim corsairs. "The same day that we were taken we saw the island of Malta, where, it is said, Paul suffered shipwreck. The Turks, being afraid of their men-of-war, made from that island, for they terrified the Turks much," wrote a prisoner taken by a Barbary pirate.[56] According to Contreras, the battle was brutal and was anyone's to win:

> They let us have a broadside. It sent seventeen of our men to the next world and wounded many others. Then we fired a broadside, and it was just as good as theirs. We then went alongside her, boarded her, and started hand-to-hand fighting. It was a hard battle. At one time, the Turks took our forecastle, and it was a long job dislodging them and forcing them back to their own ship. For the rest of the night, we parted company and we stayed in our own ships. By the morning, the captain had a plan that proved very good. He battened down all the hatches and only allowed the actual soldiers on deck, where they had either to stay and fight or jump into the sea.[57]

At dawn the battle continued, with the Maltese first capturing the Turkish forecastle then being forced to retire. Contreras's vessel then stood off and battered the Turk with her great guns, given that his crew were better seamen, their ship more maneuverable, and their guns greater. But it was not enough, and the fight lasted through another day. At dawn on the third day, Contreras's galleon furled her sails, stowed the oars she had used to help maneuver during the fight, and had her consort frigate—used as a stores vessel—tow her alongside the Turk. They fought for three more hours. The Maltese were victorious in the end. Contreras notes that "We made prisoners of the Turks who were aboard and clapped them in irons to take back as slaves. We pillaged the ship and did very well for ourselves."[58] Contreras described numerous other fights, including slave raids on the Barbary coast, made this time from Maltese galleys. The liberty enjoyed by these corsairing, pirate-hunting captains and crews to raid, plunder, kill, enslave, and punish was extreme. But it would not last forever.

Eventually, as navies grew to be fully professional bodies, the pirate and privateer were eliminated as pirate hunters. By the eighteenth century, if men like Contreras wanted to hunt pirates, they typically had to do so as naval commanders or part of their crews. Although orders to these later naval commanders were typically broad, giving them the free rein required for the typically broad tasking of naval cruisers, commanders were also more restricted by laws and regulations than their predecessors had been. As naval professionalism increased, naval commanders acted less like freebooters and rogue dispensers of justice and more like the naval professionals they were becoming. In 1671, the orders to Captain Holmes of the HMS *Diamond* stated that he could, within the limits of his station, "according as you shall be guided by your Intelligence, and as you shall judge may best further the Service on which you are sent, which is the Security of the King's Subjects, trading in those Parts, and the suppressing of the Pirates of Salley; and upon your meeting with any Ships belonging to Salley, or any other place in Hostility with his Majesty, you are to use your best endeavours to take, sink, or otherwise destroy them."[59]

And many did use their best endeavors. Only rarely did pirate-hunting men-of-war refuse engagement. In 1670, the frigate *Sapphire*, seeing four Algerian men-of-war standing toward them, ran itself aground rather than fight. "The master and one mariner onely had a sence of honour and declared their resolution to fight their way through them."[60] But this was a rare instance. Far more common were engagements such as those described by Thomas Baker: "Whereupon yᵉ Charles Gally laid her aboard and entring her men, they after a very small dispute became Masters of yᵉ Upper deck, and about halfe an hower after, the Turks, betwixt decks yielded."[61]

However, the most effective means—yet often not particularly effective in the long term—of suppressing the Barbary corsairs was not to attack their corsairs and shipping one by one, but to attack their ports by bombarding their cities and burning their docks and vessels, and occasionally by making a ground assault and capturing all or part of the port as well. This was typically followed up by negotiation followed by treaty aimed at freeing slaves, garnering restitution, and ensuring the free passage of one's merchantmen and men-of-war.

CAMPAIGNS AGAINST THE CORSAIRS

Christian states waged numerous naval campaigns against the Barbary corsair cities, of which only a few are noted here. In 1611, King James I of England ordered a campaign against Algiers, but the brief enterprise was a failure and resulted in retaliation against English shipping.[62] In 1624, Dutch Admiral "Moy" Lambert (Lambert Hendriksz) appeared in Algiers harbor with captured Algerian corsairs. ("Moy" or "Mooi" meant "Handsome," a nickname given Lambert reportedly because he was unattractive.) When the pasha refused to negotiate a treaty with the Netherlands, Lambert hanged some of his prisoners, threw the rest into the sea to drown, and sailed away. When he returned with another set of corsair prisoners, the pasha agreed to negotiate with the Dutch and released Dutch prisoners and slaves.[63] In 1655, the English admiral Blake successfully attacked Tunis, which was later attacked by the Dutch, French, and English, typically successfully. By the mid- to late-eighteenth century, the power of the corsairs was significantly diminished, and the major European navies were powerful enough to protect their shipping. Still, nations paid tribute, and small states with small navies, such as the United States, remained vulnerable.[64]

In 1804, the United States dispatched a flotilla to put a stop to Tripolitan attacks on U.S. shipping. The USS *Enterprise* defeated the *Tripoli* (a Tripolitan corsair) U.S. Navy men-of-war bombarded Tripoli, and U.S. Marines marched overland under First Lt. Presley O'Bannon and captured Derna (the harbor fortress of Tripoli), giving the U.S. Marines both its Mameluke sword and the famous line in the Marine Corps Hymn, "To the shores of Tripoli."[65] The campaign was a success. However, the most famous action of the brief war was the burning of the USS *Philadelphia* by a force under Navy Lt. Stephen Decatur.

The frigate had run aground and was captured by Tripolitan corsairs. "Cutting it out"—recapturing it and sailing it away—was determined to be too dangerous, so burning was resolved upon to deny the corsairs the use of the powerful warship. In Decatur's words, addressed to his commanding officer:

> On Board the Ketch Intrepid, at Sea, February 17, 1804. Sir: I have the honor to inform you, that in pursuance to your orders of the 31st ultimo, to proceed with this ketch off the harbor of Tripoli, there to endeavor to effect the destruction of the late United States' frigate Philadelphia, I arrived there in company with the United States' brig Syren, lieutenant

commandant Stewart, on the 7th, but owing to the badness of the weather, was unable to effect any thing until last evening, when we had a light breeze from the N.E. At 7 o'clock I entered the harbor with the Intrepid, the Syren having gained her station without the harbor, in a situation to support us in our retreat. At half past 9 o'clock, laid her alongside of the Philadelphia, boarded, and after a short contest, carried her. I immediately fired her in the store-rooms, gun-room, cock-pit, and birth-deck, and remained on board until the flames had issued from the spar-deck, hatchways . . . I boarded with sixty men and officers, leaving a guard on board the ketch for her defence, and it is the greatest pleasure I inform you, I had not a man killed in this affair, and but one slightly wounded.[66]

Nonetheless, North African corsairs remained a significant threat to merchant shipping until 1830, when the French brutally overthrew Algiers and conquered the surrounding region, finally bringing the heyday of the Barbary corsair to a close. In the end, it was a combination of modern navies, control of the sea, international agreement, and, in some cases, the capture and destruction of corsair bases that ended the Barbary threat to shipping. The last significant Christian pirate threat to shipping was largely suppressed in 1828, near the end of the Greek War of Independence. After a combined British, French, and Russian fleet destroyed the Turkish-Egyptian fleet at Navarino, many Greek privateers turned pirate. The U.S. Navy had already found it necessary to provide protection against the pirates, and their brief heyday ended when a combined English-French force, along with an independent Greek force, attacked and destroyed many of them. From the Levant west to the Americas, by 1830, large-scale piracy had been destroyed.

Even so, sea roving had not yet taken its last breath.

12

Of Frigates and Cruisers

In Pursuit of the Commerce Raiders, 1688–1865

"I put to sea, accompanied by another frigate of the same force [eighteen great guns]; we discovered thirty English merchantmen, escorted by two men-of-war of sixteen guns each, along the English coast: I fought them alone, and made myself master of one, then the other, after an hour of sufficiently lively combat; my consort in the meantime went after the merchantmen; he took twelve of them," wrote famous French *corsaire* and naval commander René Duguay-Trouin of his second command of a privateer.[1] His actions epitomized the danger of the privateer to merchant shipping, even when convoyed. Most threatening of all, some privateers were not afraid to attack men-of-war.

Through the early nineteenth century, navies were typically too busy locating and engaging the enemy and protecting commerce, and they left the capture of enemy commerce largely to private individuals and vessels. The period from King William's War in 1688 through the Napoleonic Wars was the heyday of privateering, far outstripping piracy of the same period in terms of the number of rovers putting to sea, prizes captured, and damage to shipping and trade. Every maritime nation at war during this period sent privateers to sea, making it an age of rampant greed and derring-do under the guise of national service.

The French term for commerce raiding—*la guerre de course*, which indicates a "cruising" war for profit against merchantmen—summed up the strategy best: weaken the enemy by attacking its merchant shipping and thus its economy. In the words of Admiral Alfred Thayer Mahan, the famous naval historian and strategist, the *guerre de course* was a "cruising, commerce

221

destroying warfare."[2] Licensing a privateer cost the state nothing and even provided some profit to the state, given that it received part of the plunder, typically ten percent. It should have been an ideal situation. Privateering damaged the enemy economy and tied up enemy men-of-war in convoy duty and cruising for privateers, all at no cost to the state—in theory. But as with most things "free," privateering came with a price.

THE PROBLEM WITH PRIVATEERS

Foremost, privateering invited retaliation in the form of enemy privateering, hearkening back to the Mycenaean Age. Further, and put bluntly, the enemy's privateers were not the only privateers that might threaten a state's merchant shipping. Often, one's own privateers and those of one's allies were accused of committing a variety of misdeeds, including cruelty to prisoners, embezzling from prizes (captured vessels), defrauding prize courts, plundering innocent vessels (that is, piracy), flying false colors in order to attack allies, colluding with the enemy, and smuggling. Almost anything to make a buck, and almost any violence—even to the degree of murder on occasion, as long as it did not draw too much attention—was acceptable to many privateers.[3] Privateers also tended to draw skilled mariners away from both the naval and merchant fleets, for the lure of lawful plundering was powerful.

The potential for misbehavior at sea was substantial. In 1771, for example, a combined fleet of Russian men-of-war, hired English merchantmen, small Ragusian vessels (from Ragusa, Italy), and "a large number of small Greek vessels," all under the command of Count Alexey Orloff (best known for using his bare hands to strangle Catherine the Great's husband, Peter III, in the coup that put Catherine on the throne), was sent against the Turks. The Greek participants were described as:

> for the most part, but privateers [*corsaires*], who had purchased the right to fly the Russian flag. They would have been very good for a pirate war [i.e. for privateering], but never for a great [naval] expedition; they soon demonstrated that they were but some of the true pirates who infested the Archipelago, and against which Orloff had to take precautions. Three hundred Albanians deserted the Russian squadron to join some of these pirates, who stole two transport vessels, desolated many islands, and did this while under the Russian flag; and Orloff had to send the order to capture them.[4]

Privateering often led to a rise in piracy when privateers were not well regulated and supervised and when they lacked adequate employment at the end of a major conflict. The latter was certainly a significant factor in the rise of the Anglo-American pirates in the early eighteenth century.

Privateers could also be a problem ashore. In 1705, for example, a group of privateers, probably drunk and most belonging to the "Briganteen *Dragon*," assaulted the New York sheriff, "beat and wounded several persons that came to his assistance," then attacked and murdered one Army officer and "grievously wounded" another who just happened to be walking by. The "Sheriff, Officers and Seamen of Her Majesties Ships" counterattacked and arrested several of the privateers after a fight in which men on both sides were wounded. A number of the privateers escaped the scene.[5] There are many such instances of privateers violently misbehaving ashore among their compatriots.

Such behavior gave rise to an often well-deserved mistrust of privateers, even among themselves. In the English navy, for example, officers tended to view privateers as unprofessional and sometimes as potentially criminal. Seventeenth-century naval captain Jeremy Roche referred to privateers as "skulking," for example, and defined the difference between the man-of-war and privateer when confronted simultaneously by enemy warships and rich merchantmen: "[W]e were awhile at a stand disputing the point between profit and honour. Profit showed us several merchant ships, richly laden, which we might easily take, but honour urged the baseness of so easy a conquest, and the glory of the other."[6] Naval officers were to choose duty over profit whenever there was a choice, although they too often engaged in cruising warfare and received shares of the plunder. For the privateer, it was the other way around: profit almost always came before duty. Nonetheless, the French Navy often recruited successful privateers as naval officers. René Duguay-Trouin (a Frenchman) and Jean Bart (a Fleming in the service of France) were two such officers whose fame as privateers and naval officers resounds to this day. Both were well known for their capture of numerous enemy merchantmen and their willingness to engage enemy men-of-war.

There were legal restraints against the unlawful activities of privateers. Their captains would forfeit their bonds or even lose their commissions if they exceeded the bounds of their authority, whether by cruelty against prisoners, embezzling legitimate prizes, or illegally capturing innocent vessels or otherwise engaging in piracy. But the punishments do not seem to have been severe or of long duration, especially as compared to the apparent number of incidents.[7] Many people, both mariners and "landmen," considered privateering little more than piracy legalized and privateers little more than pirates protected by the state. Of course, many privateers did not engage in these criminal behaviors, considering it an honor to fight for their country, as well as a simultaneous opportunity to get rich, or at least to earn significantly more than their naval or merchant counterparts. One need only look at the journals of Duguay-Trouin, Woodes Rogers, and Commodore George Walker, for example, or at William Hutchinson's *Treatise of Naval Architecture*, to get a sense of the professionalism, seamanship, and courage of many privateers.[8]

DEFEATING THE PRIVATEER, 1688–1846

The primary responsibility of countering privateers fell to the navy, typically to the smaller men-of-war, as opposed to the powerful "ships of the line." Larger warships were usually too slow to run down privateers, most of whom had been selected for speed and invariably had the far more important mission of engaging enemy fleets. Smaller men-of-war were more suited to cruising warfare and convoy duty. Although navies were the principal defense against privateers—after the arming of merchantmen, that is—they were also, according to Admiral Mahan, necessary in order for commerce raiding to be successful. Privateering needed to be "seconded by a squadron warfare, and by divisions of ships-of-the-line; which, forcing the enemy to unite his forces, permit the cruisers to make fortunate attempts upon his trade."[9] The usual anti-privateer tactic was simply to cruise—in other words, to patrol—and, upon discovery of a privateer, capture or destroy it.

The tactics and arms of the fight at sea between two vessels were those described in the last two chapters, and they remained largely unchanged until the end of the Napoleonic Wars. The frigate (both the lighter men-of-war of the seventeenth and early eighteenth centuries as well as the true frigate of the mid-eighteenth century and beyond) was not only the principal privateer hunter but also often a commerce raider as well. The French in particular put their smaller men-of-war to work commerce raiding. Duguay-Trouin's first commands in the French Navy, for example, were of cruisers, and his time was spent largely in seeking enemy merchantmen.[10] Most privateers were relatively small, ranging from 50 to 200 tons, and seldom larger than 250, although in the eighteenth and early nineteenth century, some privateers were as large as 400 tons or more, and some reached over 500.[11]

Where there were no warships available to defend against privateers, local vessels—usually sloops in the North American colonies—were often fitted out as a defense against them.[12] Privateers often fought enemy privateers they ran across, either for the sake of plunder or even at times out of a sense of honor, duty, or other obligation. Still, only rarely did they deliberately seek out enemy privateers, given the "hard knocks" and often minimal plunder to be had. Invariably when they did, they did so for material gain or because they had been specifically tasked to do so. Such deliberate privateer hunting by privateers was usually at the behest of colonial officials whose colonies lacked naval protection: the "Gentlemen of Her Majesties Council met and sent for Capt. Claver Commander of the Dutch Privateer, and proposed to him to go out and take said Privateer, at least to retake the Prize," for example, and "Whereupon his Honour being concerning for the Publick Weal and Safety of Her Majesties good Subjects, immediately caused the Drum to beat for Voluntiers, under the Command of Capt. *Wanton*."[13]

Raiding privateer ports was rarely done and even less rarely effective. Brazilian forces twice raided United Provinces's (today's Argentina) privateer bases in 1827 and were twice repulsed, for example. The blockading of privateer ports was always an option, but privateers were typically swift vessels and manned with the sort of men willing and able to run a blockade. Further, blockades were difficult to maintain, privateers sailed from more ports than could be blockaded (or raided), and privateers were generally a lower priority than enemy fleets. The large number of ports available to privateers made it virtually impossible to stop them anywhere but at sea—and the size of the sea made stopping them there virtually impossible.[14]

Although the merchantman's best defense against privateers and commerce-raiding men-of-war was to sail in convoy and otherwise to run (or sometimes to bluff, then run—some late-eighteenth-century English East India men even disguised themselves as French men-of-war), merchantmen often fought against privateers when they had to.[15] It is tempting to assume that they were more willing to fight a privateer than a pirate because they perceived less chance of violent retaliation in response to resistance. Even so, at times privateers of all nations committed unlawful abuses and violence, including murder, in reprisal against merchantmen who had the temerity to resist. Such violence was sometimes also committed against the loser in privateer versus privateer engagements: in 1709, "the French had taken one *Pease* of *Rhode-Island*, who stoutly resisted the Privateer, kill'd one of them, and wounded several; however being too strong for him, they boarded him, & he cry'd quarter, yet notwithstanding because of his Noble courage they barbarously kill'd him."[16] Although certainly not common, such incidents were not unknown. Much more common was occasional physical abuse and imprisonment under less than humanitarian conditions, as defined during the period.

Many of the fights against privateers were successful. "[B]ut in the interim Two French Privateers met with two Bristol men loaden with Provisions from Ireland, one of which being of some Force sunk one of the Privateers."[17] In another instance, "Capt. *Moules* Commander of a Briganteen Private Man of War from Barbadoes, has had several Rencounters with the *French* Privateers near that Island, in one of which he had kill'd *Lambert* one of their Captains, and several of his men; the next day he shot off both the Legs of another Privateer Captain."[18] According to Father Labat, the famous observer and chronicler of *boucaniers* and filibusters, among many other subjects, Captain Lambert was killed *after* the Barbadian privateer struck its colors after a bloody four-hour fight. An English sailor picked up a pistol and shot the famous French commander in the head. "This shot stunned his [Lambert's] crew, and the English, perceiving the disorder among them, raised their ensign anew and escaped."[19]

Merchantmen used closed quarters very effectively during the period, particularly in the case of a reasonably sized vessel with a reasonably trained crew willing to defend itself, and probably far more often than they actually engaged in a true "rencontre" or maneuvering engagement between ships. The defense was typically used to minimize losses to crew and passengers, rather than chance a conventional fight in the open, or because it was the only viable defense:

[A] French privateer sloop came up with her; lay by all night, and about five in the morning attacked the galley, with design to board her; but the Liverpool man having provided broken glass bottles, with which he covered his decks and retired to his close quarters, as the privateer came up so he levelled his chase guns upon him, that he made a lane fore and aft on the Frenchman's decks, who still advanced and boarded him; but finding it impossible to keep the galley's decks by reason of the warm fire from their close quarters, powder-chests, &c., they were obliged to retire.[20]

A similar, detailed account is provided by a 1706 *Boston News-Letter*:

> And Capt. Wilson judging he could not run from the Privateer, stood away for him, and soon came up with each other; whereupon Capt. Wilson halled up his Sails, he and his men retiring to their close Quarters, prepared to Fight; The Privateer presently boarded him, & clapt a considerable number of his men on board; Wilson and he were Lashed board and board about an hour. The Privateers finding it to hot for them on his Deck, their Gratings being all secured that they could not penetrate into his close Quarters, most of them went on board their own Sloop again, and from thence ply'd their small Arms on Wilson, and Wilson on them, till at last the Privateer was glad to cut his Lashings and get clear of him; and left 3 Fuzees [flintlock muskets], 3 Swords, and some Axes and Pistols behind them on Wilson's Deck and one of their men dead in his Chains; and they judge that they kill'd many of the Privateer's men, because they saw several fall and thrown down into their Hold, and the blood running very plentifully out of their Scuppers; Capt. Wilson had no men kill'd, only himself and Son received several Wounds; at parting Capt. Wilson discharged two Great Guns loaden with small Shot, which he supposes did great execution among the Privateers men.[21]

Boarders were typically well armed for breaching closed quarters: a dying pirate abandoned by his retreating comrades in the late seventeenth century was armed with "a fuzee, an axe, a cartouch-box [cartridge box], a stinkpot, a pistol, and a cutlass."[22]

In extreme cases, a merchant might use extreme tactics. In 1695, an English East Indiaman, for example, "after several hours dispute, and a 3d boarding, blew up her deck, with 70 French men, and so gott off."[23]

THE DEMISE OF THE PRIVATEER

The last significant privateering enterprises were those of the early to mid-nineteenth century. In 1823, France declined to issue commissions against Spain and vice-versa, although Spain apparently did issue a few.[24] Privateers of the United Provinces and Uruguay surged forth against the Brazilian merchantmen and men-of-war from 1825 to 1828. Peruvian privateers did likewise from 1838 to 1839 during war with Chile, as did Haitian privateers during the war with the Dominican Republic from 1845 to 1846. This last conflict largely spelled the end of privateering in the Mediterranean, northern waters, and the Americas.[25] Mexico tried to issue privateering commissions in 1846 in Havana and elsewhere during war with the United States, but the only taker, in Spain, was arrested and charged with piracy.[26] There would be one more effort at serious privateering in the West, the intention of another, and one circumstance that some would argue was a form of privateering. All three were part of a new age of seafaring created by changes in international law and, more importantly, by significant changes in naval technology. With the exception of these instances, privateering no longer existed in the sense of written commissions authorizing private vessels to attack enemy shipping.

The end of the privateer did not come through military action. Arguably it could not, for as long as there was significant maritime commerce, private vessels that could be armed, and insufficient naval resources, privateering was viable. Rather, the demise of privateering came about politically, through an international agreement that put in writing what was already largely in practice. In 1856, the Paris Declaration Respecting Maritime Law outlawed privateering among its signatories in return for the protection of private property. In the phrase of the time, "Free Ships Free Goods." War was war, but business was business, and private property was vital to every trading nation's survival. Governments and businesses wanted private property to be respected at sea as it had come to be respected ashore. Maritime trade had been brought almost to a standstill during the long Napoleonic Wars, and no nation of commerce wanted to see this occur again.[27] The depredations of privateers and the associated difficulty of regulating influenced opinion as well.

The United States, however, did not sign the declaration.[28] With its small navy and large merchant fleet, the United States preferred to keep its options open in case of war, particularly given that the declaration did not protect all private property at sea. It protected neutral and enemy goods on neutral shipping, as well as neutral goods on enemy shipping, contraband excluded in all cases.[29] But it did not protect *all* private property at sea, other than contraband, and the United States objected to this. In particular, the United States feared that in a war with a major sea power, much U.S. commerce could be blockaded in harbor (no matter that it could not be seized at sea), and seized neutral property might be held indefinitely.[30] Further, privateering had augmented the U.S. naval strategy during the American Revolution and the War of 1812 and might do so again. The position was a pragmatic one, notwithstanding that in the treaty of 1785 between the United States and Prussia, in which Benjamin Franklin was the principal U.S. negotiator, the two nations were the first to agree not to commission privateers against each other.[31] In the case of the declaration, the United States couched its decline in terms of the agreement's language and proposed a reasonable amendment that would not stand among the majority: "[P]rivate property of the subjects or citizens of a belligerent on the high seas shall be exempted from seizure by public armed vessels of the other belligerent, except it be contraband."[32] The amendment failed; Britain had lobbied heavily against it. However, the provision came to be generally recognized over time.

In 1865, Chile, whose navy consisted of one warship, intended to grant privateering commissions against Spain, and the U.S. flagged steamship *Meteor* was to be sold to Chile as a privateer, but the transaction fell through, as apparently did the rest of Chile's efforts at lawful sea roving.[33] During the Franco-Prussian War from 1870 to 1871, Prussia hired private ships and recruited seamen to man them. The vessels flew the Prussian flag, the crews wore Prussian uniforms, and the vessels were considered part of the Prussian navy. Even so, premiums were to be paid to the vessels' owners for the capture or destruction of enemy vessels, and this led some to argue that the Prussian vessels were indeed privateers.[34] But this was mere quibbling. The last real privateers sailed during the American Civil War.

COUNTERING THE CONFEDERATE RAIDERS

When the Civil War broke out, the Confederate States were at a distinct disadvantage when it came to naval warfare. The U.S. Navy remained essentially in U.S. hands, U.S. shipping was heavily invested in the North (as it had been since the nation's inception and long before) and the South lacked the shipyards and other resources to support a powerful navy. The Confederacy attempted to counter this naval superiority by means of fortified ports, blockade runners, commerce raiders, privateers, foreign assistance, and even new technology such as the submarine and the armored warship. The submarine CSS *Hunley* and the ironclads CSS *Virginia* and USS *Monitor* proved how quickly technology can progress when mankind is under duress—or at least when one part is trying to kill another. Although navies still had traditional sailing men-of-war with broadsides of conventional great guns, they were proved obsolete when the armored steam-powered CSS *Virginia* sank the large frigates USS *Congress* and USS *Cumberland* with impunity in Hampton Roads in 1862.

Practical steam power had been developed in 1807, followed swiftly by "paddle steamers" with paddlewheels astern then amidships port and starboard, then by "screw ships" or "screw steamers" with one or two screws (propellers) astern. Some steamers were coupled with sail, although in many, sail was auxiliary or even emergency propulsion at best. Iron steamships were constructed from 1822 on. However, the majority of merchantmen were still sailing vessels without auxiliary steam propulsion.

Gunnery changed as well. In the 1840s, the U.S. Navy introduced French "shell guns," and by the Civil War, U.S. Navy warships were mounted with similar guns of U.S. design. Nearly all Civil War naval ordnance was smoothbore and muzzle-loaded and often of far greater caliber than had been used in the recent past. A large variety of projectiles were used as well, ranging from solid round shot to hollow shot filled with explosives or shrapnel to rifled projectiles. Explosive shells had a variety of fuses, including concussion and percussion. The combination of greater caliber, range, and accuracy, coupled with the pivot mount (with the recoil taken up by skids) and various explosive shells, permitted warships to carry fewer guns while becoming far deadlier than their recent "wooden wall" predecessors. When armor was added to create the "ironclad," the modern warship was born.

Confederate privateers were typically schooners, usually under 200 tons, and privately outfitted and manned in the traditional manner. There were a few large privateer steamers and a variety of other vessels, including a full-rigged converted slaver and a converted revenue cutter. Crews tended to be small and armament light, often consisting of a single pivot gun, a few older "broadside guns," or both. The privateers were reasonably successful, capturing U.S. shipping throughout the war, although they were unable to significantly suppress U.S. international trade, and certainly not to the degree that the U.S. naval blockade affected Southern ports. Merchantmen could do little to counter the privateers, except try to run; they were now often unarmed except in certain waters, and even if they happened to carry small arms and light guns, these arms, along with fundamental defenses such as closed quarters, were useless against the much larger guns privateers and warships now carried. The U.S. Navy, in turn, had only a few successes against Confederate privateers: "On the day following, while standing into Charleston Harbor, she gave chase to the privateer *Petrel*, which, after firing two or three shots across the stern of the *St. Lawrence*, was sunk by a shell from that ship," for example.[35] Detecting privateers along thousands of miles of American and

European coastlines was a problem. The situation would have been worse, however, if the Confederacy had had the vessels and ports with which to flood the seas with privateers.

Confederate privateers captured U.S. merchantmen for profit, either sailing the prizes back to port (provided they could successfully run the blockade) or removing what valuables they could then sinking them. But the Confederacy also sent warships to sea as commerce raiders, not primarily to capture U.S. merchantmen, but to destroy them in what would become the principal form of commerce raiding in the age of steam. These vessels were not small, lightly armed vessels, but swift warships of 1,000 tons or more with a typically strong, modern armament.

The pursuit of the Confederate raider CSS *Tallahassee* is a good example of the problems and tactics of the pursuit of a commerce raider in this new age. In the summer of 1864, the steamer attacked U.S. shipping off New York, then ran north, entered the Gulf of St. Lawrence, and began burning U.S. fishing vessels and other maritime traffic. The raider was of approximately 1,000 tons and 230 feet long, had two engines and two screws, carried "two pivot guns and one light gun on the forecastle," had a complement of 140 men, and could make a maximum estimated fifteen knots under steam alone.[36] She could outrun almost any vessel on the water, sail or steam. The simple addition of two or three modern guns to a swift steamer created a commerce raider deadly to the merchantman and the equal of many warships.

A brief encounter with the raider by the USS *Britannia* illustrated the changes in naval warfare that had occurred in only three decades:

At 9:45 saw a rocket about N. E. thrown toward S. W., and shortly after several rockets were seen thrown in different directions, with considerable firing. Went to quarters . . . saw a stranger on our port quarter running alongshore toward Fort Fisher. Put the helm hard aport and went ahead fast, and fired as soon as the guns would bear. Continued firing and chasing until she was close under Fort Fisher, in white water, the breakers being between us and her. She fired one shrapnel at us, which burst close aboard, cutting our starboard paddle box a little . . . I feel confident that two shells took effect on her; one from 12-pounder rifled howitzer exploded directly over her, lighting up her decks and showing that she was a white propeller with two smokestacks and one mast.[37]

And from the USS *Niphon*: "At daylight saw a vessel at anchor near the Mound. She was a large screw steamer, painted light lead color, and apparently carrying three guns—two abaft and one forward; two smokestacks near together, small foremast, and had a white rebel ensign flying at her flagstaff."[38]

Besides warships dispatched in pursuit, the U.S. Navy sent small naval vessels to protect local fishing stations from the *Tallahassee*. One of them, the U.S. ship *Ino*, was ordered to disguise herself "so that she will not be taken for a man-of-war should one of the pirates happen to sight her," hoping, of course, to lure the raider within range.[39] Other tactics to protect shipping against the *Tallahassee* and other raiders included convoying local shipping, entering ports and stopping merchant ships and fishermen in order to acquire intelligence of the "pirate," blockading ports, cruising off and even entering neutral ports where Confederate raiders were known to frequent (of Britain and France especially), and putting diplomatic pressure on nations that might support the raiders by providing safe havens or naval stores—including now-vital coal. Steamers had the virtue of ignoring the wind, but only as long as they had coal, which burned quickly. Raiders could not raid far or escape pursuit for long without it. The *Tallahassee*, after a nineteen-day cruise in which it destroyed twenty-six merchant or fishing vessels and captured seven, ran into Halifax harbor, a neutral port, for coal, where it was trapped by two U.S. warships.[40] Although not captured, the *Tallahassee*'s brief commerce raid was over.

Throughout the Civil War, Union officials and naval officers often referred to the Confederate raiders, whether privateer or naval, as pirates. Even when they did not, they often referred to them as privateers rather than grant them the respect due men-of-war of a lawful state's navy. One of the great legal debates of the war, both in the United States and abroad, was whether, given that Confederate privateers and warships were commissioned by a state in rebellion, they should be considered as pirates under the law. Early in the war, Abraham Lincoln reportedly ordered that the privateers would be treated as pirates and thus hanged upon conviction. However, no Confederate privateers or raiders were ever hanged for piracy, apparently out of fear of reprisal against Union prisoners. Reasoned legal opinion generally held that the privateers and raiders were not pirates, given their commissions.[41] Indeed, because the United States had not signed the Declaration of Paris, privateering would have been legal on both sides of the conflict.

There was precedent as well: during the American Revolution, the colonies held that their privateering against Great Britain was lawful.

We cannot end the discussion of the Civil War commerce raiders without noting the pursuit and destruction of the CSS *Alabama* by the USS *Kearsarge*. In 1864, the *Kearsarge*, which had been lying in wait for the *Alabama* off the French coast, engaged her. Of note is that the battle took place under steam alone and at far longer range than "age of sail" engagements. A description of the engagement, derived from the logs and letters of the *Alabama's* captain, Raphael Semmes, provides a feel for the tactics of the day:

> "It took three-quarters of an hour for the Alabama to come within range of the Kearsarge. At the distance of one mile, the Alabama opened fire with solid shot. The Kearsarge took time to reply. After ten minutes the firing was sharp on both sides. According to the statement of the Captain of the Kearsarge, her battery consisted of seven guns–to wit, two 11-inch Dahlgrens–very powerful pieces of ordnance; four 32-pounders, one light rifle 28-pounder. She went into action with a crew of 162 officers and men. The armament of the Alabama consisted of one 7-inch Blakeley rifled gun, one 8-inch smooth-bore pivot gun, six 32-pounders, smooth-bore, in broadside. The Alabama's crew numbered not more than 120. On this head Captain Winslow speaks erroneously. He sets down the Alabama's crew at 150 officers and men. The Alabama had a formidable piece in the Blakeley rifled gun, but she was destitute of steel shot...[42]

The engagement took place within sight of land. Spectators massed on a hill at Querqueville, a few miles west of Cherbourg. What they witnessed was a hint of the future of naval warfare:

> "The crew of the Alabama, seamen and officers, were in high spirits throughout the engagement, though very early the slaughter set in and the decks were covered with blood. Their fire was rapid and admirable... Each ship fought her starboard broadside, and steamed in a circle to keep that side to the enemy. So, for an hour, this, to a distant spectator, monotonous manoeuvre continued, without perceptibly narrowing the range. Captain Semmes was standing on the quarter-deck when the chief engineer sent word to say that the ship was endangered by leakage. The first lieutenant, Mr. Kell, was sent below to inspect the damage. He returned with word that the ship was sinking. Captain Semmes at once

ordered the ship to be put about and steered towards shore. But the water was rising in her: the fires were speedily extinguished. The Alabama's shot from slackening had now ceased. It was evident to all on board that she was doomed."[43]

The *Alabama* settled beneath the surface of the sea, to be located by archaeologists more than a century later. With the end of the war, the age of the Western privateer was over, but not that of the naval commerce raider whose purpose was solely the destruction of enemy shipping. In the Middle and Far East, however, sea rovers, considered pirates by some and a form of privateer by others, still plied the seas under the colonial aegis.

13

Pirates, Rebels, and Warriors

Pirate Hunting in the East, 694 BC–AD 1896

One of the difficulties in attempting a broad subject with a wealth of research material at hand and a limited number of words in which to express facts, questions, and conclusions is that not everything, and sometimes nothing, can be covered thoroughly. Further, every culture tends to look at history through its own eyes, and the study of piracy and privateering—and in this case, of pirate hunting—is no different. The perspective is understandable: historians typically comprehend their own culture better than they do foreign ones and see best through their own experience; research material in the historian's native language, in the few others he or she may know, is more easily accessed; and scholarship in the social sciences tends to focus on one's local, national, or regional perspective, influence, or history, or on an often narrow theory or ideology. In other words, something, if only depth or detail in one or more pertinent areas, is invariably left out. This book, unfortunately, is no different. The most commonly neglected area of sea roving in Western scholarship is the vast history of Eastern sea roving, ranging from the Persian Gulf and Red Sea; west into the Indian Ocean and Indonesian waters; and north into the seas of China, the Philippines, and Japan; and even across the vast expanse of Polynesia. And when the sea roving of these regions is studied by Western scholars, it is often through the perspective of Western trade and colonialism, as opposed to that of local eyes. This is unfortunate, for the region from the Red Sea and Persian Gulf to the western Pacific comprises a third of the planet's geography, has seen multitudes of cultures rise and fall, and remains the crossroads of the world.

Most of the sea rovers who originated here preyed not only on regional vessels and towns, but also on the vessels of distant foreign traders in the region. From the sixteenth though early twentieth centuries, these vessels were often European. In the Red Sea, Persian Gulf, and waters surrounding India during the seventeenth and early eighteenth centuries, both Western and Eastern pirates and privateers plied their trade, and some crews were composed of peoples from both sides of the world. The suppression of these rovers was undertaken not only by local states or peoples, but also by those who traded from afar. As European nations gained control of Eastern trade, and at times of Eastern governments, nearly all of the sea roving in these areas came to be seen in Western eyes as piracy.

This is not to suggest that all Eastern rovers, even during times of Western colonial expansion, were privateers or patriotic insurgents. Many were in fact outright pirates who preyed on vessels indiscriminately solely for the sake of profit. But more than a few belonged to people for whom sea roving had long been a legitimate way of life, and others were in essence commerce raiders—albeit often "independent" ones—profiting from the merchant trade of nations that had more or less invaded foreign lands. In many cases, Western nations used anti-piracy operations to justify colonial expansion and, in such cases, classified all Eastern sea rovers as pirates.

Although there is plenty of tortuous legal reasoning and rumination leading to the conclusion that these rovers were indeed pirates (and also careful legal reasoning that many were *not*), we need only look at the definition of piracy in the *Oxford English Dictionary*, in which the core of the argument is repeated: piracy is committed when a sea-going plunderer does not hold "a commission from an *established civilized state*."[1] The statement is either a convenient sophistry or the expression of a reasonable justification for dealing expediently with sea rovers who fall outside the traditional late-medieval Western division of sea rovers into those commissioned by an established civilized state and thus legitimate, and those either not commissioned at all or who are sanctioned by a non-state or by an uncivilized one and thus a pirate. Still, we cannot forget the simple fact that even a lawful sea rover, whether a privateer in the Western sense or of a sea-roving people, is a threat and must be dealt with. Nor can we ignore the fact that any sea rover, commission or tradition in hand or not, who murders those he attacks must be dealt with harshly.

THE RED SEA AND THE GULF OF ADEN
Much of this long narrow seaway is bordered by desert, lacks good harbors, has prevailing north winds, and in the northern region has numerous coral islands perfect for pirates from local nomadic tribes to lie in wait for pass-

ing merchantmen. For these reasons, "Arabs developed camel routes along the whole western side of the peninsula" in early antiquity, an early example of defense against piracy.[2] Best known in the West for the depredations of Golden Age Anglo-American pirates such as Henry Every and Thomas Tew, the region had probably been infested with sea rovers since the first significant trade took to sea there. Egyptian merchantmen sailed the Red Sea as early as 2470 BC, and between 2341 and 2181 BC were trading as far as "Punt," probably the Somali coast today known as Puntland.[3] Around 1495 BC, Queen Hatshepsut sent a merchant fleet into the Red Sea, providing fodder for pirates, and Pharaoh Necho II's navy was busy protecting Egyptian shipping there circa 600 BC. Particularly notorious five centuries later were the Nabataean pirates, whose people also controlled the caravan routes of Arabia. The Nabataeans not only attacked vessels at sea but also lured them onto reefs in order to wreck and rob them. Red Sea merchantmen attempted to counter the pirates by manning their vessels with archers, but the pirates carried archers too, and their arrows were reportedly poisoned.[4] During the Middle Ages, some merchantmen were armed with Greek fire against pirates.[5]

Socotra, an island off the Horn of Africa and near which all trade from the Red Sea to the Arabian Sea had to pass, was an infamous pirate base in the Middle Ages. In the thirteenth century, Indian pirates sold their goods to the island's population, who, being Christians, purchased "of them without any scruple, justifying themselves on the ground of their being plundered from idolaters and Saracens."[6] Local residents had a novel form of pirate hunting: if "any vessel belonging to a pirate should injure one of theirs, they do not fail to lay him under a spell, so that he cannot proceed on his cruise until he has made satisfaction for the damage; and even although he should have had a fair and leading wind, they have the power of causing it to change, and thereby of obliging him, in spite of himself, to return to the island."[7] Red Sea piracy continued to be a threat right into the twentieth century when it was largely suppressed by naval patrols.

THE PERSIAN GULF

The Persian Gulf has long been frequented by pirates, and without doubt they were there long before Sennacherib and his navy swept the Gulf of Chaldean sea rovers in 694 BC, as described in chapter 3. Persian, Arab, and Indian pirates were known in the Gulf in the millennia afterward (Persian pirates also roamed the Caspian Sea for centuries), and in the seventeenth

and eighteenth centuries, European pirates cruised there as well.[8] So dangerous was the threat of piracy that Basra—famous in the voyages of Sinbad the
Sailor, and a major port that received Persian, Indian, and Chinese shipping,
thus a significant pirate target—had scaffolds erected to serve both as light-
houses and watchtowers.[9] Bahraini pirates were active in the Gulf, and Basra
sent an expedition to punish them in 825, probably one of many.[10]

In 1809, after forces of Said bin Sultan, the Sultan of Muscat and Oman,
were unable to halt Qawasim attacks—often referred to as "Wahhabi and
Joassmee piracy"—on Omani and British shipping in the Gulf, British forces
from India attacked and burned the pirate stronghold at Ras al-Khaimah,
suppressing the attacks for a few years. The Qawasim rovers had a reputation for brutality: in 1808, after a two-day fight, they captured the merchantman *Minerva* and put her captured crew to death by slitting their throats.
Reportedly only a single member of the crew was spared.[11] Roving soon increased again, and the Imam of Muscat was defeated in 1815 in an attack
on the Qawasim fleet and failed in an expedition against Ras al-Khaimah
in 1816.[12] Again, British forces crushed the "piratical" state and also aided
the ruler of Oman in his war against the Qawasim.[13] However, much of the
Qawasim "piracy" was arguably a form of privateering or commerce raiding,
albeit a bloodthirsty one, as part of a war over regional trade engaged in by
the rulers of Qawasim and Oman.[14] In Western eyes, any brutal form of sea
roving, even legitimate, had come to be considered piracy.

In 1867, Mohammed bin Khalifa of Bahrain put to sea and plundered
several nearby towns in Qatar, reportedly quite barbarically. Qatar tribes retaliated by land and sea, but unsuccessfully. In 1868, the gunboats *Clyde* and
Hugh Rose of the "Bombay Marine"—Her Majesty's Indian Navy—destroyed
the fort at al-Muharraq, and the HMS *Vigilant*'s boats burned piratical "war
dhows" belonging to bin Khalifa. A year later, bin Khalifa led a force against
Bahrain in order to regain control. He defeated the local leadership, killed
some of them, captured the towns of Manama and al-Muharraq, and plundered Manama. Britain ordered a retaliatory force to the area, destroyed the
fort at Manama, captured most of the piratical leaders, and imprisoned them
in Bombay.[15]

Again, one can argue that this was as much the pragmatic taking of sides
in a local conflict as it was an anti-piracy expedition. The problem with the
assistance of European colonial powers in anti-piracy operations was that it
came with a price: foreign influence over local government. In some cases,
Europeans assumed complete control over local government, if it had not

already been seized by virtue of conquest. With colonialism came Western navies, and with them control of local seas and the suppression not only of local piracy, but also local sea roving in any form.

INDIA

The Indian coasts were likewise long known for piracy, and Indian pirates had attacked international commerce at least since the ninth century AD, when an active trading route existed from the Red Sea and Persian Gulf to India, Indonesia, and China.[16] Indian pirates ranged not only along Indian shores, but also across the Arabian Sea and Bay of Bengal in *bawarij*, sleek thirty-nine to sixty-oared vessels, some of them armed with *naffatun* (warriors who threw naphtha incendiaries), some of them with roofs built over the rowers to protect them from projectiles.[17] Pots of unslaked lime were also a common weapon.

According to Marco Polo, in the mid-thirteenth century in Malabar:

As well here as in the kingdom of Guzzerat [Gujarat], which is not far distant, there are numerous pirates, who yearly scour these seas with more than one hundred small vessels, seizing and plundering; all the merchant ships that pass that way. They take with them to sea their wives and children of all ages, who continue to accompany them during the whole of the summer's cruise. In order that no ships may escape them, they anchor their vessels at the distance of five miles from each other; twenty ships thereby occupying a space of a hundred miles. Upon a trader's appearing in sight of one of them, a signal is made by fire or by smoke; when they all draw closer together, and capture the vessel as she attempts to pass. No injury is done to the persons of the crew; but as soon as they have made prize of the ship, they turn them on shore, recommending to them to provide themselves with another cargo, which, in case of their passing that way again, may be the means of enriching their captors a second time.[18]

John Fryar described the principal late-seventeenth century Indian rovers:

Here in this large Field of Water the *Singarian* Pirates wreak their Malice on the unarmed Merchants, who not long able to resist their unbounded Lust, become tame Slaves to their lawless Rage, and fall from the highest Hopes, to the humblest degree of Servitude: These are alike cruel, and equally savage as the *Malabars,* but not so bold as to adventure longer in these Seas than the Winter's Blasts have dismissed them, retiring with their ill-got Booty to the Coasts of *Sinda,* where they begin to rove nearer their Dens of Thievery, not daring to adventure Combat with the *Malabars,* or stir from thence till the Season makes the *Malabar* retire. No part of these Seas are without these Vermin, the Bay of *Bengal* being infested as much as the Coast of *Coromandel* by Outlaw'd *Portugals,* and are a mixture of that Race, the most accursedly base of all Mankind, who are known for their Bastard-Brood lurking in the Islands at the Mouths of the *Ganges,* by the Name of Racanners [Arakanese].[19]

Examples of seventeenth- and eighteenth-century Indian sea roving and pirate hunting shed light on the difficulties facing both the pirate hunter and the merchantman, as well as the effect of colonial empire on pirate hunting and local politics. India's internal political situation was itself complicated, composed as it was of competing regions, peoples, and religions. It was made more difficult by competing Portuguese, Dutch, and English interests, beginning with Portuguese explorer and trader Fernão Mendes Pinto's early-sixteenth-century expedition, noted among other things for acts of piracy and pirate hunting by adventurer Antonio de Faria. In the seventeenth century on the northeast coast of India, in what is today Bangladesh, were the Feringhis—the "Outlaw'd Portugals" Fryar referred to—and Arakanese rovers and their strongholds of Chittagong and Sandwip. Portuguese pirates had long been a problem in India to both Western and Eastern shipping since the mid-sixteenth century and had allied with the Arakan ruler Minbin as mercenaries. In 1665, Mogul forces captured both of the major havens of these pirates' descendents, freed thousands of prisoners, and ended the Feringhi reign.[20]

In the late seventeenth century, Indian and European merchantmen feared falling into the hands of the Malabaris, rovers of the southwest coast of India and strict Muslims said to be very cruel towards Christians. In the words of French traveler Jean-Baptiste Tavernier:

I have seen a Barefoot Carmelite Father who had been captured by these pirates. In order to obtain his ransom speedily, they tortured him to such an extent that his right arm became half as short as the other, and it was the same with one leg. The commanders only pay wages to the value of two ecus to each soldier for the six months which they generally spend at sea, and do not share with them the prizes taken; but they are allowed to keep the garments and the food of those whom they have captured. It is true that the soldiers are permitted to leave then, and if the commanders desire them to remain they are obliged to pay them afresh. They seldom venture farther to sea than from 20 to 25 leagues, and whenever the Portuguese capture any of these pirates they either hang them straight off or they throw them into the sea. These Malabaris number 200 and sometimes as many as 250 men in each vessel, and they go in squadrons of from ten to fifteen vessels to attack a big ship, and they do not fear cannon. They at once come alongside and throw numbers of fire-pots on the deck, which cause much injury if care is not taken to provide against them. For as they know the habits of the pirates, immediately they see them they close all the scuttles on deck, and cover it with water, so that these pots, which are full of fireworks, cannot take effect.[21]

In the early eighteenth century, much of the coast from Bombay (Mumbai) to the region of Goa was under the control of the Maratha navy, whose members were commonly referred to by Europeans as "Angrian pirates." More correctly, in their maritime ventures, the Hindu Maratha were opportunistic sea rovers whose vessels were authorized to prey on shipping that failed to pay tribute, and thus they were, strictly speaking, privateers or even legitimate, if plundering, men-of-war. Controlling the coast from Bombay south to Goa, the Angrians sent their *grabs* (a type of Indian sailing vessel) armed with great guns, and *gallivats* (a form of galley) to sea to, in the eyes of their victims, capture any vessel that happened by, and in their own eyes, capture any vessel without a pass—that is, any who had not paid tribute. Unfortunately for this line of reasoning, the Angrians also captured vessels and sacked towns and villages as far south as the former kingdom of Travancore, far beyond their own waters, although one could argue that this was merely a form of local warfare. After all, the "Mycenaean" sea-roving model has been a common one in many ages worldwide.

The Angrian rovers—whose ranks included not only Maratha, but also Christian and Muslim renegades and a variety of other peoples—were capable of engaging on a large scale, and often did. The British East India Company, which sustained significant financial and human losses from Angrian attacks, could not come to terms with the rovers. Naval bombardments by Britain, Portugal, and the Netherlands were failures. Angrian leaders, such as the famous Maratha admiral Kanhoji Angria, not only profited from their sea-roving lifestyle but also doubtless saw themselves as patriots, as does the state of India today, notwithstanding that their attacks ranged far beyond their own waters. By 1728, the Angrians controlled and had fortified more than one hundred miles of coast. Merchant vessels had to go heavily armed and in convoy.[22] In 1755, after a successful attack on three well-armed Dutch ships of fifty, thirty-two, and eighteen guns, in which the first two were burned and the third was captured, a joint force of East India men-of-war and allied Maratha grabs, gallivats, and soldiers set out. The British fleet bombarded the "Severndroog" (Suvarnadurg) fort and forced its surrender, then captured "Bancoote" (Bankot) but went no further, leaving the sea-roving empire largely intact. A year later, another joint expedition attacked the Angrian pirate empire and burned nearly its entire fleet. In particular, the expedition was noted for its "plundering" mentality. The spoils were divided solely among the British, who had secretly arranged the division before setting out. Maratha complaints about the division were dismissed on the grounds of an attempted bribe of a British officer, which reportedly would have permitted looting by Maratha forces, notwithstanding that the bribe attempt came long after the division of spoils had already been arranged.[23] Again, the naval presence associated with colonial empire eventually reduced sea roving to the level of nuisance.

MALAYA, BORNEO, AND THE PHILIPPINES

With its many thousands of miles of coastlines, its vital straits and passages, and its jungle-shrouded waterways, Indonesia was until recently a pirate's paradise and remains a stronghold of small-scale piracy. Predominant among the rovers of this region were the "pirates" of the Malay Peninsula, the Sea Dyaks of Sarawak (west Borneo), the rovers of Mindanao in the south Philippines, and the rovers of the Sulu Archipelago of the southwest Philippines. All were known for slave raiding and were active into the nineteenth century. Likewise, all were well noted for their daring: one of the Malay chiefs, Raga, reportedly even surprised two British sloops-of-war sent against him in the early nineteenth century.[24] The Sea Dyaks were known legitimately as warriors and headhunters and were often allied with Malay rovers. The Sulu rovers put to sea great slave-raiding fleets at the time of the southwest monsoon, known locally as the "pirate wind," and actively resisted Spanish, Dutch, and British incursions and counterattacks into the nineteenth century.[25] Largely unreported are the sea-roving and pirate-hunting expeditions of the nearby Austronesian and Polynesian peoples.

Most of these Indonesian rovers used large *proas* (long sharp-bowed vessels swift under sail and oar, sometimes fitted with a bronze cannon in the bow), armed themselves with a variety of highly effective edged weapons and spears, and lived in fortified villages. In the words of a historian who lived among them:

> The Malay fleet consisted of a large number of long war-boats, or *prahus* [proas], each about ninety or more feet long, and carrying a brass gun in the bows, the pirates being armed with swords and spears and muskets. Each boat was paddled by from sixty to eighty men . . . These piratical raids were often made with the secret sanction of the native rulers, who obtained a share of the spoil as the price of their connivance. The Dyaks of Saribas and Skrang and the Balaus gladly joined the Malays in these expeditions, not only for the sake of obtaining booty, but because they could thus indulge in their favourite pursuit, and gain glory for themselves by bringing home human heads to decorate their houses with. The Dyak *bangkongs* were long boats capable of holding as many as eighty men. They often had a flat roof, from which the warriors fought, while their comrades paddled below.[26]

Given that all of these rovers were seafaring peoples for whom raiding was a fundamental cultural practice, it is difficult to legitimately classify them as pirates, no matter their depredations. Again, they fell between the modern Western definitions of pirate and privateer, failing to fit either exactly, and thus were invariably classified as pirates by Europeans. But no matter their classification, they were a serious threat to all vessels passing through their waters. There were numerous nineteenth-century expeditions against the various Indonesian rovers, and the brief description of the most significant of them must suffice to describe the tactics of these "pirates" and their pirate hunters. In 1841, a young adventurer named James Brooke suppressed a rebellion in Sarawak and in reward was made governor of Sarawak by the Sultan of Brunei, under whose administration the region fell. Given that Sarawak did not fall under the control of any European colonial power, Brooke made himself the first of the "White Rajas" of Sarawak. Using his schooner the *Royalist*, he diligently hunted the sea-roving Dyaks in a series

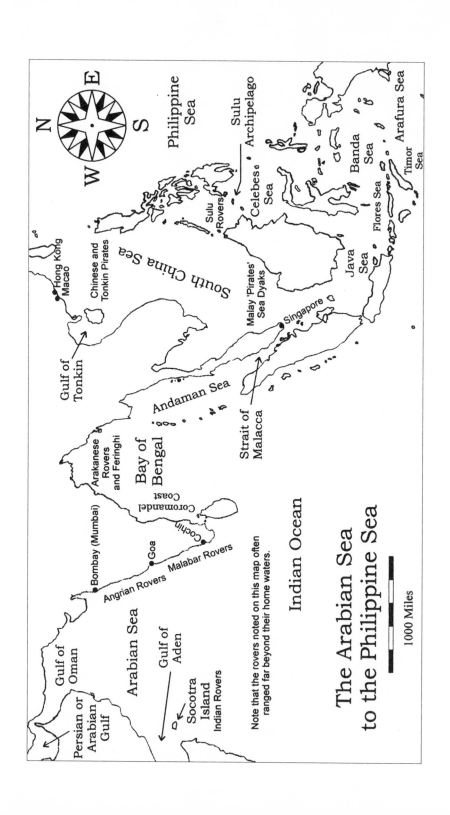

The Arabian Sea
to the Philippine Sea

1000 Miles

Note that the rovers noted on this map often
ranged far beyond their home waters.

Indian Ocean

N
E
S
W

Philippine
Sea

Sulu
Archipelago

Sulu
Rovers

Celebes
Sea

Banda
Sea

Arafura Sea

Flores Sea

Timor
Sea

Java
Sea

Hong Kong
Macao

Chinese and
Tonkin Pirates

South China Sea

Gulf of
Tonkin

Malay 'Pirates'
Sea Dyaks

Singapore

Andaman Sea

Strait of
Malacca

Arakanese
Rovers
and Feringhi

Bay of
Bengal

Coromandel
Coast

Cochin

Bombay (Mumbai)

Goa

Angrian Rovers

Malabar Rovers

Arabian Sea

Gulf of
Oman

Persian or
Arabian
Gulf

Gulf of
Aden

Socotra
Island
Indian Rovers

of bloody engagements highly romanticized at the time. He soon had the assistance of the HMS *Dido*, and together they brought Malay and Dyak roving largely to a close.

Brooke's own words, including the references common to racial prejudice at the time, provide the description of a typical fight against the Dyaks:

29th. —My birthday. Men collected, and to-morrow we start for Telang Telang. This morning, much to my relief, our fleet returned, after an encounter with thirteen Dyak boats. About one o'clock on the 28th, pulling into a bay between Morotaba and Tanjong Poe, they came unexpectedly on them. One Borneon boat had lagged behind; the Pangeran who commanded deserted the second, and sought refuge with the Tumangong, trying to induce him to fly; and the crew of the third, a large boat with my two Europeans on board, was, by their account, in a state of fear, which totally incapacitated them from acting. All rose, none would pull; all shouted, none would serve the guns; all commanded, none obeyed; most were screaming out to run; all bellowing out, in hopes of frightening the enemy; none to direct the helm. The Tumangong, with only seventeen men in all, insisted on advance; and the Borneons, encouraged by threats from the Europeans, and the good example of the Javanese, did not fly. The two boats opened their fire; the Dyaks retreated in confusion and alarm: but from the tumult, the noise, and the rocking of the boat, Mr. Crimble could only fire three times with the bow six-pounder carronade, and from other guns loaded with grape and canister, while the rascally Borneons never fired at all.

The Dyaks suffered loss, and left behind them clothes, rice, fish, cooking-pots, swords, &c.; and, considering the state of the Borneons, it was lucky the dread of our prowess put them to flight so easily. Crimble assured me that, with a Siniawan crew, he could have destroyed half their force. The Dyaks behaved very well, pulling off with great steadiness and without noise.[27]

Brooke also worked to suppress Malay, Mindanao, and Sulu sea rovers on the Borneo coast. The typical anti-piracy strategy in the region was to trap the rovers upriver where they could not escape; destroy their vessels, homes, and fortifications; and capture or kill the rovers themselves. This suppression of sea rovers via the destruction of their vessels, villages, and rovers themselves was a successful, if brutal, strategy and was the typical strategy used against indigenous or aboriginal rovers around the world, including Native Americans, the Caribs in particular.

CHINA, TONKIN, AND JAPAN

As in all of the piracies and pirate-hunting practices discussed in this chapter, an entire book could be devoted to each one, and those of China, Tonkin (Vietnam), and Japan are no exception. China experienced waves of large-scale piracy throughout much of its history, including the mid-sixteenth, mid-seventeenth, and turn of the nineteenth centuries, and constant small-scale piracy well into the twentieth century. The British made repeated pirate-hunting expeditions, jointly with Chinese forces and also unilaterally, against powerful Chinese pirates into the mid-nineteenth century, the expeditions led by the HMS *Medea* being some of the best known.[28] Chinese pirate vessels typically consisted of junks, both sea-going and riverine, often armed with small naval cannon and swivel guns. Perhaps the best known of the Chinese rovers are the seventeenth-century half-Chinese, half-Japanese patriot "pirate" Koxinga (Zheng Chenggong), who fought against the Manchus and drove the Dutch from Formosa (modern Taiwan), and nineteenth-century Lady Cheng (Cheng I Sao), who inherited her husband's pirate fleet, led a brutal piratical campaign against both Western and Eastern shipping in the early nineteenth century, defeated Chinese forces sent against her, and was eventually lured from piracy by an offer of amnesty. Her followers who failed to accept the offer were hunted down.

Mid-nineteenth-century British seaman Edward Brown served aboard a Chinese merchant *lorcha*—a European hull with a Chinese junk rig commonly used as a pirate craft—and described a chase by Chinese pirates in craft called *tymung*, which used both sail and up to forty or more sweeps (long oars) for propulsion. The lorcha prepared for possible attack by "getting our guns out of the hold, mounting them, and preparing our ammunition and stink-pots, in case of an attack, which we all expected; though, as our sailing capacities were good, and our guns and powder all of English manufacture, I should not have been the least afraid of falling in with any single piratical vessel."[29] Soon chased by pirates, and the wind falling, the merchant lorcha put out her sweeps in an effort to prolong the chase. The wind rose again and the seven pirate vessels closed. Brown pointed out a deficiency in the lorcha's defense: "The heavy guns being mostly mounted forward on swivels, and the high sterns, prevent a vessel chased from replying effectually to the fire of an enemy, without changing her course every time she fires a shot; by which she loses distance considerably."[30] The merchantman was forced to haul on the port tack to bring the enemy on the quarter. Soon she disabled one pirate vessel and hulled (shot holes in the hull at or near the waterline) several. The chase continued under both sail and sweep. When the pirates were in range, the merchantman began firing grapeshot, but it was not enough. With several of its crew dead or wounded and the rest exhausted from the sweeps, the pirates—two hundred or more—came alongside, threw stinkpots, and boarded and captured the hapless lorcha.[31]

Vietnam was harassed for centuries variously by Tonkin, Chinese, Japanese, Indonesian, and European pirates. In the late eighteenth century, Chinese pirates joined the Vietnamese Tay-son rebellion more or less as privateers. The most notable expedition against Tonkin pirates was conducted by France during the "pacification" of Tonkin from 1886 to 1896, after the Sino-French war of 1883 to 1885, in which China had used Chinese and Vietnamese pirates as auxiliaries. The French military pursued insurgents, bandits, and pirates in the region, typically referring to all of them as pirates, no matter their nationality, political affiliation, or ultimate purpose. In similar fashion, the French believed that many of the Vietnamese made no distinction between insurgents, bandits, and pirates, considering them all as patriots. These various "pirates" were armed with a motley collection of small arms, as one would expect of insurgents and pirates, ranging from early-nineteenth-century muskets to late-nineteenth-century rifles, and they were noted as being extraordinarily mobile, making their suppression a long, slow, difficult process. These "pirate" tactics of insurgency were repeated by the Vietnamese twice again in the twentieth century, first against France, then against the United States.[32]

Japan had a long history of pirates who served both independently and as mercenaries in various military ventures. In the tenth century, Fujiwara no Sumitomo led a pirate fleet against imperial forces but was defeated and beheaded. In the twelfth century, the imperial court ordered Taira no Shigemori to pursue pirates in Kyushu, apparently because they were stealing royal revenues. Korea long had problems with Japanese pirates, whose raids increased significantly in the fourteenth century. In the early fifteenth century, a Korean fleet attacked and defeated Japanese pirates on Tsushima, destroying both vessels and settlements. A more subtle form of pirate hunting was also practiced in the fifteenth century when China required all Japanese vessels to bear certificates as proof they were not pirates or smugglers. In the early sixteenth century, Japanese pirates used Formosa as a base, and defeated Chinese efforts to dislodge them.[33] Japanese piracy was largely quashed from the seventeenth century onward, in large part apparently due to the centralization of Japanese government and its suppression of feudal conflicts, combined with Chinese anti-piracy efforts.

Japanese pirates, called *wakō*, at times ranged as far as India. John Davis, the famous navigator, met a Japanese pirate crew traveling aboard a captured junk in 1605 near Singapore. A member of his crew described the encounter after they anchored at a small island near Bintan, an island twenty miles southeast of Singapore:

> [T]hey were ninetie men, and most of them in too gallant a habit for Saylers, and such an equalitie of behaviour among them that they seemed all fellowes . . . they, seeing oportunitie, and talking to the rest of their Companie which were in my ship, being neere to their Juncke, they resolved, at a watchword betweene them, to set upon us resolutely in both ships. This being concluded they suddenly killed and drave over-boord all my men that were in their ship; and those which were aboord my ship sallied out of my Cabbin, where they were put, with such weapons as they had, finding certaine Targets in my Cabbin, and other things that they used as weapons. My selfe being aloft on the Decke, knowing what was likely to follow, leapt into the waste, where, with the Boate Swaines, Carpenter, and some few more wee kept them under the halfe-decke. At their first comming forth of the Cabbin, they met Captaine Davis comming out of the Gun-roome, whom they pulled into the Cabbin, and giving him six or seven mortall wounds they thrust him out of the Cabbin before them. His wounds were so mortall that he dyed as soone, as he came into the waste.[34]
>
> They pressed so fiercely to come to us, as we receiving them on our Pikes, they would gather on our Pikes with their hands to reach us with their Swords. It was neere halfe an houre before Three o we could stone them backe into the Cabbin: In which time we had killed three or foure of their Leaders. After they were driven into the Cabbin they fought with us at the least foure houres before we could suppresse them, often fyring the Cabbin, burning the bedding, and much other stuffe that was there. And had we not with two Demy-culverings, from under the halfe decke, beaten downe the bulke head and the pumpe of the ship we could not have suppressed them from burning the ship. This

Ordnance being charged with Crosse-barres, Bullets, and Case-shot, and bent close to the bulke head, so violently marred therewith boords and splinters that it left but one of them standing of two and twentie. Their legs, armes, and bodies were so torne as it was strange to see how the shot had massacred them. In all this conflict they never would desire their lives, though they were hopelesse to escape: such was the desperatenesse of these Japonians. Only one lept over-boord, which afterward swamme to our ship againe and asked for grace; wee tooke him in, and asked him what was their purpose? He told us that they meant to take our shippe and to cut all our throates. He would say no more, but desired that he might be cut in pieces.[35]

It is no wonder that "the Japons are not suffered to land in any Port in India with weapons: being accounted a people so desperate and daring that they are feared in all places where they come."[36]

THE TECHNOLOGICAL ADVANTAGE

By the nineteenth century, much of the Western advantage over Eastern sea rovers was technological and commonly the basis of their destruction. So significant was this advantage that by the late nineteenth century, large-scale piracy had been eradicated, leaving only a few local pockets of resistance, primarily in the South China Sea and Indonesian waters. Quickly had warships gone from sail to sail and steam to steam alone, with many merchantmen quickly following suit, although much merchant sail held onto canvas alone until the early twentieth century. Wrought iron hulls (both sail and steam) appeared in the first half of the nineteenth century, followed later by steel hulls. Naval guns developed to incredible size, range, and accuracy, moving from the smoothbore Dahlgren-type guns with explosive shells in the mid-eighteenth century to the great long-range rifled artillery of the dreadnoughts and the even more powerful battleships that followed. Light artillery, suitable for pirate hunting, and as well, as did small arms.

In the case of small arms, the percussion lock replaced the flintlock in the first half of the nineteenth century, although the percussion lock remained in use in some places into the twentieth century.[37] The mid-nineteenth century saw the development of the percussion rifled-musket, followed by the breech-loading single-shot rifle, then the repeating rifle, whose modern cartridge and firing systems replaced the percussion lock. The revolver, developed mid-nineteenth century, was followed in the late nineteenth century by the magazine-fed semi-automatic pistol, although the revolver did not disappear and is unlikely to. The mid-nineteenth-century Gatling gun was followed by the first true machine gun in 1880. However, at least one simple naval weapon remained in limited use in the West throughout the introduction of new technology: the cutlass was still issued, if only in limited quantities, by most Western navies until World War II.

Even so, traditional sea-roving tactics remained largely unchanged, as did those of traditional pirate hunting. Modern warships searched for, found, overtook, and engaged pirate fleets on open waters and destroyed them or tracked them to their lairs and similarly dealt with them, as had been done for centuries. The expensive technology of engine, armor, and rifled gun, however, gave the modern pirate hunter a significant advantage over the more traditionally equipped pirate, many of whom still cruised in sailing vessels, and some of whom still mounted traditional muzzle-loading cannon—great guns, that is—into the early twentieth century. However, technology was about to significantly change the nature of the commerce raider, and with it change the nature of those hunting and destroying him.

14

Death from Beneath the Waves

Combating the Submarine Menace, 1914–1945

"Submarine Destroys Irish Fishing Fleet," read a 1918 headline. Beneath it were the details: "BELFAST, June 14.—The sinking of a considerable number of fishing boats between the County Down coast and the Isle of Man recently was one of the most wanton acts yet perpetrated by Hun pirates."[1]

A German U-boat "armed fore and aft" and bearing "no identification number" had appeared among a flotilla of twenty or so Irish fishing vessels, fired two shots across the bow of the ketch *Never Can Tell,* and ordered its crew to abandon ship and bring with them any small boats they had. The Germans sank the ketch with explosives then repeated the process until each of the fishing vessels lay at the bottom of the sea. They advised the fishermen, who now filled the small boats, to make for the Irish coast. In all, it was a routine act of modern commerce raiding, except that in this case the raider had the advantage, as necessary, of surprise from beneath the sea.[2]

The reference to submarine crews as pirates was not only typical but grossly exaggerated, just as was the similar piratical reference to commerce raiders in general. Conventional European naval forces of the age of sail had generally looked down upon the unconventional tactics and "plunder as purpose" of pirates and privateers, although conventional navies did employ unconventional tactics when necessary. Still, they often considered their unconventional adversaries to be inferior or even less than honorable—pirates, for example, and North African corsairs. "The Pyrates, tho' singly Fellows of Courage, yet wanting such a Tye of Order, some Director to unite that Force, were a contemptible Enemy, neither killed nor wounded us a man in taking them, and must ever, in the same Circumstances, be the Fate of such Rabble," wrote John Atkins in the early eighteenth century.[3]

To the conventional naval officer, such enemies did not merit "honorable" warfare, or at least were undeserving of it, not to mention that conventional tactics were often unsuitable against them. After all, most pirates and privateers typically ran from warships and fought only when they had no choice. As navies turned from sail to steam, much of the leadership of the early steel navies appears to have retained this prejudice against unconventional forces and tactics. For these officers, the greatest action was battleship fleet versus battleship fleet, in line of battle and exchanging broadsides, although with advances in the technology of weapons—increased accuracy, vastly greater range, and powerful explosive projectiles—even this romantic, heroic notion of naval warfare would fade from reality, due largely to advances in aviation. This notion did not go quietly. The U.S. Navy recommissioned four battleships in the 1980s, primarily for their shore bombardment capability, although national prestige was certainly a factor. Anyone who has ever stepped aboard any commissioned battleship, or even one preserved as a monument or museum, has probably felt the impressive, romantic lure of these great warships. Similarly, to those of the traditional mentality, the second-greatest action at sea was a single combat between two ships, as with the frigates of old. To many traditionalists, submarine warfare came across as anything but heroic.

This attitude should come as no surprise. After all, submarines attack by ambush from beneath the sea. Even when submarines attacked from the surface, as they often did in World Wars I and II by using their low profile to help conceal their movement, their initial approach was often underwater, as often was their egress or escape. Although the ambush or surprise attack from concealment has been a routine, obvious tactic of warfare, it has nonetheless often been excoriated as unfair, skulking, or even cowardly by those who—for reasons of social norms, superior conventional forces, or the natural desire to engage in battle on one's own superior terms—preferred to engage in warfare in the open. Supporting the perception is the natural tendency to believe in the nobility of the "fair fight on equal terms," something that warfare necessarily eschews. Warfare is neither sport nor ritual combat, and surprise attacks from concealment can grant a decisive advantage, putting the weaker party on equal or superior terms with a more powerful adversary or permitting a more powerful adversary to minimize losses. Like speed, surprise is one of the critical factors in warfare, and concealment is a typical, critical means of surprise. One can argue even that surprise is a form of speed in that it disconcerts the adversary, thus granting the attacker the advantage of a measure of time over him.

Surprise attacks, especially those from ambush, also sow the seeds of doubt and fear. Hyper-vigilance becomes mandatory, for the target never knows when or where an attack might come. The price of this constant, vital vigilance is continual stress and anxiety. To refer to an attacking submarine as a pirate was therefore not surprising, given the pirate's unconventional tactics, his use of surprise to minimize losses and maximize profit, and his preference for attacking the weak. In a sense, it was Odyssean: if it is acceptable to blind the Cyclops in his sleep, then it should also be acceptable to sink an unsuspecting warship by stealth. It is not a fair fight, but it was never supposed to be.

Further, because a submarine often had to do nothing more than point a deck gun at a vessel in order to compel surrender—as was the case with the Irish fishing boats—there was an obvious sea-roving aspect to submarine warfare, acknowledged by all sides. Submarine crews sometimes referred to themselves as pirates, freebooters, or buccaneers, reveling in the fact that they were indeed the modern predators of the seas. Whenever they could during World War I, German U-boat crews plundered captured ships of provisions before they sank them, again providing meat for the image.[4] During both world wars, British submarines even flew the skull and crossbones on their return to port from a cruise during which at least one enemy ship had been sunk. The practice began and has continued as a reflection of the view that submariners were more or less pirates. The British nuclear hunter-killer submarine HMS *Conqueror* flew the skull and crossbones on its return to Her Majesty's Naval Base Clyde in Scotland after sinking the Argentine cruiser *General Belgrano* in the South Atlantic during the Falklands War, and other British submarines have done so at the end of deployments related to the post-9/11 wars in Iraq and Afghanistan.[5]

So appealing was it to equate submarine warfare with piracy or piratical adventure that even a real pirate might be tempted to join a submarine crew. In 1916, Ernest Schiller, serving a life sentence for hijacking the British merchant ship *Matoppa*, scaled one of the walls of the Atlanta Federal penitentiary and made a dash for freedom amidst the prison guards' fusillade. Unfortunately for this pirate of the Dreadnought Age, just as he was nearly free of the prison grounds, an alert teamster brought him down. Interrogated by the warden, Schiller claimed his impulse to escape was brought on when he learned that the German submarine *Deutschland* was visiting the United

States. "I . . . sought freedom in order to join that gallant crew. I hate the English for their treatment of me, and I am determined to get free and seek vengeance on them."[6] Schiller, whose real name was Clarence R. Hodson, had previously been arrested in England on suspicion of espionage but maintained his innocence, although he later bragged to U.S. authorities that he had indeed been a German spy. However, a friend who had been arrested at the same time in London was convicted of signaling to raiding Zeppelin airships and put to death.[7]

Exiled from England, Schiller eventually came to New York, where, destitute, he planned an attack on the *Matoppa* with four accomplices who quickly deserted him. Arming himself with two revolvers, he stowed away aboard the ship in one of her boats, then single-handedly captured her and her crew of forty-three. Nineteen hours later, he surrendered after he was trapped by pilot and coast patrol boats as he attempted to escape to shore. Schiller's defense, perhaps inspired by his attorney, was essentially that he had acted as a privateer—that he acted for political or nationalistic purpose, and not for private purpose as a pirate would have. At the time of his arrest, however, he claimed he was after the money aboard the ship. An examining doctor described him as "mentally unbalanced."[8]

But the submarine was destined to inspire more than just quixotic crime. Its very nature inspired extreme views on strategy, tactics, and the laws of humanity. Many naïve or manipulative politicians, propagandized citizens, outraged victims or victims' families, and quite possibly a few traditional naval officers, argued during and after World War I to abolish the submarine as a weapon, and some even argued that submariners were not only pirates but should be prosecuted as such.[9] As noted in chapter 1, labeling an adversary a pirate often makes for great headlines and can have great propaganda value, the truth notwithstanding.[10] In the aforementioned "pirate" attack on twenty Irish fishing vessels, for example, none of the fishermen were harmed, the U-boat captain was described as being courteous, and the only pillage was "some ropes and a pair of sea boots."[11]

However, some acts of submarine warfare incurred violent accusations of murder and incited calls for bloody revenge. In such cases, the term *pirate* was easy to adopt. In 1915, the German submarine *U-20* torpedoed the unarmed British passenger liner *Lusitania* off the Old Head of Kinsale, a promontory in southwestern Ireland, with the loss of more than 1,000 lives, most of them civilian passengers, many of them neutrals.[12] From the German perspective, the U-boat commander had simply been following orders to enforce a blockade, and indeed, warnings that ships in the "restricted zone" around Britain were subject to attack had been issued, including in U.S. newspapers.[13] Not until 1916 would Germany warn that "armed liners" would be sunk without warning.[14]

However, no one in Britain or the United States had expected an un-armed civilian liner to be torpedoed without warning.[15] Many journalists, politicians, and common citizens—Teddy Roosevelt among them—loudly proclaimed the attack to have been an act of piracy.[16] In 1918 the Federal District Court of New York upheld the British legal view that the attack was an act of piracy, although more reasoned, less emotional opinions had correctly concluded otherwise and still do.[17] Whether the torpedoing violated international law remains open for debate, however. Certainly many people did and do view the sinking of the *Lusitania* as a barbarous act of inhumanity.[18] German U-boats sank other neutral ships as well during World War I, also resulting in the death of innocent, neutral civilians.[19] These acts were one of the main sources of anti-German and anti-submarine sentiments during the war.

There were other accusations and calls for retribution as well, often inspired by allegations of the deliberate murder of surrendered merchant and fishing crews by German submariners during World War I. According to one news report, "Sometimes the submarine moved around a raft, and German officers jeered at the misery of their victims while shrapnel tortured or killed them."[20] The British Seaman's Union boycotted Germany after the war in protest of these crimes, and the British government put U-boat commanders on trial, even if they had not been arrested and turned over by German authorities.[21] The specter of piracy was often raised: "No heartless pirate in past centuries was guilty of greater or more wanton cruelty than is shown in the record of their offenses."[22] Submarines, "as Germany uses them, 'are in effect outlaws'" wrote one commentator.[23]

However, all such acts and perpetrators of barbaric submarine warfare, real and imagined, of either world war and committed by submariners of any nation were, by all accounts, not the norm. Even warfare, a barbarous practice indeed, is expected in most modern cultures to be limited in its barbarity, even if in fact it is not. The murder of civilians, particularly of neutrals, hearkened back to a not-so-distant European past when lives were held to be of little value—one need only recall the routine slaughter of prisoners at sea during the Middle Ages. Our modern "laws of war and humanity" are relatively recent implementations and not always successful. The same disdain for human life reared its monstrous head again worldwide during World War II and several times thereafter in various parts of the world. It is surely a difficult task, that of governing humankind's capacity to slaughter its own.

At any rate, most submarine commanders of all nations appear to have done their best to avoid unnecessary loss of civilian life. Perhaps the real complaint against the submarine was not of its stealthy, "underhanded," "give no warning" form of warfare, but of the consequences of such warfare. Until World War I, and for a decade afterward in some minds, a warship's captain and crew had a legal obligation to warn a private vessel of attack and a moral obligation to render assistance to those it placed in peril of the sea. "German authorities on the laws of war at sea themselves establish beyond all doubt that, though in some cases the destruction of an enemy trader may be permissible, there is always an obligation to first secure the safety of the lives on board."[24]

The submarine, however, was often in no position to do so, and survivors had to fend for themselves. Even when it was safe to pick up survivors, submarine crews often had orders not to do so, as often did surface ships of both sides as well. A fictional observer, based on novelist Lothar-Günther Buchheim's own experiences aboard a World War II U-boat, ponders the destruction of a tanker: "How does the Old Man feel when he visualizes the mass of ships that he himself has destroyed? And when he thinks of the crowds of men who were traveling on those ships and went down with them, or were blown up by the torpedoes—scalded, drowned, smashed. Or half scalded and half smothered and then drowned." He ponders further on survivors adrift at sea: "The Old Man stands motionless: a sailor who dares not help another in distress because an order from the C-in-C [commander-in-chief] forbids rescuing surviving personnel!"[25] The concept of "total war" had begun to override the recent advances made in the laws, customs, and practices of the sea. The medieval mentality had returned.

FROM WARSHIP NEMESIS TO COMMERCE RAIDER

In the early nineteenth century—and for that matter, perhaps long before then—some insightful minds had predicted that the submarine would one day become the deadliest weapon of the seas. "I will not disguise that I have full confidence in the power which I possess, which is no less than to be the means, should I think proper, of giving to the world a system which must of necessity sweep all military marines from the ocean, by giving the weaker maritime powers advantages over the stronger, which the stronger cannot prevent," wrote Robert Fulton, inventor of the steam engine, to William Pitt, prime minister of Great Britain.[26] Fulton, who in 1806 wrote a manuscript entitled *On Submarine Navigation and Attack*, had previously been commissioned by Napoleon to build a prototype submarine of war. Named *Nautilus*, the submarine survived tests to a depth of twenty-five feet and, in a demonstration destroyed a vessel in Brest harbor. Soon after, Fulton went to Britain to prove the submarine's effectiveness as weapon. An expedition against the French fleet at Boulogne failed, but in 1805, Fulton's submarine destroyed a heavy brig in a demonstration, proving again the potential effectiveness of an underwater warship.[27]

Beyond noting its potential use in special operations, reconnaissance, and attacks on warships, one observer, Citizen St. Aubin, also pointed out its potential psychological effect: "[W]hat will become of maritime wars, and where will sailors be found to man ships-of-war when it is a physical certainty that they may at every moment be blown into the air by means of diving-boats, against which no human foresight can guard them?"[28] St. Aubin was correct regarding the potential psychological effect of the submarine but overlooked not only man's inherent ability to devise countermeasures, but also one of the most significant purposes to which the submarine would be put.

Jules Verne, author of *Twenty Thousand Leagues Under the Sea*, likewise recognized the danger of the submarine to surface ships. To harpooner Ned Land's wish that a distant warship sink the *Nautilus*, Professor Aronnax's assistant Conseil replied, "[W]hat harm can it do to the Nautilus? Can it attack it beneath the waves? Can it cannonade us at the bottom of the sea?"[29] Nemo's metal beast sank its attacker, whose struggling, drowning crew Verne described as "a human ant-heap overtaken by the sea."[30] In a literary sense, Verne's *Nautilus* fulfilled the potential of Fulton's *Nautilus*, as in reality the U.S. Navy's *Nautilus* fulfilled the potential of Verne's *Nautilus* almost a century later. But Verne also predicted the brutality of submarine warfare: only once did he have his hero Nemo rescue any of the passengers or crew of a ship he sank, and only then as a plot device so that Verne's narrator, Professor Aronnax, could tell the tale.

The reality of the submarine is perhaps best understood when watching one firsthand as it surfaces from beneath the sea, disappears into it, or, even more rarely, travels underwater. It is easy to accept the reality of the submarine intellectually, but there remains something quite amazing in the fact of a "ship" traveling beneath the sea.[31] Surface travel has probably always been comprehensible, but whenever a vessel sank beneath the sea, only rarely was it ever brought to the surface again, at least until the advent of the submarine. Even service aboard a submarine does not convey the literally incredible effect of watching one surface from or disappear into the sea.[32]

"There was no doubt about it! This monster," wrote Verne in his tale of the *Nautilus* and its misanthropic commander, "this natural phenomenon that had puzzled the learned world, and overthrown and misled the imagination of seamen of both hemispheres, was, it must be owned, a still more astonishing phenomenon, inasmuch as it was a simply human construction."[33]

Once the reality settled in, however, the submarine was recognized by all as a capital war machine of the sea. But what Fulton, St. Aubin, and even many military analysts up to World War I overlooked was the potential of the submarine as a commerce raider. A prize-winning 1912 essay, published in the British *Naval Review* in 1914, projected how a German enemy might attack British trade at sea: "Against our trade, a systematic *guerre de course* might be executed by small squadrons, single cruisers and armed merchantmen, with occasional raids directed against the east coast."[34] In other words, commerce raiding would reflect that of the past three or more centuries. No mention was made of the submarine as commerce raider. The submarine was intended to give weaker navies an advantage against stronger ones, and thus German submarines would be used primarily, along with mining craft, to "reduce our [British] supremacy in larger [war]ships."[35] And so it was in the early days of the World War I: submarines attacked only enemy warships. But as more and more warships were sunk, many retreated from the sea into harbors behind screens of patrol craft and anti-submarine nettings, and submarines began to look for other prey.

Even the German Navy did not predict the effective use of the submarine as a commerce raider. According to U-boat officer Johann Speiss, speaking of the first U-boat attack on a merchant vessel, "Attacks on commercial steamers had not been foreseen. The possibilities of that kind of warfare had not been anticipated. The U-boats were not equipped with guns, prize lists, contraband rules, or any of the paraphernalia necessary for a campaign against oceanic trade."[36]

Unfortunately, predicting even near-future warfare, particularly in the age of technology, is inherently difficult, and even the best minds filled both with practical theory and firsthand experience of warfare may still be wrong. And in the case of submarine warfare, many were, for the submarine, while never shirking its duty to sink enemy warships, was quickly destined to become the preeminent commerce raider of the twentieth century.[37]

SUBMARINE TACTICS

Submarines nearly always used torpedoes to attack enemy warships. However, merchantmen, whether steamers or sailing vessels, were small by today's standards, usually lightly armed (if at all), and so were typically attacked on the surface by the submarine's deck armament, at least in the early days of World War I. Often a warning shot and an order to abandon ship were sufficient. However, as the war progressed, many merchant ships were armed with guns of equal or greater caliber to those of the German U-boats. Some were even armed and used as decoys to lure U-boats to their doom. Very quickly, the U-boats abandoned the "restricted" warfare in which merchant ships were first warned before being attacked and instead began sinking merchant ships without warning. A postwar newspaper article pointed out what had become obvious during the war: submarines "were effective as commerce destroyers only if the old rules regarding visit and search and provision for the safety of civilian crews and passengers were disregarded."[38]

The outcry over the sinking of the *Lusitania* forced the German government to reconsider the ancient laws of commerce raiding and the sea and withdraw the unrestricted submarine campaign. But only briefly. With World War I died many traditional notions of honor and warfare. Still, according to Lowell Thomas, the famous correspondent and author of *Raiders of the Deep*, most German submarine commanders gave warning whenever they safely could, even during unrestricted warfare. There were, Thomas pointed out, practical reasons for doing so: it saved torpedoes and it helped counter anti-German propaganda.[39]

Submarine tactics developed quickly and adapted as required to the enemy's countermeasures. A single chapter, much less a short section, is insufficient to do justice to the complexity of tactics; a short summation must serve instead. Submarine commerce-raiding tactics passed from classic surface attacks using the threat of or an actual deck gun in World War I, to the stalking of a merchant target on the surface and underwater and the ship's destruction via torpedo in both world wars, to the German use of "wolf packs"—submarines that would rendezvous for a combined attack on a convoy—in World War II. The *U-Boat Commander's Handbook* of World War II described two basic attacks: the underwater attack and the night surface attack. Both were intended as short-range attacks, without warning, to take the target by surprise.[40]

The lethality of torpedoes grew quickly during the wars and between them, from those detonating only on contact to those developed in World

War II that would detonate not only on contact but also when magnetic sig-natures reached a certain magnitude.[41] Acoustic torpedoes that could "home in" on propeller noise were developed.[42] Torpedo propulsion evolved as well, from gas-operated turbines to electricity.[43] During World War II, U.S. subma-rines were fitted with air and surface search radars, greatly increasing their survivability.[44] Above all, though, the critical tactical component was the abil-ity to maintain appropriate depth, according to U-boat commander Georg Günther Freiherr von Forstner: "The principal condition for the success of a submarine attack is to steer to the exact depth required. The periscope must not rise too far above water, for it might easily be observed by the enemy; but if by clumsy steering, the top of the periscope descends below the waves, then it becomes impossible to take aim to fire the torpedo."[45] As with all maritime warfare, seamanship was the critical element.

The submarine's strength was its ability to hide beneath the surface of the water, both to attack its enemy and to escape from him. But this was also its weakness. A submarine had to come near the surface and extend a peri-scope in order to be able to see its target. It was slower than the small war-ships tasked with its destruction, it had limited means with which to defend itself if discovered, and, once located, it had little protection (other than the blanket of the sea) from the shells, bombs, and depth charges of the enemy. For many submarines, this blanket became their shroud.

MERCHANT DEFENSES

Defending against the submarine was no simple task for a warship, much less for a merchantman. Gone were the early years when the submarine was a man-powered semi-submersible, as had been Bushnell's egg-shaped *Turtle* of the American Revolution; gone were the years when the submarine was a man-powered true submersible, as had been the cigar-shaped CSS *H. L. Hunley* of the American Civil War. By World War I, the submarine was diesel-electric powered on the surface and battery powered underwater. During World War II, German U-boats began to be fitted with a snorkel, permitting them to travel at shallow depths underwater under diesel power. The speed of the latest submarines in World War II was twenty knots on the surface and nine underwater.[46] Most merchantmen, however, were slow, and even the slowest of submarines could outpace them, although submarines preferred not to waste time and fuel in chase, but to lie in wait. Again, economics con-spired with the relationship of cargo capacity to speed. In the case of the

Allied Atlantic convoys, submarines often had little need for the chase: they merely lay in wait for targets they knew had to come their way.

Early in World War I, Britain and other nations began to arm their merchantmen against German U-boats, a practice that continued throughout the war and one that was common in World War II as well. Armament was usually light, as compared to the guns of surface warships, and was typically manned by naval gun crews. However, as already noted, the practice led at least in part to the German decision to engage in unrestricted warfare. Merchant ships had some notable successes engaging U-boats, albeit few and far between. In early 1918, the skipper of a British trawler spotted a periscope a hundred yards off. He tried to ram the U-boat, but the submarine avoided the collision, leaving the trawler scraping alongside. The skipper, who had a "fighting spirit," grabbed a coal shovel and "reduced it [the periscope] to fragments."[47] In mid-1918, a British tanker attacked a German "sea pirate" after just barely avoiding two of its torpedoes. The U-boat surfaced "with her guns ready . . . and the fight started." The twenty-sixth shot from the tanker hit the submarine, at which point the submarine swung around and drifted "broadside on." The tanker made full speed away from the scene of the battle, assuming it had destroyed the U-boat.[48]

Just as likely, however, was defeat when engaging a submarine. In mid-1917, a U.S. tanker engaged a German U-boat, firing more than 150 rounds at it before being sunk. Four of the tanker's crew were lost, but the German crew rescued the remainder, and the German captain congratulated the tanker's skipper on his heroism.[49]

The most effective merchant tactic, however, was the convoy protected by naval escorts. For the merchantman, this meant steaming according to naval orders—often in a zigzag pattern—and keeping a lookout for the telltale periscope or, worse, the telltale wake of a torpedo. Warships and troopships could keep a large number of men at the lookout, changing them often before fatigue set in and diminished their value. But on "merchant ships they do not keep a lookout which combs the sea thoroughly; they do not carry men enough for that. The strain of such a lookout is great. Men cannot stand to it as to an ordinary watch; they have to be relieved frequently; and so submarines may have an advantage over merchant ships, especially if the merchant ships are slow-moving freighters."[50] The seafaring writer added that "Seeing a periscope is oftentimes a matter of luck."[51] A periscope was, after all, but a "four inch pipe" at this time.

Upon sighting a periscope, a merchant vessel would signal to its escorts and man its guns. Upon sighting a torpedo, a merchant vessel first took evasive maneuvers and notified its escorts then, if armed, engaged the source of the torpedo. In the case of a periscope or the submarine itself being spotted, all guns were trained on it and the order was given to "Open fire!" In practice, however, most merchant ships were sunk without ever having had notice of the submarine or torpedoes that attacked them.

Other strategies and tactics were proposed as well during World War I. One suggestion was to flood, so to speak, the sea with small armed wooden vessels to replace the 500,000 tons per month German U-boats were sinking, as compared to the 320,000 tons of shipping being launched monthly from U.S. shipyards. "However, the chief reliance of this argosy method of getting food and munitions to Europe is not to be in the speed or defensive power of a unit, for many of them may be lost, but in the numerical strength of the fleet, the almost endless chain of boats doing the needed work."[52] This was a commonly proposed solution to submarine commerce raiding: build more ships than can be sunk. The "Ships for Victory" program of World War II was an effective version.[53]

Another suggestion, although apparently of little effect, was proposed by ship owner and member of Parliament R. P. Houston in the *London Times* in 1916: "To encourage them [merchant crews] by deed as by word, I will present to any British-born master of a British-owned merchant ship 2,000 [pounds] for each and every German submarine that can be satisfactorily proved to have been sunk by his ship, up to the total of fifty . . . the 2,000 bonus to be divided among the master and crew in proportions satisfactory to me."[54] Yet another suggestion included increasing the watertight integrity of merchant ships via better bulkheads and pumping systems.[55] Ultimately, though, the best merchant tactic against submarine commerce raiders was the convoy, supported by vigilance, training, and, especially, professional cooperation with naval escorts. However, the tactic was not perfect. Ships were still lost, supply lines were slowed, naval assets were tied down, and fear gripped the merchant fleets.

NAVAL ANTI-SUBMARINE WARFARE

That the submarine was an invincible weapon by virtue of the shroud of the sea was soon proved wrong. As one seafarer put it in 1918: "My own notion of it is that the U-boats have many of us bluffed. They must be capable men who go in submarines; of good nerve, quick wit, and the power to withstand long nervous strain. Such men in a submarine are going to throw great scares into people of less capacity on surface ships. . . . But these men, no men, can make the submarine do impossible things."[56] And indeed it was not long before surface warships developed tactics to protect not only themselves but also their auxiliaries and the merchant fleets from the submarine menace. There is nothing like war to put humankind's courage and cunning to the test, and perhaps only in time of war does humankind's technology progress so quickly. Similarly are warriors quick to adapt to their adversary's tactics and develop new ones.

During World War I, light vessels were quickly adapted to the purpose of submarine hunting. Typical was the British eighty-foot motor launch with a speed of twenty-five knots and armed with a thirteen-pound gun and depth charges.[57] Very quickly, the hydrophone was implemented, and tactics were developed to listen for submarines and attack them with depth charges. A cat and mouse game developed, for submarines were similarly equipped with acoustical detection equipment. Submarines caught by surprise on the surface or forced to surface by depth charges were invariably engaged with guns or torpedoes and were occasionally rammed.

Although the hydrophone and depth charge were the most significant anti-submarine weapon combination of World War I, others were used as well. Aircraft sank a few U-boats. "Indicator nets" were laid in areas where submarines might be expected. When a submarine became entangled in one, an indicator float on the surface would begin to burn, signaling the location of the submarine. "Explosive sweeps"—a long loop of cable with explosive charges attached—were used to snag and destroy submarines underwater. A surface vessel would drag the sweep along the suspected location of a submarine on the bottom, and if a submarine—or anything else—were snagged, the charges would detonate on contact. Surface ships, warships especially, used smoke screens and camouflage patterns to help escape the detection of submarines.[58]

Q-ships, also called Q-boats and "mystery ships," were put to somewhat effective use by the British. Disguised as merchant vessels, they even mounted a small gun with which they would engage German U-boats, luring them in. The *U-Boat Commander's Handbook* advised skippers to know the "prize regulations" before stopping a steamer, closely examine via periscope the steamer it intended to search, keep a good watch and have small arms ready, have the steamer send a boat rather than board it, and to ruthlessly smash any attempted resistance. Resistance was described not only as engaging the submarine, but also as making any radio transmission or failing to follow instructions quickly enough or at all.[59] A German U-boat captain described being on the receiving end of what he thought was a puny shot from a small merchant vessel. "It fell so short that it meant nothing more than an irritating expression of defiance," he noted, then ordered his crew to close with and oblige the apparent merchant ship steamer that wanted to fight. But then, as the captain described it, "She turned on us. The bulkheads on her deck dropped and revealed the muzzles of two big guns." The Q-ship opened fire, and the U-boat just barely escaped under cover of a smoke screen.[60] Roughly a dozen German U-boats were sunk by Q-ships during World War I.[61] The Q-ships also contributed to the German decision to give no notice to merchant vessels prior to attack.

Anti-submarine tactics during World War II were similar, but with the advantage of higher technology. Asdic or sonar—an active listening device that sent out sound waves and located a submarine based on the reflected sound—was developed and put to effective use, as was the "Hedgehog," a weapon that fired a broad pattern of depth charges. Submarines were often located via their radio transmissions, and the development of radar gave surface warships another tool with which to locate submarines, although the submarine's low profile somewhat mitigated radar's effectiveness. Aerial patrols were highly effective and, along with escort carriers and the development of aircraft radar, provided an effective means of spotting and attacking German U-boats. In particular, the air-sea combination became quite deadly.[62]

U-boats spotted on the surface were attacked on the surface, if possible, although the development of acoustic torpedoes eventually made engaging a submarine on the surface more dangerous and resulted in the development of a towed noisemaker the British called a "foxer," intended to mislead the sound-seeking torpedo. Further, light escort vessels often had light armament, their heavier weapons having been replaced by depth charges and Hedgehogs. Submarines were still sometimes rammed on the surface, but the ensuing damage to the ramming ships led to a suspension of the practice.[63]

For the most part, the usual anti-submarine tactic was to depth charge a submarine's suspected location until the boat was destroyed. The tactics of doing so were far more complex than they might sound, given the many variables of man, ship, and sea, not to mention of measures and counter-measures, too many and too detailed to be dealt with here. Capt. Donald Macintyre, one of the most effective U-boat hunters of World War II, de-scribed the destruction of a U-boat which Allied forces had managed to maintain sonar contact with under perfect acoustic conditions. His ship and another repeatedly attacked the submarine with common depth charges, a "one-ton depth charge," and the twenty-four depth bombs of a Hedgehog. "Gaping holes torn in her hull, *U 191* plunged to the bottom with all hands."[64]

Lothar-Günther Buchheim described being on the receiving end of depth charges: "Now we are struck by a single ringing blow, like a giant cud-gel on a sheet of steel. Two or three men begin to stagger. The air is hazy, hanging in blue layers. And again the heavy explosions . . . Whoever has us on the hook now is no beginner, and we're defenseless in spite of the five tor-pedoes in our tubes. We can't surface, we can't come speeding from behind cover and throw ourselves on the enemy. We haven't even the grim assurance to be had from simply holding a weapon in your hand. We can't so much as shout at them. Just creep away. Keep going deeper."[65] And often the subma-rine did keep going deeper, to be crushed by depth charges or the depth of the sea—or both.

THE PROPAGANDA AND INTELLIGENCE BATTLES

"Centuries ago the seas were infested with pirates as fiendish in their method as the hideous modern Hun," wrote the aforementioned English ship owner to the *London Times* in 1918, describing his offer of reward to those merchant crews who sink enemy submarines.[66] Enemies are always vili-fied, peace or war notwithstanding, and effective propaganda is a strategic weapon, a capital ship so to speak. For example, anti-submarine warfare propaganda during World War I did briefly persuade the German govern-ment to suspend unrestricted submarine warfare after the sinking of the *Lusitania*. Propaganda—and even the deliberate, calculated dissemination of the truth, currently referred to as "public diplomacy"—works by motivat-ing its audiences to take action.

In the case of commerce-raiding submarines, the outcry against the death of non-combatants put sufficient pressure on the perpetrating state to briefly suspend unrestricted submarine warfare. However, in the case of pira-cy not supported by a state, as opposed to privateering or commerce-raiding supported or perpetrated by a state, both propaganda and public diplomacy work by motivating victim states to take action, and not by pressuring pirates themselves, who are largely immune to such tactics.

More effective than propaganda was intelligence gathering and analysis. During both world wars, the usual methods of espionage and reconnaissance were employed. However, during World War II, the capture of the Enigma coding machine and the associated ability of talented cryptologists at Bletchley Park to decode German submarine transmissions turned the Battle of the Atlantic in favor of the Allies. Convoys were routed around the German wolf packs, and escorts were prepared to meet and destroy U-boats.[67] After all, to be forewarned is to be forearmed.

THE "PIRATE" SUBMARINE'S DECLINE

There is no doubt that the submarine was the greatest commerce raider of the twentieth century. During World War I, for example, German U-boats sank between 5,000 and 6,000 Allied merchantmen, almost 19 million tons worth. During World War II, submarines accounted for sixty percent of the 2,117 Japanese merchant vessels (8 million tons worth) sunk by U.S. forces.[68] But in spite of submarine victories, submarine losses were significant. Of the fewer than 400 German U-boats put into active service during World War I, 178 were lost due to enemy action.[69] Of the roughly 40,000 U-boat sailors of World War II, 30,000 perished.[70] The United States lost more than forty submarines in the Western Pacific during World War II.[71] Perhaps even more tragically, as many as 50,000 Allied merchant sailors went to their graves in the sea due to World War II U-boat attacks.[72] Many Axis merchant mariners were lost to Allied submarines as well.

Fortunately or unfortunately, the attack submarines of the world's major powers today are too expensive, far too few in number, and have far too many more important missions—fleet protection, detection and destruction of enemy submarines, destruction of enemy surface warships and auxiliaries, destruction of point targets ashore, intelligence gathering, special operations support—to play as great a role in commerce raiding of the future as they did in the first half of the twentieth century, at least in the sense of sinking thousands of merchant ships. However, one or two submarines today could easily bring shipping to halt through the world's major sea lane chokepoints. The sinking of a few large merchant vessels—or perhaps even one—in one of these areas is all it would take to create panic among merchant crews and owners and bring shipping to a halt, at least until the offending submarines are located and destroyed.

THE SURFACE RAIDERS

Submarines were not the only commerce raiders of the world wars. Germany sent warships as well as disguised surface combatants called *auxiliary cruisers* to sea as commerce raiders during both wars, and Japan did so in the latter, with limited success. All German surface raiders combined, for example, sank only 130 Allied or neutral vessels from 1940 to 1943, after which raiding came to an effective end. The figure is insignificant as compared to submarine raiding. A few of the German disguised raiders, however, had notable individual successes. The *Atlantis*, for example, destroyed twenty-two vessels and the most tonnage before being sunk by the HMS *Devonshire* in 1941. A handful of other disguised raiders had similar success. However, their most notable success was not in tonnage sunk, but in tying down Allied naval forces in the search for them. Tactics used to seek and destroy the raiders were conventional, relying on patrol, search, chase, and intelligence gathering, and they were often opportunistic. Warnings by attacked ships were the most common means of locating raiders, but during World War II, raiders would attempt to jam transmissions. Once located, commerce raiders were engaged by warships, although not always successfully. In 1941, for example, the HMAS *Sydney* sank the raider *Kormoran* but was herself sunk in the engagement. Armed merchant vessels often fought back against the raiders, sometimes successfully.[73]

Only a handful of German commerce-raiding warships ever got to sea. The most famous of them, the *Bismarck*, never sank a merchantman and, after sinking the cruiser HMS *Hood* in company with the commerce raider *Prinz Eugen*, was sunk by the British navy in an epic engagement. Her grave has been located and inspected by nautical explorers and archaeologists. Her sister ship, the *Tirpitz*, never succeeded as a commerce raider either, finding it too difficult to escape port without drawing an overwhelming Allied response. She was attacked in harbor in Norway by British mini-subs, called X-craft, in a daring raid and was severely damaged, although only two of the six X-craft reached her. An earlier attempt to attack her with British "chariots"—human torpedoes—failed.[74] The *Tirpitz* was eventually destroyed by aerial attack. The few warships that actually engaged enemy commerce, such as the famous *Graf Spee* and *Scheer*, made only short cruises and none after early 1941, when surface raiding by warships was halted after the loss of the *Bismarck*. The Allied navies were simply too strong for the German surface fleet.

It would be remiss in any book on sea roving or pirate hunting not to mention the last of the great sailing commerce raiders. Commanded by Count Felix von Luckner, whose adventurous life deservedly places him among the greatest of swashbucklers, the clipper *Seeadler* (*Sea Eagle*) was fitted out in World War I as a disguised raider.[75] Formerly the *Pass of Balmaha*, she sailed with a disguised crew and a deception plan that rivaled any in the history of sea roving. The *Seeadler* captured and sank fourteen vessels totaling roughly 30,000 tons, took over 300 prisoners and treated them well, and caused the death of only one person, a British officer killed by a shell fired at the *Horngarth*.[76] She escaped, largely by accident, a British trap set for her at Cape Horn but ran aground in the South Pacific, ending her famous cruise. She was not the last of the sea rovers under sail—Chinese pirate junks still cruised in Eastern seas, for example—but her loss marked the end of an age.

15

Ships, SEALs, and Satellites

The Return of the Pirate Hunters

For generations, piracy as a significant threat seemed extinct, and commerce raiding, but for two brief violent interludes, was dormant. Pirates had become caricatures, and no one still lived who had known piracy on a grand scale. Many mariners and sea travelers, of course, were familiar with piracy on the relatively small scale of petty banditry at sea, of pirates boarding ships and robbing them of cash and supplies, and occasionally of a rusty freighter pirated, then renamed and reflagged for profit. But piracy sufficient to warrant international attention, to warrant an aggressive naval presence, to warrant the arming of commercial shipping? The idea was ludicrous, a Hollywood fantasy, a writer's idle idea for another novel.

But in 2008, reality intruded. All had forgotten what history had taught: that the passage of significant maritime trade along an unguarded coast whose population is in need or who has a tradition of roving is a recipe for piracy. Too complacent with our modern technology and image of the pirate as nothing more than an icon, we ignored the potential. The sudden upsurge in Somali piracy, and particularly its scale, caught everyone—maritime analysts, intelligence agencies, and the shipping industry, among others—off guard. In 2000, the South China Sea was considered "the most dangerous for piracy in the world," and in April 2008, just before the sudden upsurge in Somali piracy, Nigeria had been named the "number one piracy hot spot."[1] But by mid-2008, Somalia was number one, and on a scale not seen since the nineteenth century.

Before we look in detail at modern pirate hunting, it is important to note the two circumstances that have provided the modern pirate with the ability to engage in successful piracy. It is not seamanship, tactics, improved vessel design, special technology, inventiveness, or courage that equips the success-

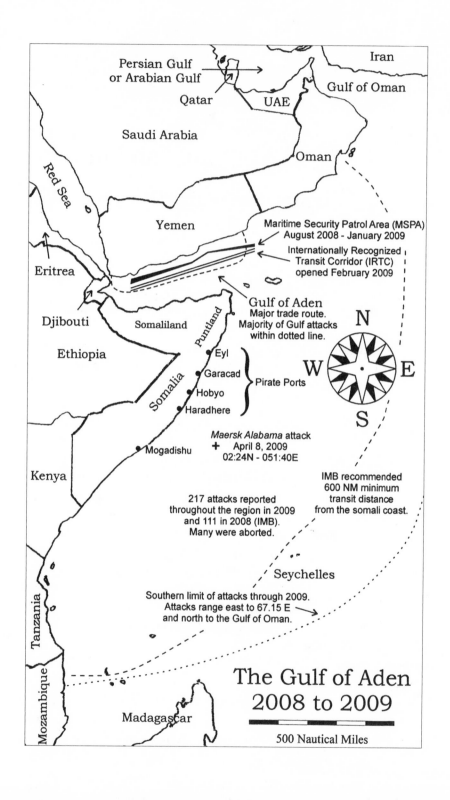

Persian Gulf or Arabian Gulf

Iran

Gulf of Oman

Qatar

UAE

Saudi Arabia

Oman

Red Sea

Yemen

Maritime Security Patrol Area (MSPA)
August 2008 - January 2009

Internationally Recognized
Transit Corridor (IRTC)
opened February 2009

Eritrea

Gulf of Aden
Major trade route.
Majority of Gulf attacks
within dotted line.

Djibouti

Somaliland

Puntland

N

Ethiopia

Somalia

Eyl

Garacad

Hobyo

Haradhere

Pirate Ports

W   E

S

Mogadishu

Maersk Alabama attack
+   April 8, 2009
02:24N - 051:40E

Kenya

IMB recommended
600 NM minimum
transit distance
from the somali coast.

217 attacks reported
throughout the region in 2009
and 111 in 2008 (IMB).
Many were aborted.

Seychelles

Southern limit of attacks through 2009.
Attacks range east to 67.15 E
and north to the Gulf of Oman.

Tanzania

Mozambique

The Gulf of Aden
2008 to 2009

Madagascar

500 Nautical Miles

ful modern pirate, although these are useful and some of them mandatory. Rather, it is the outboard motor—a common, century-old bit of engineering—combined with a lack of armed force aboard most target vessels that permits the typical modern pirate to do his dirty work.

The former, which we can do nothing about, gives him a simple, inexpensive, but highly effective means of overtaking his target. The latter, for which much can and, in my estimation, should be done, permits him to attack and board with relative impunity. Indeed, a powerful outboard or two coupled to a cheap but swift seaworthy wood or fiberglass hull—both often rented—crewed with a handful of men armed with a few assault rifles and a rented RPG (rocket propelled grenade) launcher or two, banded together with a few similar vessels, and supported by a battered "mother ship" laden with fuel, food, and water is sufficient today to capture an unarmed container ship or oil tanker and its crew and hold them for millions of dollars in ransom. The cost of sending a Somali "pirate team" to sea? Roughly six thousand dollars.[2] Merchant owners, captains, and crews of past centuries would have looked incredulously upon this state of affairs, unable to comprehend the unwillingness of owners and governments to arm shipping—and to use those arms when threatened by pirates.

THE MODERN PIRATE

Piracy today remains characterized as it was in the past, modern statements to the contrary notwithstanding: gangs of armed men in light, often small craft pursuing large, slow-moving commercial vessels whose crews are small and whose armament is light or non-existent. The tactics of lying in wait, ruse, and swift pursuit have not changed, nor has the value placed on people as plunder. The norm is still to attack weak merchant shipping, and the modern pirate's tactics are simple and virtually identical to those of past millennia, consisting primarily of lying in wait along major shipping routes or using ruse as necessary to bring a target vessel close or to distract warships, followed by a swift pursuit at speeds up to twenty-five knots. A typical Somali pirate tactic is to use two or more vessels and approach each stern quarter. Pirates then board, usually astern where the freeboard (height above water) is lowest, using poles tipped with hooks, and occasionally common ladders, as a means of access. The pirates use small arms (or in some areas even knives and machetés) to intimidate captain and crew into surrendering. Sometimes the mere threat of armed force, coupled with rounds fired from AK-47 assault rifles and perhaps an RPG launched at the hull or superstructure, is sufficient to force a surrender. In mid-2010, some Somali pirates began using "swarm" attacks, with six or more skiffs attacking a single ship.

Pirates remained active to some degree worldwide throughout the twentieth century. Chinese pirates were well known for their attacks through the 1930s, particularly on the Yangtze River and in Chinese coastal waters. Chinese attacks began to diminish afterward but are still occasionally reported.[3] Pirates, generally small scale, were active in the Red Sea, Persian Gulf, and Arabian Sea throughout the twentieth century. In 1953, for example, the HMS *Flamingo* captured twenty Arab pirates asleep aboard their prize, the Indian dhow *Naram Passa*, anchored in their hideout at Jadhib, Yemen.[4] Pirates are still occasionally encountered in these waters. In the mid- to late-1970s, Vietnamese "boat people" fleeing Vietnam were preyed upon by Thai and Cambodian pirates who would rob them of what few valuables they had and often rape the women aboard.[5] Pirate attacks are still occasionally reported in Vietnamese waters.

"Indonesian" pirates, including Indonesians, Malaysians, and Filipinos, were the most notorious of the past century until their general suppression in the early years of the new millennium. Often hired by criminal syndicates, their common targets were palm-oil tankers and other vessels whose cargoes could be readily disposed of. They occasionally murdered those who resisted, and remain active today on a much smaller scale.[6] Occasional petty piracy takes place in the Caribbean, with victims ranging from pleasure craft to small local fishing vessels. The Gulf of Guinea is rife with piracy and maritime violence and is currently the number two area for piracy. Vessels carrying oil are often the target. Small-time piracy is occasionally seen in European waters and typically consists of petty robbery in harbors and anchorages. Readers should note that under international law, piracy committed within territorial waters is considered "armed robbery at sea," although to the victim, and indeed to most of us except lawyers, piracy is piracy. Just as important to note is that many pirate attacks go unreported, for reasons ranging from fear of retaliation to fear of an increase in insurance premiums.

But it is Somali piracy that has risen to number one on the list, and the reasons are simple. Somalia is a "failed state" with no central government and no viable economy, a state in which warlords and Islamist insurgents vie for power while much of the population is left to fend for itself. It is little wonder that local fishermen, impoverished by Somalia's inability to protect itself from interloping commercial fishing vessels, eventually armed themselves and took violently to the sea. Today, Somali piracy bears little resemblance to these first self-proclaimed "Somali coastguards" who took to the sea in defense of economic rights, although they often use the same rhetoric.[7] Rather, it is a full-blown criminal operation complete with infrastructure, including a form of stock exchange, investors great and small, bankers, ransom negotiators, administrators, security personnel, outfitters, and, of course, pirates. The latter are composed primarily of former fishermen for their maritime experience, former militiamen for their experience in arms, and "technical experts" capable of operating GPS, satellite phones, and other technology.[8]

Although Somali piracy has brought much-needed capital into impoverished coastal towns, it has also brought the common vices associated with seafaring and sea-roving ports for millennia: alcohol (an especially divisive product in a largely Muslim country) and drugs, prostitution and its consequent exploitation of local women, inflation, and violent crime.[9]

PIRACY AND TERRORISM

A few words on piracy and terrorism are in order, for too often the specter of terrorism is raised in regard to piracy. Some analysts, commentators, and journalists accuse pirates of being terrorists outright or of being terrorists by virtue of engaging in "terrorism," in that they inspire terror in their victims. In fact, terrorism is a crime of political violence, while piracy is a crime of violence for material gain. If terrorism were committed any time a victim is terrorized, even the brutal armed robber would be guilty of it, and this is simply not the case.[10]

There remains the small possibility that piracy might be used to finance terrorism or that pirate tactics—the seizure of ships and crews and holding them for ransom, or even the theft and sale of cargoes, although the former is typically far easier to accomplish today—may be used by terrorists or even adapted as a weapon to be used against ports, coastal populations, shipping lanes, or the marine environment. Mariners might be held in return for terrorist demands, a toxic cargo might be spilled into coastal waters or be burned adjacent to a populated coastline, or a ship might be sunk in the channel of a major port. Cruise ships remain potential targets. But this is terrorism, not piracy, and in the view of some analysts, the threat of maritime terrorism is exaggerated.[11]

Acts of piracy for the purpose of personal gain, as well as privateering and commerce raiding—notwithstanding that they deal in fear, theft, and even destruction at sea—are not terrorism. Equating piracy with terrorism is at best a naïve means of directing resources toward its suppression and at worst may draw vital resources and attention away from the threat of real terrorism. A terrorist who practices piracy in support of political violence is foremost a terrorist and should be treated as one. But a pirate is simply a common criminal on the sea. We can disregard the argument that the violence committed by pirates purportedly "rebelling" against unjust corporate interests, or against maltreatment at the hands of merchant officers and owners, is terrorism, for if he is primarily seeking material gain for private purpose, he is a pirate, not a terrorist. It is possible in theory that pirates might ally themselves with terrorists, but pirates are financially motivated, terrorists politically. Perhaps only rarely does the combination share enough common ground to make an alliance profitable to both sides. Markedly distinct, the pirate is not interested in giving up his life in the pursuit of his goal; the terrorist often is.[12]

NAVIES AS PIRATE HUNTERS

As with piracy, pirate hunting has changed little over the millennia. The weapons reach farther and are far more accurate and deadly, communication is better, information and intelligence resources are vast, and vessels have greater size, speed, seaworthiness, and range. But the fundamentals have not changed. Convoy remains the best method of naval protection against pirates, but navies are overtasked, and convoys are expensive in terms of lost transit time. Escorts of individual vessels through danger areas have been successful, then and now. Transit corridors patrolled by warships have been largely, but not always, successful in protecting commercial shipping in the Gulf of Aden. Task forces have been established to deal with piracy, but to date their role has been primarily defensive. Naval patrols have been hit and miss, as they have been for millennia. The sea is as large as it ever was.

Modern navies do have a few more tools than they did in the past and have used them against the Somali pirates. Fixed-wing aircraft and unmanned drones patrol for pirates, helicopters are dispatched as a quick reaction force, satellite photography helps reveal pirate movement, and a submarine has even been sent to collect intelligence on pirates. Warships monitor pirate transmissions provide intelligence on pirate location and intent. Modern men-of-war also use sophisticated radar, sonar, night vision devices, and thermal imaging devices to locate pirates. But again, the sea is large, the number of warships is limited, and small vessels are very difficult to track.

Direct action against attacking pirates has been invariably successful, provided naval assets were within reach. In every one of the few instances in which Somali pirates have engaged modern naval forces, they have either surrendered or have been literally blown out of the water. In 2008, the Indian frigate INS *Tabor*, for example, engaged a fishing vessel it believed was a pirate mother ship and, upon receiving fire from the vessel, destroyed it. The vessel had apparently just been captured by pirates.[13] It is a myth, fostered by press reports that sensationalize modern piracy, that Somali pirates are well armed. Their typical armament consists of AK-47s and RPGs. Such arms are entirely inadequate against those of even the smallest offshore patrol vessels.[14]

Naval patrols and assets, including the lightly equipped but enthusiastic Somaliland Coast Guard, have had some success in arresting suspected pirates, but in many cases, naval personnel have been forced to turn Somali pirates loose for lack of evidence or for lack of venue to prosecute them in. How captured pirates are dealt with depends much on the nationality of the naval force that captures them.

Direct action against Somali pirates ashore has been minimal, the most noted instance being the French strike after pirates released the luxury yacht *Le Ponant*. French naval commandos captured several pirates and recovered part of the ransom money.[15] The search for and destruction of pirate "mother ships"—usually captured fishing vessels, or even smaller craft ferrying fuel— is a viable tactic and was used with some success beginning in 2010. Direct action in inshore waters is limited in some cases by the lack of light, shallow-draft warships designed for this purpose. The United States, for example, has a minimal capability in this area but is working to improve it. Even so, recent naval patrols in Somali waters have netted suspected Somali pirates headed out to sea.

The most notable incidents of direct action against pirates have been hostage rescues. The Commando Hubert (a French naval unit similar to the U.S. Navy SEALs) has conducted two operations, killing pirates in both instances, although in one operation a hostage was inadvertently killed by a rescuer.[16] Puntland Somali forces have stormed captured vessels and killed pirates. As described in chapter 1, U.S. Navy SEAL snipers killed three pirates holding Capt. Richard Phillips of the *Maersk Alabama*. Some analysts predicted that the use of deadly force would lead to violent reprisal by Somali pirates, but as of April 2010, no such violent response had occurred. Pirates seek profit, and the wrath of governments willing to kill pirates is bad for business.

It is important to note that hostage rescues are always dangerous to both hostages and rescuers. Not only are hostages in danger of being killed in the crossfire, but they also may be put at further risk if the rescue stalls and hostage takers retaliate by further threatening or even killing hostages. Further, the risk of political fallout—the greatest apparent concern of many political leaders—due to the failure of a rescue or the death of hostages during the rescue, is high, sometimes leading to an unwillingness to authorize a rescue under any circumstances. But rescues are never without risk, and the risks to hostages and rescuers must be balanced against the risks of doing nothing.[17]

The French Commando Hubert, for example, did not attempt a rescue of the luxury yacht *Le Ponant*. The commandos considered an underwater approach to be the most practical, but strong currents precluded it, and so the rescue was cancelled.[18] Rescues must be made with surprise and violence sufficient to overwhelm or even preclude the ability of hostage takers to respond effectively. Teams must be highly skilled and should be composed of those who train full-time for the mission. In the case of maritime hostage rescue, teams must be specialists in hostage rescue in the maritime environment.[19]

Occasionally, one hears suggestions that naval special operations forces should be used more aggressively against Somali and other pirates. However, the missions of these units—U.S. Navy SEAL Teams, British Special Boat Squadrons (SBS), and the French Commando Hubert, for example—are purposefully limited to special operations. In other words, their job is to undertake "high risk high gain" special missions that cannot or should not be undertaken by other forces or assets. They cannot be the lead element in the fight against pirates, except to board and recapture ships, whether hostages are aboard or not; rescue hostages; capture pirates, their leaders, and financiers ashore in regions not under government control; and conduct other various special operations against pirates as required. Modern conventional naval forces are perfectly suited to handling most anti-piracy operations.[20]

One of the more successful naval anti-piracy operations of the modern age has been the joint suppression of piracy in Southeast Asia. Beginning in the 1990s, joint agreements between Malaysia, Indonesia, and Singapore established fairly effective naval and coast guard patrols, although they did not allow for "hot pursuit" into a neighbor's territory, but only for a "hand off" of the pursuit to local forces. Similar agreements were established between these states and the Philippines, Thailand, and Japan, although the littoral states of the Strait of Malacca are averse to patrols by outside states, given that no part of the vital strait is part of the open sea. Due to air patrols begun in 2005 in combination with sea patrols by Malaysian, Indonesian, Singapore, and Thai maritime forces, no pirate attacks were reported in the Strait of Malacca in 2007, and pirate attacks were down elsewhere in the region. Yet in spite of the reported success of naval and coast guard efforts, piracy in the area may be on the rise again, perhaps in response to the success of the Somali pirates.[21]

MERCHANT DEFENSES

As in past centuries, in the absence of naval or private armed escort or convoy, the modern commercial vessel's primary defense against pirates is speed; in other words, it must outrun the attacker. Failing this, its secondary defense must be a combination of physical barriers to boarding combined with the use of deadly force against attackers. In general, if attackers can reach a ship, they can probably board it, and once aboard, if they are armed and the crew is not, capture is usually a result. The effective use of firearms at long range will in most circumstances deter the attack. To date, no ship that has used firearms against Somali pirates has been captured.

However, in spite of many successful Somali pirate attacks and the millions paid in ransoms, many governments, shipping companies, and affiliated agencies and businesses still strongly recommend only non-lethal defensive measures to protect commercial shipping. Fundamental methods include anti-piracy training; proper implementation of a ship's security plan; the use of satellite tracking systems; strengthening bridge protection against bullets and shrapnel; fortifying a space as a "citadel" or "panic room;" keeping a good watch, which includes monitoring radio traffic, radar, and surveillance camera systems; and keeping an increased lookout with binoculars in the daytime and night vision devices at night.[22]

Transit tactics include sailing as far from pirate waters as possible; transiting at night; transiting under full sea speed (the standard ship handling term for full speed), in particular sailing at more than sixteen knots, given that pirates have been unsuccessful attacking at these speeds; using bow wave and stern wash to impede pursuing boats; for vessels whose maximum speed is under seventeen knots, zigzagging when chased in order to create a stern wash that makes it difficult for pirates to board; and heading into wind and swell, which makes boarding more difficult. Other "unarmed" tactics include sounding alarms, making distress calls, contacting naval authorities, and using barriers to boarding. Barriers can include stringing barbed wire, concertina wire, or electric fencing along the gunwales, or at least along areas where boarding is likely; expanding the width of gunwales to prevent grappling hooks from taking hold; using "slippery paint" on areas where boarding is likely; spraying slippery foam on deck and on gunwales; trailing mooring lines, cargo nets, and anti-boat nets alongside and astern in order to foul boat propellers; and spreading broken glass on deck, given that many pirates are barefoot. Ships with high freeboard—high "sides," that is—are more difficult to attack due to the difficulty in climbing them.[23]

More aggressive tactics include using fire hoses and fire-fighting foam monitors on pirates and their craft; firing flares at pirates; using sonic lasers; (which project painful, focused sound) against pirates in boats; creating water barriers by activating fire-fighting systems (which some captains object to if done routinely, fearing wear and tear on a vital life-saving system); and using sophisticated systems that spray a hot water barrier around the vessel. Used effectively and immediately by trained crews, these various "non-lethal" tactics can be successful, forcing pirates to seek another target.[24]

Recently, much emphasis has been placed on "panic rooms" or "citadels" aboard commercial vessels as a means of protecting the crew during attack and preventing capture of the vessel. These fortified rooms, along with the physical barriers described above, the securing of access to vessel spaces as well as to tools that might be of use to pirates, and the disabling of the ship's propulsion, are nothing more than the modern version of "closed quarters" used by merchant sail for centuries. However, closed quarters were designed for use in conjunction with armed force. They were designed to protect crews while they engaged the enemy, forcing them from their decks. Similarly, the use of "citadels" without the associated use of deadly force will likely result in the capture of the vessel unless a naval presence is nearby. In February 2010, for example, the crew of the bulk carrier *Ariella* barricaded themselves within a "citadel" when attacked by pirates. Their captain contacted NATO forces, which dispatched a helicopter and the Danish frigate *Absalon*. The pirates fled before the frigate arrived. In this case, the vessel was in a transit corridor with naval forces nearby. On April 5, 2010, Dutch marine commandos boarded the MS *Taipan*, rescued its barricaded crew, and captured ten pirates. Similarly, Russian forces boarded a Russian tanker a month later and rescued its barricaded crew, killing one pirate in the process and capturing ten. In another instance, pirates inexplicably abandoned a captured Turkish vessel whose crew members had barricaded themselves in a safe room. In all cases, unarmed crews barricading themselves must be able to contact naval forces for assistance, and all members of the crew must barricade themselves to prevent pirates from taking hostages. To be completely effective, "citadels" and fortified spaces should be augmented by trained, armed security personnel, or a warship must be nearby. Sooner or later, pirates will develop the means of breaching fortified spaces.

The crews of some attacked vessels have successfully supplemented non-lethal measures with more aggressive ones. In December 2008, the crew of the Chinese commercial vessel *Zhenhua 4* successfully defended itself from Somali pirate attack not only by using fire hoses, but also with a tried-and-true method used for millennia, that of incendiary devices. In this case, the crew made firebombs from bottles—Molotov cocktails, in other words—and threw them down upon their attackers.[25] In April 2009, Somali pirates attacked the Antigua and Barbuda-flagged cargo ship *Boularibank*. When the pirates came alongside to board, Capt. Peter Stapleton ordered his crew to "release the port-side battery"—and immediately they dumped ten-foot-long heavy timbers over the side and down upon the attacking pirate craft. The *Boularibank* escaped.[26] In October 2007, the crew of a North Korean vessel overpowered their eight Somali pirate captors and reclaimed their ship.[27] Egyptian fishermen overpowered their captors in 2009 and sailed their vessels home, although there is some dispute as to how much help they may have had from Egyptian private or national security forces.[28] Recall also that the crew of the *Maersk Alabama* used a knife against an attacking pirate. It is important to note that these tactics, although they did not employ firearms, either were or could have been lethal. We have already seen that merchant seamen have a long, proud history of defending themselves against attack by pirates and other sea rovers, and many are willing to maintain it. If crews are willing to use potentially deadly force against pirates, they should have the proper tools—arms, that is—to do so.

It is a fact that none of the existing non-lethal defenses will always stop a determined attack by pirates armed with assault rifles and RPGs if the vessel's speed is below sixteen knots and pirates are capable of maintaining position alongside, if gunwales are within reach of pirate boarding tools, and if pirates are capable of using their arms aggressively and effectively, although doubtless the manufacturers of some recent anti-pirate systems might disagree. Non-lethal methods send the message to pirates that they may attack with near-impunity. Critics of the use of armed security aboard merchant shipping typically cite the cost of maintaining security teams; the difficulty of getting around restrictions on armed personnel in the territorial waters of most nations; the concern that private security has no legal right to board a threatening pirate vessel; a predicted increase in "flags of convenience" which would permit armed security aboard; the potential for legal claims and criminal charges in the case of the death or injury of "an innocent party"; and the potential for the escalation of violence.[29]

However, some analysts, the author included, note that these objections disregard the right to self-defense on the high seas and have the implication, or at least appearance, of suggesting that mariners' lives and well-being are secondary to legal, financial, and logistical convenience. No reasonable person wants to see the oceans turned into an armed free-for-all, but much of the east coast of Africa, from the Gulf of Aden to the Seychelles, is already one—it's just one-sided. Most of the objections do not hold water. The issue of restrictions on arms has already been managed by many security companies. In general, agreements and exceptions designed to regulate armed security may be worked out among transit route nations in order to address specific circumstances, Somali piracy for example, and can be limited in scope and duration.

Regarding the question of the right of private escort vessels or security to board suspected pirate vessels, the author is unaware of any intention of security forces to do so. Their job would be strictly defense, not arrest or search and seizure. "Flags of convenience" have not increased as a means of arming ships, although it may be too soon to tell. Regarding liability, it is hard to imagine that shipping companies will not be sued for providing inadequate security in the case of the death of mariners at the hands of pirates, and perhaps even in the case of capture alone. The use of security teams aboard commercial shipping increased significantly in 2009 and into 2010, yet there was no related escalation of violence or of a move by Somali pirates to arm themselves better.

Many merchant seamen support arms aboard ship, to be handled by either themselves or by a trained security force. In a typical response, when asked what he would have liked to have had as a means of defending against pirates, a former LNG (liquefied natural gas) captain who had transited the Strait of Malacca for decades replied immediately and without hesitation: "Firepower on the bridge wings."[30] The fact is, armed security can be reasonably maintained aboard commercial shipping if the principals involved—shipping companies, insurers, navies, governments, the United Nations, mariners' unions, and maritime NGOs—are willing to put forth the effort.

From a tactical perspective, ships and large patrol vessels are much more stable platforms than small boats, and it is easier to hit a small target, such as a man aboard a pirate skiff, from a ship or patrol vessel than it is to hit a small target, such as a man aboard a ship or large vessel, from a small craft. Large vessels with their high freeboard provide better cover from fire coming from boats at sea level and provide a good angle of fire against such craft. The bridge wings are an excellent position on many vessels as an observation and firing platform. Further, as has always been the case (and which has been used to good advantage for millennia), the higher freeboard of larger vessels permits defenders to fire down into pirate craft, which are often open vessels with neither cover nor concealment for pirate crews. As small pirate craft come alongside, they are also vulnerable to grenades and other hand-thrown missiles, as well as to "dunnage" in the form of timbers, pallets, oil drums, and other heavy items.

The often unspoken concern, of course, is that private contractors might run amok and not be held accountable. This is a legitimate issue given the tendency in past centuries of privateers to act unlawfully and privateer pirate hunters to exceed their commissions, but the opportunity for security contractors to run amok aboard commercial vessels is limited. Further, the vast majority are professionals who invariably behave responsibly. Some commentators have raised the specter of private contractor excesses in Iraq and Afghanistan as reasons not to arm commercial shipping with private contractors, but the rationale is more fear-mongering than substantial. Others have accused private contractors, many of whom began looking for new work as the Iraq war wound down, of exaggerating the Somali pirate threat as a means of finding business. The use of military security teams may minimize much of the concern over the use of armed private security in some territorial waters and is the ideal way to go, although properly trained and screened private professionals, with proper government monitoring, are also capable of providing more than adequate protection, and they have.

But, as many shipping company executives would probably concede, the real downside to private security is expense: $10,000 to $15,000 per day for three to six armed professionals who might be paid as much as $500 each per day, plus per diem and travel, is a sum that makes many shipping companies think twice.[31] More costly, albeit more effective, is the use of private escort vessels or hired naval warships. Yemen's navy, for example, offered to provide a naval escort to individual vessels at a cost of $35,000 to $45,000 for three days.[32] Shipping companies and insurers must balance the cost of security against the cost of ransom and, more importantly, against the suffering of a crew assaulted and imprisoned by pirates.

However, in any case in which armed personnel are placed aboard vessels as a means of defense against pirates, they absolutely must be equal to the task. It will only embolden pirates if they are able to capture a vessel that puts up an inadequate armed defense. Similarly, all security forces, military or private, must be authorized to use lawful deadly force when conditions warrant. Bluffing—the threat of force without the intention of using it—will lead eventually to the discovery that the threat is not viable and will thus embolden pirates.

Granted, many maritime professionals in all capacities are squeamish about the use of deadly force—and deadly force should never be used irresponsibly. Circumstances in which deadly force is reasonable include the defense by crew, security personnel, and naval vessels and aircraft against direct attack by pirates. Deadly force is also reasonable during the attempted rescue of hostages held by pirates; in self-defense by police or military forces (each of which has different rules of engagement) conducting anti-piracy operations; and in hot pursuit of armed suspected pirates. Some might go further and argue that deadly force is reasonable in retaliation for the murder of a state's citizens by pirates. If such retaliatory violence is used, it must be used carefully, without harm to the innocent and with respect to law and rules of engagement. In general, arrest and prosecution, with deadly force used strictly in self-defense or in the defense of others, is the preferred means of dealing with individual pirates. And this should include the use of deadly force as a means of self-defense by merchant crews.

For men seeking quick riches, the very real possibility of death or lengthy incarceration may be enough to deter many. In the words of John Smith almost four centuries ago: "Yea, and many times a Pirat who are commonly the best manned, but they fight only for wealth, not for honour or revenge, except they bee extremely constrained."[33] Men who seek wealth through force of arms tend to seek the easiest prospects, for they want to survive long enough to spend the money they risk their lives for.

BROADER STRATEGIES

The use of deadly force notwithstanding, the problem of piracy will never be solved by capturing or killing every pirate on the sea. Rather, it will be solved by attacking its roots—that is, in the case of Somalia for example, by returning Somalia to a functioning state, including a viable economy and the means of policing its streets, shores, and seas. Similarly, piracy in the Gulf of Guinea will not disappear entirely until the region is politically and economically stabilized. Unfortunately, there is understandably neither international nor unilateral political will to do so under current conditions. The costs of nation-building in these areas would be high. Further, some knowledgeable analysts and commentators argue that the threat of piracy is actually overblown—"a very minor problem in the large scheme of things."[34]

Even so, there are plenty of supplemental, synergistic means of pirate hunting suitable to the "modern" age, beyond those of armed force at sea. Pirate amnesty, if combined with realistic economic prospects, should be a viable part of any serious anti-piracy strategy. Arms embargos, particularly on large crew-served weapons that could do significant damage to a vessel's hull and superstructure, should be in place and enforced, although this will do nothing to prevent the use of small arms and RPGs, both of which are widespread in piracy-prone areas. The assets of persons or groups funding and profiting from piracy should be frozen or seized whenever possible, but money is difficult, some say impossible, to track in Somalia.[35] In some circumstances, the capture, arrest, and trial of pirate leaders, financiers, and other major profit takers ashore might be warranted. Pressure on pirates from local groups and leaders should be supported without becoming too intrusive, lest it seem that the pressure is not local but external.

The use of covert operations to foment unrest between pirate factions or between pirates and insurgents, militias, or other organized criminals— Somali piracy has had several violent incidents between militias and pirates, for example—is probably an unwise tactic, as it might drive pirates into the hands of insurgents, create more crime or greater criminal cooperation, and create greater hardship among the local population, making them more supportive of piracy or insurgency.

Similarly, attacks on pirate bases, located as they are among local populations, would likely lead to more problems than solutions, as just described. Blockades can be put in place, but pirates will likely take to the seas again as soon as a blockade is lifted if local economic conditions are not improved. Perhaps more ominous in the long term is the possibility of a takeover of Somalia by Islamist insurgents, whose government might shield terrorists and thus become a greater danger to the international community than Somali pirates are today. In the short term, however, Islamists might suppress piracy—in May 2010, for example, pirates in Haradhere fled when Islamists captured the pirate port.

Importantly, issues of jurisdiction and venue must be resolved so that pirates can be tried speedily and fairly. At present, there are far too many disagreements over where and how to prosecute pirates. A court was established in Kenya to try Somali pirates, but in March 2010, Kenya stopped prosecuting pirates, claiming that the international community had not provided the assistance it promised. Proposals are afoot to create an international court to try pirates, but the process has so far moved very slowly. Suspected pirates are still often released rather than being prosecuted. Further, a piracy database combining naval intelligence and law enforcement records, and accessible to both military forces and law enforcement, must be established in order to aid in the prosecution of pirates.

Ultimately, though, the ancient, fundamental means must be in place, for they are the best not only in the interim, but overall. Foremost, commercial vessels likely to be successfully targeted by pirates must not only have effective passive countermeasures in place but also must be armed or otherwise have the protection of force of arms. Second, navies must aggressively seek out and deter, capture, or destroy pirates and their craft as the threat warrants (but it is well to remember that navies remain heavily tasked). Third, the arrest, trial, and, upon conviction, incarceration of pirates, along with the use of deadly force when appropriate, sends a message that piracy has consequences. Last, pirate bases—better yet, the conditions that support them and piracy itself—must be rendered harmless, preferably by establishing local physical and economic security.

THE FUTURE

Unfortunately, Somali pirate successes have reminded the world just how vast the seas are, how difficult it is to track criminals on the sea, and, worst of all, how easy it can be to get away with piracy. No one, as the cliché goes, can predict the future, and even the best "expert" estimates can be horribly wrong. Still, some possibilities are more likely than others. If significant maritime environmental changes predicted by global warming come to pass, for example, the consequent displacement of many coastal societies might virtually ensure a significant rise in piracy, both as a means of survival of some populations, as well a means of opportunistic exploitation of the situation by individuals not in immediate need or danger. Even local disasters might result in an increase in piracy. (Although piracy in Indonesian waters very briefly diminished in the immediate aftermath of the 2004 tsunami, it soon reappeared in fewer but more effective larger-scale attacks.[36]) Again, all that would be needed is a light skiff, a pair of powerful outboards, and a few rusty but reasonably serviceable AK-47s. Privateering might even rear its head again as hard-hit nations and populations seek the resources they require for survival. Blackmail or "tribute seeking," such as that practiced by many Mediterranean peoples of the past three millennia, would likely be seen as well on some scale.

In the near term, there is a small but reasonable potential for an increase in the sophistication of pirate attacks. With the appropriate resources—specifically training, motivated personnel, and equipment which, because I do not intend to promote piracy, will remain unspecified here—Somali pirates could significantly extend their range, the types of vessels they could successfully attack, and their ability to defend against counterattack. Such tactics, though, would doubtless bring an aggressive response from governments willing to send their navies in harm's way.

Overall, though, the best prediction is that, in one form or another, piracy—perhaps great, perhaps petty—will remain for generations to come. The sea is great, nations will trade, and the motives of need and greed are unlikely to go away.

OF PIRATES AND PIRATE HUNTERS

It is well to remind ourselves again of the need for pirate hunting, of viewing pirates not through romantic lenses but through reality. An early-eighteenth-century judgment against pirates is particularly apt, even today:

> The crime of piracy of which all of ye have been justly convicted, is of all other robberies the most aggravating and inhuman, in that being removed from the fears of surprise, in remote and distant parts, ye do in wantonness of power often add cruelty to theft. Pirates, unmoved at distress or poverty, not only spoil and rob, but do it from men needy, and who are purchasing their livelihoods through hazards and difficulties which ought rather to move compassion; and what is still worse, do often, by persuasion or force, engage the inconsiderate part of them to their own and families' ruin, removing them from their wives and children, and by that, from the means that should support them from misery and want.[37]

That pirates themselves may be victims is no excuse for using violence against other men and women trying hard to make a decent living.

Those who fear the consequences of direct action against pirates—whether by arming their commercial shipping or directing their navy to seek out, engage, and capture or destroy pirates—should consider the words of Capt. Jeremy Roche upon his being taken for a well-armed, well-manned pirate when his boat—aboard which was only Roche, another man, and a dog—landed at Lyme, England, in the late seventeenth century: "[S]uch is the nature of Fear to multiply or magnifie objects through her false Optics."[38] The modern pirate is no great threat to those willing to defend themselves.

And if these words fail to move them, perhaps recalling those of William Mountaine will: "And when a Merchant Ship cannot otherwise well discharge herself, the Necessity of Fighting is evident; for no Man is so devoid of Reason as not to know, that it is his peculiar Interest to defend his Property, unless he will toil and labour for others, and like the Sheep patiently endure the Shearing of his Fleece." Or, perhaps, endure the taking of his or her life as well, at least as long as one can endure the loss of one's life.

It is obvious that piracy and pirate hunting have changed little in several millennia, right up to the present. Pirates remain for the most part small gangs of lightly armed men in swift, light vessels in pursuit of large, slow-moving, poorly armed merchant vessels. The tactics of lying in wait, ruse, and swift pursuit have not changed, nor has the value placed on people as plunder. Likewise, the tactics of pirate hunting have changed little. Above all, the defense of a merchant vessel by its crew, in particular the ability of the crew to prevent boarding, remains the ultimate defense against piracy. The words of nineteenth-century naval strategist Admiral Alfred Thayer Mahan remain valid today: "The attack and defense of commerce is still a living question."[39]

Early in this book, I described Odysseus as the archetype of the pirate and pirate hunter, and so he remains. Pirate hunting requires courage and cunning in equal measure, but Odyssean cunning—that of the fox—must be ever at the forefront in the hunt for pirates. Courage takes its place in the will to stand up to and defend against pirates, as naval seamen, merchant sailors, and sea-going travelers have done for thousands of years and still do today.

Our world is three-quarters water, its society complex and interdependent, and its population all too human. The seas are vital for trade and travel, vital to the preservation and advancement of our society, and vital ultimately to our individual survival. The fight to protect ourselves, our property, and our freedoms from those who would take them from us on the sea remains both a mandate and a challenge, and the history of pirate hunting offers us a means of reminding ourselves how we may do this, as well as a way of honoring those who have.

Notes

Abbreviations

CLB: Calendar of Letter-Books Preserved Among the Archives of the Corporation of the City of London

CPR: Calendar of the Patent Rolls Preserved in the Public Record Office

CSPC: Calendar of State Papers, Colonial

CSPD: Calendar of State Papers, Domestic

CSPE: Calendar of State Papers, East Indies

CSPV: Calendar of State Papers, Venice

OCIMF: Oil Companies International Marine Forum

UNCLOS: United Nations Convention on the Law of the Sea

Chapter 1: Of Black Flags and Bloody Banners
The Pursuit of Pirates and Privateers

1. John Taylor, "Apologie for Sea-men," in *The Works of John Taylor the Water Poet Not Included in the Folio of 1630* (Manchester: The Spenser Society, 1878), 15.

2. Charles May, "An Account of the wonderful Preservation of the Ship *Terra Nova* of London" (1694), in Awnsham Churchill and John Churchill, eds., *A Collection of Voyages and Travels* (London: John Walthoe et al., 1732), vol. 6:345.

3. In general, see David Cordingly, *Under the Black Flag* (New York: Random House, 1995).

4. Charles Johnson is no longer generally believed to have been Daniel Defoe. See, for example, Philip Nicholas Furbank and W. R. Owens, "The Defoe that Never Was: A Tale of De-Attribution," *The American Scholar* 66, no. 2 (1997).

5. Charles Johnson, *A General History of the Robberies and Murders of the Most Notorious Pirates* (1726; repr., New York: Dodd, Mead, 1926), 145.

6. Philip Ashton and John Barnard, *Ashton's Memorial*, 1725, reprinted in Donald P. Wharton, *In the Trough of the Sea* (Westport, CT: Greenwood, 1979), 177; George Roberts, *The Four Years Voyages of Capt. George Roberts; Being a Series of Uncommon Events Which Befell Him* (1726; repr., London: Traveller's Library, 1930), 38; William Snelgrave, *A New Account of some parts of Guinea and the Slave Trade*, 1727, excerpted in *Captured by Pirates* ("The Bloody-Minded Villain Came on to Kill Me"), John Richard Stephens, ed. (Cambria Pines by the Sea, CA: Fern Canyon, 1996), 159–160.

7. J. M. Barrie, *Peter Pan and Wendy* (1906), reprint, illustrated by Edmund Blampied (New York: Charles Scribner's Sons, 1940), 55 (chapter 4).

8. Robert Fisk, "Pirates of the high seas," *The Independent*, October 5, 2008; Somali piracy: "We're defending our waters," *Mail & Guardian Online*, April 16, 2009, http://www.mg.co.za/article/2008-10-14-somali-piracy-were-defending-our-waters.

9. "Crewman who stabbed pirate says he won't go back," *Associated Press*, April 19, 2009; "Maersk Alabama crew recalls pirate attack," *USA Today*, April 17, 2009; Mark Mazetti and Sharon Otterman, "U.S. Captain Is Hostage of Pirates; Navy Ship Arrives," *New York Times*, April 8, 2009; Jason Miller, "We heard pirates' footsteps," *Toronto Star*, May 7, 2009.

10. For the complete modern definition, see UNCLOS 1982, art. 101.

11. Charles Molloy, *De Jure Maritimo Et Navali: Or, A Treatise of Affairs Maritime, and of Commerce* (London: John Walthoe Junior, 1722), 55.

12. Montague Bernard, *A Historical Account of the Neutrality of Great Britain During the American Civil War* (London: Longmans, Green, Reader, and Dyer, 1870), 119.

13. Matthew Tindall, *An Essay Concerning the Laws of Nations, and the Rights of Soveraigns* (London: Richard Baldwin, 1694) 25–26.

14. Ibid., 25.

15. Marcus Tullius Cicero, *Select Orations of Marcus Tullius Cicero*, translated by C. D. Young (Philadelphia: David McKay, 1898), 433.

16. See, for example, Alfred P. Rubin, *The Law of Piracy* (Newport, RI: Naval War College Press, 1988); Zou Keyuan, "Seeking Effectiveness for the Crackdown of Piracy at Sea," *Journal of International Affairs* 59, no. 1 (2005); Michael Bahar, "Attaining Optimal Deterrence at Sea: A Legal and Strategic Theory for Naval Anti-Piracy Operations," *Vanderbilt Journal of Transnational Law* 40 (January 2007); and Joshua Michael Goodwin, "Universal Jurisdiction and the Pirate: Time for an Old Couple to Part," *Vanderbilt Journal of Transnational Law* 39 (2006). For a thorough but succinct description of the legal definitions of piracy and of modern piracy in general, see Jack A. Gottschalk et al., *Jolly Roger with an Uzi: The Rise and Threat of Modern Piracy* (Annapolis, MD: Naval Institute Press, 2000), 28–43. For a thorough analysis of the legal definition of piracy and its historical basis, see Rubin, *Law of Piracy*.

17. "The Lords of the Council to [Sir Henry Crispe . . .], 21 October 1571," in F. C. Loder-Symonds, E. R. Wodehouse, et al., eds. *The Manuscripts of Rye and Hereford Corporations*, Historical Manuscripts Commission, Thirteenth Report, Appendix, Part IV (London: Eyre and Spottiswoode for Her Majesty's Stationery Office, 1892), 8–9; *CSPD 1547–1580*, no. 68.

18. *CSPC 1717–1718*, no. 760.

19. "Thomas Greene Mayor of Lynn to Lord Townshend," in Great Britain: Royal Commission on Historical Manuscripts, *Manuscripts of the Marquess Townshend*, (London: Eyre and Spottiswoode, 1887) 27; "Declaration of Jeremiah Tay and Others, March 1691," in J. Franklin Jameson, *Privateering and Piracy in the Colonial Period* (New York: Macmillan, 1970), 147.

20. Tom Goldstein and Jethro Koller Lieberman, *The Lawyer's Guide to Writing Well*, 2nd ed. (Berkeley: University of California Press, 2003), 124.

21. Louis XIV, "Declaration du Roy contre les corsaires ennemis. Donnée à Versailles au mois de Juillet 1691." (Paris: Guillaume Desprez, 1691), ii.

22. Thomas Gage, *Thomas Gage's Travels in the New World*, 1648, reprint, edited by J. Eric S. Thompson (Norman: University of Oklahoma Press, 1969), 335–336.

23. "*Proditor et pirate nequissimus*," "*vir flagitiosissimus*," "*archipirata*," "*apostata*," "*tyrannus ex Hispania*," quoted in Anon., "Our One Hundred Questions," *Lippincott's Monthly Magazine*, vol. 42 (July–December 1888), 570.

24. Mazetti and Otterman, *New York Times*, April 8, 2009.

25. *Monty Python's The Meaning of Life* (Universal Studios, 1997). Similarly, in the *South Park* "Fatbeard" episode (2009), Cartman recruits a crew to join the Somali pirates.

26. For example, the Royal Navy's *Blackburn Buccaneer* fighter-bomber and *Buccaneer* VSTOL fighter-bomber, and the U.S. Navy's Vought F-4U *Corsair* fighter and its first jet fighter, the short lived Vought F-6U *Pirate*.

27. Regarding submarines and the Jolly Roger, see chapter 14. Regarding insignia, author's experience as a Navy SEAL working with various military and law enforcement units.

28. Théodore Ortolan, *Règles internationales et diplomatie de la mer*, 4th ed. (Paris: Librarie de Henri Plon, 1864), vol. 2:74.

29. For a description of the most significant terms for piracy and privateering, see Peter R. Galvin, *Patterns of Pillage: A Geography of Caribbean-based Piracy in Spanish America, 1536–1718* (New York: Peter Lang, 2000), 2–8, and Benerson Little, *The Sea Rover's Practice: Pirate Tactics and Techniques 1630–1730* (Washington, D.C.: Potomac Books, 2005), 10–17, 221–223.

30. See, for example, Marcus Rediker, *Between the Devil and the Deep Blue Sea* (Cambridge: Cambridge University Press, 1987) and Rediker, *Villains of All Nations: Atlantic Pirates in the Golden Age* (Boston: Beacon Press, 2004).

31. See, for example, J. L. Anderson, "Piracy and World History: An Economic Perspective on Maritime Predation," *Journal of World History* 6, no. 2 (1995).

32. Thucydides, *The History of the Peloponnesian War*, in *Great Books of the Western World: 6, Herodotus, Thucydides*, 1952, translated by Richard Crawley, reprint, revised by R. Feetham (Chicago: Encyclopedia Britannica, 1982), 350.

33. Charles Johnson, *A General History of the Robberies and Murders of the Most Notorious Pirates*, 1726, reprint (New York: Dodd, Mead, 1926), vii–viii.

34. Niccolò Machiavelli [Nicholas Machiavel], *The Art of War*, 1520, reprinted in *The Works of Nicholas Machiavel.* 2 vols., translated by Ellis Farnworth (London: Thomas Davies, 1762), vol. 2:8.

35. See, for example, Elizabeth A. Kennedy, "Somali pirates find booming business," *Associated Press*, April 23, 2008, and Chege Mbitiru, "There and About: Somali pirates face new offensive," *Daily Nation* (Kenya), May 5, 2008, http://allafrica.com/stories/200805051368.html.

36. See, for example, Plutarch [Lucius Mestrius Plutarchus], *The Lives of the Noble Grecians and Romans: The Dryden Translation*, translated by John Dryden (Chicago: Encyclopedia Britannica, 1952), 510.

37. Gottschalk, Flanagan, Kahn, and Larochelle list three conditions for successful piracy: worthwhile rewards, a geographic area where the risk of detection is acceptable, and, if possible, safe havens. See Gottschalk, et al. *Jolly Roger with an Uzi*, 5.

38. For modern examples, see Tony Iltis, "The real story of the Somali pirates," *Green Left Online*, April 18, 2009, http://www.greenleft.org.au/node/41491, and

Olivier Laurent, "Why did France resort to violence off the coast of Somalia?" *World Socialist Web Site*, May 1, 2009, http://www.wsws.org/node/41491.

39. Cicero [Marcus Tullius Cicero], *Orations of Marcus Tullius*, translated by C. D. Young, (London: George Bell and Sons, 1878), vol. 1:84.

40. International Maritime Bureau Piracy Reporting Centre, "IMB 2008 Piracy Report," http://www.icc-ccs.org, 22; David McKenzie, "No way to stop us, pirate leader says," *CNN.com*, December 4, 2008; "Pirates of the high seas," *The Independent*, October 5, 2008. Estimated annual losses were in British pounds. I converted them to U.S. dollars using the published exchange rate for October 2008 and updated the figure per the rate for April 2010.

41. Taylor, John, "An Apologie for Sea-men," 15.

42. Thomas Fuller, *The History of the Worthies of England*, 1662, reprint (London: Thomas Tegg, 1860), vol. 2:117.

43. Johnson, *General History*, 164–166; William Snelgrave, *A New Account of some parts of Guinea and the Slave Trade*, 1727, excerpted in *Captured by Pirates* ("The Bloody-Minded Villain Came on to Kill Me"), John Richard Stephens, ed. (Cambria Pines by the Sea, CA: Fern Canyon, 1996), 172–173.

44. Ibid.

45. Johnson, *General History*, 164–166.

46. Snelgrave, *New Account*, 143, 151, 172–173.

47. Ibid., 161, 174. Snelgrave's account is given; Johnson's account describes stronger retaliation against the local Portuguese after Davis's death.

48. Kennedy, "Somali pirates"; "It's a pirate's life for me," *BBC News*, April 22, 2009, http://news.bbc.co.uk/2/hi/8010061.stm.

49. Richard Phillips, *A Captain's Duty: Somali Pirates, Navy SEALs, and Dangerous Days at Sea*, with Stephan Talty and George K. Wilson (New York: Hyperion, 2010), 167–263; Howard Altman, "Rescued captain praises heroism of crew, SEALs," *Tampa Tribune*, April 28, 2009; John Crane, "Dry Fork sailor a witness to high-seas drama," *Danville News* (Virginia), April 23, 2009; Bill Gertz, "EXCLUSIVE: Obama OK'd 2 SEAL teams for pirates," *Washington Times*, April 22, 2009; Abdiqani Hassan, "Somali pirate families ask for U.S. pardon," *Reuters UK*, April 22, 2009; Jamie Kinton, "Local sailor part of heroic Navy crew," *Mansfield News Journal* (Ohio), April 19, 2009; Robert D. McFadden and Scott Shane, "In Rescue of Captain, Navy Kills 3 Pirates," *New York Times*, April 12, 2009; Howard Pankratz, "Colorado sailor aids U.S. captain's rescue from pirates," *Denver Post*, May 6, 2009; Buddy Wellborn, "Real story of Obama and the hostage," email forwarded to author.

50. Ibid.

51. Ibid.; "New charges against Maersk Alabama pirate suspect," *MarineLog.com*, January 12, 2010.

Chapter 2: Heroes of the Fantastic
Pirate Hunting in the Age of the Iliad

1. Horace, *Carmina* 1.3.9–12; Horace [Quintus Horatius Flaccus], *Odes and Epodes*, Charles E. Bennett, ed., 1934, revised edition (Boston: Allyn and Bacon, 1968), 4–5, 148. The translation is from Norbert Guterman, ed., *The Anchor Book of Latin Quotations* (1966; repr. New York: Doubleday, 1990), 155.

2. Homer, *Odyssey*, translated by S. H. Butcher and Andrew Lang, in *The Complete Works of Homer* (New York: The Modern Library, 1935), 112.

3. "The Trial of Captain John Quelch," in John D. Lawson, ed., *American State Trials* (St. Louis: F. H. Thomas Law Book Co., 1916), vol. 5:335. See also Edward Coke, quoted in William Blackstone, *Commentaries on the Laws of England*, 1765–1769, facsimile reprint (Chicago: University of Chicago Press, 1979), vol. 4:71, and Rubin, *Law of Piracy*, 66–113.

4. Homer, *Odyssey*, 1, 203.

5. Marcus Tullius Cicero, *Select Orations*, 95 (*Pro Lege Manilia Oratio*, XI). He repeats the similar sentiment in the fifth book of the second pleading against Verres (LX).

6. Heliodorus of Emesa, *Aethiopian Adventures: or, the History of Theagenes and Chariclea*, translated by "a Person of Quality" and Nahum Tate (Dublin: R. Main, 1753), 146.

7. Taylor, "Apologie for Sea-men," in Taylor, *Works*, vol. 5:16.

8. Paul Johnstone, *The Sea-craft of Prehistory*, 2nd ed. (London: Routledge, 1988) 55–56; John Noble Wilford, "On Crete, New Evidence of Very Ancient Mariners," *New York Times*, February 15, 2010. A few researchers believe that some hominids took to the sea as many as 800,000 years ago.

9. Homer, *Odyssey*, 1.

10. Hesiod, *Hesiod: The Homeric Hymns and Homerica*, translated by Hugh. G. Evelyn-White (London: William Henemann, 1920), 488–505, 530–531. In chronological order, the cycle includes *Cypria*, the *Iliad*, *Aethiopis*, the *Little Iliad*, the *Sack of Troy*, *Nostoi*, the *Odyssey*, and *Telegony*. Conceivably one could attach the *Aeneid* as well.

11. Michael M. Sage, *Warfare in Ancient Greece: A Sourcebook* (New York: Routledge, 1996) 23.

12. Homer, *Odyssey*, 100.

13. Thucydides, *Peloponnesian War*, 350–351; Alastar Jackson, "War and Raids for Booty in the World of Odysseus," in *War and Society in the Greek World*, John Rich and Graham Shipley, eds. (New York: Routledge, 1995) 64–65; Tracey Rihll, "War, Slavery, and Settlement in Early Greece," in Rich and Shipley, *War and Society*, 79–82.

14. Herodotus, *The Histories of Herodotus*, in *Great Books of the Western World:6, Heroditus, Thucydides*, 1952, translated by George Rawlinson, reprint (Chicago: Encyclopedia Britannica, 1982) 1–2.

15. Homer, *Odyssey*, 127.

16. Ibid., 47–48.

17. Virgil [Publius Vergilius Maro], *The Aeneid*, translated by Robert Fagles, 2006 (New York: Penguin, 2008 reprint).

18. Herodotus, *History*, 2.

19. Homer, *Odyssey*, 216.

20. Apollonius Rhodius, *The Argonautica*, translated by R. C. Seaton (New York: Macmillan, 1912), 235.

21. Lionel Casson, *The Ancient Mariners: Seafarers and Sea Fighters of the Mediterranean in Ancient Times* 2nd ed. (Princeton, NJ: Princeton University Press, 1991), 38.

22. See, for example, Homer, *Odyssey*, 128.

23. Casson, *Ancient Mariners*, 26–29, 38–43; Casson, *Ships and Seamanship in the Ancient World* (Princeton, NJ: Princeton University Press, 1971), 43–48; Homer, *Odyssey*, 24, 26–27; Robert Graves, *The Greek Myths*, 1955, 1960 (London: Folio Society, 1996 reprint) 532.

24. Homer, *Odyssey*, 215–216.

25. Thomas Day Seymour, *Life in the Homeric Age* (New York: Biblo and Tannen, 1963),

629–674; Chrestos Tsountas and J. Irving Manatt, *The Mycenaean Age: A Study of the Monuments and Culture of Pre-Homeric Greece* (Boston: Houghton Mifflin, 1897), 191–212.

26. Tsountas and Manatt, *Mycenaean Age*, 199.
27. See, for example, Homer, *Odyssey*, 272.
28. Graves, *Greek Myths*, 317.
29. Homer, *Odyssey*, 272.
30. Graves, *Greek Myths*, 317.
31. Homer, *Odyssey*, 286; Seymour, *Homeric Age*, 673–674.
32. Homer, *Odyssey*, 65.
33. Casson, *Ancient Mariners*, 85, 103.
34. Paul W. Bamford, *Fighting Ships and Prisons* (Minneapolis: University of Minnesota Press, 1973), 39.
35. Thucydides, *Peloponnesian War*, 350; Henry A. Ormerod, *Piracy in the Ancient World: An Essay in Mediterranean History*, 1924 (Totowa, NJ: Rowman and Littlefield, reprint 1978), 44–45.
36. Graves, *Greek Myths*, 486.
37. Ibid., 533, 531; Apollonius, *Argonautica*, 45.
38. Graves, *Greek Myths*, 484; Josiah Burchett, *A Complete History of the most Remarkable Transactions at Sea* (London: J. Walthoe, 1720), 43; Homer, *Iliad*, 211–224.
39. Homer, *Odyssey*, 127–128.
40. Ibid., 272.
41. Virgil *Aeneid* 5.199–200, trans. Fagles.
42. Burchett, *Remarkable Transactions*, 42.
43. Homer, *Odyssey*, 286.
44. William Gilkerson, *Boarders Away: With Steel: Edged Weapons and Polearms of the Classical Age of Fighting Sail, 1626-1826* (Lincoln RI: Andrew Mowbray Publishers, 1991), 56.
45. Georges Guillet de Saint-Georges, *Les arts de l'homme d'epée, ou, Le dictionnaire du gentil-homme* (Paris: Chez la veuve Gervais Clouzier, 1682), 743 ; Jacques Bourdé de Villehuet, *Le Manoeuvrier, ou essai sur la théorie et la practique de mouvements du navire et des évolutions navales* (Paris: H. L. Guerin and L. F. Delatour, 1765), 224.
46. Homer, *Odyssey*, 292; Seymour, *Homeric Age*, 633.
47. Casson, *Ships and Seamanship*, plate 61; Casson, *Ancient Mariners*, 35, figure 4.
48. Homer, *Odyssey*, 287.
49. Ibid., 484–485, 535.
50. Plutarch, *Lives*, 6–7; Graves, *Greek Myths*, 316.
51. Homer, *Odyssey*, 31.
52. Graves, *Greek Myths*, 484–496.
53. *CSPC 1685–1688*, no. 476; John Taylor, *Jamaica in 1687: The Taylor Manuscript at the National Library of Jamaica*, edited by David Buisseret (Kingston, Jamaica: University of West Indies Press, 2008), 108; "Le commissaire Jolinet au ministre Colbert [extrait]," 19 December 1678, Archives nationales, Colonies, C8 A rec. 1, fol. 130–131, reproduced in *Les Archives de la Flibuste*, http://us.geocities.com/trebutor/archives/D1670/D7808lemoign.html; Benerson Little, *The Buccaneer's Realm: Pirate Life on the Spanish Main, 1674–1688* (Washington, D.C.: Potomac Books, 2007), 99, 203, 205, 237, 239.
54. Graves, *Greek Myths*, 524, 529, 530; Apollonius, *Argonautica*, 5, 29, 31, 39.

55. Elijah H. Burritt, *The Geography of the Heavens, and Class Book of Astronomy* (New York: Huntington and Savage, 1843), 75–76.
56. Apollonius, *Argonautica*, 1–17, 31; Graves, *Greek Myths*, 525–526.
57. Graves, *Greek Myths*, 484.
58. In general, see Apollonius, *Argonautica*, and Graves, *Greek Myths*, 523–562.
59. Thucydides, *Peloponnesian War*, 350; Graves, *Greek Myths*, 316.
60. Plutarch, *Lives*, 6.
61. Ibid.; Graves, *Greek Myths*, 316.
62. Plutarch, *Lives*, 2–3, 6. Plutarch, citing Demon, notes that Taurus, "the chief captain of Minos," was killed by Theseus. Taurus may have been one of Minos's pirate hunting captains, but nowhere is this stated. See Plutarch, *Lives*, 6.
63. François Leguat, *The Voyage of François Leguat of Bresse to Rodriguez, Mauritius, Java, and the Cape of Good Hope*, 1708, reprint edited by Pasfield Oliver (London: Hakluyt Society, 1891), vol. 1:38.
64. Burritt, *Geography of the Heavens*, 43; Dava Sobel, *Longitude: The True Story of a Lone Genius Who Solved the Greatest Scientific Problem of His Time* (New York: Penguin, 1996), 51–53, 59–60.
65. The *Argo* is now broken into four constellations: *Carina*, *Puppis*, *Vela*, and *Pyxis* (*Keel*, *Poop*, *Sail*, and *Compass*). *Volans* and *Columba* (*Flying Fish* and *Dove*) are associated with the ship.
66. T. B. L. Webster, *From Mycenae to Homer* (London: Methuen, 1958), 136.
67. Virgil, *Aeneid* 3.9, trans. Fagles; Homer, *Odyssey*, 165.

Chapter 3: In the Age of Ancient Empires
Pirate Hunting in the Mediterranean, 1450–700 BC

1. For a discussion of geography's effect on piracy in the Mediterranean, see Henry Mainwaring, *The Life and Works of Sir Henry Mainwaring*, edited by G. E. Manwaring and W. G. Perrin (London: Navy Records Society, 1922), vol. 2:25–35, and Galvin, *Patterns of Pillage*, 1–19.
2. Homer, *Odyssey*, 125.
3. Casson, *Ancient Mariners*, 108. In general regarding maritime trade, seafarers, and pirates during this period, see Casson, *Ancient Mariners*; Casson, *Ships and Seamanship*; Phillip de Souza, *Piracy in the Graeco-Roman World* (Cambridge: Cambridge University Press, 2002); and Ormerod, *Piracy in the Ancient World*.
4. See Casson, *Ancient Mariners*, 6–22.
5. Ormerod, *Piracy in the Ancient World*, 59–79.
6. Ibid., 59; *Oxford English Dictionary*, 2nd ed., s.v. "pirate."
7. Rubin, *Law of Piracy*, 5; Thucydides, *Peloponnesian War*, 350.
8. Ibid, 352 . See also Ormerod, *Piracy in the Ancient World*, 96–97.
9. W. M. Flinders Petrie, *Syria and Egypt: From the Tell el Amarna Letters* (London: Methuen, 1898), 46; Trevor Bryce, *The Trojans and Their Neighbours* (London: Routledge, 2006), 148–150.
10. Casson, *Ancient Mariners*, 34.
11. Ibid.
12. Ibid., 33–34; Barry Strauss, *The Trojan War: A New History* (New York: Simon & Schuster, 2006), 188–189.
13. E. A. Wallis Budge, *Egypt Under the Priest-Kings, Tanites, and Nubians* (London: Kegan Paul, Trench, Trübner, 1902), 10–16; Ormerod, *Piracy in the Ancient World*, 74–75; Casson, *Ancient Mariners*, 52–53.

14. Thucydides, *Peloponnesian War*, 350; Ormerod, *Ancient Piracy*, 89, 93–97.
15. Thucydides, *Peloponnesian War*, 350.
16. Ibid.
17. Casson, *Ancient Mariners*, 32.
18. Thucydides, *Peloponnesian War*, 350–351.
19. Ormerod, *Piracy in the Ancient World*, 88.
20. Strauss, *Trojan War*, 91.
21. Thucydides, *Peloponnesian War*, 353.
22. Casson, *Ancient Mariners*, 33–34.
23. James Henry Breasted, ed., *Ancient Records of Egypt* Vol. IV (Chicago: University of Chicago Press, 1906), 45–47.
24. Ibid.
25. Ormerod, *Piracy in the Ancient World*, 94; Gaston Maspero, *The Passing of the Empires, 850 B.C. to 330 B.C.*, edited by Archibald Henry Sayce, translated by M. L. McClure (London: Society for Promoting Christian Knowledge, 1900), 298, 300–304.
26. Casson, *Ancient Mariners*, 74; Thucydides, *Peloponnesian War*, 353; Herodotus, *History*, 115; Polyaenus, *Stratagems of War*, translated by Richard Shepherd (London: George Nicol, 1793), 206–207.
27. Casson, *Ancient Mariners*, 76–79.
28. Ibid., 78.
29. Thucydides, *Peloponnesian War*, 353.
30. Casson, *Ships and Seamanship*, 53–54.
31. L'Abbat [Monsieur L'Abbat], *The Art of Fencing, or, the Use of the Small Sword*, 1734, translated by Andrew Mahon, reprint (n.p.: Kessinger Reprints, n.d.), 61.
32. See Edward Latham, *Famous Sayings and Their Authors: A Collection of Historical Sayings in English, French, German, Greek, Italian, and* Latin 2nd ed. (London: Swan Sonnenschein, 1906), 218.
33. Ibid.
34. Casson, *Ancient Mariners*, 144.

Chapter 4: Of Laurel Leaves and Pirate Princes
Pirate Hunting in the Mediterranean, 700 BC–AD 476

1. George Cary, *The Medieval Alexander*, edited by D. J. A. Ross (Cambridge: Cambridge University Press, 1956), 95–96.; Pierre Dan, *Histoire de Barbarie et de ses Corsaires, des royaumes et des villes d'Alger, de Tunis, de Salé, & de Tripoly* 2nd ed. (Paris: Pierre Rocolet, 1649), 14.
2. St. Augustine, *City of God*, 4.4.
3. Cary, *Medieval Alexander*, 95–96.
4. Thucydides, *Peloponnesian War*, 352.
5. Douglas Kelly, "Alexander's *Clergie*," in Donald Maddox and Sara Sturm-Maddox, eds., *The Medieval French Alexander* (Albany: State University Press of New York, 2002), 46.
6. See, for example, Noam Chomsky, *Pirates and Emperors, Old and New: International Terrorism in the Real World* (Montreal: Black Rose Books, 1986), 9–16.
7. Alexandre Dumas, *The Black Tulip* (New York: Walter J. Black, 1932), 27.
8. Ormerod, *Ancient Piracy*, 122.
9. Rubin, *Law of Piracy*, 1–13.

10. Polybius, *The Histories*, translated by W. R. Paton (New York: G. P. Putnam's Sons, 1922), 269.
11. In general, see Thucydides, *Peloponnesian War*.
12. Thucydides, *Peloponnesian War*, 394.
13. Casson, *Ancient Mariners*, 178.
14. Ibid., 405.
15. Ibid., 385–386.
16. Herodotus, *History*, 131.
17. Ormerod, *Ancient Piracy*, 102; de Souza, *Piracy*, 92.
18. Livy [Titus Livius], *Livy*, translated by George Baker (New York: Harper and Brothers, 1836), 32.22, 37.27; Ormerod, *Ancient Piracy*, 116–117.
19. Casson, *Ancient Mariners*, 179.
20. Ormerod, *Ancient Piracy*, 70, 259.
21. Ibid.
22. Polybius, *Histories*, 261.
23. Ormerod, *Ancient Piracy*, 113.
24. Casson, *Ancient Mariners*, 178.
25. Ormerod, *Ancient Piracy*, 113, 119–120, 123.
26. Casson, *Ancient Mariners*, 112.
27. Ormerod, *Ancient Piracy*, 98.
28. Casson, *Ancient Mariners*, 178.
29. Polybius, *Histories*, 267.
30. Casson, *Ancient Mariners*, 83–84.
31. Sextus Julius Frontinus, *Strategematicon, or Greek and Roman Anecdotes, Concerning Military Policy and Science of War*, translated by Robert B. Scott (London: Thomas Goddard, 1811), 288.
32. Ibid., 287.
33. Ibid., 287–288.
34. Casson, *Ships and Seamanship*, 137–140, 152–153; Casson, *Ancient Mariners*, 146.
35. Casson, *Ancient Mariners*, 87.
36. Thucydides, *Peloponnesian War*, 2:92.
37. Casson, *Ships and Seamanship*, 300–309, 322–325.
38. Thucydides, *Peloponnesian War*, 2:89.
39. Casson, *Ancient Mariners*, 88.
40. Livy, *Livy*, 37.27.
41. Casson, *Ancient Mariners*, 92.
42. de Souza, *Piracy*, 91–92.
43. Thomas Dew, *A Digest of the Laws, Customs, Manners, and Institutions of the Ancient and Modern Nations* (New York: D. Appleton and Company, 1872), 243; Casson, *Ancient Mariners*, 179.
44. Livy, *Livy*, 40.27.
45. Ibid., 40.28.
46. Ibid.
47. Ormerod, *Ancient Piracy*, 110.
48. Casson, *Ancient Mariners*, 112–113.
49. Ormerod, *Ancient Piracy*, 122.
50. Casson, *Ancient Mariners*, 138–139.
51. Polyaenus, *Stratagems of War*, 212.

52. In general, see the pleadings against Verres in Cicero, *Orations*.
53. Livy [Titus Livius], *The History of Rome*, translated by D. Spillan and Cyrus Edmonds (London: George Bell and Sons, 1887), 22.19.
54. Thucydides, *Peloponnesian War*, 2:25.
55. Casson, *Ancient Mariners*, 179; Casson, *Ships and Seamanship*, 125–132. See also Polybius, *Histories*, 263. Some maritime historians consider the *lembos* and the *liburnian* as essentially the same vessel.
56. Polybius, *Histories*, 263.
57. Casson, *Ancient Mariners*, 91.
58. Casson, *Ships and Seamanship*, 129–131.
59. Ibid., plate 80.
60. Pliny the Elder [Caius Plinius Secundus], *The Natural History of Pliny*, edited by John Bostock and H. T. Riley (London: George Bell & Sons, 1890), 6:101.
61. Cicero, *Orations*, vol. 1:505.
62. Ibid.
63. Ibid.
64. Thucydides, *Peloponnesian War*, 410.
65. Ibid., 557.
66. Polybius, *Histories*, 249–259.
67. Ibid.
68. Ormerod, *Piracy in the Ancient World*, 186.
69. Ibid., 191–192.
70. Plutarch, *Lives*, 510; Florus, *Epitome of Roman History*, in Watson, *Sallust*, 361–362.
71. Ormerod, *Piracy in the Ancient World*, 185.
72. Huzar, *Mark Anthony*, 13–14.
73. Ibid., 15–16.
74. Florus, *Epitome of Roman History*, in John Selby Watson, ed., *Sallust, Florus, and Velleius Paterculus* (London: George Bell and Sons, 1889), 362.
75. Plutarch, *Lives*, 577; Velleius Paterculus, *Remains of His Compendium of the History of Rome*, in Watson, *Sallust*, 479–480; Suetonius [Gaius Suetonius Tranquillus], *Suetonius*, edited by J. C. Rolfe (London: William Heinemann, 1914), vol. 1:5, 7, 95.
76. Plutarch, *Lives*, 577; Velleius Paterculus, *Remains of His Compendium of the History of Rome*, in Watson, *Sallust*, 479–80; Suetonius, *Suetonius*, vol. 1:5, 7, 95.
77. Ibid.
78. Plutarch, *Lives*, 510–512.
79. Florus, *Epitome of Roman History*, in Watson, *Sallust*, 363–364.
80. Ibid., 363.
81. Caesar [Gaius Julius Caesar], *The Civil War: together with The Alexandrian War, The African War, and The Spanish War by other Hands*, translated by Jane F. Mitchell (New York: Penguin, 1980), 63–64; Caesar, *Alexandrian War*, 14.
82. Lucan [Marcus Annaeus Lucanus], *The Pharsalia of Lucan*, translated by H. T. Riley (London: Henry G. Bohn, 1853), 119.
83. Ormerod, *Piracy in the Ancient World*, 250.

Chapter 5: The Scourge from the North
Standing Against the Norsemen, 780–1066

1. Ambrose Bierce, *The Devil's Dictionary*, 1911 (New York: Dover, 1958 reprint), s.v. "piracy."

2. *The Complete Oxford English Dictionary*, 2nd ed. (Oxford: Clarendon Press, 1989), s.v. "brigantine."

3. From "The Dying Ode of Regner Lodbrog," in Alfred, King of England, *The Whole Works of Alfred the Great*. (London: Bosworth & Harrison, 1858), vol. 1:377. A coat of mail was body armor made of small interlinked rings.

4. Jane Smiley, *The Sagas of Icelanders: A Selection*, Introduction by Robert Kellogg (New York: Penguin, 2000), 190.

5. Lee M. Hollander, trans., *The Saga of the Jómsvíkings* (Austin: University of Texas Press, 1955), 61–62.

6. Archibald R. Lewis and Timothy J. Runyan, *European Naval and Maritime History, 300–1500* (Bloomington: Indiana University Press, 1990), 91. In "Egil's Saga," Egil is not only a fierce pillaging Viking warrior, but also a merchant trader who trades from Iceland to Norway. See Smiley, *Sagas of Icelanders*, 148, and "Egil's Saga" in general.

7. In general, see Smiley, *Sagas of Icelanders*.

8. See, for example, ibid., 12.

9. Lewis and Runyan, *European Naval and Maritime History*, 90; Dirk Meier, *Seafarers, Merchants and Pirates in the Middle Ages*, translated by Angus McGeoch (Woodbridge, UK: Boydell Press, 2006), 98. Regarding the Carolingian empire, the expansion of empires often forces neighbors to expand their own boundaries.

10. Florence of Worcester, *The Chronicles of Florence of Worcester*, translated by Thomas Forester (London: Henry G. Bohn, 1854), 156–157.

11. John Davies, *A History of Wales* (London: Penguin, 1993), 81; R. F. Foster, *The Oxford Illustrated History of Ireland* (Oxford: Oxford University Press, 2001), 31; F. Logan, *The Vikings in History* 2nd ed. (New York: Routledge, 1992), 112.

12. Davies, *History of Wales*, 81; Foster, *History of Ireland*, 33; F. Donald Logan, *The Vikings in History* 2nd ed. (New York: Routledge, 1992), 114.

13. See, for example, Hollander, *Saga of the Jómsvíkings*, 73.

14. Smiley, *Sagas of Icelanders*, 630. See, for example, Smiley, *Sagas of Icelanders* and Alfred, *Whole Works*.

15. Foster, *History of Ireland*, 34–37. In general, see Thomas Walsh, *History of the Irish Hierarchy* (New York: D. & J. Sadlier, 1854) for detailed chronologies of Viking attacks on Irish monasteries and clergy.

16. Smiley, *Sagas of Icelanders*, 105.

17. Hollander, *Saga of the Jómsvíkings*, 89–90. Debate continues over whether *Jómsvíkings* were a real or fictional order of Vikings, or a fictional order based to some degree in fact.

18. See, for example, Smiley, *Sagas of Icelanders*, 102.

19. Martina Sprague, *Norse Warfare: Unconventional Battle Strategies of the Ancient Vikings* (New York: Hippocrene, 2007), 80–81; Smiley, *Sagas of Icelanders*, 741–742.

20. Anon., *Beowulf*, translated by William Ellery Leonard (Norwalk, CT: Heritage Press, 1967), 9, 71.

21. Florence of Worcester, *Chronicle*, 90–91.

22. "Chronicle of Florence," in Alfred, *Whole Works*, 127.

23. Florence of Worcester, *Chronicle*, 85.

24. Ibid.

25. John Asser, "Life of King Alfred," in Alfred, *Whole Works*, vol. 1:80. Some scholars have questioned the authenticity of Asser's work, but in this instance, other Alfred chronicles corroborate Asser's work.

26. Logan, *Vikings in History*, 143–148.
27. Lewis and Runyan, *European Naval and Maritime History*, 93–94.
28. Ibid., 94; Susan Rose, *Medieval Naval Warfare 1000–1500* (London: Routledge, 2002), 25–26.
29. Florence of Worcester, *Chronicle*, 84.
30. "The Huntingdon Chronicle," in Alfred, *Whole Works*, 127.
31. In the *Saga of the Jómsvíkings*, the wind, perhaps aided by an ogress, turns back arrows and other missiles. Hollander, *Saga of the Jómsvíkings*, 101.
32. Judith Jesch, *Ships and Men in the Late Viking Age: The Vocabulary of Runic Inscriptions and Skaldic Verse* (Suffolk, England: Boydell Press, 2001), 208–209.
33. "Egil's Saga," in Smiley, *Sagas of Icelanders*, 101.
34. Jesch, *Ships and Men*, 209–210.
35. Snorri Sturluson, *The Heimskringla: A History of the Norse Kings*, translated by Samuel Laing (London: Norroena Society, 1907), 296.
36. "Egil's Saga," in Smiley, *Sagas of Icelanders*, 100.
37. Hollander, *Saga of the Jómsvíkings*, 76.
38. "Egil's Saga," in Smiley, *Sagas of Icelanders*, 17.
39. "*Saga of the People of Laxardal*," in Smiley, *Sagas of Icelanders*, 307–308.
40. Jesch, *Ships and Men*, 209.
41. Ibid., 210.
42. Sturluson, *Heimskringla*, 254, 298.
43. Ibid.
44. Hollander, *Saga of the Jómsvíkings*, 98.
45. "Heimskringla," Saga VII, quoted in William Ledyard Rodgers, *Naval Warfare Under Oars, 4th to 16th Centuries*, 1940 (Annapolis, MD: Naval Institute Press, 1967 reprint), 80; Hollander, *Saga of the Jómsvíkings*, 98.
46. "Egil's Saga," in Smiley, *Sagas of Icelanders*, 105.
47. See Jesch, *Ships and Men*, 211, for descriptions from runic inscriptions and skaldic verse.
48. Sturluson, *Heimskringla*, 239–240.
49. Oddr Snorrason, *The Saga of King Olaf Tryggwason Who Reigned Over Norway A.D. 995 to A.D. 1000*, translated by John Sephton (London: David Nutt, 1895), 413.
50. Ibid., 242.
51. See, for example, Jesch, *Ships and Men*, 210; Rodgers, *Naval Warfare*, 79–87; and Hollander, *Saga of the Jómsvíkings*, 57, 102.
52. Geoffrey Vaughan Scammel, *The World Encompassed: The First European Maritime Empires c. 800–1650* (Berkeley: University of California Press, 1981), 205; Rodgers, *Naval Warfare*, 140.
53. Rodgers, *Naval Warfare*, 99.
54. John Fryer, *A New Account of East India and Persia, Being Nine Years' Travels 1672–1681*, 1698, reprint edited by William Crooke (Millwood, NY: Kraus Reprint, 1967), vol. 3:89.
55. Little, *Sea Rover's Practice*, 159.
56. Rodgers, *Naval Warfare*, 79.
57. Joseph Anderson, ed., *The Orkneyinga Saga*, translated by Jon A. Hjaltalin and Gilbert Goudie (Edinburgh: Edmonston and Douglas, 1873), 142–146.
58. See, for example, "Egil's Saga," in Smiley, *Sagas of Icelanders*, 22, 86, 146.
59. Hollander, *Saga of the Jómsvíkings*, 45–46.
60. "The Saga of Ref the Sly," in Smiley, *Sagas of Icelanders*, 617.

61. See, for example, Rodgers, *Naval Warfare*, 80–86, and Lewis and Runyan, *European Naval and Maritime History*, 94–95.
62. Meier, *Seafarers, Merchants, and Pirates*, 114–115.

Chapter 6: A Sea Roving Free-for-All
Pirate Hunting in the Northern Seas, 1066–1492

1. *CPR Henry VI*, 21 November 1444, vol. 4:338; *Oxford English Dictionary*, 2nd ed., s.v. "rover."
2. Enguerrand de Monstrelet, *The Chronicles of Enguerrand de Monstrelet*, translated by Thomas Johnes (London: George Routledge and Sons 1867), vol. 2:345; N. A. M. Rodger, *The Safeguard of the Sea: A Naval History of Great Britain 660–1649* (New York: W. W. Norton, 1999), 115.
3. *CPR Edward II*, 29 January 1321, vol. 3:557.
4. Quoted in William Cunningham, *The Growth of English Industry and Commerce During the Early and Middle Ages* (Cambridge: Cambridge University Press, 1896), 302.
5. *CPR Henry VI*, 28 October 1436, vol. 3:83.
6. Ibid., 3 February 1441, vol. 3:506.
7. Manuel Lucena Salmoral, *Piratas, Bucaneros, Filibusteros y Corsarios en América* (Caracas: Grijalbo, 1994), 22; "Stay of letters of marque," in R. G. Marsden, ed., *Documents Relating to Law and Custom of the Sea* (London: Navy Records Society, 1916), vol. 1:19–20.
8. Marsden, *Law and Custom of the Sea*, vol. 1:111; *CPR Henry VI*, vol. 2, 28 February 1436, 509.
9. See, for example, "Letters of marque and reprisal against the Genoese," in Marsden, *Law and Custom of the Sea*, vol. 1:121–124.
10. "Letters of reprisal, to obtain payment of a debt," in ibid., vol. 1:126–127.
11. *CPR Henry VI*, 28 June 1442, vol. 4:80.
12. Ibid., 28 December 1439, vol. 3:373.
13. Matthew of Paris, *Matthew Paris's English History from the Year 1235 to 1273*, translated by J. A. Giles (London: Henry G. Bohn, 1852–1854), vol. 1:418–419.
14. Montague Burrows, *The Cinque Ports* (London: Longmans, Green, 1892), 105–106.
15. E. Keble Chatterton, *Sailing Ships: The Story of Their Development from the Earliest Times to the Present Day* (Philadelphia: J. B. Lippincott, 1915), 148–149; László and Woodman, *Story of Sail*, 44–46.
16. Casson, *Illustrated History*, 63–68.
17. Nicolas, *History of the Royal Navy*, vol. 2:265.
18. Howard, *Sailing Ships of War*, 14–16; Veres László and Richard Woodman, *The Story of Sail* (Annapolis, MD: Naval Institute Press, 1999), 57–59.
19. R. C. Anderson, *Oared Fighting Ships: From Classical Times to the Coming of Steam* (London: Percival Marshall, 1957), 42–51.
20. Edward L. Cutts, *Scenes and Characters of the Middle Ages* (London: Virtue & Co., 1872), 476–77; Matthew of Paris, *Flowers of History*, vol. 2:399; Rodgers, *Naval Warfare*, 94.
21. Cutts, *Scenes and Characters*, 475–476.
22. "Commission to Henry Paye," in Marsden, *Law and Custom of the Sea*, vol. 1:112–114.
23. Anderson, *Oared Fighting Ships*, 50.
24. *CPR Henry VI*, 18 October 1431, vol. 2:128; *CPR Henry VI*, 10 June 1431, vol. 2:152;

Rodgers, *Naval Warfare*, 98; William Durrant Cooper, *The History of Winchelsea, One of the Ancient Towns Added to the Cinque Ports* (London: John Russell Smith, 1850), 101; Harris Nicolas, ed., *Proceedings and Ordinances of the Privy Council of England* (London: Commissioners of the Public Records, 1835), vol. 5:cxxviii; "Writ for a Balinger," in Mary Bateson, ed., *Records of the Borough of Leicester* (London: C. J. Clay and Sons, 1901), vol. 2:161–162; J. W. Sherborne, "English Barges and Balingers of the Late Fourteenth Century," *Mariner's Mirror* 63, no. 2 (1977): 109–114; W. J. Carpenter-Turner, "The building of the *Gracedieu, Valentine,* and *Falconer* at Southampton, 1416–1420," *Mariner's Mirror* 40 (1954), no. 1: 55–72; Julian S. Corbett, *Drake and the Tudor Navy* (Longmans, Green, 1898), 19–20.

25. Brian Lavery, *Ship: The Epic Story of Adventure* (New York: DK Publishing, 2004), 44; Rodger, *Safeguard of the Sea*, 166–167.

26. See, for example, *CPR Henry VI*, 14 June 1432, 201–202 and 25 October 1433, 348.

27. Other candidates include the dusack as well as the shorter-bladed versions of the shamshir. It is also possible that the cutlass was developed independently to fill a need and was based on lessons learned from a variety of previous sea-going swords.

28. Peter D. Bryson, *Comprehensive Review in Toxicology for Emergency Clinicians* 3rd ed. (Washington, DC: Taylor & Francis, 1996), 278.

29. For an overview, see John F. Guilmartin Jr., *Galleons and Galleys* (London: Cassell, 2002), 52–63.

30. The author had the opportunity to test firepots filled with combustibles mixed from a medieval recipe at the Medieval Center in Denmark in 2007. The devices burned intensely.

31. Casson, *Illustrated History*, 91; Guilmartin, *Galleons and Galleys*, 60–61.

32. Casson, *Illustrated History*, 91.

33. In general see Guilmartin, *Galleons and Galleys*, 52–63.

34. Sherborne, "English Barges," 112; Carpenter-Turner, "Building of the *Gracedieu,* 70.

35. Charles de la Roncière, "Un Inventaire de Bord en 1294," in *Bibliothéque de l'École des Chartres, LVIII* (Paris: Librarie d'Alphonse Picard et Fils, 1897), 394–395, 408–409. The inventory is also discussed in David Hannay, *The Sea Trader: His Friends and Enemies* (Boston: Little, Brown, 1912), 29–38.

36. *CPR Henry VI*, 24 February 1442, vol. 4:77.

37. *CPR Henry VI*, 28 February 1436, vol. 2:509.

38. Travers Twiss, ed., *Monumenta Juridica: The Black Book of the Admiralty.* (London: Longman, 1873), vol. 1:5.

39. Geoffrey Chaucer, *The Canterbury Tales*, translated by J. U. Nicolson (Garden City, NY: Garden City Books, 1934), Prologue, "The Sailor."

40. Enguerrand, *Chronicles*, vol. 1:25.

41. Matthew of Paris, *English History*, 329.

42. Lucena Salmoral, *Piratas*, 21; Cutts, *Scenes and Characters*, 481; Florence of Worcester, *Chronicle*, 366.

43. *CPR Henry VI*, 2 May 1440, vol. 3:411.

44. Philip Gosse, "Piracy," *Mariner's Mirror* 36 (1950), no. 4:338.

45. "Agreement entered into at Bruges," in Marsden, *Law and Custom of the Sea*, vol. 1:46–48; "Order to the Warden of the Cinque Ports," in Marsden, *Law and Custom of the Sea*, vol. 1:59–61.

46. James Hamilton Wylie, *History of England Under Henry the Fourth* (London: Longmans, Green, 1884), vol. 2:68.

47. "Security for the good behavior of Newcastle ships," in Marsden, *Law and Custom of the Sea*, vol. 1:141–144.
48. *CPR Henry VI*, 28 February 1436, vol. 2:509.
49. "Proclamation against piracy," in Marsden, *Law and Custom of the Sea*, vol. 1:136–38.
50. Marsden, *Law and Custom of the Sea*, vol.1:xv.
51. Proclamation against harbouring pirates," in Marsden, *Law and Custom of the Sea*, vol.1:145–146.
52. "Rolle of Olayron," in Twiss, *Monumenta Juridica*, vol. 2:480–481.
53. *CPR Henry VI*, 4 July 1445 and 11 June 1445, vol. 4:370, and in general.
54. *CPR Edward II*, 29 January 1321, vol. 3:557.
55. "Petition of Robert de Morley," in Marsden, *Law and Custom of the Sea*, vol. 1:74–75.
56. "Pardon to pirates," in Marsden, *Law and Custom of the Sea*, vol. 1:31–35; *CPR Henry VI*, 4 July 1445, vol. 4:370.
57. "Commission of oyer and terminer," in Marsden, *Law and Custom of the Sea*, vol. 1:10–12.
58. Marsden, *Law and Custom of the Sea*, vol. 1:xi–xiv.
59. Matthew of Paris, *English History*, vol. 1:449.
60. *CPR Henry VI*, 17 May 1437, vol. 3:64.
61. "Ships convoying the wine fleet," in Marsden, *Law and Custom of the Sea*, vol.1:92–94. See also Marsden, vol. 1:xii.
62. Matthew of Paris, *English History*, vol. 1:419.
63. Ibid., vol. 1:442.
64. Burrows, *Cinque Ports*, 105–106.
65. Matthew of Paris, *English History*, vol. 1:449.
66. Gutierre Díaz de Gámez [Gutierre Diez de Games], *Chronica de Don Pedro Niño, Conde de Buelna, Por Gutierre Diez de Games su Alferez* (Madrid: Don Antonio de Sancha, 1782), 93–111; *Le Victorial: Chronique de Don Pedro Niño, Comte de Buelna par Gutierre Diaz de Gamez, son Alferez (1379–1449)*, 1782, reprint, translated by Labert de Circourt and the comte de Puymaigre (Paris: Victor Palmé, 1867), 274–314; *The Unconquered Knight: A Chronicle of the Deeds of Don Pero Niño, Count of Buelna*, translated by Joan Evans (Suffolk, England: Boydell Press, 2004), 107–130; Wylie, *History of England* (1894), vol. 2:321–327.
67. Wylie, *History of England* (1884), vol. 1:443–444.
68. Díaz de Gámez, *Chronica*, 93–111; *Le Victorial*, 274–314; *Unconquered Knight*, 107–130; Wylie, *History of England* (1894), vol. 2:321–327.
69. Ibid.
70. *CLB, Letter-Book H, 1375–1399*, 269.
71. Díaz de Gámez, *Unconquered Knight*, 176.
72. Díaz de Gámez, *Chronica*, 93–111; *Le Victorial*, 274–314; *Unconquered Knight*, 107–130; Wylie, *History of England* (1894), vol. 2:321–327.
73. Matthew of Paris, *Flowers of History*, vol. 2:441–442, 447.
74. Matthew of Paris, *English History*, vol. 1:406–409; Cutts, *Scenes and Characters*, 484.
75. Matthew of Paris, *Flowers of History*, vol. 2:399–401.
76. Ibid.
77. Ibid.
78. See, for example, in Meier, *Seafarers*, 148, and Lewis and Runyan, *European Maritime and Naval History*, 123.
79. See, for example, in Lewis and Runyan, *European Maritime and Naval History*, 124.

Regarding lime pots shot from bows, see Matthew of Paris, *English History*, vol. 3:413.

80. Matthew of Paris, *English History*, vol. 3:413.
81. Rose, *Medieval Naval Warfare*, 30.
82. Rodgers, *Naval Warfare*, 94. See also Rose, *Medieval Naval Warfare*, 30.
83. Meier, *Seafarers*, 146–159; Rose, *Medieval Naval Warfare*, 72–73. Dates of the naval expedition have been given variously as 1400, 1401, and 1402.
84. "German pirate skull snatched from museum: police," *Agence France Presse*, January 19, 2010. Period accounts do not appear to mention the execution of Störtebeker.
85. Enguerrand, *Chronicles*, vol. 1:25.
86. Robert Southey, *The British Admirals* (London: Longman, Rees, Orme, Brown, Green, Longman, and John Taylor, 1833), 162–63; Patrick Fraser Tytler, *The History of Scotland from the Accession of Alexander III to the Union* (Edinburgh: W. P. Nimmo, Hay, & Mitchell, 1887), vol. 1:251–252; Alfred Spont, *La Marine Française Sous le Règne de Charles VIII, 1483–1493* (Paris: Bureaux de la Revue, 1894), 37.
87. Díaz de Gámez, *Chronica*, 142–149, *Le Victorial*, 373–379, *Unconquered Knight*, 160–166.
88. Ibid.
89. Ibid.
90. Ibid.
91. Ibid.
92. Ibid.; Wylie, *History of England* (1894), vol. 2:449.
93. "Petition of Jehan Maulpetit," in Spont, *Marine Française*, 37–38.
94. Ibid. Author's translation.
95. Richard of Devises, *Chronicles of the Crusades*, 130.

Chapter 7: Of Faith, Galleys, and Greed
Defeating the Mediterranean Corsairs, 476–1492

1. "Chronicle of Richard of Devizes," in Richard of Devises, Geoffrey de Vinsauf, and John de Joinville, *Chronicles of the Crusades, Being Contemporary Narratives of the Crusade of Richard Coeur de Lion* (London: Henry G. Bohn, 1848), 115–116.
2. Jean Foissart, *The Chronicles of Froissart*, translated by John Bourchier, edited by G. C. Macaulay (London: Macmillan, 1908), 62.
3. Dominique Buhours, *The Life of the Renowned Peter D'Aubusson, Grand Master of Rhodes* (London: George Wells and Samuel Carr, 1679), 66.
4. George Fadlo Hourani, *Arab Seafaring in the Indian Ocean in Ancient and Early Medieval Times*, 1951 (Beirut: Khayats, 1963 reprint), 53.
5. Lewis and Runyan, *European Naval and Maritime History*, 16–20.
6. Abbé de Vertot, *The History of the Knights Hospitallers of St. John of Jerusalem, Styled Afterwards the Knights of Rhodes* (Dublin: J. Christie, 1818), vol. 2:124–125.
7. Roger de Hoveden, [Roger of Hoveden], *The Annals of Roger de Hoveden*, translated by Henry T. Riley (London: H. G. Bohn: 1853), vol. 2:248, 250, 254.
8. Behâ Ed-dîn, *The Life of Saladin* (London: Committee of the Palestine Exploration Fund, 1897), 241.
9. Ibid., 235–236
10. Ibid.
11. Ibid., 26.

12. "Chronicle of Richard of Devizes," in Richard of Devies et al., *Chronicles of the Crusades*, 130.
13. "Joinville's Memoirs of Saint Louis IX," in Richard of Devies et al., *Chronicles of the Crusades*, 438.
14. Ibid., 442.
15. "Chronicle of Richard of Devizes," in Richard of Devies et al., *Chronicles of the Crusades*, 116.
16. Ibid., 199.
17. Horace K. Mann, *The Lives of the Popes in the Early Middle Ages* (London: Kegan Paul, Trench, Trübner, 1906), vol. 3:322–323.
18. See, for example, Rose, *Medieval Naval Warfare*, 35.
19. Ibid., 39.
20. Guilmartin, *Galleons and Galleys*, 39.
21. Hourani, *Arab Seafaring*, 104; Anderson, *Oared Fighting Ships*, 40–41.
22. Anderson, *Oared Fighting Ships*, 36–41; Rodgers, *Naval Warfare*, 27–29.
23. *History of the Wars*, in Procopius, *Procopius*, translated by H. B. Dewing (London: William Heinemann, 1916), vol. 2:105 (III.xi).
24. Rodgers, *Naval Warfare*, 63–68.
25. "Chronicle of Richard of Devizes," in Richard of Devies et al., *Chronicles of the Crusades*, 115.
26. László and Woodman, *Story of Sail*, 41.
27. Casson, *Illustrated History*, 71–72.
28. Ibid., 70.
29. Ibid., 83–88.
30. See, for example, Buhours, *Life*, 347.
31. Rodgers, *Naval Warfare*, 126.
32. Ibid., 43.
33. "Chronicle of Richard of Devizes," in Richard of Devies et al., *Chronicles of the Crusades*, 115. See also Rodgers, *Naval Warfare*, 41–45.
34. Rodgers, *Naval Warfare*, 112–126.
35. de Hoveden *Annals*, vol. 2:206.
36. Rodgers, *Naval Warfare*, 62.
37. Ibid., 132.
38. Douglas Haldane, "The Fire-Ship of Al-Sālih Ayyūb and Muslim Use of "'Greek Fire,'" in *The Circle of War in the Middle Ages: Essays on Medieval Military and Naval History*, edited by Donald J. Kagay and L. J. Andrew Villalon (Suffolk: Boydell, 1999), 142.
39. "Chronicle of Richard of Devizes," in Richard of Devies et al., *Chronicles of the Crusades*, 197.
40. Rodgers, *Naval Warfare*, 112.
41. Helen Nicholson and David Nicolle, *God's Warriors: Knights Templar, Saracens and the Battle for Jerusalem* (New York: Osprey, 2006), 130–134; Michael D. Coe, et al., *Swords and Hilt Weapons* (New York: Barnes and Noble, 1993), 139–140.
42. Procopius, *History of the Wars*, in *Procopius*, vol. 2:106–107.
43. Lewis and Runyan, *European Naval and Maritime History*, 68–69.
44. Buhours, *Life*, 66.
45. Guilmartin, *Galleons and Galleys*, 39.
46. Ruy Gonzalez de Clavijo, *Narrative of the Embassy of Ruy Gonzalez de Clavijo to*

the Court of Timour, at Samarcand, A.D. 1403–6, translated by Robert Markham
Clements (London: Hakluyt Society, 1856), 9.

47. Vassilios Christides, "Military Intelligence in Arabo-Byzantine Naval Warfare" (Athens: Institute for Byzantine Studies, 1996), 271.
48. Buhours, *Life*, 66–67.
49. Díaz de Gámez, *Unconquered Knight*, 57–58, 84–89.
50. Buhours, *Life*, 93
51. Ibid.
52. See, for example, Lewis and Runyan, *European Naval and Maritime History*, 51.
53. Vassilios Christides, "Some Remarks on the Mediterranean and Red Sea Ships in Ancient and Medieval Times, Part II," *Proceedings of the 2nd International Symposium on Ship Construction in Antiquity* (Delphi: Tropis II, 1987), 89.
54. Lewis and Runyan, *European Naval and Maritime History*, 46; Fernand Braudel, *The Mediterranean and the Mediterranean World in the Age of Philip II*, translated by Sian Reynolds (Berkeley: University of California Press, 1996), vol. 1:133.
55. Lewis and Runyan, *European Naval and Maritime History*, 22.
56. Lucena Salmoral, *Piratas*, 21.
57. Scammel, *World Encompassed*, 205.
58. William Hunt, *Bristol* (London: Longmans, Green, 1889), 96–97.
59. Buhours, *Life*, 227.
60. See, for example, Lewis and Runyan, *European Naval and Maritime History*, 24, and Procopius, *History of the Wars*, in *Procopius*, vol. 2:61.
61. de Hovedon, *Annals*, vol. 2:206.
62. "Chronicle of Richard of Devizes," in Richard of Devies et al., *Chronicles of the Crusades*, 114–116.
63. Ibid.
64. Ibid., 115–116.
65. Matthew of Paris, *English History*, 413.
66. "Chronicle of Richard of Devizes," in Richard of Devies et al., *Chronicles of the Crusades*, 199 (chapter XLI).
67. Behâ Ed-dîn, *Life of Saladin*, 249–250.
68. Buhours, *Life*, 202.
69. Ibid., 347–348
70. Ibid..
71. Díaz de Gámez, *Unconquered Knight*, 51–52.
72. Ibid., 54–62.
73. Ibid., 62–64.
74. Ibid., 68–72.
75. Ibid., 72–73.
76. Ibid., 73–75.
77. *CSPV 1202–1509*, no. 492, 499; *CSPV 1509–1519*, no. 851.
78. *CSPV 1202–1509*, nos. 419, 498, 499, 547, and page lxviii; Domenico Malpiero, *Annali Veneti dall' Anno 1457 at 1500 del Senatore Domenico Malipiero* (Firenze: Gio. Pietro Vieusseux, 1844), xx, 620–21; Fernando Colón, *Historia del almirante don Cristóbal Colón*, 1571 (Madrid: T. Minuesa, 1892 reprint), 22–23. An intelligence report notes eight ships and balingers lying in wait for the galleys.
79. *CSPV 1202–1509*, no. 547.

80. Ibid., no. 609.
81. Colón, *Historia del almirante*, 23.

Chapter 8: Spanish Galleons and Portuguese Carracks
Plunderers Fighting Plunderers, 1492–1654
1. Bernal Díaz del Castillo, *The Discovery and Conquest of Mexico 1517–1521*, 1632, reprint, translated by A. P. Maudslay (New York: Farrar, Straus and Cudahy, 1956), 4.
2. In general, see Cruz Apestegui, *Pirates of the Caribbean*, translated by Richard Lewis Rees (Edison, NJ: Chartwell Books, 2002), and A. P. Newton, *The European Nations in the West Indies 1493–1688*, 1933 (New York: Barnes and Noble, 1967 reprint).
3. See, for example, Mainwaring, *Life and Works*, vol. 2:119.
4. Casson, *Ships and Boats*, 91–97; Guilmartin, *Galleons and Galleys*, 62–69.
5. Fryer, *New Account*, vol. 1:153.
6. J. H. Parry, *The Spanish Seaborne Empire* (London: Hutchinson & Co., 1966), 251–262; C. R. Boxer, *The Portuguese Seaborne Empire 1415–1825* (New York: Knopf, 1969), 205–220; José de Veita Linaje [Ioseph de Veitia Linage], *Norte de la Contratacion de las Indias Occidentales* (Seville: Juan Francisco de Blas, 1672), 192–194. In general, see also Galvin, *Patterns of Pillage*; C. H. Haring, *Trade and Navigation Between Spain and the Indies* (Cambridge: Harvard University Press, 1918); Philip Ainsworth Means, *The Spanish Main* (New York: Charles Scribner's Sons, 1935); and Parry, *Spanish Seaborne Empire*.
7. Gage, *Travels in the New World*, 333.
8. Ibid., 336.
9. Nicholas Downton, *The sinking of the Carrack, The Five Wounds*, 1600, reprinted in C. Raymond Beazley, *An English Garner: Voyages and Travels mainly during the 16th and 17th Centuries, Vol. II* (New York: E. P. Dutton, 1902), 150.
10. Parry, *Spanish Seaborne Empire*, 257, 261.
11. Richard Hawkins, *The Observations of Sir Richard Hawkins, Knight in His Voyage into the South Sea in the Year 1593*, 1622, reprint, edited by C. R. Drinkwater Bethune (London, Hakluyt Society, 1847), 221; Mainwaring, *Life and Works*, vol. 2:121; Rodgers, *Naval Warfare*, 144; Cesáreo Fernández Duro, *Armada Español desde la unión de los reinos de Castilla y de León* (Madrid: Sucesores de Rivadeneyra, 1895–1903), 379–380.
12. Hawkins, *Observations*, 206.
13. John Smith, *The Sea-mans Grammar and Dictionary* (London: Randal Taylor, 1691), 58.
14. Corbett, *Drake*, vol. 2:366–367 (illustration), vol. 1:159, note 3 (comments); Richard Hakluyt, *The Principal Navigations, Voyages, Traffiques & Discoveries of the English Nation* (Glasgow: James MacLehose and Sons, 1903–1905), xiv–xv.
15. Apestegui, *Pirates of the Caribbean*, 142.
16. Mainwaring, *Life and Works*, 147.
17. See, for example, Smith, *Sea-mans Grammar*, 58.
18. See, for example, Francis Drake, *Sir Francis Drake revived; Calling upon this dull or effeminate Age, to follow his noble steps for gold and silver*, 1626, reprinted in C. Raymond Beazley, *An English Garner: Voyages and Travels mainly during the 16th and 17th Centuries, Vol. II* (New York: E. P. Dutton, 1902), 262.
19. Rodgers, *Naval Warfare*, 144; Chavez, "Espejo de Navegantes" in Fernández Duro, *Armada Española*, vol. 1:379.
20. Hawkins, *Observations*, 206; Francis Pretty, "The Admirable and Prosperous Voyage

of the worshipful Master Thomas Cavendish" in Edward John Payne, ed., *Voyages of Elizabethan Seamen* (London: Oxford, n.d.)

21. Smith, *Sea-mans Grammar*, 57–58.
22. Hawkins, *Observations*, 194.
23. See, for example, Mainwaring, *Life and Works*, 147; and Nathaniel Boteler, *Boteler's Dialogues*, 1685, reprint, edited by W. G. Perrin (London: Navy Records Society, 1929), 240.
24. Rodgers, *Naval Warfare*, 144; Chavez, "Espejo de Navegantes" in Fernández Duro, *Armada Española*, vol. 1:379.
25. Rodgers, *Naval Warfare*, 144; Chavez, "Espejo de Navegantes" in Fernández Duro, *Armada Española*, vol. 1:383; Hawkins, *Observations*, 199.
26. Mainwaring, *Life and Works*, 147.
27. Hawkins, *Observations*, 185.
28. Pretty, "Admirable and Prosperous Voyage," 107; Hawkins, *Observations*, 206, 221; John Smith, "Accidence for Young Seamen" in John Smith, *Works: 1608–1631*, edited by Edward Arber (Westminster: Archibald Constable, 1895), vol. 2:800.
29. Rodgers, *Naval Warfare*, 145; Chavez, "Espejo de Navegantes," in Fernández Duro, *Armada Española*, vol. 1:383.
30. Rodgers, *Naval Warfare*, 144–45; Chavez, "Espejo de Navegantes," in Fernández Duro, *Armada Española*, vol. 1:379, 384; Clements R. Markham, ed., *The Hawkins' Voyages During the Reigns of Henry VIII, Queen Elizabeth, and James I* (London: Hakluyt, 1888), 345.
31. Rodgers, *Naval Warfare*, 144; Chavez, "Espejo de Navegantes," in Fernández Duro, *Armada Española*, 381.
32. See, for example, Francis Drake, *The World Encompassed by Sir Francis Drake Being his next Voyage to that to Nombre de Dios*, reprint (London: Hakluyt Society, 1854), 56, 57; Drake, *Sir Francis Drake Revived*, 233, 235, 236, 262; Hawkins, *Observations*, 199; Pretty, "Admirable and Prosperous Voyage," 107; Rodgers, *Naval Warfare*, 144–145; Chavez, "Espejo de Navegantes," in Fernández Duro, *Armada Española*, 379–384.
33. Rodgers, *Naval Warfare*, 145; Chavez, "Espejo de Navegantes," in Fernández Duro, *Armada Española*, 383; Hawkins, *Observations*, 185.
34. Smith, "Accidence for Young Seamen" in Smith, *Works*, vol. 2:800; Smith, *Sea Grammar*, in Smith, *Generall Historie*, vol. 2:294; Hawkins, *Observations*, 237.
35. Hawkins, *Observations*, 216.
36. Boteler, *Dialogues*, 262; Hawkins, *Observations*, 216–218.
37. Hawkins, *Observations*, 216–217.
38. Ibid., 194, 217.
39. Jacques Bourdé de Villehuet, *Le Manoeuvrier, ou essai sur la théorie et la practique de mouvements du navire et des évolutions navales* (Paris: H. L. Guerin and L. F. Delatour, 1765), 262. John Paul Jones reportedly wore armor during his engagement with the *Serapis*. See Harold L. Peterson, *Arms and Armor in Colonial America 1526–1783* (New York: Bramhall House, 1956), 309–311.
40. Hawkins, *Observations*, 216.
41. See, for example, Hawkins, *Observations*, 193–194.
42. See, for example, Drake, *World Encompassed*.
43. Markham, *Hawkins' Voyages*, 336.
44. Pretty, "Admirable and Prosperous Voyage," 107.
45. Ibid., 108.

46. Markham, *Hawkins' Voyages,* 337. English accounts do not mention the hanging.
47. See, for example, Braudel, *Mediterranean,* vol. 1:300, on the original advantages of large merchant ships.
48. Drake, *World Encompassed,* 110–111, 241–242.
49. Anon., "Destruction, capture, &c. of Portuguese Carracks," 1600, reprinted in C. Raymond Beazley, *An English Garner: Voyages and Travels mainly during the 16th and 17th Centuries Vol. II* (New York: E. P. Dutton, 1902), 134–136.
50. Downton, "Firing and sinking," 145–150.
51. Anon., "Destruction, capture, &c. of Portuguese Carracks," 137–143.
52. Samuel Purchas, *Hakluytus Posthumus or Purchas His Pilgrimes Contayning a History of the World in Sea Voyages and Lande Travells by Englishmen and others* (Glasgow: James MacLehose and Sons, 1907), 114.
53. Parry, *Spanish Seaborne Empire,* 254.
54. Baptista Antonio, "A relation of the ports..." in Hakluyt, *Principal Navigations,* vol. 10:152. Haring quotes the same passage in *Trade and Navigation,* 244.
55. John Steinbeck, *Cup of Gold* (New York: Covici Friede, 1936), 153.
56. Ibid., 254–255, 261–262; Bibiano Torres Ramirez, *La Armada de Barlovento* (Seville: Escuela de Estudios Hispano-Americanos de Sevilla, 1981), 1–68; José de Veita Linaje, *The Spanish Rule of Trade to the West-Indies,* 1702, translated and edited by John Stevens, facsimile reprint (New York: AMS Press, 1977), 203–205.
57. Markham, *Hawkins' Voyages,* 346; Hawkins, *Observations,* 181–220.
58. Hawkins, *Observations,* 181–220. See also Markham, *Hawkins' Voyages,* 333–349, for a translation of the Spanish account of the action.
59. Hawkins, *Observations,* 195–196, 207; Markham, *Hawkins' Voyages,* 345.
60. Hawkins, *Observations,* 213–214, 221–222; Rodgers, *Naval Warfare,* 144; Chavez, "Espejo de Navegantes," in Fernández Duro, *Armada Española,* vol. 1:381.
61. Rodgers, *Naval Warfare,* 144; Chavez, "Espejo de Navegantes," in Fernández Duro, *Armada Española,* 383.
62. Hawkins, *Observations,* 213–214, 221–222.
63. Ibid., 230.
64. William Monson, *Sir William Monson's Naval Tracts,* edited by M. Oppenheim (London: Navy Records Society, 1902), vol. 1:247–278.
65. Hawkins, *Observations,* 232.
66. Hakluyt, *Principal Navigations,* 156–157.
67. Hawkins, *Observations,* 204–205.
68. Markham, *Hawkins' Voyages,* 347.

Chapter 9: Of Blind Eyes and Opportunity
An Introduction to the "Golden Age," 1655–1725

1. William Beeston, "A journal kept by colonel Beeston, from his first coming to Jamaica," in Anon., *Interesting Tracts, Relating to the Island of Jamaica* (St. Jago de la Vega, Jamaica: Lewis, Lunan, and Jones, 1800), 285. Captain "Munroe" was filibuster Jean Moreau.
2. Ibid.
3. *CSPC 1675–1676,* no. 236.
4. Regarding Garrett Garretson, see *CSPC 1661–1668,* no. 1894, and Hans Sloane, *A Voyage To the Islands Madera, Barbados, Nieves, S. Christophers and Jamaica* (London: B. M. for the author, 1707), vol. 1: lxxiii.

5. See also Little, *The Buccaneer's Realm*, which covers the period 1674 to 1688.

6. Transported criminals were usually pardoned in recompense. See, for example, *CSPC 1661–1668*, no. 292.

7. Beeston, "Journal," 276.

8. Regarding those tricked into their indentures, see for example, *CSPC 1661–1669*, nos. 331, 739.

9. *CSPC 1574–1660*, vol. xii, no. 30, October 19.

10. *CSPC 1661–1668*, no. 1892.

11. Robert C. Ritchie, *Captain Kidd and the War Against the Pirates* (Cambridge: Harvard University Press, 1986), 233–234.

12. Alexander Exquemelin [John Esquemeling], *The Buccaneers of America*, 1684 (New York: Dorset, 1987 reprint), 254–256; *CSPC 1669–1674*, no. 1226iii.

13. *CSPC 1677–1680*, nos. 1094, 1118, 1129, 1188, 1498, 1516; Beeston, "Journal," 298.

14. Snelgrave, *New Account*, 143.

15. *CSPC 1677–1680*, no. 1425.

16. See, for example, Lucena Salmoral, *Piratas*, 248.

17. "Letters Concerning the English Expedition into the Spanish West Indies in 1655," in C. H. Firth, ed., *The Narrative of General Venables* (London: Longmans, Green, 1900), 130.

18. [John Cox]. *The Adventures of Capt. Barth. Sharp, And Others, in the South Sea* (London: P. A. Esq. [Philip Ayers], 1684), 70.

19. *CSPC 1661–1668*, no. 1212.

20. Henry Whistler, "Extracts from Henry Whistler's Journal of the West India Expedition," in C. H. Firth, ed., *The Narrative of General Venables* (New York: Longmans, Green, 1900), 156.

21. Little, *Buccaneer's Realm*, 90–91.

22. Charles Johnson, *A General History of the Robberies and Murders of the Most Notorious Pirates*, 1726 (New York: Dodd, Mead, 1926 reprint), 152; Snelgrave, *New Account*, 151.

23. Johnson, *History of the Pirates*, 200, 294.

24. Ibid., 150, 213; "Ogle to Admiralty," in C. H. Green, *The Historical Register, Containing An Impartial Relation of all Transactions, Foreign and Domestick*, vol. 7. (London: H. Meere, 1722), 346.

25. Johnson, *General History*, 240.

26. Livy, *Livy*, vol. 1:342; Ormerod, *Piracy in the Ancient World*, 157–158.

27. M. de Pouancey [au comte d'Estrées, 1 April 1677, Archives nationales, Colonies, C9 A rec. 1, reprinted in *Les Archives de la Flibuste*, http://members.tripod.com/diable_volant/archives/D1670/D7704pouancey.html; Johnson, *History of the Pirates*, 194.

28. See, for example, Clive Senior, *A Nation of Pirates: English Piracy in Its Heyday* (New York: Crane, Russak, 1976), 31.

29. In general, see Little, *Buccaneer's Realm*, 223–229. Medical care and disability were common among seamen long before the Golden Age of pirates. See the *Laws of Oleron*, for example, as described in Estienne Cleirac, *Us, et coutumes de la mer* (Bordeaux: Guillame Millanges, 1647).

30. Homer, *Odyssey*, 127.

31. See, for example, Smiley, *Sagas of Icelanders*, 646; Meier, *Seafarers, Merchants, and Pirates*, 147.

32. Little, *Buccaneer's Realm*, 223–224.
33. For a generally Marxist perspective on piracy, see the following works by Marcus Rediker: *Between the Devil and the Deep Blue Sea* (Cambridge: Cambridge University Press, 1987); "The Seaman as Pirate: Plunder and Social Banditry at Sea," in C. R. Pennell, ed., *Bandits at Sea: A Pirate Reader* (New York: New York University Press, 2001); and *Villains of All Nations: Atlantic Pirates in the Golden Age* (Boston: Beacon Press, 2004). For the pirate as rebel, see Christopher Hill, *Liberty Against the Law: Some Seventeenth-Century Controversies* (London: Penguin, 1996), 114–122.
34. Mainwaring, "Of the Beginnings," vol. 2:11, and vol. 2:11, note 1.
35. *Swashbuckler* (Universal Studios, 1976); *Pirates of the Caribbean: At World's End* (Walt Disney Studios, 2007).
36. Johnson, *History of the Pirates*, 168.
37. Henry Pitman, "A Relation of the Great Sufferings and Strange Adventures of Henry Pitman," 1689, reprinted in *An English Garner: Stuart Tracts 1603–1693*, vol. 8 (New York: E. P. Dutton, n.d.), 453, 463.
38. See Rafael Sabatini, *Captain Blood: His Odyssey* (New York: Grosset and Dunlap, 1922). Sabatini took his inspiration for Captain Peter Blood, the physician who becomes a pirate, from Dr. Henry Pitman, transported for rebellion to Barbados; Pitman described the aforementioned "rebel" pirates.
39. *CSPC 1685–1688*, nos. 210, 212, 505, 596, 602, 1209; "Letter from Col. Cony to the Committee," in J. H. Lefroy, ed., *Memorials of the Discovery and Early Settlement of the Bermudas or Somers Islands 1511–1687* (London: Longmans, Green, 1879), 549.
40. Ibid.; *CSPC 1685–1688*, no. 552i; "At the Committee of Trade and Plantations, 25 July, 1685," 552, and "Artickels of complaint," 544–546, in Lefroy, *Memorials of the Discovery*.
41. *CSPC 1685–1688*, nos. 532, 533, 852.
42. *CSPC 1681–1685*, no. 1522; *CSPC 1685–1688*, nos. 602, 617, 617i–x, 618, 635iii, 709, 840, 925, 949, 1022, 1533; "Letter to ye Committee from Coll Coney, January 3, 1685/6," in Lefroy, *Memorials of the Discovery*, 562.
43. *CSPC 1685–1688*, no. 618.
44. Little, *Buccaneer's Realm*, 216–217; Christopher Lloyd, "Bartholomew Sharp, Buccaneer," in *The Mariner's Mirror* 42, no. 4 (1956) 297–298; *CSPC 1685–1688*, no. 1136iii.
45. *CSPC 1685–1688*, nos. 602, 925.
46. *CSPC 1685–1688*, nos. 949, 1111; Little, *Buccaneer's Realm*, 216–217.
47. Plutarch, *Lives*, 443.
48. Basil Ringrose, "The Buccaneers of America: The Second Volume," in Exquemelin, *Buccaneers of America* (1684), 307–308; Roberts, *Four Years Voyages*, 85.
49. Saleban Aadan Barqad, quoted by the Associated Press, "US Navy attacks Somali 'pirates,'" *TimesOnline*, March 20, 2006, http://www.timesonline.co.uk/tol/news/world/article743166.ece.
50. Anon., *Mery Tales, Wittie Questions and Quicke Answeres, Very pleasant to be Readde*, 1567, reprinted in *Shakespeare Jest-Books*, edited by W. Carew Hazlitt (London: Willis and Sotheran, 1864), 134–136.
51. "Deposition of Jeremiah Tay, July 6, 1694" and "Deposition of Samuel Perkins, August 25, 1698," in Jameson, *Privateering and Piracy*, 150, 177; *CSPC 1697–1698*, nos. 473, 473ii, 473xvii, 904.
52. See Simon Tyssot de Patot, *Voyages et Avantures de Jaques Massé* (Bordeaux: Jaques

l'Aveugle, 1710). The book's title page indicates a 1710 publication, but it may have been published as late as 1717, still plenty early enough for Johnson to have read it. See Aubrey Rosenberg, *Tyssot de Patot and his work 1655–1738* (The Hague: Nijhoff, 1972), 84–85.

53. Johnson, *General History*, 340–372, 397–416; "Deposition of Samuel Perkins, August 25, 1698," in Jameson, *Privateering and Piracy*, 176–177; "Deposition of Adam Baldridge, May 5, 1699," in Jameson, *Privateering and Piracy*, 186–187. Regarding Red Sea piracy and the pirate settlements at Madagascar and St. Mary's, see Jan Rogozinski, *Honor Among Thieves: Captain Kidd, Henry Every, and the Pirate Democracy in the Indian Ocean* (Mechanicsburg: PA, Stackpole Books, 2000). Rogozinski does not mention Misson or Libertalia.

Chapter 10: The Real Pirates of the Caribbean
Pirate Hunting in the "Golden Age," 1655–1725

1. John Atkins, *A Voyage to Guinea, Brazil, and the West Indies*, 1735, facsimile reprint (London: Frank Cass, 1970), 191–192.
2. "Instructions to Mr. Heathcote" in *Interesting Tracts*, 241.
3. *CSPC 1699*, no. 740.
4. In general, see Peter Earle, *The Pirate Wars* (New York: Thomas Dunne, 2003), and Donald Shomette, *Pirates on the Chesapeake* (Centreville, MD: Tidewater Publishers, 1985), for discussions of the difficulties of pirate hunting in this period.
5. *CSPC 1661–1668*, no. 786; *CSPC 1675–1676*, no. 1129.
6. *CSPC 1661–1668*, no. 786.
7. See, for example, *CSPC 1685–1688*, no. 148.
8. See Philippe Hrodej, "La flibuste domingoise à la fin du XVIIe siècle: une composante économique indispensable," in Michel Le Bris, ed., *L'Aventure de la Flibuste* (Paris: Éditions Hoëbeke, 2002), 289–312.
9. Charles Howard [Earl of Carlisle], "The Earl of Carlisle's Answer to a Charge Against Him," in *Interesting Tracts, Relating to the Island of Jamaica* (St. Jago de la Vega, Jamaica: Lewis, Lunan, and Jones, 1800), 153.
10. Ibid., 156–157.
11. "Instructions to Mr. Heathcote" in *Interesting Tracts*, 242.
12. In general, see Little, *Sea Rover's Practice*, 41–56, and Little, *Buccaneer's Realm*, 13–20.
13. Regarding the lug sail, early nineteenth century sources note that the Spanish *barcalonga* was rigged with one on each mast (for example, J. J. Moore, *The Midshipman's or British Mariner's Vocabulary* [London: Vernor and Hood, 1805] s.v. "barcalonga"), and an earlier, probably seventeenth century illustration in the Museo Naval de Madrid (reprinted in Apestegui, *Pirates of the Caribbean*, 56) indicates a "*virga al tercio*" or lug spar for a lug sail. This sail plan would make the *barcalonga* an excellent vessel for chasing or escaping to windward.
14. *CSPC 1681–1685*, no. 1866.
15. Little, *Sea Rover's Practice*, 41–56, and Little, *Buccaneer's Realm*, 13–20.
16. William Dampier, *A New Voyage Round the World*, 1697 (New York: Dover, 1968 reprint), 135–136.
17. Edmond Wright, "A True & Exact account of an Engagement maintained by the Ship *Caesar*, Capt. Edm^d. Wright Comand^r. against Five Shipps (being Pyrates)...," in John Horsley Mayo, *Medals and Decorations of the British Army and Navy, Vol. 1* (Westminster: Archibald Constable, 1897), 65.

18. The issue is discussed without solid conclusion in L. G. Carr Laughton, "Gunnery, Frigates, and the Line of Battle," *Mariner's Mirror* 14, no. 4 (1928): 339–363.

19. Little, *Sea Rover's Practice*, 134–147.

20. Ibid., 134–152.

21. Ibid., 57–74, 153–161. Regarding seventeenth-century references to the fire-pike, see for example, Smith, *Sea-mans Grammar*, 88, "Pikes of Wild-fire."

22. Little, *Sea Rover's Practice*, 57–74, 153–611. See William Mountaine, *The Seaman's Vade-Mecum and Defensive War by Sea*, 1756 (London: Conway Maritime, 1971 reprint), 106–115, for a detailed exposition of closed quarters.

23. See, for example, Earle, *Pirate Wars*, 188–189; Ritchie, *Captain Kidd*, 157; and Shomette, *Pirates on the Chesapeake*, in general.

24. "Randolph to Blathwayt Complaining of George and Dudley," August 23, 1686, in Alfred Thomas Scrope Goodrick, ed., *Edward Randolph; Including His Letters and Official Papers from the New England, Middle, and Southern Colonies in America, and the West Indies. 1678–1700* (Boston: Prince Society, 1909), vol. 6:198–199.

25. "Instructions to Mr. Heathcote" in *Interesting Tracts*, 241.

26. Johnson, *General History*, ix.

27. Dampier, *Voyages and Discoveries*, 210.

28. Juan Juarez Moreno, *Corsarios y Piratas en Veracruz y Campeche* (Seville: Escuela de Estudios Hispano-Americanos de Sevilla, 1972), 286–287; Little, *Buccaneer's Realm*, 207.

29. Johnson, *General History*, 294–296, 302; Earle, *Pirate Wars*, 202.

30. Ibid; Charles Johnson, *Histoire des Pirates Anglois* (Utrecht: Jacques Broedelet, 1725), 276. Regarding Low alive in 1726, see "Extract of a Letter from on Board the Diamond Man of War" in C. H. Green, ed., *The Historical Register, Containing an Impartial Relation of All Trasactions Foreign and Domestick*, vol.11 (London: H. Meere, 1726) 327; and Abel Boyer, *The Political State of Great Britain*, vol. 32 (London: privately printed, 1726), 273. One of the reports is almost certainly the result of a false claim made as a joke by William Fly and his pirate crew, while the other likely refers to events in 1724.

31. In general, see Little, *Sea Rover's Practice*, for a detailed description of the preparation and tactics of the fight at sea.

32. *CSPC 1699*, nos. 693, 740.

33. Ibid, nos. 746, 802; A. S. Salley, Jr., ed., *Commissions and Instructions from the Lords Proprietors of Carolina to Public Officials of South Carolina 1685–1715* (Columbia, SC: Historical Commission of South Carolina, 1916), 134.

34. Johnson, *General History*, 178, 185, 195, 196, 206–213, 226–227; Atkins, *Voyage to Guinea*, 191–193, 262–263; "Ogle to Admiralty" in [Green], *Historical Register*, 344–346.

35. Ibid. The pirates were George Lowther and a member of Charles Harris's crew. See Johnson *General History*, 283; *CSPC 1724–1725*, 102i and *The American Weekly Mercury*, June 20–June 27, 1723.

36. Taylor, *Jamaica in 1687*, 106; *CSPC 1685–1688*, no. 475.

37. Taylor, *Jamaica in 1687*, 106.

38. Ibid., 47–48.

39. *CSPC 1685–1688*, no. 754.

40. Ibid., no. 1127.

41. Johnson, *General History*, 50–59; "The Weekly Journal or British Gazetteer," April 25, 1719.
42. Torres Ramirez, *Armada de Barlovento*, 90–94.
43. *CSPC 1681–1685*, no. 1163.
44. Dampier, *New Voyage*, 12, regarding the Darien guard ship.
45. Lucena Salmoral, *Piratas, Bucaneros*, 22–23.
46. Ibid., 256.
47. Ibid., 249–253.
48. Haring, *Trade and Navigation*, 256.
49. Linaje, *Spanish Rule of Trade*, 206.
50. *CSPC 1669–1674*, no. 182.
51. Little, *Buccaneer's Realm*, 207.
52. *CSPC 1685–1688*, no. 1733.
53. *CSPC 1669–1674*, no. 799.
54. Ibid., nos. 310i, 310ii.
55. *CSPC 1719–1720*, no. 34.
56. See also H. M. Chapin, *Privateer Ships and Sailors, The First Century of American Colonial Privateering 1625–1725* (Toulon: Imprimerie G. Mouton, 1926), 96–100.
57. John Henry Edmonds, *Captain Thomas Pound* (Cambridge, MA: John Wilson and Son, 1918), 35–37. This short book contains an excellent collection of related primary documents.
58. Ibid., 38–39, 81–83.
59. Johnson, *General History*, 71–81.
60. In general see Ritchie, *Captain Kidd*, and Don C. Seitz, ed., *The Tryal of Capt. William Kidd for Murther and Piracy*, 1936 (Mineola, NY: Dover Publications, 2001 reprint). The former is a thorough description and analysis, the latter the trial's transcript.
61. Ibid.
62. *CSPC 1681–1685*, no. 1839; *CSPC 1685–1688* nos. 963, 1010; *CSPC 1669–1674*, no. 908.
63. *CSPC 1669–1674*, nos. 705, 709, 883, 888, 908, 945, 1115; Marley, *Pirates and Engineers*, 49–54.
64. *CSPC 1685–1688*, nos. 768, 913, 1356, 1382, 1733; *CSPC 1696–1697*, nos. 371, 1201.
65. Mountaine, *Seaman's Vade-Mecum*, 133.
66. Juarez Moreno, *Corsarios y Piratas*, 151.
67. In general see Frederick Parkes Weber, *Aspects of Death and Correlated Aspects of Life in Art, Epigram, and Poetry*, 3rd ed. (New York: Paul B. Hoeber, 1918).
68. John Francis, ed., *Notes and Queries: A Medium of Intercommunication for Literary Men, General Readers, Etc.* 5ᵗʰ ser., vol. 1 (January–June) (London: John Francis, 1874), 195; Anders Franzén, "Kronan: Remants of a Warship's Past," *National Geographic* 175, no. 4 (April 1989), 455. A photograph of the charm recovered from the *Kronan* is posted online on the Kalmar Läns museum website at http://www.regalskeppetkronan.se.
69. Anon., *Journal de Bord d'un Flibustier (1686–1693)*, edited by Edouard Ducéré, in *Bulletin de la Société des Sciences & Arts de Bayonne, Année 1894* (Bayonne: A. Lamaignère, 1894), 516, author's translation.

70. Anon., *A Pacquet from Parnassus: or, a Collection of Papers*, vol. 1, no. 1 (London: J. How and J. Nutt, 1702), 16.

71. Henri Martin, *Martin's History of France: The Age of Louis XIV*, vol. 2, translated by Mary L. Booth (Boston: Walker, Wise, 1865), 515.

72. In general see Cordingly, *Under the Black Flag*, for a discussion of the origin, symbolism, and myths of the black flag or "Jolly Roger," 117–118.

73. Samuel Sewall, *The Diary of Samuel Sewall: 1714–1729* (Boston: Massachusetts Historical Society, 1882), 325, note 2. See also Clifford Beal, *Quelch's Gold: Piracy, Greed, and Betrayal in Colonial New England* (Westport, CT: Praeger, 2007), 52–53.

74. Sewall, *Diary*, 325, note 2, quoting the Boston *News-Letter of* July 25, 1723; Johnson, *General History*, 196, 202, 213; Capt. Richard Hawkins, quoted in C. H. Firth, *Naval Songs and Ballads* ([London]: Navy Records Society, 1908), 347.

75. Henry Playford, *Pills to Purge Melancholy* vol. 1 (London: W. Pearson for J. Tonson, 1719), 19–21.

76. *Oxford English Dictionary*, 2nd ed., s.v. "roger"; *A Classical Dictionary of the Vulgar Tongue* (London: Hooper and Wegstead, 1796), 3rd ed., s.v. "roger."

77. Little, "The Origin of the Dread Pirate Banner, the Jolly Roger," *Pirates Magazine*, no. 12 (April 2010), 9–14.

78. "Voyage of Commodore Roggewein," in Samuel Johnson, Oliver Goldsmith, and Christopher Smart, eds., *The World Displayed; or, a Curious Collection of Voyages and Travels* (London: J. Newberry, 1760), vol. 9:101.

79. Robert Everard, "A Relation of Three Years Sufferings of Robert Everard, Upon the Coast of Assada Near Madagascar, in a Voyage to India, in the Year 1686," in Awnsham Churchill and John Churchill, eds., *A Collection of Voyages and Travels, Vol. 6* (London: John Walthoe et al., 1732), 259.

80. Anon., *Journal de Bord*, 481.

81. See, for example, Jean Baptiste Labat [Labat, R. P.], *Voyages aux Isles De L'Amerique*, 1722, reprint edited by A. t'Serstevens (Paris: Editions Duchartre, 1931) vol. 1:97–99.

82. See Alexandre Exquemelin [Joseph Exquemeling], *The Buccaneers of America* (1699) (Boston: Sanborn, Carter and Bazin, 1856 reprint), 84–85; Exquemelin, *Les Flibustiers du Nouveau Monde*, 1699, with additional passages from the 1688 edition, reprint edited by Michel Le Bris (Paris: Éditions Phébus, 1996), 139; Exquemelin [Alexandre Olivier O'Exquemelin], *Histoire des Avanturiers Flibustiers qui se sont Signalez dans les Indes* (Paris: Jacques Le Febvre, 1699), vol. 1:275–276; Little, *Buccaneer's Realm*, 79–81.

83. Edward Barlow, *Barlow's Journal*, edited by Basil Lubbock (London: Hurst & Blackett, 1934), vol. 2:456, 484–485.

84. Wright, "True & Exact account," 64–65. This is the same action noted earlier in which pirates loaded "outboard."

85. Mountaine, *Seaman's Vade-Mecum*, 134.

86. "The Buccaneers on the Isthmus and in the South Sea. 1680–1682," in John F. Jameson, ed., *Privateering and Piracy in the Colonial Period: Illustrative Documents* (New York: Macmillan, 1923), 124, [author unknown, but believed to be Edward Povey]; Cox, *Adventures*, 88–89.

87. Little, *Buccaneer's Realm*, 213.

88. Marcus Tullius [Tully] Cicero, *Tully's Offices* [*de Officii*], *in Three Books*, 6th ed., translated by R. L'Estrange (London: D. Browne et al., 1720), vol. 3:29.107.

89. Dampier, *New Voyage*, 160.
90. Amy Turner Bushnell, "How to Fight a Pirate: Provincials, Royalists, and the Defense of Minor Ports During the Age of Buccaneers," *Gulf Coast Historical Review* 5 (1990):18.
91. Little, *Sea Rover's Practice*, 190–195, *Buccaneer's Realm*, 171–187.
92. Sloane, *Voyage*, vol. 1:lxxxix.
93. Beeston, "Journal," 279.
94. Ibid., 284.
95. Ibid., 296.
96. See, for example, Francis B. C. Bradlee, *Piracy in the West Indies and its Suppression* (Salem, MA: Essex Institute, 1923), in general, and Thomas Arnold, *The American Practical Lunarian, and Seaman's Guide* (Philadelphia: Robert Desilver, 1822), 355–364, 372–390.
97. It is popularly claimed that José Gasparilla was a pirate of great renown in this later time and place, but some historians doubt he even existed. Even so, a minor pirate named José Gaspar was active at this time.

Chapter 11: From the Mediterranean to the North Sea
The War Against Pirates and Corsairs, 1493–1830

1. Regarding Lepanto, see Guilmartin, *Galleons and Galleys*, 126–151. In general regarding corsairs in this period, see Jacques Heers, *The Barbary Corsairs: Warfare in the Mediterranean, 1480–1580*, translated by Jonathan North (London: Greenhill Books, 2003); Clive Senior, *A Nation of Pirates: English Piracy in Its Heyday* (New York: Crane, Russak, 1976); and Stanley Lane-Poole, *The Story of the Barbary Corsairs* (New York: G. P. Putnam's Sons, 1890).
2. Henry Boyde, *Several Voyages to Barbary*, 2nd ed. (London: Olive Payne, 1736), 6; Richard Bulstrode, *The Bulstrode Papers* (London: privately printed, 1897), vol. 1, no. 109.
3. *CSPV 1581–1591*, no. 348.
4. Heers, *Barbary Corsairs*, 44–45.
5. Richard Hasleton, *Strange and Wonderful Things*, 1595, reprinted in C. Raymond Beazley, *An English Garner: Voyages and Travels mainly during the 16th and 17th Centuries, Vol. II* (New York: E. P. Dutton, 1902), 151–180.
6. "Antiquity of the Trade" in Hakluyt, *Principal Navigations*, vol. 5:63.
7. Ibid.
8. Ibid.
9. Smith, *Generall Historie*, 43, 45.
10. Ibid., 202–203.
11. *CSPV 1581–1591*, no. 981.
12. Thomas Baker, *Piracy and Diplomacy in Seventeenth Century North Africa: The Journal of Thomas Baker, English Consul in Tripoli, 1677–1685*, edited by C. R. Pennell (London: Associated University Presses, 1989), 103.
13. Heers, *Barbary Corsairs*, 68–69.
14. "Discourse on Piracy" in Mainwaring, *Works*, vol. 2:25.
15. Baker, *Journal*, 106.
16. Edward Coxere, *Adventures by Sea of Edward Coxere*, edited by E. H. W. Meyerstein (London: Oxford University Press, 1946), 87.
17. Ibid.

18. Nabil Matar, *Turks, Moors, and Englishmen in the Age of Discovery* (New York: Columbia University Press, 1999), 57.

19. Samuel Purchas, *Hakluytus Posthumus or Purchas His Pilgrimes Contayning a History of the World in Sea Voyages and Lande Travells by Englishmen and others* (Glasgow: James MacLehose and Sons, 1907), vol. 10:497.

20. Pennell, in the introduction to Baker, *Journal*, 27.

21. Casson, *Illustrated History*, 119.

22. See, for example, Alonso de Contreras, *The Adventures of Captain Alonso de Contreras: A 17th Century Journey*, translated and annotated by Philip Dallas (New York: Paragon House, 1989), 24–26; Purchas, *Hakluytus Posthumus*, vol. 10:497; [Giovanni Paolo Marana], *Letters Writ by a Turkish Spy, Who liv'd Five and Forty Years Undiscover'd at Paris* (London: A Wilde, 1753), vol. 2:200–201; Baker, *Journal*, 132; and Narcissus Luttrell, *A Brief Historical Relation of State Affairs From September 1678 to April 1714* (Oxford: Oxford University Press, 1857), vol. 3:474.

23. *CSPV 1581–1591*, no. 668.

24. See Michael Strachan, "*Sampson's* Fight with Maltese Galleys, 1628," *Mariner's Mirror* 55, no. 3 (1969), 281–289.

25. Baker, *Journal*, 106–107.

26. "Discourse on Piracy," in Mainwaring, *Works*, vol. 2:14.

27. *CSPV 1592–1603*, no. 950; Daniel Goffman, *The Ottoman Empire and Early Modern Europe* (Cambridge: Cambridge University Press, 2002), 194.

28. Baker, *Journal*, 120; Henry Teonge, *The Diary of Henry Teonge*, edited by G. E. Manwaring (New York: Harper & Brothers, 1927) 128. Regarding the definition here of brigantine as half-galley, see P. J. Guéroult du Pas, *Recuëil de Veües des tous les differns Bastimens de la Mer Mediterranie, et de l'Ocean; avec leurs noms et usages,*1710 (repr. Nice: A.N.C.R.E., 2004), book III, plate 24.

29. Baker, *Journal*, 106.

30. Anon., "*A Fight at Sea,* famously fought by the Dolphin of London, against Five of the Turks' Men of War," in Beazley, *An English Garner*, 217.

31. Ibid., 218.

32. Contreras, *Adventures*, 81.

33. "Discourse on Piracy," in Mainwaring, *Works*, vol. 2:23–24.

34. Ibid.

35. Anon., *Fight at Sea*, 215–220.

36. Ibid.

37. "Discourse on Piracy," in Mainwaring, *Works*, vol. 2:31.

38. Ibid., vol. 2:30–31.

39. Boyde, *Several Voyages to Barbary*, 6.

40. "Discourse on Piracy," in Mainwaring, *Works*, vol. 2:44, note 3.

41. *CSPV 1581–1591*, no. 846.

42. "Discourse on Piracy," in Mainwaring, *Works*, vol. 2:21.

43. *CSPV 1592–1603*, no. 950.

44. *CSPV 1581–1591*, no. 368.

45. James Maidment, ed., *Analecta Scotica: Collections Illustrative of the Civil, Ecclesiastical, and Literary History of Scotland*, 2nd ser. (Edinburgh: Thomas G. Stevenson, 1837), no. 116.

46. Ibid.

47. "Discourse on Piracy," in Mainwaring, *Works*, vol. 2:42.

48. Ibid., vol. 2:40–49.
49. *CSPD 1611–1618*, no. 35.
50. John Smith, *The Generall Historie of Virginia, New England, & The Summer Isles* (Glasgow: James MacLehose and Sons, 1907), vol. 2:205–205.
51. "Discourse on Piracy," in Mainwaring, *Works*, vol. 2:46.
52. Ibid., 44.
53. Contreras, *Adventures*; Lope de Vega, *El rey sin reyno tragicomedia famosa de Lope de Vega Carpio*, dedication, in Lope de Vega, *Segunda Parte de la Parte Veinte de las Comedias de Lope de Vega Carpio* (Madrid: La Viuda de Alonso Martín, 1625).
54. "Discourse on Piracy," in Mainwaring, *Works*, vol. 2:20.
55. Contreras, *Adventures*, 44–45.
56. Coxere, *Adventures by Sea*, 82.
57. Contreras, *Adventures*, 21.
58. Ibid., 21–23.
59. James, Duke of York, *Memoirs of the English Affairs, Chiefly Naval, From the Year 1660, to 1673. Written by His Royal Highness James Duke of York* (London: n.p., 1729), 233–234.
60. Bulstrode, *Bulstrode Papers*, vol. 1, no. 109.
61. Baker, *Journal*, 85.
62. Matar, *Moors, Turks, and Englishmen*, 150–151.
63. Dan, *Histoire de Barbarie*, 124–126.
64. Joseph Wheelan, *Jefferson's War: America's First War on Terror* (New York: Carroll & Graf, 2003), 27–31. The Mameluke hilt was copied from North African scimitar hilts.
65. "Lieut. Commandant S. Decatur's Report to Com. Preble," in Department of the Navy, *Documents, Official and Unofficial, Relating to the Case of the Capture and Destruction of the Frigate Philadelphia, at Tripoli, on the 16th February, 1804* (Washington, [DC]: John T. Towers, 1850), 13–14.
66. W. Alison Phillips, *The War of Greek Independence, 1821 to 1833* (New York: Charles Scribner's Sons, 1897), 293. See also Peter M. Swartz, "US-Greek Naval Relations Begin: Antipiracy Operations in the Aegean Sea," COP D0008571.A1 (Alexandria, VA: Center for Strategic Studies, 2003).

Chapter 12: Of Frigates and Cruisers
In Pursuit of the Commerce Raiders, 1688–1865

1. René Duguay-Trouin, *Mémoires de Duguay-Trouin, Lieutenant général des Armées Navales*, 1741, reprint edited by Philippe Clouet (Paris: Éditions France-Empire, 1991), 20.
2. Alfred Thayer Mahan, *The Influence of Sea Power Upon History, 1660–1783* 12th ed. (Boston: Little, Brown, 1918), 196.
3. See G. N. Clark, *The Dutch Alliance and the War Against French Trade 1688–1697* (London: Longmans, Green, 1923), 46–48.
4. Antoine-François-Claude Ferrand, *Histoire des Trois Démembrements de la Pologne* (Paris: Deterville, Librarie, 1820), vol. 1:438–439.
5. "Boston News-Letter, October 1, 1705," in Lyman Horace Weeks and Edwin M. Bacon, eds., *A Historical Digest of the Provincial Press* (Boston: Society for Americana, 1911), 248.
6. Ibid., 35, 112.

7. Clark, *Dutch Alliance*, 46–48.
8. Rogers was, however, sued over the division of plunder.
9. Mahan, *Influence of Sea Power*, 196.
10. Duguay-Trouin, *Mémoires*, 21–27.
11. See, for example, J. W. Damer Powell, *Bristol Privateers and Ships of War* (Bristol: J. W. Arrowsmith, 1930).
12. See, for example, "Boston News-Letter, February 5, 1705" and "Boston News-Letter, August 7, 1704," in Weeks and Bacon, *Historical Digest*, 161, 115.
13. "Boston News-Letter, August 7, 1704," in Weeks and Bacon, *Historical Digest*, 115.
14. Julian S. Corbett, *Some Principles of Maritime Strategy* (London: Longmans, Green, 1918), 242.
15. Regarding the disguise, see [George Walker], *The Voyages and Cruises of Commodore Walker*, 1760 (London: Cassell, 1928 reprint), 115.
16. "Boston News-Letter, May 29, 1709 [1704]," in Weeks and Bacon, *Historical Digest*, 80.
17. Ibid., 79.
18. "Boston News-Letter, May 12, 1705," in Weeks and Bacon, *Historical Digest*, 173.
19. Labat, *Voyages aux Isles*, vol. 2:443. Author's translation.
20. "J. D., at Antigua, to J. A., in London, March 5th, 1710–11," in *The Penn and Logan Correspondence, Volume 2*, in *Memoirs of the Historical Society of Pennsylvania* Vol. 10 (Philadelphia: J. B. Lippincott, 1872), 433.
21. Everard, *Relation*, 259.
22. Ibid.
23. Luttrell, *Brief Historical Relation*, vol. 3:505. Smith noted the tactic in the early seventeenth century in his *Sea Grammar* (Smith, *Works*, vol. 2:282).
24. Henry Wheaton, *Elements of International Law*, 8th ed., edited by Richard Henry Dana, Jr. (London: Sampson Low, Son, 1866), 358; Dmitrii Ivanovich Katchenovsky [Professor Katchenovsky], *Prize-Law: Particularly with Reference to the Duties and Obligations of Belligerents and Neutrals*, translated by Frederic Thomas Pratt (London: Stevens and Sons, 1867), 130.
25. Regarding the United Provinces-Brazil conflict specifically, see Earle, *Pirate Wars*, 235–36. Regarding eighteenth-century Latin American privateering in general, see Scheina, *Latin America's Wars*.
26. Katchenovsky, *Prize Law*, 130–131.
27. Corbett, *Principles of Maritime Strategy*, 242.
28. Raymond Francis Stark, *The Abolition of Privateering and the Declaration of Paris* (New York: Columbia University Press, 1897), 147.
29. Ibid., 141.
30. Ibid., 149–150.
31. Wheaton, *Elements of International Law*, 358.
32. Stark, *Abolition of Privateering*, 147–148.
33. Wheaton, *Elements of International Law*, 358.
34. Stark, *Abolition of Privateering*, 153, 157–158.
35. Navy Department, *Official Records*, ser. 1, vol. 6:63. See also John Thomas Sharf, *History of the Confederate States Navy from Its Organization to the Surrender of Its Last Vessel* 2nd ed. (Albany, NY: Joseph McDonough, 1894), in general.
36. In general, see Navy Department, *Official Records*, ser. 1, vol. 3:137–196, for original records of the search for the *Tallahassee*, and also Department of the Navy,

Dictionary of American Naval Fighting Ships, s.v. *Tallahassee*, http://www.history.navy.
mil/danfs.

37. Navy Department, *Official Records*, ser. 1, vol. 3:152, 173–174.
38. Ibid., 184.
39. Ibid., ser. 1, vol. 3:178.
40. Department of the Navy, *Dictionary of American Naval Fighting Ships*, s.v. *Tallahassee*,
    http://www.history.navy.mil/danfs.
41. See, for example, Charles P. Daly, *Are the Southern Privateersmen Pirates?* (New York:
    James B. Kirker, 1862).
42. Rafael Semmes, *The Cruise of the Alabama and the Sumter* (New York: Carleton
    Publisher, 1864), 234–236.
43. Ibid.

Chapter 13: Pirates, Rebels, and Warriors
Pirate Hunting in the East, 694 BC–AD 1896

1. *Oxford English Dictionary*, 2nd ed., s.v. "piracy" (emphasis added). See Rubin, *Law
   of Piracy*, 201–291, for an evaluation of British imperial law and the treatment of
   "pirates."
2. George Fadlo Hourani, *Arab Seafaring in the Indian Ocean in Ancient and Early
   Medieval Times*, 1951 (Beirut: Khayats, 1963 reprint), 5.
3. Ibid., 7.
4. Casson, *Ancient Mariners*, 161; Omerod, *Piracy in the Ancient World*, 258; Hourani,
   Arab Seafaring, 20.
5. Hourani, *Arab Seafaring*, 70.
6. Marco Polo, *The Travels of Marco Polo, the Venetian*, edited by Thomas Wright
   (London: Henry G. Bohn, 1854), 426.
7. Ibid.
8. Hourani, *Arab Seafaring*, 5, in regard to the Caspian reference.
9. Ibid., 66, 69.
10. Ibid., 66.
11. William Heude, *A Voyage Up the Persian Gulf and a Journey Overland from India to
    England in 1817* (London: Longman, Hurst, Rees, Orme, and Brown, 1819), 38.
12. Sultan ibn Muhammad al-Qasimi, *The Myth of Arab Piracy in the Gulf*, 2nd ed.
    (London: Croom Helm, 1986), 195–196.
13. James H. Noyes, *The Clouded Lens: Persian Gulf Security and U.S. Policy*, 2nd ed.
    (Stanford: Hoover Institution Press, 1982), 5–6.
14. See, for example, ibid., and al-Qasimi, *Myth of Arab Piracy*, in general.
15. *A Collection of Treaties, Engagements, and Sanads Relating to India and Neighbouring
    Countries*, 3rd. ed., compiled by C. U. Aitchison (Calcutta: Office of the
    Superintendent of Government Printing, 1892), vol. 10:108–110.
16. Hourani, *Arab Seafaring*, 70–79.
17. Ibid., 114, note 113.
18. Polo, *Travels*, 416–417.
19. Fryer, *New Account*, vol. 2:152–153.
20. John Stewart Bowman, ed., *Columbia Chronologies of Asian History and Culture* (New
    York: Columbia University Press, 2000), 283.
21. Jean Baptise Tavernier, *Travels in India*, 1676, translated by Valentine Bell
    (London: MacMillan, 1889), vol. 1:177.

22. Henry Beveridge, *A Comprehensive History of India, Civil, Military, and Social* (London: Blackie and Son, 1867), vol. 1:509–516.
23. Ibid.
24. Charles Elms, *The Pirates Own Book: or, Authentic Narratives of the Lives, Exploits, and Executions of the Most Celebrated Sea Robbers* (Portland, ME: Francis Blake, 1855), 208.
25. Stefan Eklöf, *Pirates in Paradise: A Modern History of Southeast Asia's Maritime Marauders* (Copenhagen: NIAS Press, 2006), 9–11.
26. Edwin H. Gomes, *Seventeen Years Among the Sea Dyaks of Borneo* (Philadelphia: J. B. Lippincott, 1911), 23–24.
27. Henry Keppel and James Brooke, *The Expedition to Borneo of H.M.S. Dido for The Suppression of Piracy: With Extracts from the Journal of James Brooke, Esq., of Sarawak,* 1846 (New York: Harper & Brothers, 1861 reprint), 185–186.
28. Regarding mid-nineteenth-century expeditions from the British point of view, see, for example Beresford Scott, *An Account of the Destruction of the Fleets of the Celebrated Pirate Chieftains Chui-apoo and Shap-ng-tsai on the Coast of China, in September and October, 1849* [No publication data: 1851?].
29. Edward Brown, *A Seaman's Narrative of His Adventures During a Captivity Among Chinese Pirates On the Coast of Cochin-China* (London: Charles Westerton, 1861), 23
30. Ibid., 25.
31. Ibid., 23–31.
32. See, for example, G. Romilly, *Étude sur la Guerre contre les Pirates au Tonkin* (Angoulême, France: Imprimerie Militaire L. Coquemard, 1910).
33. Bowman, *Columbia Chronologies,* 129, 131, 136, 183; James Hoare and Susan Pares, *Korea: An Introduction* (New York: Routledge, 1988), 33–34.
34. "The Last Voyage of John Davis with Sir Edward Michelborne," in John Davis, *The Voyages and Work of John Davis the Navigator,* edited by Albert Hastings Markham (London: Hakluyt Society, 1880), 178–182.
35. Ibid.
36. Ibid.
37. The author's great-great-grandfather, Philip P. Seale, used his percussion lock rifle well into the 1930s, for example. The rifle was almost a century old by then. Percussion firearms based on the old buccaneer gun were produced and shipped to some parts of Africa as late as the 1950s. In a personal communication to the author, editor Don McKeon noted that he observed buccaneer guns in ceremonial use in West Africa in the 1970s and believes that they were still actively used by hunters and night watchmen.

Chapter 14: Death from Beneath the Waves
Combating the Submarine Menace, 1914–1945

1. "Submarine Destroys Irish Fishing Fleet," *New York Times,* June 15, 1918.
2. Ibid.
3. Atkins, *Voyage to Guinea,* 192–193.
4. Lowell Thomas, *Raiders of the Deep,* 1928 (Annapolis, MD: Naval Institute Press, 2004 reprint), 85, 264–265.
5. Henry Stanhope and Jonathan Wills, "All clear for the Jolly Roger," *London Times,* July 5, 1982.
6. "Schiller Tries to Flee," *New York Times,* July 11, 1916.
7. "German Stowaway Captures Steamer," *New York Times,* March 31, 1916; "'Schiller'

Plotted to Sink Pannonia," *New York Times*, April 1, 1916; "Pirate Schiller Coming to New York," *New York Times*, April 2, 1916.

8. Ibid.

9. See, for example, "The Ethics of Piracy," *London Times*, August 20, 1917; "No Peace with Piracy," *New York Times*, October 14, 1918; "Find Kaiser is Culpable," *New York Times*, November 30, 1918; and R. L. Duffus, "Submarine Again Becomes a World Issue," *New York Times*, November 22, 1925.

10. See, for example, "Germany's Policy 'Piracy,'" *New York Times*, May 8, 1915; "The Ethics of Piracy," *London Times*, August 20, 1917; "Finds Lusitania the Victim of an Act of Piracy," *New York Times*, August 26, 1918; "No Peace with Piracy," *New York Times*, October 14, 1918.

11. "Submarine Destroys Irish Fishing Fleet," *New York Times*, June 15, 1918.

12. "The Lusitania Sunk One Year Ago Today," *New York Times*, May 7, 1916; Thomas, *Raiders of the Deep*, 93.

13. "The Lusitania Sunk One Year Ago Today," *New York Times*, May 7, 1916; Thomas, *Raiders of the Deep*, 101.

14. "Teutons to Sink All Armed Liners," *New York Times*, February 11, 1916.

15. Thomas, *Raiders of the Deep*, 100.

16. Regarding Roosevelt, see "Roosevelt Calls it an Act of Piracy," *New York Times*, May 8, 1915.

17. "Lusitania Attack Miscalled 'Piracy,'" *New York Times*, May 17, 1915; "Finds Lusitania the Victim of an Act of Piracy," *New York Times*, August 26, 1918. In general regarding the comparison of submarine warfare to piracy, see Rubin, *Law of Piracy*, 295–297.

18. See, for example, "Press Calls Sinking of Lusitania Murder," *New York Times*, May 18, 1915.

19. "The Ethics of Piracy," *London Times*, August 20, 1917.

20. "The Submarine Murders," *New York Times*, February 27, 1919.

21. Ibid; "Tells How U-boat Drowned 35 Sailors," *New York Times*, August 31, 1921.

22. "The Submarine Murders," *New York Times*, February 27, 1919.

23. "The Ethics of Piracy," *London Times*, August 20, 1917.

24. "The Lusitania Sunk One Year Ago Today," *New York Times*, May 7, 1916.

25. Lothar-Günther Buchheim, *Das Boot*, 1973, reprint of 1975 translated edition (London: Cassell Military Paperbacks, 1999), 373, 377.

26. Robert Fulton to William Pitt, January 6, 1806, quoted in Georg Günther Freiherr von Forstner, *The Journal of Submarine Commander von Forstner*, 1916, reprint, translated and edited by Mrs. Russell Codman (New York: Houghton Mifflin, 1917), xi.

27. Robert H. Thurston, *Robert Fulton: His Life and Its Results* (New York: Dodd, Mead, 1891), 69–75. Fulton's manuscript is preserved in the Library of Congress.

28. Ibid., 74–75.

29. Jules Verne, *Twenty Thousand Leagues Under the Sea*, 1870, reprint translated by Mercier Lewis (Norwalk, CT: Easton, 1977), 310.

30. Ibid., 316.

31. In this case, the term *ship* must be enclosed in quotation marks, lest its use provoke the wrath of the submariner. A submarine may always be referred to as a boat (preferred), submarine, or sub, but never as a ship.

32. The author's experience has been that, except on the surface, there is little sense of the sea in a submarine, at least not in modern boats.

33. Verne, *Twenty Thousand Leagues*, 40.

34. Anon., "The Influence of Commerce in War," *Naval Review* 2 (August 1914): 160.

35. Ibid.

36. Johann Speiss, quoted in Thomas, *Raiders of the Deep*, 34.

37. Not all submarine fleets focused on commerce raiding. The Japanese in World War II, for example, focused on attacking warships and on other missions. See, for example, Samuel Eliot Morison, *The Two-Ocean War: A Short History of the United States Navy in the Second World War* (Boston: Little, Brown and Company, 1963), 496.

38. R. L. Duffus, "Submarine Again Becomes a World Issue," *New York Times*, November 22, 1925.

39. Thomas, *Raiders of the Deep*, 80.

40. See High Command of the Navy, *The U-Boat Commander's Handbook*, 1943, reprint translated by the U.S. Navy (Gettysburg, PA: Thomas Publications, 1989), 40–73.

41. Morison, *The Two-Ocean War*, 495.

42. Donald Macintyre, *U-Boat Killer: Fighting the U-Boats in the Battle of the Atlantic*, 1956 (London: Rigel Publications, 2004 reprint), 92.

43. Ibid.

44. Ibid.

45. Forstner, *Journal*, 27–28.

46. Morison, *Two-Ocean War*, 494.

47. "Shovel Routed U-Boat," *New York Times*, March 10, 1918.

48. "Certain Tanker's Shot Ended U-Boat's Career," *New York Times*, August 21, 1918.

49. "American Tanker Sunk in Battle," *New York Times*, June 16, 1917.

50. James B. Connolly, *The U-Boat Hunters* (New York: Charles Scribner's Sons, 1918), 53–54.

51. Ibid., 129.

52. "Submarine's Nemesis," *New York Times*, April 29, 1917.

53. David Fairbank White, *Bitter Ocean: The Battle of the Atlantic, 1939–1945* (New York: Simon & Schuster, 2006), 200–201.

54. "Shipowner Offers $10,000 for Each U-Boat Sunk; Would Pay Out $500,000 to Help the Warfare," *New York Times*, November 21, 1916, quoting the *London Times*.

55. John Hays Hammond, Jr., in Forstner, *Journal*, xlix.

56. Connolly, *U-Boat Hunters*, 53.

57. Charles W. Domville-Fife, *Submarine Warfare of To-Day: How the Submarine Menace Was Met and Vanquished* (Philadelphia: J. B. Lippincott, 1920), 57–61.

58. In general regarding World War I anti-submarine weapons and warfare, see Domville-Fife, *Submarine Warfare*.

59. High Command of the Navy, *U-Boat Commander's Handbook*, 89–91.

60. Thomas, *Raiders of the Deep*, 75–76.

61. Ibid., 351.

62. In general, see Macintyre, *U-Boat Killer*. To maintain secrecy, British researchers referred to their active sound detection work as ASDics, ASD standing for Anti-Submarine Division. SONAR is an acronym for Sound Navigation And Ranging.

63. Ibid., 91–93.

64. Ibid., 109–110.

65. Buchheim, *Das Boot*, 198, 199.

66. "Shipowner Offers $10,000 for Each U-Boat Sunk," *New York Times*, November 21, 1916, quoting the *London Times*.
67. White, *Bitter Ocean*, 122–123, 196–200.
68. Morison, *Two-Ocean War*, 511.
69. Thomas, *Raiders of the Deep*, 351–352.
70. Buchheim, *Das Boot*, introduction (n.p.).
71. Morison, *Two-Ocean War*, 498.
72. In general see Philip Kaplan and Jack Currie, *Convoy: Merchant Sailors at War, 1939–1945* (Annapolis, MD: Naval Institute Press, 2000).
73. In general, see David Woodward, *The Secret Raiders: The Story of the German Armed Merchant Raiders in the Second World War* (New York: W. W. Norton, 1955).
74. In general, see C. E. T. Warren and James Benson, *The Midget Raiders: The Wartime Story of Human Torpedoes and Midget Submarines* (New York: William Sloane Associates, 1954).
75. In general, see Thomas, *Raiders of the Deep*, and Felix Graf von Luckner, *Seeteufel: Abenteuer aus meinem Leben* (Leipzig: R. F. Koehler, 1921).
76. See Tony Bridgland, *Sea Killers in Disguise: Q Ships & Decoy Raiders of WWI* (Annapolis, MD: U.S. Naval Institute Press, 1999), 253–254, regarding the single death.

Chapter 15: Ships, SEALs, and Satellites
The Return of the Pirate Hunters

1. "Modern pirates: Armed and ruthless," *BBC News*, April 24, 2000, <http://news.bbc.co.uk>; Craig Eason, "Nigeria named number one piracy hot spot," *Lloyd's List*, April 17, 2008.
2. Rob Walker, "Inside story of Somali pirate attack," *BBC News*, June 4, 2009, <http://news.bbc.co.uk>.
3. See, for example, "With the Chinese Pirates," *Popular Mechanics* (February 1932): 266–271; "Ramos pushes Navy modernization," *Manila Standard*, February 1, 1996; and "IMB Piracy Reports" in general.
4. "British Frigate Captures Pirates Who Stole a Dhow in Arabian Sea," *New York Times*, December 7, 1953.
5. See, for example, James P. Sterba, "The Agony of Vietnam Refugee Boat 0105," *New York Times*, July 25, 1979.
6. See Alex Perry, "Buccaneer Tales in the Pirates' Lair," *TIMEasia.com* (Asian Journey 2001), http://www.time.com/time/asia/features/journey2001/pirates.html.
7. See, for example, Andrew Harding, "Postcard from Somali pirate capital," *BBC News*, June 16, 2009, http://news.bbc.co.uk/2/hi/africa/8103585.stm.
8. Robyn Hunter, "Somali pirates living the high life," *BBC News*, October 28, 2008, http://news.bbc.co.uk/2/hi/Africa/7650415.stm. Regarding the stock exchange, see "Somali sea gangs lure investors at pirate lair," *Reuters*, December 1, 2009, http://www.reuters.com/article/idUSGEE5AS0EV. My thanks to Rachel Lindstrom for forwarding me that latter article.
9. Hunter, "Somali pirates."
10. Little, "Terrorists and Pirates," 80–84.
11. See, for example, Sam Bateman, "The Threat of Maritime Terrorism and Piracy Is Exaggerated," in Noah Berlatsky, ed., *Piracy on the High Seas* (Detroit: Greenhaven, 2010), 95–107.

12. Little, "Terrorists and Pirates," 80–84. See also Peter Lehr, *Violence at Sea: Piracy in the Age of Global Terrorism* (New York: Routledge, 2007), 85.

13. "Indian navy destroys pirate ship as super-tanker ransom demanded," *AFP*, November 19, 2008, http://www.afp.com; "Indian navy 'sank Thai trawler,'" *BBC News*, November 25, 2008, http://news.bbc.co.uk/india/Thai-company-says-INS-Tabar-sank-its-vessel/articleshow/3757449.cms; "Thai company says INS Tabar sank its vessel," *Times of India*, November 26, 2008, http://timesofindia.indiatimes.com/india/Thai-company-says-ins-Tabar-sank-its-vessel/articleshow/3757449.cms; Press Information Bureau, Government of India, "Anti Piracy Action at High Seas," November 19, 2008.

14. Author's experience.

15. Arnaud de La Grange, "Le Ponant: l'histoire secrète d'une liberation," *Le Figaro*, April 14, 2008.

16. "French man killed in front of his son as commandos storm yacht held by pirates," *Telegraph.co.uk*, April 10, 2009, http://www.telegraph.co.uk/news/worldnews/piracy/5138317/French-man-killed-in-front-of-his-son-as-commandos-storm-yacht-held-by-pirates.html; James Gordon Meek, "Fatal French commando rescue of pirate hostages underscores risk of sneak attack," *New York Daily News*, April 11, 2009, http://www.nydailynews.com/news/national/2009/04/11/2009-04-11_fatal_french_commando_rescue_of_pirate_hostages_underscores_risk_of_sneak_attack.html; "Russian Special Forces Storm Captured Ship," *AP*, May 6, 2010.

17. Author's experience.

18. de La Grange, "Le Ponant," April 14, 2008.

19. Author's experience.

20. Ibid.

21. Marcus Hand, "Joint patrols cut Malacca attacks to 'zero per cent,'" *Lloyd's List*, April 14, 2008, http://www.lloydslist.com; Anders C. Sjaastad, "Southeast Asian SLOCS and Security Options," in Kwa Chong Guan and John K. Skogan, eds., *Maritime Security in Southeast Asia* (New York: Routledge, 2007), 11–12; Adam J. Young, *Contemporary Maritime Piracy in Southeast Asia: History, Causes, and Remedies* (Singapore: Institute of Southeast Asian Studies, 2007), 83; Adam J. Young and Mark J. Valencia; "Conflation of Piracy and Terrorism in Southeast Asia: Rectitude and Utility," *Contemporary Southeast Asia* 25, no. 2 (2003): 269–283.

22. See, for example, Oil Companies International Marine Forum, "Piracy: The East Africa/Somalia Situation. Practical Measures to Avoid, Deter or Delay Piracy Attacks" (London: OCIMF, 2009); and "Fighting off the Somali pirates," *BBC News*, April 14, 2008, http://news.bbc.co.uk/2/hi/7999974.stm.

23. Ibid.

24. Regarding the around the clock use of fire fighting systems, John Dorozynski, a retired master of liquefied natural gas (LNG) vessels, personal communication, September 17, 2008.

25. "Chinese sailors fend off pirates in Gulf of Aden," December 19, 2008, *China Daily*, http://www.chinadaily.com.cn/world/2008-12/19/content_7325314.htm.

26. Fergal Keane, "British captain's Somali pirate nightmare," *BBC Radio 4*, January 19, 2010, http://news.bbc.co.uk/2/hi/africa/8465770.stm.

27. "Crew of a ship in Somalia thwarts pirate attack," *AP*, October 30, 2007.

28. "Freed Egypt sailors cheered home," *BBC News*, August 23, 2009, http://news.bbc.co.uk/2/hi/africa/8216732.stm.
29. See, for example, Peter Chalk, "Opposing View: Keep Arms Off Ships," *USA Today*, May 4, 2009.
30. John Dorozynski, personal communication, September 17, 2008.
31. Figures provided to author by maritime security professionals.
32. "Yemen Navy rents out antipiracy services," *MarineLog*, January 8, 2010, http://www.marinelog.com/DOCS/NEWSMMIX/2010jan00080.html.
33. Smith, *Sea Grammar*, vol. 2:281.
34. Rear Adm. Terence McKnight, USN (Ret.), quoted in "Media Dramatizes Somali Piracy," *Military.com*, December 8, 2009, http://www.military.com/news/article/navy-news/media-dramatizes-somali-piracy.html. See also Bateman, "Threat of Maritime Terrorism," 95–107.
35. Mary Harper, "Chasing the Somali piracy money trail," *BBC News*, May 24, 2009, http://news.bbc.co.uk/2/hi/Africa/8061535.htm.
36. Gordon Corera, "Resurgence of piracy on tsunami-hit seas," *BBC News*, May 11, 2005, http://news.bbc.co.uk/2/hi/asia-pacific/4535677.stm.
37. Johnson, *General History*, 231.
38. Roche, "Journals", 99.
39. Mahan, *Influence of Sea Power*, 194.

Bibliography

Alfred. *The Whole Works of Alfred the Great.* 3 vols. London: Bosworth & Harrison, 1858.

al-Qasimi, Sultan ibn Muhammad. *The Myth of Arab Piracy in the Gulf.* 2nd ed. London, Croom Helm, 1986.

Anderson, J. L. "Piracy and World History: An Economic Perspective on Maritime Predation." *Journal of World History* 6, no. 2 (1995): 175–199.

Anderson, Joseph, ed. *The Orkneyinga Saga.* Translated by Jon A. Hjaltalin and Gilbert Goudie. Edinburgh: Edmonston and Douglas, 1873.

Anderson, R. C. *Oared Fighting Ships: From Classical Times to the Coming of Steam.* London: Percival Marshall, 1957.

Anon. *Beowulf.* Translated by William Ellery Leonard. Norwalk, CT: Heritage Press, 1967.

Anon. "The destruction, capture, &c. of Portuguese Carracks, by English seamen," 1600. Reprinted in C. Raymond Beazley. *An English Garner: Voyages and Travels mainly during the 16th and 17th Centuries, Vol. 2.* New York: E. P. Dutton, 1902.

Anon. "A Fight at Sea, famously fought by the Dolphin of London, against Five of the Turks' Men of War." In C. Raymond Beazley. *An English Garner: Voyages and Travels mainly during the 16th and 17th Centuries, Vol. 2.* New York: E. P. Dutton, 1902.

Anon. "The Influence of Commerce in War." *Naval Review* 2 (August 1914): 159–164.

Anon. *Journal de Bord d'un Flibustier (1686–1693).* Edited by Edouard Ducéré. In *Bulletin de la Société des Sciences & Arts de Bayonne, Année 1894.* Bayonne: A. Lamaignère, 1894.

Anon. *Mery Tales, Wittie Questions and Quicke Answeres, Very pleasant to be Readde.* 1567. Reprinted in *Shakespeare Jest-Books.* 2 vols. Edited by W. Carew Hazlitt. London: Willis and Sotheran, 1864.

Anon. "Our One Hundred Questions." *Lippincott's Monthly Magazine,* vol. 42 (July–December 1888), 567–578.

Anon. *A Pacquet from Parnassus: or, a Collection of Papers.* Vol. 1, no. 1. London: J. How and J. Nutt, 1702.

Anon. "The Submarine Menace: Sir Percy Scott and His Critics." *Naval Review* 2, (August, 1914): 178–180.

Apestegui, Cruz. *Pirates of the Caribbean.* Translated by Richard Lewis Rees. Edison, NJ: Chartwell Books, 2002.

Apollonius Rhodius. *The Argonautica.* Translated by R. C. Seaton. New York: Macmillan, 1912.

Archer, William. *The Pirate's Progress: A Short History of the U-Boat.* New York: Harper & Brothers, 1918.

Arnold, Thomas. *The American Practical Lunarian, and Seaman's Guide.* Philadelphia: Robert Desilver, 1822.

Ashton, Philip, and John Barnard. *Ashton's Memorial.* 1725. Reprinted in Donald P. Wharton. *In the Trough of the Sea.* Westport, CT: Greenwood, 1979.

Atkins, John. *A Voyage to Guinea, Brazil, and the West Indies.* 1735. Facsimile reprint, London: Frank Cass, 1970.

Augustine. *The City of God.* Translated by Marcus Dods. In *Great Books of the Western World: 18. Augustine.* 1952. Reprint, Chicago: Encyclopedia Britannica, 1982.

Bacon, Matthew. *A New Abridgement of the Law.* 10 vols. Philadelphia: Thomas Davis, 1846.

Bahar, Michael. "Attaining Optimal Deterrence at Sea: A Legal and Strategic Theory for Naval Anti-Piracy Operations." Nashville, TN: Vanderbilt University School of Law, *Vanderbilt Journal of Transnational Law* 40 (January 2007).

Baikouzis, Constantino, and Marcelo O. Magnasco. "Is an eclipse described in the Odyssey?" *Proceedings of the National Academy of Sciences* 105, no. 26 (July 1, 2008): 8823–8828.

Baker, Thomas. *Piracy and Diplomacy in Seventeenth Century North Africa: The Journal of Thomas Baker, English Consul in Tripoli, 1677–1685.* Edited by C. R. Pennell. London: Associated University Presses, 1989.

Bamford, Paul W. *Fighting Ships and Prisons.* Minneapolis: University of Minnesota Press, 1973.

Barlow, Edward. *Barlow's Journal.* 2 vols. Edited by Basil Lubbock. London: Hurst & Blackett, 1934.

Barrie, J. M. *Peter Pan and Wendy.* 1906. Reprint, illustrated by Edmund Blampied. New York: Charles Scribner's Sons, 1940.

Bateman, Sam. "The Threat of Maritime Terrorism and Piracy Is Exaggerated." In Berlatsky, *Piracy on the High Seas,* 95–107.

Bateson, Mary, ed. *Records of the Borough of Leicester.* 5 vols. London: C. J. Clay and Sons, 1901.

Beal, Clifford. *Quelch's Gold: Piracy, Greed, and Betrayal in Colonial New England.* Westport, CT: Praeger, 2007.

Beeston, William. "A journal kept by colonel Beeston, from his first coming to Jamaica." In *Interesting Tracts, Relating to the Island of Jamaica.* St. Jago de la Vega, Jamaica: Lewis, Lunan, and Jones, 1800.

Behâ Ed-dîn. *The Life of Saladin.* London: Committee of the Palestine Exploration Fund, 1897.

Benton, Elbert Jay. *International Law and Diplomacy of the Spanish-American War.* Baltimore: Johns Hopkins University Press, 1908.

Berlatsky, Noah, ed. *Piracy on the High Seas.* Detroit: Greenhaven, 2010.

Bernard, Montague. *A Historical Account of the Neutrality of Great Britain During the American Civil War.* London: Longmans, Green, Reader, and Dyer, 1870.

Beveridge, Henry. *A Comprehensive History of India, Civil, Military, and Social.* 3 vols. London: Blackie and Son, 1867.

Bierce, Ambrose. *The Devil's Dictionary.* 1911. Reprint, New York: Dover, 1958.

Blackstone, William. *Commentaries on the Laws of England*. 1765–1769. 4 vols. Facsimile reprint, Chicago: University of Chicago Press, 1979.

Boteler, Nathaniel. *Boteler's Dialogues*. 1685. Reprint, edited by W. G. Perrin. London: Navy Records Society, 1929.

Bourdé de Villehuet, Jacques. *Le Manoeuvrier, ou essai sur la théorie et la practique de mouvements du navire et des évolutions navales*. Paris: H. L. Guerin and L. F. Delatour, 1765.

Bowman, John Stewart, ed. *Columbia Chronologies of Asian History and Culture*. New York: Columbia University Press, 2000.

Boxer, C. R. *The Portuguese Seaborne Empire 1415–1825*. New York: Knopf, 1969.

Boyde, Henry. *Several Voyages to Barbary*. 2nd ed. London: Olive Payne, 1736.

Boyer, Abel, ed. *The Political State of Great Britain*. Vol 32. London: privately printed, 1726.

Bradlee, Francis B. C. *Piracy in the West Indies and its Suppression*. Salem, MA: Essex Institute, 1923.

Braudel, Fernand. *The Mediterranean and the Mediterranean World in the Age of Philip II*. Translated by Sian Reynolds. 2 vols. Berkeley: University of California Press, 1996.

Breasted, James Henry, ed. *Ancient Records of Egypt*. Vol. IV. Chicago: University of Chicago Press, 1906.

Bridgland, Tony. *Sea Killers in Disguise: Q Ships & Decoy Raiders of WWI*. Annapolis, MD: U.S. Naval Institute Press, 1999.

Brown, Edward. *A Seaman's Narrative of His Adventures During a Captivity Among Chinese Pirates On the Coast of Cochin-China*. London: Charles Westerton, 1861.

Bryce, Trevor. *The Trojans and Their Neighbours*. London: Routledge, 2006.

Bryson, Peter D. *Comprehensive Review in Toxicology for Emergency Clinicians*. 3rd ed. Washington, DC: Taylor & Francis, 1996.

Buchheim, Lothar-Günther. *Das Boot*. 1973. Reprint of 1975 translated edition. London: Cassell Military Paperbacks, 1999.

Budge, E. A. Wallis. *Egypt Under the Priest-Kings, Tanites, and Nubians*. London: Kegan Paul, Trench, Trübner, 1902.

[Buhours, Dominique.] *The Life of the Renowned Peter D'Aubusson, Grand Master of Rhodes*. London: George Wells and Samuel Carr, 1679.

Bulstrode, Richard. *The Bulstrode Papers*. 2nd ser. 2 vols. London: privately printed, 1897.

Burchett, Josiah. *A Complete History of the most Remarkable Transactions at Sea*. London: J. Walthoe, 1720.

Burnett, John S. *Dangerous Waters: Modern Piracy and Terror on the High Seas*. New York: Dutton, 2002.

Burritt, Elijah H. *The Geography of the Heavens, and Class Book of Astronomy*. New York: Huntington and Savage, 1843.

Burrows, Montague. *The Cinque Ports*. London: Longmans, Green, 1892.

Bushnell, Amy Turner, "How to Fight a Pirate: Provincials, Royalists, and the Defense of Minor Ports During the Age of Buccaneers," *Gulf Coast Historical Review* 5 (1990): 18–35.

Caesar [Gaius Julius Caesar]. *The Civil War: together with The Alexandrian War, The African War, and The Spanish War by other Hands*. Translated by Jane F. Mitchell. New York: Penguin, 1980.

Calendar of Letter-Books Preserved Among the Archives of the Corporation of the City of London at the Guildhall. Edited by Reginald R. Sharpe. London: John Edward Francis, 1907.

Calendar of the Patent Rolls Preserved in the Public Record Office, Henry VI. 6 vols. London: Mackie, 1907.

Calendar of State Papers and Manuscripts, Relating to English Affairs, Existing in the Archives and Collections of Venice, and in other Libraries of Northern Italy, 1202–1675. 38 vols. Edited by Rawdon Brown et al. London: Eyre and Spottiswoode, et al, 1864–1947.

Calendar of State Papers, Colonial Series, America and West Indies, 1574–1738. 44 vols. Edited by Noel W. Sainsbury, J. W. Fortescue, et al. London: 1860–1969.

Calendar of State Papers, Domestic Series, of the Reigns of Edward VI, Mary, Elizabeth and James I, 1547–[1625]. 12 vols. London:, Longman, Brown, Green, Longmans & Roberts; [etc.], 1865–72.

Carpenter-Turner, W. J. "The Building of the *Gracedieu, Valentine* and *Falconer* at Southampton, 1416–1420," *Mariner's Mirror* 40 (1954), no. 1: 55–72.

Carr Laughton, L. G. "Gunnery, Frigates, and the Line of Battle." *Mariner's Mirror* 14, no. 4 (1928): 339–363.

Cary, George. *The Medieval Alexander.* Edited by D. J. A. Ross. Cambridge: Cambridge University Press, 1956.

Casson, Lionel. *The Ancient Mariners: Seafarers and Sea Fighters of the Mediterranean in Ancient Times.* 2nd ed. Princeton, NJ: Princeton University Press, 1991.

———. *Illustrated History of Ships & Boats.* New York: Doubleday, 1964.

———. *Ships and Seamanship in the Ancient World.* Princeton, NJ: Princeton University Press, 1971.

Caulfield, Richard. *The Council Book of the Corporation of Youghal.* Guildford, Surrey [England]: J. Billing and Sons, 1878.

Chalk, Peter. "The Maritime Dimension of International Security: Terrorism, Piracy, and Challenges for the United States." Prepared for the United States Air Force by the RAND Corporation, 2008.

Chapelle, Howard I. *The History of American Sailing Ships.* New York: Bonanza Books, 1935.

———. *The Search for Speed Under Sail 1700–1855.* New York: W. W. Norton, 1967.

Chapin, H. M. *Privateer Ships and Sailors, The First Century of American Colonial Privateering 1625–1725.* Toulon: Imprimerie G. Mouton, 1926.

Chatterton, E. Keble. *Sailing Ships: The Story of Their Development from the Earliest Times to the Present Day.* Philadelphia: J. B. Lippincott, 1915.

Chaucer, Geoffrey. *The Canterbury Tales.* Translated by J. U. Nicolson. Garden City, NY: Garden City Books, 1934.

Chomsky, Noam. *Pirates and Emperors, Old and New: International Terrorism in the Real World.* Montreal: Black Rose Books, 1986.

Christides, Vassilios. "Military Intelligence in Arabo-Byzantine Naval Warfare." Athens: Institute for Byzantine Studies, 1996.

———. "Some Remarks on the Mediterranean and Red Sea Ships in Ancient and Medieval Times, Part II." *Proceedings of the 2nd International Symposium on Ship Construction in Antiquity.* Delphi: Tropis II, 1987.

Churchill, Awnsham, and John Churchill, eds. *A Collection of Voyages and Travels.* 6 vols. London: John Walthoe et al., 1732.

Cicero, Marcus Tullius [Tully]. *Orations of Marcus Tullius Cicero.* Translated by C. D. Yonge. *Orations of Marcus Tullius Cicero.* London: George Bell and Sons, 1878.

———. *Select Orations of Marcus Tullius Cicero.* Translated by C. D. Yonge. Philadelphia: David McKay, 1898.

———. *Tully's Offices [de Officii], in Three Books.* 6th ed. 3 vols. Translated by R. L'Estrange. London: D. Browne et al., 1720.

Clark, G. N. *The Dutch Alliance and the War Against French Trade 1688–1697.* London: Longmans, Green, 1923.

Cleirac, Estienne. *Us et Coutumes de la Mer.* Bordeaux: Guillaume Millanges, 1647.

Coe, Michael D., et al., *Swords and Hilt Weapons.* New York: Barnes and Noble, 1993.

A Collection of Treaties, Engagements, and Sanads Relating to India and Neighbouring Countries. 3rd. ed. 11 vols. Compiled by C. U. Aitchison. Calcutta: Office of the Superintendent of Government Printing, 1892.

Colón, Fernando. *Historia del almirante don Cristóbal Colón.* 1571. 2 vols. Reprint, Madrid: T. Minuesa, 1892.

Connolly, James. B. *The U-Boat Hunters.* New York: Charles Scribner's Sons, 1918.

Cooper, William Durrant. *The History of Winchelsea, One of the Ancient Towns Added to the Cinque Ports.* London: John Russell Smith, 1850.

Corbett, Julian S. *Drake and the Tudor Navy.* 2 vols. Longmans, Green, 1898.

———. *Some Principles of Maritime Strategy.* London: Longmans, Green, 1918.

Cordingly, David. *Under the Black Flag.* New York: Random House, 1995.

[Cox, John]. *The Adventures of Capt. Barth. Sharp, And Others, in the South Sea.* London: P. A. Esq. [Philip Ayers], 1684.

Coxere, Edward. *Adventures by Sea of Edward Coxere.* Edited by E. H. W. Meyerstein. London: Oxford University Press, 1946.

Cunningham, William. *The Growth of English Industry and Commerce During the Early and Middle Ages.* Cambridge: Cambridge University Press, 1896.

Cutts, Edward L. *Scenes and Characters of the Middle Ages.* London: Virtue & Co., 1872.

Daly, Charles. P. *Are the Southern Privateersmen Pirates?* New York: James B. Kirker, 1862.

Damer Powell, J. W. *Bristol Privateers and Ships of War.* Bristol: J. W. Arrowsmith, 1930.

Dampier, William. *A New Voyage Round the World.* 1697. Reprint, New York: Dover, 1968.

Dan, Pierre. *Histoire de Barbarie et de ses Corsaires, des royaumes et des villes d'Alger, de Tunis, de Salé, & de Tripoly.* 2nd ed. Paris: Pierre Rocolet, 1649.

Davies, John. *A History of Wales.* London: Penguin, 1993.

Davis, John. *The Voyages and Work of John Davis the Navigator.* Edited by Albert Hastings Markham. London: Hakluyt Society, 1880.

de Contreras, Alonso. *The Adventures of Captain Alonso de Contreras: A 17th Century Journey.* Translated and annotated by Philip Dallas. New York: Paragon House, 1989.

———. *Vida de Capitan Alonso de Contreras, Caballero del Habito de San Juan, Natural de Madrid, Escrita por él Mismo (Años 1582 a 1633).* Madrid: Establecimiento Tipográfico de Fortnanet, 1900.

de Monstrelet, Enguerrand. *The Chronicles of Enguerrand de Monstrelet.* Translated by Thomas Johnes. 2 vols. London: George Routledge and Sons, 1867.

de Pouancey, M. [au comte d'Estrées], 1 April 1677, Archives nationales, Colonies, C9 A rec. 1, reprinted in *Les Archives de la Flibuste,* http://members.tripod.com/diable_volant/archives/D1670/D7704pouancey.html.

Department for Transport. "The UK Government's strategy for tackling Piracy and Armed robbery at sea." London: Msc 80/5/17, March 4, 2005.

Department of the Navy. *Documents, Official and Unofficial, Relating to the Case of the Capture and Destruction of the Frigate Philadelphia, at Tripoli, on the 16th February, 1804.* Washington [DC]: John T. Towers, 1850.

———. [Navy Department]. *Official Records of the Union and Confederate Navies in the War of the Rebellion.* 30 vols. Washington: Government Printing Office, 1896.

de Souza, Phillip. *Piracy in the Graeco-Roman World.* Cambridge: Cambridge University Press, 2002.

Dew, Thomas. *A Digest of the Laws, Customs, Manners, and Institutions of the Ancient and Modern Nations.* New York: D. Appleton and Company, 1872.

Díaz de Gámez, Gutierre [Gutierre Diez de Games]. *Chronica de Don Pedro Niño, Conde de Buelna, Por Gutierre Diez de Games su Alferez.* Madrid: Don Antonio de Sancha, 1782.

———. *Le Victorial: Chronique de Don Pedro Niño, Comte de Buelna par Gutierre Diaz de Gamez, son Alferez (1379–1449).* 1782. Reprint, translated by Labert de Circourt and the comte de Puymaigre. Paris: Victor Palmé, 1867.

———. *The Unconquered Knight: A Chronicle of the Deeds of Don Pero Niño, Count of Buelna.* Translated by Joan Evans. Suffolk, England: Boydell Press, 2004.

Díaz del Castillo, Bernal. *The Discovery and Conquest of Mexico 1517–1521.* New York: Farrar, Straus and Cudahy, 1956.

[Dick, William.] "A Brief Account of Captain Sharp..." In *Buccaneers of America.* See Exquemelin 1684.

Domville-Fife, Charles W. *Submarine Warfare of To-Day: How the Submarine Menace Was Met and Vanquished.* Philadelphia: J. B. Lippincott, 1920.

Downton, Nicholas. *The sinking of the Carrack, The Five Wounds.* 1600. Reprinted in C. Raymond Beazley. *An English Garner: Voyages and Travels mainly during the 16th and 17th Centuries, Vol. II.* New York: E. P. Dutton, 1902.

Drake, Francis. *Sir Francis Drake revived; Calling upon this dull or effeminate Age, to follow his noble steps for gold and silver.* 1626. Reprinted in C. Raymond Beazley. *An English Garner: Voyages and Travels mainly during the 16th and 17th Centuries, Vol. II.* New York: E. P. Dutton, 1902.

———. *The World Encompassed by Sir Francis Drake Being his next Voyage to that to Nombre de Dios.* Reprint, London: Hakluyt Society, 1854.

Duguay-Trouin, René. *Mémoires de Duguay-Trouin, Lieutenant général des Armées Navales.* 1741. Reprint, edited by Philippe Clouet. Paris: Éditions France-Empire, 1991.

Dumas, Alexandre. *The Black Tulip.* New York: Walter J. Black, 1932.

Durant, Will, and Ariel Durant. *The Story of Civilization.* 11 vols. New York: Simon and Schuster, 1935–1975.

Earle, Peter. *The Pirate Wars.* New York: Thomas Dunne, 2003.

Edge, Frederick Milnes. *An Englishman's View of the Battle Between the Alabama and the Kearsarge.* New York: Anson D. F. Randolph, 1864.

Edmonds, John Henry. *Captain Thomas Pound.* Cambridge, MA: John Wilson and Son, 1918.

Eklöf, Stefan. *Pirates in Paradise: A Modern History of Southeast Asia's Maritime Marauders.* Copenhagen: NIAS Press, 2006.

Elms, Charles. *The Pirates Own Book: or, Authentic Narratives of the Lives, Exploits, and Executions of the Most Celebrated Sea Robbers.* Portland, ME: Francis Blake, 1855.

Everard, Robert. "A Relation of Three Years Sufferings of Robert Everard, Upon the Coast of Assada Near Madagascar, in a Voyage to India, in the Year 1686." In Awnsham Churchill and John Churchill, eds. *A Collection of Voyages and Travels, Vol. 6.* London: John Walthoe et al., 1732.

Exquemelin, Alexandre [John Esquemeling]. *The Buccaneers of America.* 1684. Reprint, New York: Dorset, 1987.

———. [A. O. Oexmelin]. *Les Flibustiers du Nouveau Monde.* 1699, with additional passages from the 1688 edition. Reprint, edited by Michel Le Bris. Paris: Éditions Phébus, 1996.

———. [Alexander Olivier O'Exquemelin]. *Histoire des Avanturiers Flibustiers qui se sont Signalez dans les Indes.* 2 vols. Paris: Jacques Le Febvre, 1699.

———. [Joseph Esquemeling]. *The History of the Buccaneers of America.* 1699. Reprint, Boston: Sanborn, Carter and Bazin, 1856.

Fernández Duro, Cesáreo. *Armada Español desde la unión de los reinos de Castilla y de León.* 9 vols. Madrid: Sucesores de Rivadeneyra, 1895–1903.

Ferrand, Antoine-François-Claude. *Histoire des Trois Démembrements de la Pologne.* 3 vols. Paris: Deterville, Librarie, 1820.

Firth, C. H. *Naval Songs and Ballads.* London: Navy Records Society, 1908.

Flinders Petrie, W. M. *Syria and Egypt: From the Tell el Amarna Letters.* London: Methuen, 1898.

Florence of Worcester. *The Chronicles of Florence of Worcester.* Translated by Thomas Forester. London: Henry G. Bohn, 1854.

Foissart, Jean. *The Chronicles of Froissart.* Translated by John Bourchier. Edited by G. C. Macaulay. London: Macmillan, 1908.

Forstner, Georg Günther, Freiherr von. *The Journal of Submarine Commander von Forstner.* 1916. Reprint, translated and edited by Mrs. Russell Codman. New York: Houghton Mifflin, 1917.

Foster, R. F. *The Oxford Illustrated History of Ireland.* Oxford: Oxford University Press, 2001.

Frances, John, ed. *Notes and Queries: A Medium of Intercommunication for Literary Men, General Readers, Etc.* 5th ser., vol. 1 (January–June). London: John Francis, 1874.

Franzén, Anders. "Kronan: Remants of a Warship's Past." *National Geographic* 175, no. 4 (April 1989), 438–465.

Frontinus, Sextus Julius. *Strategematicon, or Greek and Roman Anecdotes, Concerning Military Policy and Science of War.* Translated by Robert B. Scott. London: Thomas Goddard, 1811.

Fryer, John. *A New Account of East India and Persia, Being Nine Years' Travels 1672–1681.* 1698, 1909–1915. Reprint, edited by William Crooke. 3 vols. Millwood, NY: Kraus Reprint, 1967.

Fuller, Thomas. *The History of the Worthies of England.* 1662. Reprint, 3 vols. London: Thomas Tegg, 1860.

Furbank, Philip Nicholas, and W. R. Owens. "The Defoe that Never Was: A Tale of De-Attribution." *The American Scholar* 66, no. 2 (1997): 276–284.

Gage, Thomas. *Thomas Gage's Travels in the New World.* 1648. Reprint, edited by J. Eric S. Thompson. Norman: University of Oklahoma Press, 1969.

Galvin, Peter R. *Patterns of Pillage: A Geography of Caribbean-based Piracy in Spanish America, 1536–1718.* New York: Peter Lang, 2000.

Gilkerson, William. *Boarders Away: With Steel: Edged Weapons and Polearms of the Classical Age of Fighting Sail, 1626–1826.* Lincoln, RI: Andrew Mowbray Publishers, 1991.

Gill, Charles Clifford. *Naval Power in the War (1914–1917).* New York: George H. Doran, 1918.

Goffman, Daniel. *The Ottoman Empire and Early Modern Europe.* Cambridge: Cambridge University Press, 2002.

Goldstein, Tom, and Jethro Koller Lieberman. *The Lawyer's Guide to Writing Well.* 2nd ed. Berkeley: University of California Press, 2003.

Gomes, Edwin H. *Seventeen Years Among the Sea Dyaks of Borneo.* Philadelphia: J. B. Lippincott, 1911.

Goodwin, Joshua Michael. "Universal Jurisdiction and the Pirate: Time for an Old Couple to Part." *Vanderbilt Journal of Transnational Law* 39 (2006), no. 3:973–1012.

Gonzalez de Clavijo, Ruy. *Narrative of the Embassy of Ruy Gonzalez de Clavijo to the Court of Timour, at Samarcand, A.D. 1403–6.* Translated by Robert Markham Clements. London: Hakluyt Society, 1856.

Goodrick, Alfred Thomas Scrope, ed. *Edward Randolph; Including His Letters and Official Papers from the New England, Middle, and Southern Colonies in America, and the West Indies. 1678–1700.* 7 vols. Boston: Prince Society, 1909.

Gosse, Philip. "Piracy," *Mariner's Mirror* 36 (1950), no. 4:337–349.

Gottschalk, Jack A., Brian P. Flanagan, Lawrence J. Kahn, and Dennis M. Larochelle. *Jolly Roger with an Uzi: The Rise and Threat of Modern Piracy.* Annapolis, MD: Naval Institute Press, 2000.

Graves, Robert. *The Greek Myths.* 1955, 1960. Reprint, London: The Folio Society, 1996.

Great Britain: Royal Commission on Historical Manuscripts. *Manuscripts of the Marquess Townshend.* London: Eyre and Spottiswoode, 1887.

Green, C. H., ed. *The Historical Register, Containing An Impartial Relation of All Transactions, Foreign and Domestick.* Vol. 7. London: H. Meere, 1722.

———. *The Historical Register, Containing an Impartial Relation of All Transactions, Foreign and Domestick.* Vol. 11. London: H. Meere, 1726.

Guéroult du Pas, Jacques. *Recüeil de Veües de Tous les Differens Bastimens de la Mer Mediterranée, et de l'Ocean; avec Leurs Noms et Usages.* 1710. Facsimile reprint, Nice: A.N.C.R.E., 2004.

Guillet de Saint-Georges, Georges. *Les arts de l'homme d'epée, ou, Le dictionnaire du gentil-homme.* Paris: Chez la veuve Gervais Clouzier, 1682.

Guilmartin, John F., Jr. *Galleons and Galleys.* London: Cassell, 2002.

Guterman, Norbert, ed. *The Anchor Book of Latin Quotations.* 1966. Reprint, New York: Doubleday, 1990.

Hakluyt, Richard. *The Principal Navigations, Voyages, Traffiques & Discoveries of the English Nation.* 12 vols. Glasgow: James MacLehose and Sons, 1903–1905.

Haldane, Douglas. "The Fire-Ship of Al-Sālih Ayyūb and Muslim Use of 'Greek Fire.'" In *The Circle of War in the Middle Ages: Essays on Medieval Military and Naval History.* Edited by Donald J. Kagay and L. J. Andrew Villalon. Suffolk: Boydell, 1999.

Hannay, David. *The Sea Trader: His Friends and Enemies.* Boston: Little, Brown, 1912.

Haring, C. H. *Trade and Navigation Between Spain and the Indies.* Cambridge: Harvard University Press, 1918.

Hasleton, Richard. *Strange and Wonderful Things.* 1595. Reprinted in C. Raymond

Beazley. *An English Garner: Voyages and Travels mainly during the 16th and 17th Centuries, Vol. II.* New York: E. P. Dutton, 1902.

Hattendorf, John B., and Richard W. Unger, eds. *War at Sea in the Middle Ages and the Renaissance.* Rochester, NY: Boydell Press, 2003.

Haywood, John. *Dark Age Naval Power: A Re-assessment of Frankish and Anglo-Saxon Seafaring.* London: Routledge, 1991.

Hawkins, Richard. *The Observations of Sir Richard Hawkins, Knight in His Voyage into the South Sea in the Year 1593.* 1622. Reprint, edited by C. R. Drinkwater Bethune. London, Hakluyt Society, 1847.

Herbert-Burns, Rupert, Sam Bateman, and Peter Lehr, eds. *Lloyd's MIU Handbook of Maritime Security.* Boca Raton, FL: CRC Press, 2008.

Heers, Jacques. *The Barbary Corsairs: Warfare in the Mediterranean, 1480–1580.* Translated by Jonathan North. London: Greenhill Books, 2003.

Heliodorus of Emesa. *Aethiopian Adventures: or, the History Theagenes and Chariclea.* Translated by "a Person of Quality" and Nahum Tate. Dublin: R. Main, 1753.

Herodotus. *The History of Herodotus.* In *Great Books of the Western World: 6, Herodotus, Thucydides.* Translated by George Rawlinson. Reprint, Chicago: Encyclopedia Britannica, 1982.

Hesiod. *Hesiod: The Homeric Hymns and Homerica.* Translated by Hugh G. Evelyn-White. London: William Henemann, 1920.

Heude, William. *A Voyage Up the Persian Gulf and a Journey Overland from India to England in 1817.* London: Longman, Hurst, Rees, Orme, and Brown, 1819.

High Command of the Navy. *The U-Boat Commander's Handbook.* 1943. Translated by the U.S. Navy. Reprint, Gettysburg, PA: Thomas Publications, 1989.

Hill, Christopher. *Liberty Against the Law: Some Seventeenth-Century Controversies.* London: Penguin, 1996.

Hoare, James, and Susan Pares. *Korea: An Introduction.* New York: Routledge, 1988.

Hollander, Lee M., trans. *The Saga of the Jómsvíkings.* Austin: University of Texas Press, 1955.

Homer. *Iliad.* Translated by Andrew Lang, Walter Leaf, and Ernest Myers. In *The Complete Works of Homer.* New York: The Modern Library, 1935.

———. *Odyssey.* Translated by S. H. Butcher and Andrew Lang. In *The Complete Works of Homer.* New York: The Modern Library, 1935.

Horace [Quintus Horatius Flaccus]. *Odes and Epodes.* Edited by Charles E. Bennett. 1934. Revised edition, Boston: Allyn and Bacon, 1968.

Hourani, George Fadlo. *Arab Seafaring in the Indian Ocean in Ancient and Early Medieval Times.* 1951. Reprint, Beirut: Khayats, 1963.

Hoveden, Roger de [Roger of Hoveden]. *The Annals of Roger de Hoveden.* 2 vols. Translated by Henry T. Riley. London: H. G. Bohn: 1853.

Howard, Charles [Earl of Carlisle]. "The Earl of Carlisle's Answer to a Charge Against Him." In *Interesting Tracts, Relating to the Island of Jamaica.* St. Jago de la Vega, Jamaica: Lewis, Lunan, and Jones, 1800.

Howard, Frank. *Sailing Ships of War 1400–1800.* New York: Mayflower Books, 1979.

Hrodej, Philippe. "La flibuste domingoise à la fin du XVIIe siècle: une composante économique indispensable." In Michel Le Bris, ed. *L'Aventure de la Flibuste.* Paris: Éditions Hoëbeke, 2002.

Hunt, William. *Bristol.* London: Longmans, Green, 1889.

Hutchinson, William. *A Treatise on Naval Architecture*. 1794. Reprint, Annapolis, MD: Naval Institute Press, 1969.

Huzar, Eleanor Goltz. *Mark Antony: A Biography*. Minneapolis, MN: University of Minnesota Press, 1979.

International Maritime Bureau. "Best Management Practices to Deter Piracy in the Gulf of Aden and off the Coast of Somalia. (Version 2 - August 2009)." London: ICC International Maritime Bureau, 2009.

———. "Piracy and Armed Robbery Against Ships, 2008 Report." London: ICC International Maritime Bureau, 2008.

———. "Piracy and Armed Robbery Against Ships Annual Report 1 January–31 December 2007." London: ICC International Maritime Bureau, 2008.

International Maritime Organization (IMO). *International Convention for the Safety of Life at Sea (SOLAS), Consolidated Edition*. London: International Maritime Organization, 2004.

———. "Measures to Enhance Maritime Security." MSC/Circ.1073, June 10, 2003. http://www.imo.org/.

———. "Piracy and Armed Robbery Against Ships: Guidance to shipowners and ship operators, shipmasters and crews on preventing and suppressing acts of piracy and armed robbery against ships." MSC/Circ.623/Rev.1, June 16, 1999. http://www.imo.org/.

———. "Piracy and Armed Robbery Against Ships: Recommendations to Governments for preventing and suppressing piracy and armed robbery against ships." MSC/Circ.622/Rev.1, June 16, 1999. http://www.imo.org/.

Jackson, Alastar. "War and Raids for Booty in the World of Odysseus." In *War and Society in the Greek World*. Edited by John Rich and Graham Shipley. New York: Routledge, 1995.

James, Duke of York. *Memoirs of the English Affairs, Chiefly Naval, From the Year 1660, to 1673. Written by His Royal Highness James Duke of York*. London: n.p., 1729.

Jameson, J. Franklin. *Privateering and Piracy in the Colonial Period*. New York: Macmillan, 1970.

Jesch, Judith. *Ships and Men in the Late Viking Age: The Vocabulary of Runic Inscriptions and Skaldic Verse*. Suffolk, England: Boydell Press, 2001.

Johnson, Charles. *A General History of the Robberies and Murders of the Most Notorious Pirates*. 1726. Reprint, New York: Dodd, Mead, 1926.

———. *Histoire des Pirates Anglois*. Utrecht: Jacques Broedelet, 1725.

Johnson, Samuel, Oliver Goldsmith, and Christopher Smart, eds. *The World Displayed; or, a Curious Collection of Voyages and Travels*. 20 vols. London: J. Newberry, 1760.

Johnstone, Paul. *The Sea-craft of Prehistory*. 2nd ed. London: Routledge, 1988.

Juarez Moreno, Juan. *Corsarios y Piratas en Veracruz y Campeche*. Seville: Escuela de Estudios Hispano-Americanos de Sevilla, 1972.

Justinus, Marcus Junianus [M. J. Justini]. *ex Trogi Pompeii Historiis Externis*. Translated by N. Bailey. Reprint, London: Brotherton, J. Hazard, W. Meadows, et al., 1732.

Kaplan, Philip, and Jack Currie. *Convoy: Merchant Sailors at War, 1939–1945*. Annapolis, MD: Naval Institute Press, 2000.

Katchenovsky, Dmitrii Ivanovich [Professor Katchenovsky]. *Prize Law: Particularly with Reference to the Duties and Obligations of Belligerents and Neutrals*. Translated by Frederic Thomas Pratt. London: Stevens and Sons, 1867.

Kelly, Douglas. "Alexander's *Clergie*." In Maddox, Donald, and Sara Sturm-Maddox, eds. *The Medieval French Alexander.* Albany: State University Press of New York, 2002.

Keppel, Henry, and James Brooke. *The Expedition to Borneo of H.M.S. Dido for The Suppression of Piracy: With Extracts from the Journal of James Brooke, Esq., of Sarawak.* 1846. Reprint, New York: Harper & Brothers, 1861.

Keyuan, Zou. "Seeking Effectiveness for the Crackdown of Piracy at Sea." *Journal of International Affairs* 59, no. 1 (2005): 117–134.

Labat, Jean Baptiste [Labat, R. P.]. *Voyages aux Isles De L'Amerique.* 1722. Reprint, edited by A. t'Serstevens. 2 vols. Paris: Editions Duchartre, 1931.

L'Abbat [Monsieur L'Abbat]. *The Art of Fencing, or, the Use of the Small Sword.* 1734. Translated by Andrew Mahon. Reprint, n.p.: Kessinger Reprints, n.d.

Ladd, George Trumbull. *In Korea with Marquis Ito.* New York: Charles Scribner's Sons, 1908.

Lane-Poole, Stanley. *The Story of the Barbary Corsairs.* New York: G. P. Putnam's Sons, 1890.

László, Veres, and Richard Woodman. *The Story of Sail.* Annapolis, MD: Naval Institute Press, 1999.

Latham, Edward. 2nd. ed. *Famous Sayings and Their Authors: A Collection of Historical Sayings in English, French, German, Greek, Italian, and Latin.* London: Swan Sonnenschein, 1906.

Lavery, Brian. *Ship: The Epic Story of Adventure.* New York: DK Publishing, 2004.

Lawson, John D., ed. *American State Trials.* 17 vols. St. Louis: F. H. Thomas Law Book Co., 1916.

Lefroy, J. H., ed. *Memorials of the Discovery and Early Settlement of the Bermudas or Somers Islands 1511–1687.* 2 vols. London: Longmans, Green, 1879.

Lehr, Peter. *Violence at Sea: Piracy in the Age of Global Terrorism.* New York: Routledge, 2007.

Leguat, François. *The Voyage of François Leguat of Bresse to Rodriguez, Mauritius, Java, and the Cape of Good Hope.* 1708. Reprint, edited by Pasfield Oliver. 2 vols. London: Hakluyt Society, 1891.

———. *Voyage et Avantures de Francois Leguat, & de ses Compagnons, en deux isles deserted des Indies Orientales.* 2 vols. Amsterdam: Jean Louis de Lorme, 1708.

Lepers, Jean-Baptiste [P. le Pers]. *La Tragique Histoire des Flibustiers: Histoire de Saint-Domingue et de l'Ile de la Tortue, Repaires des Flibustiers, écrite vers 1715 par le Rév. P. Lepers.* Edited by Pierre-Bernard Berthelot. Paris: Éditons G. Crès, nd.

"Letters Concerning the English Expedition into the Spanish West Indies in 1655." In C. H. Firth, ed., *The Narrative of General Venables.* London: Longmans, Green, 1900.

Lewis, Archibald R., and Timothy J. Runyan. *European Naval and Maritime History, 300–1500.* Bloomington: Indiana University Press, 1990.

Linaje, José de Veita [Ioseph de Veitia Linage]. *Norte de la Contratacion de las Indias Occidentales.* Seville: Juan Francisco de Blas, 1672.

———. *The Spanish Rule of Trade to the West-Indies.* 1702. Translated and edited by John Stevens. Facsimile reprint, New York: AMS Press, 1977.

Little, Benerson. *The Buccaneer's Realm: Pirate Life on the Spanish Main, 1674–1688.* Washington, DC: Potomac Books, 2007.

———. "The Origin of the Dread Pirate Banner, the Jolly Roger." *Pirates Magazine,* no. 12 (April 2010): 9–14.

———. *The Sea Rover's Practice: Pirate Tactics and Techniques 1630–1730.* Washington, DC: Potomac Books, 2005.

———. "Terrorists and Pirates Are Similar But Not the Same." In Berlatsky, *Piracy on the High Seas,* 80–84.

Livy [Titus Livius]. *The History of Rome.* Translated by D. Spillan and Cyrus Edmonds. 3 vols. London: George Bell and Sons, 1887.

———. *Livy.* Translated by George Baker. 5 vols. New York: Harper and Brothers, 1836.

Lloyd, Christopher. "Bartholomew Sharp: Buccaneer," *Mariner's Mirror* 42, no. 4 (1956), 291–301.

Loder-Symonds, F. C., E. R. Wodehouse, et al., eds. *The Manuscripts of Rye and Hereford Corporations.* Historical Manuscripts Commission, Thirteenth Report, Appendix, Part IV. London: Eyre and Spottiswoode for Her Majesty's Stationery Office, 1892.

Logan, F. *The Vikings in History.* 2nd ed. New York: Routledge, 1992.

Louis XIV. "Declaration du Roy contre les corsaires ennemis. Donnée à Versailles au mois de Juillet 1691." Paris: Guillaume Desprez, 1691.

Lucan [Marcus Annaeus Lucanus]. *The Pharsalia of Lucan.* Translated by H. T. Riley. London: Henry G. Bohn, 1853.

Lucena Salmoral, Manuel. *Piratas, Bucaneros, Filibusteros y Corsarios en América.* Caracas: Grijalbo, 1994.

Luckner, Felix, Graf von. *Seeteufel: Abenteuer aus meinem Leben.* Leipzig: R. F. Koehler, 1921.

Luttrell, Narcissus. *A Brief Historical Relation of State Affairs From September 1678 to April 1714.* 6 vols. Oxford: Oxford University Press, 1857.

Lydgate, John. *The Pilgrimage of the Life of Man.* 1426. Reprint, translated by F. J. Furnivall. 2 vols. London: Keagan Paul, Trench, Trübner, 1901.

Machiavelli, Niccolò [Nicholas Machiavel]. *The Art of War.* 1520. Reprinted in *The Works of Nicholas Machiavel.* 2 vols. Translated by Ellis Farnworth. London: Thomas Davies, 1762.

Macintyre, Donald. *U-Boat Killer: Fighting the U-Boats in the Battle of the Atlantic.* 1956. Reprint, London: Rigel Publications, 2004.

Mahan, Alfred Thayer. *The Influence of Sea Power Upon History, 1660–1783.* 12th ed. Boston: Little, Brown, 1918.

Maidment, James, ed. *Analecta Scotica: Collections Illustrative of the Civil, Ecclesiastical, and Literary History of Scotland.* 2nd ser. Edinburgh: Thomas G. Stevenson, 1837.

Mainwaring, Henry. *The Life and Works of Sir Henry Mainwaring.* Edited by G. E. Manwaring and W. G. Perrin. 2 vols. London: Navy Records Society, 1922.

———. "Of the Beginnings, Practices, and Suppression of Pirates." 1617. Reprinted in *The Life and Works of Sir Henry Mainwaring.* See Mainwaring 1922.

———. *The Seaman's Dictionary.* Reprinted in *The Life and Works of Sir Henry Mainwaring.* 1644. See Mainwaring 1922.

Malpiero, Domenico. *Annali Veneti dall' Anno 1457 at 1500 del Senatore Domenico Malipiero.* Firenze: Gio. Pietro Vieusseux, 1844.

Mann, Horace K. *The Lives of the Popes in the Early Middle Ages.* 5 vols. London: Kegan Paul, Trench, Trübner, 1906.

[Marana, Giovanni Paolo]. *Letters Writ by a Turkish Spy, Who liv'd Five and Forty Years Undiscover'd at Paris.* 8 vols. London: A Wilde, 1753.

Maritime and Coastguard Agency (MCA). "Maritime Guidance Note 298: Measures to Counter Piracy, Armed Robbery and other Acts of Violence against Merchant Shipping." London: Maritime and Coastguard Agency, November 16, 2005.

Markham, Clements R., ed. *The Hawkins' Voyages During the Reigns of Henry VIII, Queen Elizabeth, and James I.* London: Hakluyt, 1888.

Marley, David F. *Pirates and Engineers.* Windsor, Ontario: Netherlandic Press, 1992.

Marsden, R. G., ed. *Documents Relating to Law and Custom of the Sea.* 2 vols. London: Navy Records Society, 1916.

Maspero, Gaston. *The Passing of the Empires, 850 B.C. to 330 B.C.* Edited by Archibald Henry Sayce, translated by M. L. McClure. London: Society for Promoting Christian Knowledge, 1900.

Martin, Henri. *Martin's History of France: The Age of Louis XIV.* Vol. 2. Translated by Mary L. Booth. Boston: Walker, Wise, 1865.

Matar, Nabil. *Turks, Moors, and Englishmen in the Age of Discovery.* New York: Columbia University Press, 1999.

Matthew of Paris, et al [Matthew of Westminster]. *The Flowers of History.* Translated by C. D. Yonge. 2 vols. London: Henry G. Bohn, 1853.

———. *Matthew Paris's English History from the Year 1235 to 1273.* Translated by J. A. Giles. 3 vols. London: Henry G. Bohn, 1852–1854.

May, Charles. "An Account of the wonderful Preservation of the Ship *Terra Nova* of London." 1694. In Churchill, *Collection of Voyages*, vol. 6:345–354.

Means, Philip Ainsworth. *The Spanish Main.* New York: Charles Scribner's Sons, 1935.

Meier, Dirk. *Seafarers, Merchants and Pirates in the Middle Ages.* Translated by Angus McGeoch. Woodbridge, UK: Boydell Press, 2006.

Molloy, Charles. *De Jure Maritimo Et Navali: Or, A Treatise of Affairs Maritime, and of Commerce.* London: John Walthoe Junior, 1722.

Monson, William. *Sir William Monson's Naval Tracts.* 5 vols. Edited by M. Oppenheim. London: Navy Records Society, 1902.

Moore, J. J. *The Midshipman's or British Mariner's Vocabulary.* London: Vernor and Hood, 1805.

Morison, Samuel Eliot. *The Two-Ocean War: A Short History of the United States Navy in the Second World War.* Boston: Little, Brown and Company, 1963.

Mountaine, William. *The Seaman's Vade-Mecum and Defensive War by Sea.* 1756. Reprint, London: Conway Maritime, 1971.

Newbolt, Henry. *Submarine and Anti-Submarine.* New York: Longmans, Green and Co., 1919.

Newton, A. P. *The European Nations in the West Indies 1493–1688.* 1933. Reprint, New York: Barnes and Noble, 1967.

Nicholson, Helen, and David Nicolle. *God's Warriors: Knights Templar, Saracens and the Battle for Jerusalem.* New York: Osprey, 2006.

Nicolas, Harris, ed. *A History of the Royal Navy from the Earliest Times to the Wars of the French Revolution.* 2 vols. London: Richard Bentley, 1847.

———. *Proceedings and Ordinances of the Privy Council of England.* 7 vols. London: Commissioners of the Public Records, 1835.

Noyes, James H. *The Clouded Lens: Persian Gulf Security and U.S. Policy.* 2nd ed. Stanford: Hoover Institution Press, 1982.

Oddr Snorrason. *Olap Tryggvasonar Saga.* Excerpted in *Collectanea de Rebus Albanicis:*

Consisting of Original Papers and Documents Relating to the History of the Highlands and Islands of Scotland. Edinburgh: Thomas G. Stevenson, 1847.

Oil Companies International Marine Forum. "Piracy: The East Africa/Somalia Situation. Practical Measures to Avoid, Deter or Delay Piracy Attacks." London: OCIMF, 2009.

Ormerod, Henry A. *Piracy in the Ancient World: An Essay in Mediterranean History.* 1924. Reprint, Totowa, NJ: Rowman and Littlefield, 1978.

Ortolan, Théodore. *Règles internationales et diplomatie de la mer.* 4th ed. 2 vols. Paris: Librarie de Henri Plon, 1864.

Parry, J. H. *The Spanish Seaborne Empire.* London: Hutchinson & Co., 1966.

The Penn and Logan Correspondence, Volume 2. In *Memoirs of the Historical Society of Pennsylvania.* Vol. 10. Philadelphia: J. B. Lippincott, 1872.

Peterson, Harold L. *Arms and Armor in Colonial America 1526–1783.* New York: Bramhall House, 1956.

Phillips, Richard. *A Captain's Duty: Somali Pirates, Navy SEALs, and Dangerous Days at Sea.* With Stephan Talty. New York: Hyperion, 2010.

Phillips, W. Alison. *The War of Greek Independence, 1821 to 1833.* New York: Charles Scribner's Sons, 1897.

Pitman, Henry. "A Relation of the Great Sufferings and Strange Adventures of Henry Pitman." 1689. Reprinted in *An English Garner: Stuart Tracts 1603–1693,* vol 8. New York: E. P. Dutton, n.d.

Playford, Henry. *Pills to Purge Melancholy.* Vol. 1. London: W. Pearson for J. Tonson, 1719.

Pliny the Elder [Caius Plinius Secundus]. *The Natural History of Pliny.* Edited by John Bostock and H. T. Riley. London: George Bell & Sons, 1890.

Plutarch [Lucius Mestrius Plutarchus]. *The Lives of the Noble Grecians and Romans: The Dryden Translation.* Translated by John Dryden. Chicago: Encyclopedia Britannica, 1952.

Polo, Marco. *The Travels of Marco Polo, the Venetian.* Edited by Thomas Wright. London: Henry G. Bohn, 1854.

Polyaenus. *Stratagems of War.* Translated by Richard Shepherd. London: George Nicol, 1793.

Polybius. *The Histories.* Translated by W. R. Paton. 6 vols. New York: G. P. Putnam's Sons, 1922.

[Povey, Edward]. "The Buccaneers on the Isthmus and in the South Sea. 1680–1682." In John F. Jameson, ed. *Privateering and Piracy in the Colonial Period: Illustrative Documents.* New York: Macmillan, 1923.

Pretty, Francis. "The Admirable and Prosperous Voyage of the Worshipful Master Thomas Cavendish." In Edward John Payne, ed. *Voyages of Elizabethan Seamen.* London: Oxford, n.d.

Procopius. *Procopius.* Translated by H. B. Dewing. 6 vols. London: William Heinemann, 1916.

Purchas, Samuel. *Hakluytus Posthumus or Purchas His Pilgrimes Contayning a History of the World in Sea Voyages and Lande Travells by Englishmen and others.* 20 vols. Glasgow: James MacLehose and Sons, 1907.

Rediker, Marcus. *Between the Devil and the Deep Blue Sea.* Cambridge: Cambridge University Press, 1987.

———. "The Seaman as Pirate: Plunder and Social Banditry at Sea." In C. R. Pennell, ed., *Bandits at Sea: A Pirate Reader.* New York: New York University Press, 2001.

————. *Villains of All Nations: Atlantic Pirates in the Golden Age.* Boston: Beacon Press, 2004.

Richard of Devises, Geoffrey de Vinsauf, and John de Joinville. *Chronicles of the Crusades, Being Contemporary Narratives of the Crusade of Richard Coeur de Lion.* London: Henry G. Bohn, 1848.

Rihll, Tracey. "War, Slavery, and Settlement in Early Greece." In *War and Society in the Greek World.* Edited by John Rich and Graham Shipley. New York: Routledge, 1995 (77–107).

Ringrose, Basil. "The Buccaneers of America: The Second Volume." In Alexander Exquemelin [John Esquemeling]. *The Buccaneers of America.* 1684. Reprint, New York: Dorset, 1987 (285–475).

Ritchie, Robert C. *Captain Kidd and the War Against the Pirates.* Cambridge: Harvard University Press, 1986.

Roberts, George. *The Four Years Voyages of Capt. George Roberts; Being a Series of Uncommon Events Which Befell Him.* 1726. Reprint, London: Traveller's Library, 1930.

Roche, Jeremy. "The Journals of Jeremy Roch." In *Three Sea Journals of Stuart Times.* Edited by Bruce Ingram. London" Constable & Co. Ltd., 1936.

Rodger, N. A. M. *The Safeguard of the Sea: A Naval History of Great Britain 660–1649.* New York: W. W. Norton, 1999.

Rodgers, William Ledyard. 1940. *Naval Warfare Under Oars, 4th to 16th Centuries.* Reprint, Annapolis, MD: Naval Institute Press, 1967.

Rogers, Woodes. *A Cruising Voyage Round the World.* 1712. Facsimile reprint, New York: Da Capo Press, 1969.

Rogoziński, Jan. *Honor Among Thieves: Captain Kidd, Henry Every, and the Pirate Democracy in the Indian Ocean.* Mechanicsburg: PA, Stackpole Books, 2000.

Rolt-Wheeler, Francis. *The Wonder of War at Sea.* Boston: Lothrop, Lee & Shepard, 1919.

Romilly, G. *Étude sur la Guerre contre les Pirates au Tonkin.* Angoulême, France: Imprimerie Militaire L. Coquemard, 1910.

Roncière, Charles de la. "Un Inventaire de Bord en 1294" in *Bibliothéque de l'École des Chartres, LVIII.* Paris: Librarie d'Alphonse Picard et Fils, 1897, 394–409.

Rose, Susan. *Medieval Naval Warfare 1000–1500.* London: Routledge, 2002.

Rosenberg, Aubrey. *Tyssot de Patot and his work 1655–1738.* The Hague: Nijhoff, 1972.

Rubin, Alfred P. *The Law of Piracy.* Newport, RI: Naval War College Press, 1988.

Ruhe, William J. 1994. *War in the Boats: My WWII Submarine Battles.* Reprint, Washington, D.C.: Potomac Books, 2005.

Sabatini, Rafael. *Captain Blood: His Odyssey.* New York: Grosset and Dunlap, 1922.

Sage, Michael M. *Warfare in Ancient Greece: A Sourcebook.* New York: Routledge, 1996.

Salley, A. S., Jr., ed. *Commissions and Instructions from the Lords Proprietors of Carolina to Public Officials of South Carolina 1685–1715.* Columbia, SC: Historical Commission of South Carolina, 1916.

Savérien, Alexandre. *Dictionnaire Historique, Théorique et Pratique de Marine.* 2 vols. Paris: Charles-Antoine Jombert, 1758.

Scammel, Geoffrey Vaughan. *The World Encompassed: The First European Maritime Empires c. 800–1650.* Berkeley: University of California Press, 1981.

Scheina, Robert L. *Latin America's Wars: The Age of the Caudillo, 1791–1899.* Washington: Brassey's, 2003.

Scott, Beresford. *An Account of the Destruction of the Fleets of the Celebrated Pirate Chieftains*

Chui-apoo and Shap-ng-tsai on the Coast of China, in September and October, 1849. [No publication data: 1851].

Seymour, Thomas Day. *Life in the Homeric Age.* New York: Biblo and Tannen, 1963.

Seitz, Don C., ed. *The Tryal of Capt. William Kidd for Murther and Piracy.* 1936. Reprint, Mineola, NY: Dover Publications, 2001.

Semmes, Rafael. *The Cruise of the Alabama and the Sumter.* New York: Carleton Publisher, 1864.

Senior, Clive. *A Nation of Pirates: English Piracy in Its Heyday.* New York: Crane, Russak, 1976.

Seutonius [Gaius Suetonius Tranquillus]. *Suetonius.* 2 vols. Edited by J. C. Rolfe. London: William Heinemann, 1914.

Sewall, Samuel. *The Diary of Samuel Sewall: 1714–1729.* Boston: Massachusetts Historical Society, 1882.

Sharf, John Thomas. *History of the Confederate States Navy from Its Organization to the Surrender of Its Last Vessel.* 2nd ed. Albany, NY: Joseph McDonough, 1894.

Sherborne, J. W. "English Barges and Balingers of the Late Fourteenth Century," *The Mariner's Mirror* 63, no. 2 (1977): 109–114.

Shomette, Donald. *Pirates on the Chesapeake.* Centreville, MD: Tidewater Publishers, 1985.

Sjaastad, Anders C. "Southeast Asian SLOCS and Security Options." In Guan, Kwa Chong and John K. Skogan, eds. *Maritime Security in Southeast Asia.* New York: Routledge, 2007 (3–14).

Sloane, Hans. *A Voyage To the Islands Madera, Barbados, Nieves, S. Christophers and Jamaica.* 2 vols. London: B. M. for the author, 1707.

Smiley, Jane. *The Sagas of Icelanders: A Selection.* Introduction by Robert Kellogg. New York: Penguin, 2000.

Smith, John. *The Generall Historie of Virginia, New England & The Summer Isles.* 2 vols. Glasgow: James MacLehose and Sons, 1907.

———. *The Seaman's Grammar and Dictionary.* London: Randal Taylor, 1691.

———. *Works: 1608–1631.* 2 vols. Edited by Edward Arber. Westminster: Archibald Constable, 1895.

Snelgrave, William. *A New Account of some parts of Guinea and the Slave Trade.* 1727. Excerpted in *Captured by Pirates* ("The Bloody-Minded Villain Came on to Kill Me"). Edited by John Richard Stephens. Cambria Pines by the Sea, CA: Fern Canyon, 1996.

Snorrason, Oddr. *The Saga of King Olaf Tryggwason Who Reigned Over Norway A.D. 995 to A.D. 1000.* Translated by John Sephton. London: David Nutt, 1895.

Sobel, Dava. *Longitude: The True Story of a Lone Genius Who Solved the Greatest Scientific Problem of His Time.* New York: Penguin, 1996.

Southey, Robert. *The British Admirals.* 2 vols. London: Longman, Rees, Orme, Brown, Green, Longman, and John Taylor, 1833.

Spont, Alfred. *La Marine Française Sous le Règne de Charles VIII, 1483–1493.* Paris: Bureaux de la Revue, 1894.

Sprague, Martina. *Norse Warfare: Unconventional Battle Strategies of the Ancient Vikings.* New York: Hippocrene, 2007.

Stark, Francis Raymond. *The Abolition of Privateering and the Declaration of Paris.* New York: Columbia University Press, 1897.

Steinbeck, John. *Cup of Gold.* New York: Covici Friede, 1936.

Strachan, Michael. "*Sampson*'s Fight with Maltese Galleys, 1628." *Mariner's Mirror* 55, no. 3 (1969) 281–289.

Sturluson, Snorri. *The Heimskringla: A History of the Norse Kings.* Translated by Samuel Laing. 3 vols. London: Norroena Society, 1907.

Strauss, Barry. *The Trojan War: A New History.* New York: Simon & Schuster, 2006.

Swartz, Peter M. "US-Greek Naval Relations Begin: Antipiracy Operations in the Aegean Sea." COP D0008571.A1. Alexandria, VA: Center for Strategic Studies, 2003.

Tavernier, Jean Baptiste. *Travels in India.* 1676. Translated by Valentine Bell. 2 vols. London: MacMillan, 1889.

Taylor, John. *Jamaica in 1687: The Taylor Manuscript at the National Library of Jamaica.* Edited by David Buisseret. Kingston, Jamaica: University of West Indies Press, 2008.

Taylor, John. *The Works of John Taylor the Water Poet Not Included in the Folio of 1630.* [Manchester]: The Spenser Society, 1878. Teonge, Henry. *The Diary of Henry Teonge.* Edited by G. E. Manwaring. New York: Harper & Brothers, 1927.

Thomas, Lowell. *Raiders of the Deep.* 1928. Reprint, Annapolis, MD: Naval Institute Press, 2004.

———. [and Graf Felix von Luckner]. *Count Luckner, the Sea Devil.* Garden City, NY: Doubleday, Page, 1927.

Thomson, Byerley. *The Laws of War, Affecting Commerce and Shipping.* New ed. London: Smith, Elder, 1854.

Thucydides. *The History of the Peloponnesian War.* In *Great Books of the Western World: 6. Herodotus, Thucydides.* 1952. Translated by Richard Crawley. Reprint, revised by R. Feetham. Chicago: Encyclopedia Britannica, 1982.

Thurston, Robert H. *Robert Fulton: His Life and Its Results.* New York: Dodd, Mead, 1891.

Tindall, Matthew. *An Essay Concerning the Laws of Nations, and the Rights of Soveraigns.* London: Richard Baldwin, 1694.

Torres Ramirez, Bibiano. *La Armada de Barlovento.* Seville: Escuela de Estudios Hispano-Americanos de Sevilla, 1981.

Tsountas, Chrestos, and J. Irving Manatt. *The Mycenaean Age: A Study of the Monuments and Culture of Pre-Homeric Greece.* Boston: Houghton Mifflin, 1897.

Twiss, Travers, ed. *Monumenta Juridica: The Black Book of the Admiralty.* 2 vols. London: Longman, 1873.

Tyssot de Patot, Simon. *Voyages et Avantures de Jaques Massé.* Bordeaux: Jaques l'Aveugle, 1710.

Tytler, Patrick Fraser. *The History of Scotland from the Accession of Alexander III to the Union.* 4 vols. Edinburgh: W. P. Nimmo, Hay, & Mitchell, 1887.

United Nations. "Convention on the High Seas." New York: 1958.

———. "Convention on the Law of the Sea." December 10, 1982, entered into force November 16, 1994.

———. "Report of the Monitoring Group on Somalia pursuant to Security Council resolution 1811 (2008)." S/2008/769, December 10, 2008.

United States National Security Council. "Countering Piracy Off the Horn of Africa: Partnership & Action Plan." December, 2008.

Valencia, Mark. "Piracy and Politics in Southeast Asia." In Johnson, Derek, and Mark Valencia, eds. *Piracy in Southeast Asia: Status, Issues, and Responses.* Singapore: Institute of Southeast Asian Studies, 2005 (103–121).

Vega, Lope de. *El rey sin reyno tragicomedia famosa de Lope de Vega Carpio.* In *Segunda Parte de la Parte Veinte de las Comedias de Lope de Vega Carpio.* Madrid: La Viuda de Alonso Martín, 1625 (fol. 226v–252v).

Venables, Robert. *The Narrative of General Venables.* C. H. Firth, ed. New York: Longmans, Green, 1900.

Verne, Jules. *Twenty Thousand Leagues Under the Sea.* 1870. Reprint, translated by Mercier Lewis. Norwalk, CT: Easton, 1977.

Vertot, Abbé de. *The History of the Knights Hospitallers of St. John of Jerusalem, Styled Afterwards the Knights of Rhodes.* 3 vols. Dublin: J. Christie, 1818.

Virgil [Publius Vergilius Maro]. *The Aeneid.* Translated by Robert Fagles. 2006. Reprint, New York: Penguin, 2008.

———. *The Aeneid of Virgil: Books 1–6.* Edited by R. D. Williams. 1972. Reprint, London: MacMillan Education, 1977.

[Walker, George] *The Voyages and Cruises of Commodore Walker.* 1760. Reprint, London: Cassell, 1928.

Walsh, Thomas. *History of the Irish Hierarchy.* New York: D. & J. Sadlier, 1854.

Warren, C. E. T., and James Benson. *The Midget Raiders: The Wartime Story of Human Torpedoes and Midget Submarines.* New York: William Sloane Associates, 1954.

Watson, John Selby, ed. *Sallust, Florus, and Velleius Paterculus.* London: George Bell and Sons, 1889.

Weber, Frederick Parkes. *Aspects of Death and Correlated Aspects of Life in Art, Epigram, and Poetry.* 3rd ed. New York: Paul B. Hoeber, 1918.

Webster, T. B. L. *From Mycenae to Homer.* London: Methuen, 1958.

Weeks, Lyman Horace, and Edwin M. Bacon, eds. *A Historical Digest of the Provincial Press.* Boston: Society for Americana, 1911.

Wheaton, Henry. *Elements of International Law.* Edited by Richard Henry Dana, Jr. 8th ed. London: Sampson Low, Son, 1866.

Wheelan, Joseph. *Jefferson's War: America's First War on Terror.* New York: Carroll & Graf, 2003.

Whistler, Henry. "Extracts from Henry Whistler's Journal of the West India Expedition." In C. H. Firth, ed. *The Narrative of General Venables.* New York: Longmans, Green, 1900.

White, David Fairbank. *Bitter Ocean: The Battle of the Atlantic, 1939–1945.* New York: Simon & Schuster, 2006.

Wilkins, Harold T. "Chasing Chinese Pirates." *Popular Mechanics* (October 1929): 554–57.

"With the Chinese Pirates." *Popular Mechanics* (February 1932): 266–71.

Woodward, David. *The Secret Raiders: The Story of the German Armed Merchant Raiders in the Second World War.* New York: W. W. Norton, 1955.

Wright, Edmond. "A True & Exact account of an Engagement maintained by the Ship *Caesar,* Capt. Edm^d· Wright Comand^r· against Five Shipps (being Pyrates)..." In John Horsley Mayo. *Medals and Decorations of the British Army and Navy, Vol. 1.* Westminster: Archibald Constable, 1897.

Wylie, James Hamilton. *History of England Under Henry the Fourth.* 2 vols. London: Longmans, Green, 1884.

———. *History of England Under Henry the Fourth.* 3 vols. London: Longmans, Green, 1894.

Young, Adam J. *Contemporary Maritime Piracy in Southeast Asia: History, Causes, and Remedies.* Singapore: Institute of Southeast Asian Studies, 2007.

Index

Abbasid Caliphate, 113
Abney, Paul, 157-58
Acaponeta, Mexico, 191
Achaea, 64
Achilles, 19, 29
Adriatic Sea, 58
Aegean Sea, 39
Aenead, 20
Aeson, 30
Afghanistan War, 253
Agamemnon, 19
Agyllians, 39
Ajax, 19, 25, 28
aircraft: named after pirates, 7; used for
    pirate hunting, 14, 267-68, 274, 277
Alasiya, 37
Albania, Albanians, 206
Albanian sea rovers, 222
Albici, 67
Alexander the Great, 47-48, 50, 58
Alexandria, 67, 122
Alfred the Great, 78-79
Algarve, 137
Algiers, 206, 212-13, 219
alla sensile, 119
al-Muharraq, 238
Alopeconnesos, 53
Amarna letters, 37
Amazons, 31
Ameinias, 53
Amenhotep III, 37
American Revolution, 167, 228, 233
Amon-Re, 40
Amphoterus, 58
Ancaeus, 31

Andalusia, 137
Andron, 58
Anglian sea rovers, 74
Anglo-Hanseatic War, 89
Angrian sea rovers, 241-42. *See also*
    Indian sea rovers
Anguilla, 182
Antinous, 25
Antioch, king of, 55
anti-submarine warfare, 260-67
Antonio, Baptista, 147
Apollonius Rhodius, 26
Arab expansion, 113
Arabian Sea, 239
Arab navies, rise of, 115
Aragon, 128
Arakanese pirates, 240. *See also* Indian
    sea rovers
Arawak language, 154
Arcon, 26
Argentinean privateers. *See* United
    Provinces privateers
Argonauts, 26, 30-33
Argus the Thespian, 22, 30
Arica, 137
Armada de Barlovento, 147, 175, 181
Armada de Galicia, 96
Armada del Nuestra Señora de Guía, 195
Armada de Vizcaínos, 183
Armada do Malabar. *See* Armada do Sol
Armada do Norte, 137
Armada do Sol, 137
armament of ships and vessels: antiquity,
    23, 42-43, 54-55, 60-61, 66-67,
    237; "Golden Age," 165, 173-74;

About the Author

B enerson Little was born in Key West, the son of a Navy man. At age ten, he read *Treasure Island*. Since then he has been a SEAL officer and an analyst for the Naval Special Warfare Strategy and Tactics Group. He is the author of *The Sea Rover's Practice: Pirate Tactics and Techniques, 1630–1730* and *The Buccaneer's Realm: Pirate Life on the Spanish Main, 1674–1688*. He lives in Huntsville, Alabama, where his daughters, writing, consulting, and teaching fencing occupy most of his time.